Given on the occasion of the beginning of your medical school training at NYMC. Congratulations on reaching this point in your life odyssey. I am proud to be your teacher, and rejoice in your accomplishments.

William Frishman

TRIUMPH OVER TRAGEDY

THE ODYSSEY OF AN ACADEMIC PHYSICIAN

TRIUMPH OVER TRAGEDY

THE ODYSSEY OF AN ACADEMIC PHYSICIAN

WILLIAM H. FRISHMAN, M.D., M.A.C.P.
CHAIRMAN AND PROFESSOR OF MEDICINE
NEW YORK MEDICAL COLLEGE OF TOURO COLLEGE AND UNIVERSITY
DIRECTOR OF MEDICINE
WESTCHESTER MEDICAL CENTER HEALTH NETWORK
VALHALLA, NEW YORK

VISITING PROFESSOR OF MEDICINE
ALBERT EINSTEIN COLLEGE OF MEDICINE
BRONX, NEW YORK

 Science International • New York

Publisher: Science International Corporation
Developmental Editor: Shireen Dunwoody
Production/Design: Dunwoody Consulting
Cover Design: Renee Horner
Cover Illustration: Mila Karavai

Printed in the United States of America
Printing/binding by The Sheridan Group

Science International Corporation
70 Forest Street, Suite 5S
Stamford, Connecticut 06901
203-329-0842
www.scienceinternational.org

FIRST EDITION

ISBN 978-0-692-66509-1

To my beloved wife, Esther, and our children and grandchildren, who inspire me every day by their personal examples.

And in memory of my father,
Aaron H. Frishman, the inspiration for my life's work.

FOREWORD

How little we often know about others with whom we interact.

I have known Bill Frishman for more than 40 years, meeting him initially as a first year cardiology fellow in the New York Hospital-Cornell Program. He not only did very well clinically, but authored important papers during his fellowship. These accomplishments required considerable extra effort, and his tenacity was early in evidence.

A true story. When Bill completed the propranolol study he brought a draft of the proposed paper to me and we conferred. The red pencil was much in evidence with resultant major changes in the draft. When Bill left he appeared discouraged, but the next morning he returned with a completely new version. Again the red pencil. Again Bill looking dismayed. Over the next couple of weeks this cycle repeated itself several times. The result: a finished manuscript that was submitted and accepted for publication with only minor changes.

As his career developed we became friends and professional colleagues. We meet only occasionally, but often call or email to exchange comments, request assistance and interact professionally. As a long-time transplanted New Yorker, I thought I understood a bit about Bill's background, not atypical for growing up and being educated in the public schools of New York City. This memoir, however, quickly convinced me otherwise.

How little we know about the origins, backgrounds, triumphs, barriers encountered, personal losses and tragedies of our friends and acquaintances, including those with whom we have spent many hours. Our life stories generally are known only to a few, mostly family. Fortunately, Bill has chosen to share his with us. The singular mix of family dynamics, ethnic background, faith, education, unexpected adversities and successes challenge our character and make us who we are. Bill's widespread family, their immigration from Eastern Europe and assimilation into the American scene within one or two generations is not unusual. (Note he is a baseball addict and a Yankee fan!) He takes justified pride in this heritage, and I do not doubt that it has supported him through many adventures.

And then there is his well-described encounter with education, much in the news these days. In typically American fashion we discuss (perhaps argue would be a better word) the issues of local versus state versus national control and the fundamental challenge of how we measure performance for both student and teacher. Often forgotten in the argument about local control, a tradition passed directly from the founding fathers, is that the current system has produced a highly variable primary and secondary education nationwide which is failing a significant portion of our population. There are good teachers and bad teachers, even in medical school, yet a solution to the need for sharply increasing the number of good teachers is not readily available. The key question that can be asked of Bill, as for many other outstanding graduates of our public school system, "How did you turn out so well?" The answer for Bill, and for other fortunate students in the New York City public school system, is, in part, the magnet school he attended, the Bronx High School of Science. Bill made it through with skill, perseverance, character and dedication. No doubt a little bit of luck should be thrown in the mix also. He was not going to be turned down (see Louis Pasteur quote). Whether the selection process for these special schools is the best it could be is a question being asked currently as society increasingly focuses on the need to distribute our educational resources more equitably and widely. For Bill, it worked.

Dr. Frishman fairly, in my opinion, describes the problems inherent in the structure of his training more than four decades ago as a house officer in internal medicine. Chiefs not paying attention to the workload, as well as the hours of servitude and the variability, were at times punitive of the medical trainees. Opinions, not evidence, set the standards for care. Would any of us who endured this rite of passage want to return to the "good old days?" Not me, nor Dr. Frishman I suspect. Although problems of coverage and transfer of responsibility persist, the house staff years are better now following relatively recent reforms. Of course, there are always new challenges. For example, the computer-generated record with its "cut and paste" errors transferred forward as gospel can create issues that have yet to be resolved. Dr. Frishman is an experienced, highly competent chief. These new problems will be resolved by his team and others.

Another important aspect that Dr. Frishman narrates is the wild ride during the last four to five decades that those of us in academic cardiology have been privileged to enjoy as clinical science, technology and pharmacology have surged forward with new knowledge. Additionally, the results of carefully managed randomized clinical trials now applied in the diagnosis, treatment and prevention of cardiovascular disease have become the standard of care revolutionizing the practice of medicine based on evidence.

Although cardiovascular diseases are the leading cause of death in adults worldwide, the mortality rate of the major killer, coronary artery disease, has been falling despite the inevitable growth of our aging population. Professor Frishman's role in academic cardiology has been outstanding. From the beginning he recognized the value of the clinical trial, and was involved in early randomized studies of the then new beta-blocker propranolol. He has taken an active, expansive role in studying the clinical pharmacology of newly developed, effective cardiovascular drugs. His participation in randomized trials has continued apace with important and significant results. In addition, he has had an important role in studies of aging individuals in a select population in the Bronx, illustrating the value of long term population registries. Such trials are of great importance from a public health point of view since they objectively describe what happens over time, documenting numerous medical and social factors which demand attention.

Professor Frishman has also been an active participant in the medical school educational process for years. The department of medicine is a critically important clinical department in a medical school. For medical students and young house officers it focuses on the key aspects involved in the care of the patient: careful history taking, evaluation of the emotional state, skilled physical examination, selection of appropriate laboratory tests and ultimately integrating these acquired data into a work plan for diagnosis and treatment. It takes good organization and strong leadership to teach this part of the job well.

Departments of medicine are large, with many specialty divisions competing for space, time and money. Being a successful chair requires administrative and diplomatic skills. Additionally, it is especially important to be a good clinician as a role model for the entire department as well as to critically understand what clinical investigation is all about. Ultimately, there is only one boss and you can't keep everybody happy. It's a tough job. Professor Frishman's outstanding success in this role is evident.

My congratulations to Professor William Frishman for this fascinating memoir describing his adventures and point of view in fashioning a useful and productive career. It is a good read. I am proud to have known him from the beginning of his introduction to the study and care of cardiovascular disease and the practice of clinical science.

Thomas Killip, M.D.
Professor of Cardiology
Mt. Sinai School of Medicine
New York, New York

IF

by Rudyard Kipling

If you can keep your head when all about you
   Are losing theirs and blaming it on you,
If you can trust yourself when all men doubt you,
   But make allowance for their doubting too;
If you can wait and not be tired by waiting,
   Or being lied about, don't deal in lies,
Or being hated, don't give way to hating,
   And yet don't look too good, nor talk too wise:

If you can dream—and not make dreams your master;
   If you can think—and not make thoughts your aim;
If you can meet with Triumph and Disaster
   And treat those two impostors just the same;
If you can bear to hear the truth you've spoken
   Twisted by knaves to make a trap for fools,
Or watch the things you gave your life to, broken,
   And stoop and build 'em up with worn-out tools:

If you can make one heap of all your winnings
   And risk it on one turn of pitch-and-toss,
And lose, and start again at your beginnings
   And never breathe a word about your loss;
If you can force your heart and nerve and sinew
   To serve your turn long after they are gone,
And so hold on when there is nothing in you
   Except the Will which says to them: 'Hold on!'

If you can talk with crowds and keep your virtue,
   Or walk with Kings—nor lose the common touch,
If neither foes nor loving friends can hurt you,
   If all men count with you, but none too much;
If you can fill the unforgiving minute
   With sixty seconds' worth of distance run,
Yours is the Earth and everything that's in it,
   And—which is more—you'll be a Man, my son!

CONTENTS

PROLOGUE

THE MESSENGER

I woke up shivering uncontrollably. My family and I were living in a two-room tenement apartment on the second floor of a walk-up building in the South Bronx. My sister and I shared the one bedroom, and my parents slept in the other room, which also served as our living room, kitchen and dining room. The apartment had little to no heat in winter. My mother would often leave a glass of water on my night table, and the following morning it would be frozen solid.

My shivering on that frigid morning in February of 1954 was due to more than the winter storm raging outside; I was very ill with both a sore throat and a high fever. These were the years when such an illness in a child was thought to be a prelude to polio or rheumatic fever, scourges of youth that had affected some children in our building and at school. My mother was in a panic, and my father was absent, as was often the case, at work in his clothing business. Unable to see the doctor in his office, my mother called on the phone, and asked if he could possibly make a house visit. Despite the terrible weather, he agreed to come over that evening after his office hours were finished.

Our family physician was Dr. Albert Goodman, an appropriate surname, to be sure. The waiting room in his office was always full, and no appointment was necessary to see him. He was of medium build, with thick, wavy brown hair. With his large pale blue eyes and kind face, there was a serene manner about him that put his patients instantly at ease. When he greeted me, I always felt as if I were a long lost relative or friend he was seeing again after a long absence. He had an accent foreign to the Bronx, having been raised in a small town in Western Pennsylvania. He had married his secretary later in life, in his early fifties, and they had young children. He drove the only Cadillac in the neighborhood, and lived in a large house in the Pelham Parkway section of the Bronx.

When he arrived that February night, I was still sick in bed, having undergone the usual alcohol and witch hazel sponge bath to bring down my fever. The apartment was freezing cold with the howling wind penetrating the window cracks, and I was doing my best to be brave, despite lingering fears my illness would get far worse before it got better.

The poverty of our existence in the Bronx was aggravated by the constant arguments of my parents over money. Every night my sister and I were awakened by a barrage of insults that my mother would throw at my father as soon as he walked through the door, after a hard day at work. The other sounds of the night were no better, which I clearly heard from our bedroom window overlooking a cement courtyard in the rear; the din of the above ground subway trains, other parents arguing, beggars pleading for charity, cries of babies and children, drunken revelers, loud music and televisions playing, and the squeals of passion, which I would learn to appreciate in later years.

At eight o'clock in the evening we heard footsteps on the stairs outside. Dr. Goodman knocked on the door and was let in by my mother. He came into the bedroom and with the ice and the snow covering his hair, face and overcoat, he appeared like an apparition. I don't know if it was the fever, or my fear, or the desperation I felt about my family's situation, but on that night I began to believe in angels. Not the chubby-cheeked cherubim that adorn greeting cards with golden halos and wings, but an emissary of healing, good will and kindness that walks among us. The Hebrew word for angel is "malach" which also means "messenger." That evening, Dr. Goodman was my angel, a sublime messenger who not only comforted and soothed me, but also awakened me to my destiny and an escape from the poverty that surrounded me.

After removing his outer clothes, Dr. Goodman came to my bedside to begin my examination. He looked around the room, sensing the cold, and began asking questions to both my mother and I about my symptoms. He was pensive as he began examining my throat, glands, lungs and heart. His stethoscope felt cold against my skin. Dr. Goodman began the abdominal exam with his hands, and while probing me asked a simple question, "Billy, what do you want to be when you grow up?" Not sure of what to answer, I heard myself reply, "a doctor." When he heard my answer, Dr. Goodman smiled and nodded his head while he completed his exam with the reflex hammer. He then reassured my mother that I only had a virus, and would soon recover. I was not going to die, and even the dreaded penicillin injection was not necessary.

He put on his overcoat, with the snow now melted, picked up his black medical bag and walked toward the door. My mother brought out her purse to pay him his customary five dollar fee for a house call. Surprisingly, he paused, pushed her hand away and looked at me steadily with his kind blue eyes while saying, "Billy is going to be a doctor. I am giving him professional courtesy." He then walked out of our apartment, down the stairs and into the blustery storm. My mother started to cry, and said, "an angel has just visited us." It was as if she had read my mind. She was correct, of course. I knew from that point forward what I wanted to do with my life – devote it to service and to easing the suffering of my fellow man. Little did I know at the tender age of seven what would be asked of me in following that destiny. What I do know, is that I would never recall a kinder act in my entire life.

CHAPTER

ORIGINS

"If I didn't mold my reality then I'd still be in the ghetto where people like me are supposed to stay. You have to dream your way out of the nightmare."

- will I. am

My story, like all who are a product of the immigrant experience, begins with a dream of being somewhere better - a safe place to call home. I come from a family of Jewish garment workers, not well educated, who arrived in New York City during the early 1900s from central Europe, before the onset of World War I. From 1880 through 1924 an increasingly steady flow of Jews made their way to America. Close to two million migrated from central Europe and the Russian Empire due to political upheavals and economic hardships. They all arrived seeking the "American Dream." This intense period of immigration came to an end with the passage of restrictive laws in the 1920s.

My paternal great grandparents (Frishman) and grandfather came from Belchatow, Poland, a small textile manufacturing town just south of Lodz that was then under Russian jurisdiction (Fig. 1A). During the early part of the 19th century, the family had migrated to Poland from Prussia for job opportunities hence my Germanic last name and my Yiddish-speaking forebears (Yiddish is a German-Hebrew dialect). Sadly, most of the Jewish population that remained in Belchatow during World War II were gassed in the concentration camps at Chelmno and Auschwitz.

My great grandparents Ezekiel (Iksil) and Shandil (Jenny) Markowitz Frishman (Fig. 1B) and their young children first settled in Hoboken, New Jersey (near Frank Sinatra's family home) (Fig. 1C). There were eight grown children, and my grandfather William (1891-1942) was the oldest. Like his father, he was a tailor who would open a small men's clothing factory and retail store in New York (Fig. 1D). The entire family would ultimately move to the Bronx, which was being developed after World War I, with the extension of the subways to the northern borough from Manhattan.

It is believed that the first European contact with the Bronx was in the early 1600s when Henry Hudson sought cover from a storm for his vessel the Halve Maen (Half Moon) in Spuyten Duyvil Creek. In 1639, the land was settled by Jonas Bronck, a Swedish sea captain from the Netherlands who built a farm and homestead at what became 132nd Street and Lincoln Avenue. He wrote of his new home, "The invisible hand of the Almighty Father, surely guided me to this beautiful country, a land covered with virgin forest and unlimited opportunities. It is a veritable paradise and needs but the industrious hand of man to make it the finest and most beautiful region in the entire world." Later, the area that had become known as "the Bronck's farm" and the "the Bronck's river" was shortened to "the Bronx."

In 1898 the Bronx became part of the consolidated City of New York and the borough became part of New York County, having been annexed from Westchester County which was located north of Manhattan. In 1914, Bronx County was created, and the borough experienced a boom period with an explosion in population growth to 1.3 million in 1930, largely due to the expansion of the subway system.

The borough is 25% parkland including the Bronx Zoo, the Botanical Gardens, and the largest

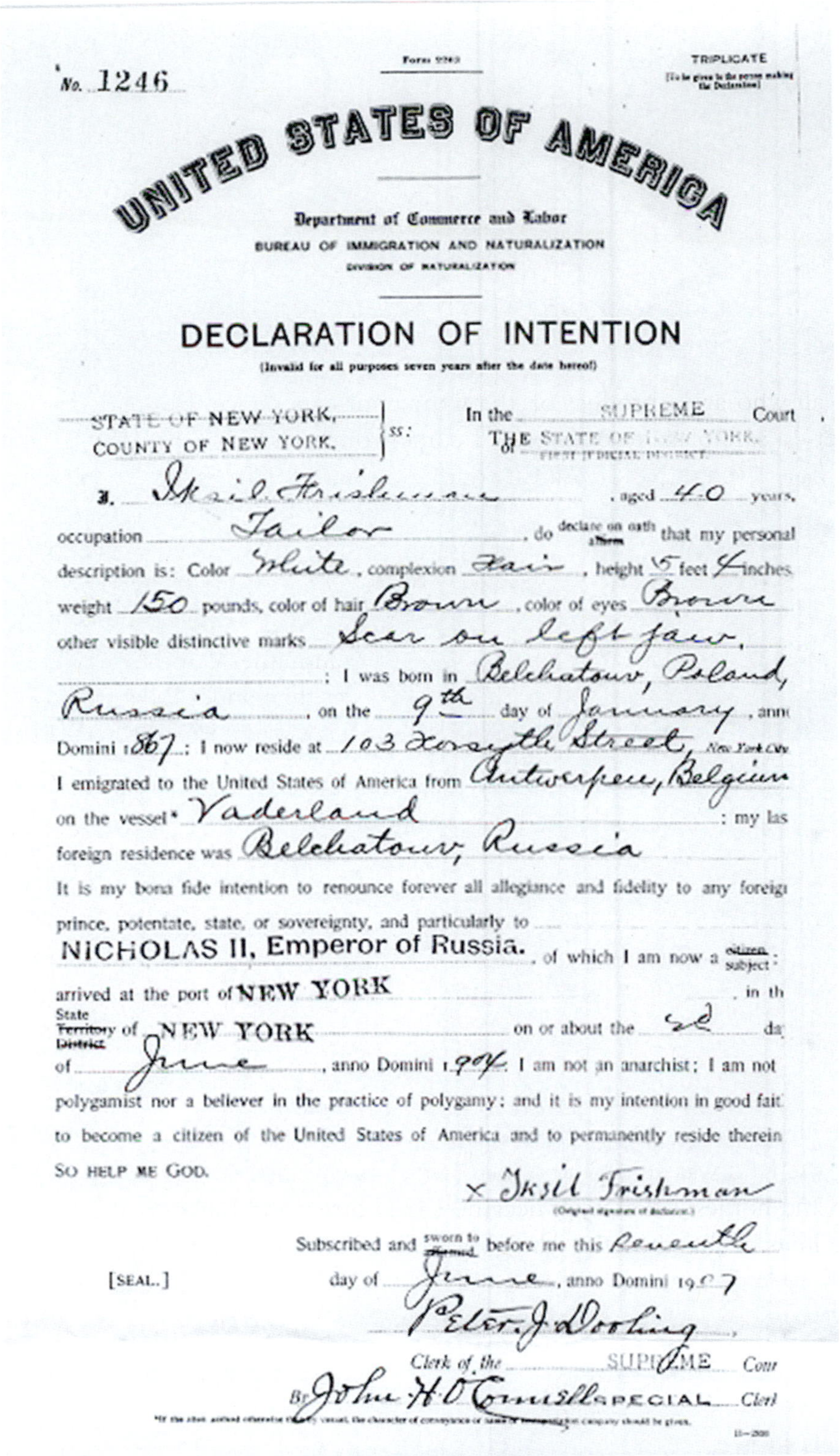

No. 1246

Form 2203

TRIPLICATE
[To be given to the person making the Declaration]

UNITED STATES OF AMERICA

Department of Commerce and Labor
BUREAU OF IMMIGRATION AND NATURALIZATION
DIVISION OF NATURALIZATION

DECLARATION OF INTENTION

(Invalid for all purposes seven years after the date hereof)

~~STATE OF NEW YORK,~~ } ss: In the SUPREME Court
COUNTY OF NEW YORK, } of THE STATE OF NEW YORK,
FIRST JUDICIAL DISTRICT

I, Iksil Frishman, aged 40 years, occupation Tailor, do declare on oath that my personal description is: Color White, complexion Fair, height 5 feet 4 inches, weight 150 pounds, color of hair Brown, color of eyes Brown other visible distinctive marks Scar on left jaw.; I was born in Belchatouv, Poland, Russia, on the 9th day of January, anno Domini 1867; I now reside at 103 Forsythe Street, New York City I emigrated to the United States of America from Antwerpen, Belgium on the vessel* Vaderland; my last foreign residence was Belchatouv, Russia It is my bona fide intention to renounce forever all allegiance and fidelity to any foreign prince, potentate, state, or sovereignty, and particularly to NICHOLAS II, Emperor of Russia, of which I am now a ~~citizen~~ subject; arrived at the port of NEW YORK, in the State of NEW YORK on or about the 2d day of June, anno Domini 1904; I am not an anarchist; I am not a polygamist nor a believer in the practice of polygamy; and it is my intention in good faith to become a citizen of the United States of America and to permanently reside therein. SO HELP ME GOD.

x Iksil Frishman
(Original signature of declarant.)

Subscribed and sworn to before me this Seventh day of June, anno Domini 1907

[SEAL.]

Peter J. Dooling,
Clerk of the SUPREME Court
By John H. O'Connell SPECIAL Clerk

*If the alien arrived otherwise than by vessel, the character of conveyance or name of transportation company should be given.

Figure 1A: The immigration papers of my great-grandfather, Iksil Frishman (1904). Belchatow was previously part of the Russian Empire (now it is part of Poland). Many Jews emigrated to Belchatow from Prussia for job opportunities in the textile industry as their settlement in other parts of the Russian Empire was forbidden.

Figure 1B: My great-grandmother Jenny Markowitz Frishman with six of her children after their arrival in the United States (1905).

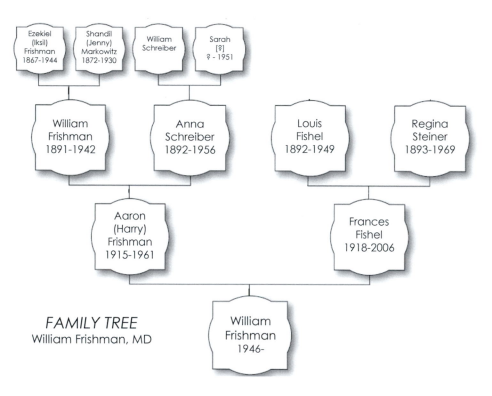

FAMILY TREE
William Frishman, MD

Figure 1C: Schematic of my family tree.

Figure 1E: Rear, center; the house on Bronx River Avenue where I spent the first two years of my life. Behind the house was a junkyard that lay adjacent to the river. My Uncle Phil is in the foreground with his glove, playing a game of baseball in the street.

Figure 1D: My paternal grandfather, Chaim Wolf (William Howard) Frishman. He owned a small men's clothing factory and a retail store in the Bronx. He died of a heart attack in 1942, years before my birth. I am named after him.

Figure 1F: On the left is my great-grandmother, Sarah Schreiber. In the rear is my grandmother, Anna Schreiber Frishman. To her right is my great-grandfather, William Schreiber with a full beard in the Jewish tradition.

Figure 1G: My maternal grandparents, Louis Fishel and Regina Steiner Fishel, dressmakers who settled in the Bronx after emigrating from Europe. My grandfather owned a small dress factory in New York that failed during the Great Depression.

park in New York City, Pelham Bay Park which includes Orchard Beach, one of the recreational projects of Robert Moses, the "Master Builder" of New York State. One of the spectacular architectural wonders of the Bronx and New York City is the Grand Concourse. This 182-foot wide Boulevard was modeled after the Champs-Élysées in Paris. It was completed in 1909 and has eight miles of "art deco" apartment houses from one end to the other. It also became the premier shopping area in the Bronx, competing with Fifth Avenue in Manhattan.

Another one of the great edifices of the Bronx, known all over the world, is Yankee Stadium. Built in 1923, it was the first athletic ballpark in America to be called a stadium. Previously, the Yankees played baseball at the Polo Grounds across the Harlem River in Manhattan, sharing the park with the New York Giants who had defeated them in the 1921-22 World Series. The Giants evicted the Yankees, so the team owners built their own ballpark in the Bronx. During the first season in 1923, Governor Alfred Smith (who ran for President in 1928) threw out the first ball on opening day, and Babe Ruth hit a home run. The Yankees would win their first of many world championships that same year. Every Bronxite has enormous pride in the Yankees, the greatest American professional baseball team in history. The stadium has always been a shrine for my family, and I have attended multiple games there with friends and relatives for over 60 years (*see Chapter 3*).

In 1925, my grandfather bought a four-family house in the Bronx on Bronx River Avenue where my father and his brothers were raised (Fig. 1E). Behind the house was a scrap metal business that bordered the river. My grandfather's men's clothing business would suffer during the Great Depression, but survived. He would die of a probable heart attack in 1942, and I am named for him. He married my paternal grandmother, Anna Schreiber, in 1913. Her family came to the United States from Austria (Fig. 1F). Her parents had seven children, all of whom were garment workers who settled in the Bronx. My grandmother Anna could not read or write English, only Yiddish and Hebrew.

My maternal great grandparents (Fishel) and their eight children emigrated from Western Russia, first settling on the Lower East Side in Manhattan before moving to the Bronx in the 1920s. My maternal grandfather, Louis Fishel, was a dressmaker who opened a small factory in Manhattan that failed during the Great Depression. He reopened another factory in the garment center of Boston. There is a story that my grandfather's workers in Boston loaned him the money to stay in business during a downturn, because they enjoyed working for him. He would die in 1949 of a heart attack at age fifty-seven, when I was three.

My grandfather married my maternal grandmother, Regina Steiner, in 1912 (Fig. 1G). My grandmother, the daughter of an innkeeper, came to the United States from the Carpathian Mountain region of Hungary with her three siblings. Her mother died when she was a young girl, and her father remarried and stayed in Hungary. Most of her family who stayed in Hungary died in the Holocaust during World War II. My grandmother was also a dressmaker who first settled in Ballston Spa, just outside of Albany, New York, eventually moving to Manhattan where she met my grandfather in the factory where they both worked. In time, they moved to the St. Lawrence Avenue section of the Bronx where they rented an apartment in a two-family house. After my grandfather's death, she lived with my aunt and uncle in the Bronx. She was fluent in English and Yiddish in both the spoken and written word, and was extremely kind to me. She also never lost her temper. In Yiddish she would always tell my parents to "let him be" with regards to my childhood antics.

My paternal great grandmother, Sarah Schreiber, was still alive when I was born but I don't remember her. My paternal grandmother, Anna, would live in our apartment building. She was short in stature, with a warm good nature and a kind laugh. I also never saw her angry. She would often babysit for me when my mother had to resume working to help with the family finances. Although

Figure 1H: My mother, Frances, as a young woman in the St. Lawrence area of the Bronx.

Figure 1I: My father, Aaron (Harry), with cigarette in hand, at Fort Sill, Oklahoma. He and all of my uncles were drafted to serve in the Army or the Navy during World War II. My Uncle Phil (Frishman) later received a purple heart for multiple combat wounds sustained in Europe.

she spoke English, she could only write in Hebrew. I was her only grandson.

I never knew my paternal grandfather, William, but he was said to be a stern individual who did not suffer fools gladly. My maternal grandfather, Louis, was a kind-hearted man, always with a joke, but he never was a success in business.

My father, Aaron (Harry) Herschel, who was born in Hoboken, New Jersey, and my mother, Frances, who was born in the Lower-East Side of Manhattan, were part of the "Greatest Generation," having grown up during the Great Depression and then living through World War II. They were both born in their homes. My parents first met at James Monroe High School in the Bronx. After high school, they both went to work during the heart of the Great Depression. My father worked in the family clothing store as a salesman and tailor, and my mother was a bookkeeper and secretary for various companies, including the original Sheraton Hotel (Fig. 1H). My father was drafted during World War II, and my parents married during the war in 1943 (Fig. 1I).

I was born after the war, the first among the "baby boomers," in Bronx Hospital (9 lbs., 12 ounces) located in the South Bronx, on November 9, 1946 (Fig. 1J). I was delivered by Dr. Jacob Clahr, who years later would become my patient. Bronx Hospital subsequently merged with Lebanon Hospital on the Grand Concourse to form the Bronx Lebanon Hospital, which is still thriving as an affiliate of Mount Sinai Medical School.

My mother had multiple miscarriages before my birth, and had to spend much of her pregnancy in bed. Years ago, during the time of my birth, the mother and newborn would spend at least a week in the hospital after the delivery. I was discharged with my mother after my ritual "bris" (Bris Milah, which is a Jewish ritual circumcision), performed at the hospital by a mohel (pronounced MOIL), eight days after my birth. A Mohel has expertise in the surgical performance of the circumcision, as well as religious training regarding the history and laws of the bris.

My original home was at 1239 Bronx River Avenue, not far from where the Pelham Bay subway line emerged from the underground, making a sharp turn over the river and continuing on over Westchester Avenue. The Pelham Bay line would be the subject of the movie, *The Taking of Pelham 123*. For the first two years of my life, I lived with my parents and paternal grandmother in the house my grandfather had purchased in 1925. My only faint recollection of that time was a visit to my maternal grandparents who were then living in Dorchester, Massachusetts.

In 1948 my parents moved two train stops east to 1134 Stratford Avenue in the Soundview area of the Bronx off Westchester Avenue (Fig. 1K). A short distance away, on Bruckner Boulevard, were prefabricated homes known as Quonset huts (Fig. 1L). Because of a housing shortage after World War II, these temporary shelters were used to house returning veterans and their families. The units were corrugated metal domes that got their name from the place where they were constructed, Quonset Point, Rhode Island. They were originally made by Seabees during World War II for military use. I remember walking among these homes with my father on his day off. Ultimately, as the housing shortage abated, these structures were all torn down.

We are also related to two other Frishman clans from Chicago and Denver. Jewish immigrants would often settle in Denver, Colorado if relatives had tuberculosis. A distant relative from the past was David Frishman (1861-1922), a famous Hebrew and Yiddish author (also spelled Frischmann) from Poland who edited multiple Jewish and Zionist publications. Frishman Street in Tel Aviv, Israel, one of the largest in the city, is named after David Frishman, and the street ends at Frishman Beach on the Mediterranean Sea. Anyone from the family who visits Israel gets their photograph taken on Frishman Street and then get their suntan on the Frishman beach. Once, while visiting Israel, I had my car "booted" in front of a McDavid's restaurant on Frishman Street. At the stationhouse, the police

Figure 1J: An early childhood picture, at age four, at the Bronx Zoo.

Figure 1K: Tenement buildings on Stratford Avenue in the South Bronx where I lived until age nine. Our two-room apartment faced the rear. We had little heat in winter and no air-conditioning. Note the fire escapes at the front of the buildings. Many apartment homes in the Bronx were burned to the ground by arsonists during the 1960s and 1970s, one of the great urban tragedies.

Figure 1L: Quonset Huts in the Bronx near our apartment. These temporary shelters housed families during severe building shortages after World War II. (Image courtesy of the Leonard Lief Library at Lehman College. Reprinted with permission.)

apologized, and waved the fine when they found out my last name was Frishman.

The neighborhood where we lived at this time consisted of walk-up apartment houses where struggling families were doing their best just to get by. It was a tough area, and we would form block gangs for protection. We were organized not by nationality or religion, but by location, so a gang could include Catholics and Jews who lived in the same building or on the same block. Fights were a common occurrence among the gangs, and it often related to the frustrations of poverty. However, it was vital to remain part of the neighborhood crew. One didn't wander too far from your apartment house unless you were in a group. It simply wasn't safe.

My experiences growing up on Stratford Avenue sensitized me to the profound impact of poverty on physical as well as mental health. I was a witness, both within my family and without, to the devastating consequences of limited resources and opportunities, and the stress of a daily struggle for security. What I have since learned is that coping with instability greatly inhibits one's capacity to self-regulate unhealthy behaviors such as smoking, drinking, gambling, poor diet and so on. I truly believe smoking and stress caused the early and tragic deaths of many members of my family from heart disease. While poverty gave me a deep empathy for all who must confront and survive it, my main consideration, especially in those early years, was how best to escape it.

CHAPTER

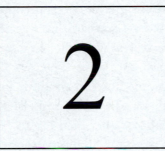

2

GREAT EXPECTATIONS

"Our lives are shaped not as much by our experience, as by our expectations."

- George Bernard Shaw

In truth, I had no right to expect anything. I was poor, shy and awkward (Fig. 2A), but my imagination defied the reality of my situation and insisted I was meant for greater things. Looking back, it is difficult now to determine which was the superior force; my intellect or my imagination. If I had to choose, I would say the latter. A vital part of my early life was going to the public library. My mother and father were avid readers, and once a week my mother would take me to browse through this amazing repository of knowledge, inspiration and kindred spirits. My favorite section was history. My interest in the presidents came from reading their biographies in the library or from books I had borrowed. I have always considered the library a center for intellectual life, for study, contemplation and doing research. I still enjoy holding a book rather than reading e-books. In later years, I would make a list of 300 classic novels and plays to read (my "Literary Bucket List"), and by now I have read them all (e.g. all of Shakespeare, Dickens, Eliot, Faulkner, Hemingway, Hardy, Dumas, Scott, Cooper etc.).

Since we lived in a small apartment, a lot of our recreational activities took place on the street. We played games that were passed down from one generation to the next, which included Johnny on the pony where one jumps onto a chain made by the bodies of your friends, stickball, punchball played with a pink "spaldeen" (a Spalding rubber ball), skelly played with bottle caps on the sidewalk, hopscotch or potsie, flip the card, hit the penny, boxball, king-queen played with a rubber ball against the apartment building wall, jump rope and stoopball. The local park had swings and monkey bars for climbing.

We had metal roller skates which we clamped to our shoes and tightened with a skate key. Other games included ring-o-levio, playing with a Duncan yoyo and marbles (small hard balls). Marbles was a seasonal game that we would suddenly start playing in the neighborhood; and for one or two weeks, we would compete in various activities, accumulating them as currency. We were always busy playing on the sidewalk, usually waiting for our parents to call us in for dinner. When it rained, we would play board games like Monopoly, Candyland or Chutes and Ladders in our small apartments.

On weekends in the winter, our fathers would take us ice skating on the frozen lake in Van Cortlandt Park, and in the spring to play baseball at Ferry Point Park located under the Whitestone Bridge where they had grass ball fields. There were few ball fields with grass in the Bronx, so we usually played ball in the street, including touch football. We always had to watch out for moving cars.

Along with the library, the candy store and the movie theatre were important neighborhood centers for me. The candy store near Stratford Avenue was called Jenny's. The store, which was open seven days a week, had a soda fountain to make egg creams, malted milk and ice cream sodas. They sold bottled soda kept cold in an ice box (we drank Pepsi and Mission soda because they came in 12-ounce bottles at the same price as Coca Cola which came in 7-ounce bottles – cans were not available). I still favor Pepsi over Coca Cola even today. The candy store sold cigars and cigarettes in packs

Figure 2A: At the Bronx Zoo with my grandmother, Regina, my sister, Randy and my mother..

and in cartons. At the age of six I could buy cigarettes for my parents at 24 cents a pack.

The candy store also sold newspapers, and people would wait for the evening editions to be delivered. Of course, the candy store sold all types of packaged candy, as well as school supplies, "Spaldeens," crayons, magazines and comic books. The store served as a reading room for children, and we could skim the magazines and comic books without buying them. I was a great fan of the classic comic book series that depicted classic novels, and the DC comic book series that featured Superman and Batman. The classic comics sold for 15 cents a copy, all other comics were 10 cents each. My love of reading comes not only from reading books, but also from the comics (although some said reading comics was a distraction).

I also went to the movies almost every week, usually on Saturday. In my neighborhood, we had the Ward Theater and there were chains like RKO and Loews that had movie theaters all over the borough. There was a drive-in theater near the Whitestone Bridge. The movie theater would feature two movies, five to ten cartoons, a newsreel and the coming attractions. The movie theaters were also the first places to use air conditioning, and people often went there just to cool off. Some of the theaters in the Bronx were truly majestic, like the Loews Paradise on the Grand Concourse with almost 4000 seats. The movie theater was the one place where you could escape the problems of the streets, and enter a fantasy world, and that is why many of the theaters were so grand in scale and design.

Television was also in its early days. We had one of the first television sets in our apartment house. The screen was 10 inches in size. People would also watch TV in the windows of appliance stores that sold the sets. My paternal grandmother, who now lived in our building, loved to watch TV in our apartment. Her favorite program featured Milton Berle. Other popular shows in the early years featured Ed Sullivan, Jackie Gleason and Sid Caesar. For children, there was the *Howdy Doody Show* with Buffalo Bob (who actually came from Buffalo, New York) and my favorite, *The Lone Ranger*, who never shot to kill. He was another role-model for me, as I have always abhorred violence. From early childhood, I recognized the need for peaceful negotiation, which was often difficult to accomplish in my neighborhood.

Other evening TV shows in the early years were *I Love Lucy* and my father's favorites, *Sergeant Bilko* and *Jack Benny*. I also enjoyed the quiz shows. One of my father's cousins, Herbert Stempel, was a contestant on *Twenty One*. He was one of the whistleblowers who reported the feeding of answers to the contestants, and was one of the antiheros in the movie *Quiz Show.*

The major sports programs on television were baseball, roller derby and wrestling. I learned to appreciate baseball by watching TV and have been a lifelong fan of wrestling. I don't' know what happened to roller derby.

We had an RCA record player that only played 45 rpm phonograph records. My mother tried to teach me to dance, playing Strauss waltz music. Radio was also a source of music, however, the radio mystery serials like *The Shadow* were dying out and were being replaced by television shows.

One favorite pastime was waiting for Jimmy, the ice cream man in the Bungalow Bar truck. I also remember the truck where women would bring out their knives to be sharpened, and the junk-rag man who pulled his wagon with a horse. Another memory of the Stratford Avenue neighborhood was the seltzer man who delivered carbonated water in recycled glass syphons along with bottles of Hoffman's soda.

I lived on Stratford Avenue until I was nine. Despite the crowded apartment we lived in, I did my best to be happy and productive. However, I always lived with a lurking fear of the threat of being attacked by a rival gang. To defend myself, I took boxing lessons in the local YMHA (Young Men's Hebrew Association) where my mother worked part-time, but I always tried to avoid fights and unnecessary confrontations.

My parents had attended public schools in the Bronx, as did my sister and I right through high school. I began my studies at Public School 77 (P.S. 77) at the age of four and a half in 1951. I had not attended preschool, as they were not popular at the time. My kindergarten class was large, about 70 students, and we had two teachers, Mrs. Jones, who was an African-American and would later become my patient, and, Mrs. Berman, who was married to an otolaryngologist, Dr. Herman Berman, who performed tonsillectomies on the many children in the class. Tonsillectomy was a highly prevalent procedure at the time, used as a means of preventing streptococcal infections and rheumatic fever. It has since been shown to be ineffective, and is rarely performed today for this indication.

P.S. 77 was built in the 1920s and was structurally similar to other public schools with similar numbers. P.S. 75, where my cousins and the author Herman Wouk attended, was almost a mirror image of P.S. 77. Our building had five stories, no elevator and a large common playground and yard covered with concrete. The school was on Ward Avenue, a four- block walk from our apartment on Stratford Avenue. I walked back and forth to school every day.

I have no major recollections of kindergarten except for not crying on the first day, and my tonsillectomy performed by Dr. Berman at the Bronx Eye and Ear Infirmary. The anesthetic was ether, and I was given the usual bowl of ice cream to relieve the postoperative sore throat.

My first grade teacher, and the woman who I believe awakened me to my academic potential, was Miss Rose Haber, who had also been my father's teacher at P.S. 77. The school principal, Mr. Fennell, had also been my father's principal. Miss Haber taught a class of about 40 students and spent a lot of time emphasizing self-discipline (sitting still). She would walk around the room with a ruler and rap us on the knuckles if our clasped hands were trembling. Our introduction to reading was from the book, *Alice and Jerry*, and we used bound notebooks for our writing and math. My homework was reviewed by my mother at night.

I have two major recollections of first grade. First, Miss Haber told my parents during open-school week that I would be "a student." The second, as mentioned, related to my love of reading and libraries. I had a fascination with presidents at an early age. Dwight Eisenhower had just been elected president in 1952 over Adlai Stevenson, and I remember watching his inauguration and the McCarthy Hearings in 1953 on the television. With my prodigious memory, which has never failed me, I would memorize the names of all the presidents, the years they were born and died, their spouses and vice-presidents, and soon Miss Haber would take me (her prize pupil) to all the classes at P.S. 77 where I would do a recitation of what I had memorized. I remember her picking me up in front of the class to show how proud she was of me. Miss Haber tried to get my parents to put me on a TV quiz show. I began to understand that my intellect was a tool, not only for survival, but for gaining adoration and respect.

My second grade (1953-1954) teacher was Mrs. Rose Stein, a soft-spoken woman who also believed in corporal punishment. I was given the prestigious job of delivering the mid-morning snack of cookies and milk. One of my substitute teachers that year was a former girlfriend of my Uncle Ken. He jilted her to marry my aunt Arlene, and the teacher made sure I never forgot what had happened to her. About two-thirds of the students were Jewish at P.S. 77, one-third were Italian and Irish, with one or two were African-American. Most of the Catholic children in the neighborhood went to parochial school. I don't know how we learned anything in such large classes, but I do remember that the students who had academic difficulties were severely chastised and punished.

The most significant event of that year (1954), as I have described, was the visit to my bedside by Dr. Albert Goodman. In mythology, every hero is called to their destiny by a messenger. I think it was my burgeoning academic abilities that had given me the courage to dream of being a doctor, and to verbalize that dream to Dr. Goodman. When he looked at me, with his piercing blue eyes, I knew he could "see" me. He knew I was serious about my intentions, even at such a young age. When he said, "Billy is going to be a doctor. I am giving him professional courtesy," I knew what he said was true; I would be a doctor.

Mythology also describes the hero's journey as an adventure in which the hero must undergo a series of tests. Each successful test further proves the hero's ability and advances the journey toward its apex. Without a doubt, my trials were harrowing. Physically, I had my deficits. We rarely used medical specialists, but once a year I visited with an ophthalmologist, Dr. Steinbach, who was following me for amblyopia (lazy eye) that was never totally corrected despite my wearing a patch over my good eye.

Dental care was provided by the local dentist, Dr. Milton Bonart. He would blast classical music in his office, and accompany opera singers performing on the radio. My orthodontists were the Fingeroth brothers. I started to wear dental braces when I was seven. Straightening teeth was a much longer process than it is today. I wore braces, or one of a number of other dental appliances, until I was in medical school.

Third grade (1954-1955) was also a bit traumatic. First, I had to attend speech therapy because of a lisp, a problem with the letter "s" (sibilant "s"), probably related to my dental braces. I will always remember my speech teacher's name, Mrs. Marshack. I was introduced to punch ball during recess, which I wasn't very good at. We learned to write script, and I always had a terrible handwriting.

President Eisenhower had a heart attack in 1955, and I remember saying a prayer in class for his recovery. My third grade teacher, Mrs. Plager, didn't like me as much as other students in the class. It bothered her that I was not a fighter, and would often avoid direct conflict. However, I was smart enough to know there was nothing to be gained by fighting back. The next day, four or five students would then attack you.

Mrs. Plager once called my mother to school, and I remember them talking, sitting alongside a fence, while I played punch ball. My Uncle Sydney, my mother's brother, had just died weeks before at the age of 41 from a heart attack, and when I returned home from school that day, my mother went into a tirade because Mrs. Plager had told her how I would grasp my hands under the desk when under stress. My mother told me this was a terrible behavior, and that my Uncle Sydney, in heaven, was upset with me. I would learn later that the hand squeezing was just a way of relieving anxiety, but my mother's extreme and inappropriate reaction affected me deeply. Childhood traumas can affect you for all the years of your life. More than ever, I was determined to overcome all of my difficulties, and my dream of being a doctor was never far from my mind.

By the fourth grade (1955-1956), I had really shown myself to be a good student. Once again, I had a kind and supportive teacher, Mrs. Gaffney, who also tried to get me on the *$64,000 Question* TV show on the subject of presidents. I used to walk with her to the subway every day at the end of school. That year our class put on a play for Armistice-Veterans Day. For the performance, I had borrowed a neighbor's Boy Scout uniform and I carried my Daisy air rifle. A big event in fourth grade was the start of the Salk polio vaccination program. Jonas Salk was a native of the Bronx who had gone to New York University Medical School. For the vaccination, we lined up in the school gymnasium to receive the injections in our arms. Polio was a terrible scourge, feared by all. The vaccine was a miracle.

In 1955, my mother went back to work full-time. She worked as a bookkeeper in a South Bronx ceramics factory. In 1956, with the increased income from my mother, we moved two more subway stops east to the Parkchester area to a three-room apartment at 1366 White Plains Road. Our old neighborhood was changing in its demography, with an influx immigrants from Puerto Rico. We moved on Wednesday, March 15, 1956. On March 14 I was still at P.S. 77. I remember walking with Mrs. Gaffney to the train station that day, crying, and she kissed me good-bye. She gave me a scroll depicting all the presidents as a farewell gift. I would never see her again. She was the best teacher I ever had in elementary school, and she gave me a great deal of courage and inspiration.

Parkchester was built by the Metropolitan Life Insurance Company (they also built Stuyvesant Town in Manhattan). It was built on property previously owned by the Catholic Church called the "Catholic Protectorate" between Tremont and Westchester Avenues. It housed 40,000 people, the largest middle-class housing development in the U.S. at the time. Unlike most of the Bronx neighborhoods, Parkchester had lawns and playgrounds. Macy's opened its first satellite store in Parkchester, and the Loews American, Art, and Circle movie theaters served the community. At the time, Parkchester was also racially segregated, and one could only obtain an apartment in the community after an intensive application process. The largest numbers of residents in Parkchester were Irish and Jewish, and east of the development was a large Italian community that extended for miles to Pelham Bay Park (the city's largest park) and the Long Island Sound.

Our apartment was also located one block from the new Cross Bronx Expressway (built by Robert Moses), which would have a great impact on the Bronx, since its construction hurt and dismantled many neighborhoods along its route. The road would be completed in 1960. Our block and its immediate vicinity had the usual candy store (Mr. Dave's), a luncheonette (Graber's), two grocery stores, a butcher shop, a bicycle repair shop, a cleaning store, a Chinese laundry, a barbershop, a beauty parlor and a launderette. The synagogue was around the corner, the Young Israel of Parkchester, and beyond that the beautiful expanse of Parkchester with Macy's and other fashionable stores.

Our apartment itself faced the front of the building and the heavy traffic on White Plains Road. There was one bedroom in the apartment where my sister and I slept; my parents slept in the living room. We had a kitchen and a small den where we had the TV, now with a 21-inch black and white screen. What was always of interest to me were the thick plastic covers that one used to protect the couch and chairs. We had no air conditioner, and used a window fan to cool the apartment in hot weather.

When we moved to Parkchester, I was in a new school, P.S. 102, where I did not know a soul. A boy can fit in right away if he is a good athlete, however, I was a terrible ball player and sports were never where I excelled. I did have a kind teacher, Mrs. O'Melia, who wore a large religious medal around her neck, and I found a friend, Steven Salgo, who was very kind to me. Moving to a new neighborhood as a shy, awkward youngster was traumatic. It was even worse to move in the middle of the school year, and in the middle of the week. In addition, my paternal grandmother had just died of metastatic breast cancer, at the age of 64, another family curse. She never saw our new apartment.

My father was 5'8" with dark blue eyes, brown hair, and had a physique like the late Yogi Berra (Fig. 2B). Like Yogi, he was a great ball player. He was also artistic, creative and could fix anything. He was kind and good-natured, and never had a bad word to say about anybody. My father was also the leader of the extended family, president of the family cousins-club and the author of the family cousins-club constitutions. Rarely did he lose his temper. He worked hard, and was extremely honest, always exhibiting a high level of integrity. Nobody had an unkind word to say about him, and he always taught me to be respectful and understanding of the other person's point of view. He was also very bright. Relatives said that if he had the opportunity, and had not been distracted by the economic depression of the 1930s and the war, he could have been a physician or an attorney. He went to night school for two years at the City College of New York.

Since my birth, my father had a men's clothing store in the Simpson Street area of the Bronx,

Figure 2B: My father and mother at a family wedding (the marriage of my Uncle Ken and Aunt Arlene, 1950).

an area that would later become known as Fort Apache, because of its high crime rate (ultimately, a movie was made with that title). My father's store was initially located in a Jewish neighborhood that would become predominantly Puerto Rican. I would often spend time with my father at the store, especially when I was off from school. In the 1940s and 1950s business was relatively good, but with the changing of the neighborhood demography, the business began to falter. Although my father was not successful in his business career, he was a great success as a family man and as a human being. Unfortunately, he was also a heavy smoker of Chesterfield unfiltered cigarettes, and his diet was definitely not low cholesterol.

My mother was 5'5" and had a thin frame, curly brown hair and piercing blue eyes. She was extremely bright and organized. She always dressed in an impeccable manner, and was demanding of herself as well as of others. During the 1950s she was one of the first married women in our neighborhood, with young children, to go to work. As a teenager, during the Great Depression, she had supported her family when her father was unemployed. Mom now worked on the top floor of an old loft building, a fire trap. Each day she would wake up early to prepare my sister and me for school, and provide each of us with a brownbag lunch. She would then take the Westchester Avenue bus to her job in the South Bronx. She would return home in the early evening after food shopping and would prepare dinner. After helping us with homework, she washed the dishes and scrubbed the floor on her hands and knees. Throughout her life, she never had outside household help. Mom had a hair-trigger temper and was the disciplinarian in the family. Although she was extremely devoted to my father and always concerned about his health, they argued frequently about finances. Unlike my father, she stopped smoking cigarettes in her mid-thirties.

The Parkchester area was a relatively safe place to live, and there was no need to form gangs to protect oneself. I learned how to ride a bicycle, a girl's bike which I shared with my sister. We would ride on the sidewalk because the automobile traffic was so great. I was active in the Boy Scouts although I did not advance very far in rank. The neighborhood also had two bowling alleys. Bowling as a sport was becoming very popular, although I was not very good at it. Sunday nights were reserved for dinners out at the local Chinese restaurant. The Chinese restaurants and the bakeries in the community were usually closed for the Jewish holidays, since Jews usually didn't eat out on those days or eat bread on Passover.

My fifth grade teacher was Mrs. Baker (1956-1957), and I had a good year with her, mastering fractions. What was changing now was the psychological cruelty that children were beginning to show one another that would continue to express itself into junior high school. I was a member of the school glee club, but didn't qualify for a musical instrument. I struggled in punch ball, but improved somewhat by changing my stance. I no longer bounced the Spalding ball before hitting it. In 1956, Eisenhower was re-elected president. Since the residents of the Bronx, always support the Democratic Party, I found it hard to believe that Eisenhower had defeated Stevenson again.

Sixth grade (1957-1958) was also a very good experience for me. I was appointed as a hall monitor and wore a special badge. I had a teacher, Mrs. Sybil Mellor, who loved to teach history. We were taught how to read and fold the *New York Times* (which I still read daily). Sputnik was launched by Russia and the space race began. This was a time when the Cold War was at its height. We had weekly air-raid drills requiring us to go under our desks to prepare ourselves for a nuclear attack from Russia. Sixth grade ended on a high note. Based on my academic record and math and reading scores, I was accepted into the special progress class for junior high school, and I danced with Susan Cowens at a daytime graduation party held at the gym. I was not sociable with the girls but Susan, a redhead and one of the pretty ones, came over to dance with me. I would never see her again after 6th grade, but

I would never forget her kindness that day.

I can go on with my adventures in the Bronx. I had lived in a tough neighborhood, and then in a less threatening neighborhood. I had good friends, the Yankees and the joy of having a large family around me. I was very successful in school. One of my friends and I wrote our own comic book, *Cutchie Brothers*, that made fun of people in the neighborhood. Had we pursued it in our older years, we would have had our own version of *South Park*.

Overall, I was grateful for the education I received in public elementary school. My only complaint was that there was no formal science curriculum. As a result, I was very deficient in science compared to some of my peers when I entered junior high school. We also had no real outdoor sports in school other than punch ball played in the school yard, while dodge ball and basketball were our indoor sports in the gym. The Bronx had few grass fields for sports, so we never played soccer or real baseball. It is hard for me to imagine how three other Bronxites, Hank Greenberg, Rocky Colavito and Ed Kranepool, ever made it as baseball stars in the major leagues.

CHAPTER

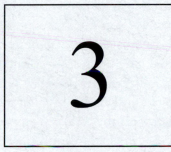

PARADISE

"It is in games that many men discover their paradise."

- Robert Lynd

Baseball and football require their own chapter and discussion, because for a Bronx-born and bred boy there is nothing more exciting than living in the same place as Yankee Stadium where Babe Ruth, Lou Gehrig, Joe DiMaggio, Whitey Ford, Mickey Mantle, Elston Howard, Yogi Berra and Derek Jeter played (Fig. 3A). The Bronx also had the likes of The New York Giants, Frank Gifford, Charlie Conerly, Roosevelt Grier, and Kyle Rote who all played football in the stadium.

It's hard to believe now, but I had little interest in watching baseball until 1954, when I turned eight. I had never played on any formal little league baseball teams, but was familiar with throwing, hitting and catching from my father. He bought me my first glove in 1958, a Rawlings Bob Turley model. (Bob Turley won the Cy Young award that year). You had to use both hands to catch with it. It was during the World Series of 1954 that I began to appreciate baseball. I clearly recall watching the fourth game between the New York Giants and Cleveland Indians with my father. I remember Dusty Rhodes hitting a twelfth inning, pinch hit, home run to help win the series for the Giants in four games. That was the game when Willie Mays made his great catch off the bat of Vic Wertz.

I had a burgeoning interest in baseball in 1954, but I became a devotee of the game in 1955, and have been ever since. I remember the exact day and the exact game. I was home sick from school, watching a Yankee game on television. Andy Carey, the third baseman for the Yankees, hit a home run and they won four to three. It was as if I had been asleep, and suddenly woke up to a whole new, amazing world. I could escape all of my troubles and get lost in each moment of the game and in all the possibility of each pitch. I could forget about illness, bullies and poverty and get lost in the game of baseball.

I went to my first game with my father in 1955, a Tuesday night game. Multiple generations of a family can watch a baseball game together and all get something out of the experience. Many of my most precious memories include going to baseball games with my father and my uncles as a child. Night lights were installed at Yankee Stadium in 1946, so before that time there were only day games. My father always bought upper grandstand seats which at the time cost $1.30 for a ticket. I remember walking up the stadium ramps and suddenly seeing the field, the lights, the spectacular green grass, and noticing the matted brown dirt in the infield and the smell of beer in the air. The Yankee team sponsors were Ballantine and Knickerbocker beers and Winston cigarettes. The Brooklyn Dodgers had Schaefer beer, and the New York Giants baseball team had Knickerbocker beer. Ultimately, the Mets would have Rheingold beer. None of these breweries are in business now, but some local microbreweries are coming back into the area.

At that first game I attended with my father, the Yankees won seven to six over the Detroit Tigers in extra innings. Irv Noren, a utility outfielder, hit two homeruns, Mickey Mantle hit one and Gil McDougald, the shortstop, also hit one. Dad and I went to a second night game that year where

Figure 3A: The old Yankee Stadium with the support poles that often blocked the view (1962). The stadium was a Bronx shrine where I spent many happy times with friends and family. (Image courtesy of the Inge Morath Foundation. Reprinted with permission.)

the Yankees won one to nothing against the White Sox. Yogi Berra, who died recently, at age 90, hit a homerun in the sixth inning. It's as if it all happened yesterday.

Going to games with my father was so special because I had very little time with him. He worked six days a week until nine o'clock at night at his clothing store. His only evening off was Tuesday, which is how we could go to the night games. The only day of the week I was able to see my father was on Sunday. I got to spend some time with him in his store. When business was good, it was wonderful. As business began to wane, I remember sitting by the store window and praying for customers to come in.

I was very close to my dad, in many ways he was a model father. Although he tried to coach me in baseball, he never criticized me for not being a good player. He always said, just try your best. He used military aphorisms like "double-time" when I did not hustle on the ball field. The only time he was critical of me was when I continued to shoot underhand in basketball, when he wasn't looking, and not overhand.

My father was the only sports coach I ever had until high school and as a baseball player, and a hitter, I did have a good "batting eye" (I was very hard to strike out), although I did not hit the ball very far. My father was also an outstanding handball player (once a popular city sport in New York City and Chicago), where gloved players hit a hard black ball against a wall. When I was growing up, handball was played less often.

Since my father had a "heart condition," I was always worried about something happening to him, especially when he played ball. When he would fall asleep with a book in his hand, I would watch his breathing to make sure he was all right. Sports are often a way boys bond with their fathers. I will always be appreciative of the love of sports that I acquired by being the son of my father and a son of the Bronx. Today, I constantly use baseball metaphors when I teach my students (*see "Aphorisms" in Chapter 14*). I am, and will always remain a "diehard" Yankee fan.

The seasons from 1955-1964 were a wonderful time to be a Yankee fan. The team won nine American League pennants and four World Series under Casey Stengel, Ralph Houk and Yogi Berra. Despite these glory years for Yankee fans, one of the most devastating moments in Yankee history was the seventh and final game of the 1960 World Series. I was listening to the game on a transistor radio with friends in a local park. Bill Mazeroski, the second basement for the Pittsburgh Pirates hit a game winning homerun in the ninth inning off the Yankee pitcher, Ralph Terry; the first World Series victory in history decided by a walk-off home run. The Yankees lost ten to nine. Yankee fans grieved at the time, and many still grieve to this day. After 1964, the Yankees suffered as competitors, but ultimately resumed their former glory under Billy Martin and then Joe Torre during the last quarter of the twentieth century. The Yankees are the greatest professional sports franchise in history with 27 World Series' wins. More contemporary Yankee stars include Derek Jeter and Mariano Rivera, both of whom I saw play in countless games.

The first joy of baseball is the actual game. The second joy of baseball is the cards. I was a big collector from 1955 to 1958 with complete sets. In our neighborhood baseball cards were like currency. In the words of Penny Marshall, another child of the Bronx, "We all used to collect baseball cards that came with bubble gum. You could never get the smell of gum off your cards, but you kept your Yankees cards pristine." I remember trading 50 duplicate cards I had for a Camilo Pascual rookie card I was missing from my collection. I memorized all the information on the back of the cards, as well as statistics from baseball almanacs, and it was by this process that I began to hone my skills and memory for academics.

One key event in the history of baseball in the Bronx was the 2008 closing of Yankee Stadium (the first ball park to be called a stadium). There was great controversy about closing the ball park despite its age (built in 1923) and the paucity of toilets, especially for women. The old stadium used to have support poles that often blocked the views of fans. I must say, the new stadium is beautiful (see Fig. 3B).

I never had an interest in the national league baseball teams, the Brooklyn Dodgers and the New York Giants who played in Manhattan. When both teams left in 1957 for the West Coast, it was devastating for Brooklynites and Manhattanites; as a Bronxite, I was not affected since the Yankee's stayed. The New York Mets eventually replaced the Dodgers and Giants in 1962.

During the years 1955-1964, the New York Giants football team also played in Yankee Stadium. Marty Glickman was the great announcer for the Giants, as were Mel Allen and Phil Rizzuto for the Yankees. The Giants won the NFL football championship in 1956 and five divisional championships in 1958, 1959, 1961, 1962 and 1963.

I also cheer for the New York Knickerbocker basketball team and the New York Rangers ice hockey team who both play in Madison Square Garden in Manhattan. College sports were never popular in New York, because we have so many professional teams. During 1955-1964 both the Knicks and the Rangers were weak contenders. Hockey was dominated by the Montreal Canadiens, and basketball by the Boston Celtics.

Figure 3B: The new Yankee Stadium. (By Groupe Canam - Own work, CC BY-SA 3.0.)

Knowledge of baseball and other sports trivia also helped me survive during the neighborhood confrontations with other groups of boys. Sometimes a tough baseball question would come up, and my friends could always count on me to answer it. I was always protected in my circle of friends, not because of my baseball prowess on the field, but by my knowledge of baseball statistics off the field. Yes, baseball has been good to me; over the years, it has provided me with a worldly paradise and a refuge.

CHAPTER

COURAGE

"It takes a lot of courage to become who you really are."

- e. e. cummings

I began junior high school in September 1958. Castle Hill Junior High School (J.H.S. 127) was a co-educational school located on Castle Hill Avenue, directly east of Parkchester and just outside its boundaries (Fig. 4A). When my parents attended school, in the Bronx, there were no junior highs. For them, elementary school ended in the eighth grade, and high school would follow with grades nine to twelve. J.H.S. 127 covered grades seven through nine.

I was chosen for the special progress classes (SPs) where a student would complete seventh grade and then skip to ninth grade, essentially completing three years in two. A student was chosen for the SPs if both their reading and math levels were two years ahead of grade. In my junior high school years, there were eleven regular classes and seven SP classes. I was assigned to 7SP2 which was the journalism specialty class, with French as the assigned foreign language. The science specialty class was 7SP1, and 7SP4 was the orchestral music class, with Spanish as the assigned foreign language. Looking back, I think learning Spanish would have been much more practical than French, especially in the Bronx.

In junior high school, for the first time, we moved period by period to enable us to learn different subjects from a series of teachers. Subjects included French, math, a combination social studies and English course called "Core," general science, typing, gym, hygiene and shop. Shop was included in the curriculum to teach vocational skills to boys. Girls were not assigned to shop, but to home economics classes.

For the first term of seventh grade I was assigned to metal shop, taught by Mr. Vogel, where I made a metal tie clip for my father. I didn't have a lot of skill in this area, and kept on breaking the blade of the jeweler's saw. I received a grade of 70 for my tie clip (passing was 75), but scored higher for doing extra polishing work in the class. I also won my first election; I was chosen shop foreman by my classmates.

During the second term of seventh grade, I was assigned to printing shop where we set type using individual metal letters (movable type) and learned how to print various documents. In order to create a template, we had to carefully set each letter by hand into metal trays, which was a detailed, meticulous process. Our teacher, Mr. Farber, had a habit of sneaking up behind a student and slamming a chair on the floor, often causing the hapless student to throw his type into the air.

In ninth grade I was assigned to wood shop where we made a wood lamp. My project looked nothing like a lamp, and I don't know how I passed the course. I think our teacher, Mr. Avy, took pity on me. For the last term of ninth grade, I was again assigned to Mr. Farber in printing shop.

J.H.S. 127 was a fairly new school, about five years old. It was a long building with a large concrete schoolyard. It also had handball courts where we played with a pink spaldeen rubber ball, rather than the regulation black handball. During recess, we would also play punch ball. We didn't play softball or baseball. During this time, again, girls didn't participate in sports, only jump rope, or they would watch the boys play.

In junior high, the teachers of the academic subjects were excellent. I did well in all my courses, except for shop and typing, and made the honor roll each term. I especially liked my seventh grade teacher, Mrs. Dancis, who emphasized social studies in the Core class. History was always my favorite subject. In seventh grade, we studied New York State history, and I remember doing particularly well on my book report on the *Last of the Mohicans* by James Fenimore Cooper.

My time in junior high was somewhat awkward, as it is for most young people. All of my classmates were at different stages of physical development. Some had reached puberty and some hadn't. The boys were often involved in discussions about sex, and were obsessed with female anatomy. I had my growth spurt in junior high, and would reach my adult height of 5'11".

Because students were at different levels of development, junior high could be a cruel place. Some students, including me, were often bullied. There were days when it took a lot of courage just to attend my classes. I think it was even worse for some of the girls who were treated very poorly, especially by the boys. I remember two girls in particular who were constantly teased and taunted. The Italian students were often picked on by some of the Jewish students who, at the time, were more plentiful in the public schools. There were often fights after school between the different boys. I avoided fighting by not being confrontational, and by removing myself from trouble as fast as I could. There was an exception to this - I was very shy around girls, but rose to their defense when they were being bullied. I have to say I am still very proud of the way I defended them.

I think it may have been these early experiences that encouraged me always to be on the side of the underdog, and never be part of any heckling, bullying or gossip. I also remain grateful to those individuals who stood up for me when I was the target of bullying. In this way, there may be some slight upside to being bullied, as it instills a great deal of empathy for others who are suffering. In truth, I also think it created a powerful drive in me – to prove to the bullies I could be successful. It gave me resilience and courage, because I knew I could go through hell and survive. I think it was Winston Churchill who said, "If you're going through hell, keep going." I kept going.

In ninth grade I was made *The New York Times* monitor, and was responsible for receiving the newspapers from the delivery truck and making sure they were distributed to the classes. It was a prestigious position, much better than being the milk monitor in elementary school. *The New York Times* sold for five cents an issue at the newsstand, and was sold for three cents at the school. We were all encouraged in school to read *The New York Times* and not the *Daily News* or *Mirror*.

In junior high, I also learned about personal finance. I received a two-dollar weekly allowance from my parents; one dollar and seventy five cents was spent on school lunches which were thirty-five cents a day. At the end of the week, I had an extra twenty five cents for bubble gum and baseball cards. I also tried to put a little aside from the remainder of my allowance.

Junior high also broadened and facilitated my interest in science. Science was not taught well in my elementary school. However, my ninth grade general science teacher, Mr. Smolar, was one of the best teachers I would ever have. He was both funny and informative, and really made the subject of science come alive. He also inspired me to one day be a teacher.

The individual who helped me the most with schoolwork during this time was my father. Dad was a good writer and an avid reader, and he corrected my writing assignments. He also helped illustrate my general science notebooks. With what little time he had with his long work schedule, Dad was there for me. I was always self-propelled in school, but Dad really made the experience of learning meaningful. I probably adopted his writing style for prose. My mother was also helpful, making sure

Figure 4A: Junior High School 127 on Castle Hill Avenue in the Bronx.

my homework was complete, but she did not have the patience with me that Dad had. I realize now how important it is for a young student to have parents who care and take an interest in their child's studies.

During my years in junior high, I didn't have many friends outside of my apartment building. My best friend was transferred to a public boarding school in Pleasantville, New York. My mother would often encourage me to find outside friends. There were twin brothers in my class who were from a different neighborhood, Pelham Parkway, and who were brought to our school by bus. The Kramer twins became my good friends, as well as another friend from Parkchester, Carl Buchman.

Of course, there were also a few embarrassing moments for me during junior high school. In seventh grade our science teacher, Mr. Monaco, went around the class asking each of us what our parents did for a living. I knew my father was struggling in his business, and when asked to speak I blatantly lied saying that my father sold Lincoln Continental cars. Why I said this I don't know, because other people knew that my father had a clothing store. Until this day, I feel ashamed that I didn't tell the truth about my father, and there would be other stories I would recite that were not true. Perhaps it was because I was a bit insecure during this time and lacked self-confidence, but I would like to think that, like many of the great writers I admire, I just had a very vivid imagination and a budding gift for storytelling. I still enjoy making up stories for my grandchildren.

During my junior high school years, the Yankees won the World Series in 1958 behind the pitching of Bob Turley. In 1959, the Yankees fell short during the season and the Los Angeles Dodgers beat the Chicago White Sox in the World Series. Larry Sherry, a Jewish relief pitcher, was the star player for the Dodgers.

I also had my Bar Mitzvah (*see Chapter 5*), but the crowning point of my junior high school years was passing the exam for the Bronx High School of Science, the most prestigious public high school in New York, and, I believe, in the whole country. To be accepted into Bronx Science, you had to be recommended by your junior high school, especially your math and science teachers, and pass a difficult written exam that included vocabulary and math.

I had prepared well for the vocabulary portion of the exam by reading a wonderful book on word derivations from Greek and Latin word roots. During the exam I thought I was doing well until I realized, with 10 minutes to go, that I missed a page of vocabulary words. I barely completed the exam. In March 1960, three months before I graduated junior high school, I was admitted to Bronx Science. My homeroom teacher, Mr. Bloom, made the announcement. It was one of the happiest days of my life, and I felt especially good because I had made my parents so proud. I graduated junior high in June with honors because I had made the honor roll every term, and had no conduct demerits. The graduation ceremony took place in the Loews American movie theater in Parkchester. I was seated in the last row of the graduates, with my parents sitting right behind me. Indeed, it took a lot of courage to get there, but I felt I was finally on my way to becoming the man I dreamed I could be.

CHAPTER

TRADITIONS

"Traditions, traditions. Without our traditions, our lives would be as...as shaky as a fiddler on the roof!"

- Tevye, *Fiddler on the Roof*

I come from a family of secular Jews who were more observant when they had lived in Europe. At least in my generation, and including those before me, there was very little intermarriage with people of other religions. I never remember going to synagogue with both of my parents, but we celebrated the holidays of Rosh Hashanah, Yom Kippur, Hanukkah and Passover with family get-togethers and traditional dinners. For those who aren't familiar with Jewish holidays, Rosh Hashanah, which translates to "head of the year" or, New Year, is the beginning of the Jewish calendar year inspiring repentance from sin and the hope of renewal. It is celebrated over two days in early autumn (September or October). Traditional foods include apples dipped in honey, circular challah bread (special Jewish braided bread served on the Sabbath and holidays) as well as pomegranates and pumpkins and other round foods, which are said to represent the unending life cycle. Other traditions includes foods that are gold-colored, like carrots (and honey). Some unique activities that are associated with the holiday include the sounding of the shofar, or ram's horn. Many Jews send New Year's cards for this holiday.

Nine days after the first day of Rosh Hashanah is the solemn holiday of Yom Kippur, or "day of atonement." According to Jewish tradition, on Rosh Hashanah God initially inscribes each person's fate for the coming year into the Book of Life, and then waits until Yom Kippur to finalize the inscription. There are no specific foods associated with this holiday as it is a day of fasting. Yom Kippur is one of the most culturally significant Jewish holidays, and is observed by many secular Jews who may not observe other holidays. During this time, it is widely observed that attendance at synagogue significantly increases.

Two weeks after Rosh Hashanah, the Jewish New Year, the eight-day holiday of Succoth (tabernacles) takes place. As part of this holiday, Jews are required to take their meals in a temporary booth (a sukkot) to commemorate the protection given to the Israelites during the forty wandering years after the exodus from Egypt. In our crowded neighborhood, nobody had space to build a sukkot, except in the synagogue, so we could not celebrate the holiday at home. As mentioned previously, this holiday is very memorable to me because Bill Mazeroski hit his game winning home run to beat the Yankees in the 1960 World Series on the first day of Succoth. The Succoth holiday ends with Simhat Torah where Jews celebrate the Torah (the five books of Moses), and restart the year-long Torah reading beginning with the first book of Genesis and the story of creation. I remember holding the Torah in synagogue on this holiday as we celebrated the giving of the Torah to the Jewish people.

Hanukkah literally translates to "dedication." It is a holiday celebrated over eight days that commemorates the Jewish recapture and rededication of the Temple in Jerusalem in 164 BCE. It is also known as the "Feast of Lights." The holiday is observed by lighting the Hanukkah lamp, or menorah. The Hanukkah lights are said to be for "illumination of the house" so that those who pass by may observe the lights and be reminded of the holiday's miracle. It is also associated with gift-giving,

1935

Figure 5A: Frishman family Passover seder (1935).

Figure 5B: At my Bar Mitzvah, age 13 (1959).

and it falls at roughly the same time of year as the celebration of Christmas.

Passover, which celebrates the exodus of the Jewish people from slavery in Egypt to freedom in Israel, centers around festive meals served over two nights, with each food having its own religious symbolism. It is the holiday that evokes some of the fondest memories of my youth, and its celebration continues to energize my spirit each year. Celebrated for over 3,000 years (Fig. 5A), the traditional Passover festive meal was also the last supper that Jesus Christ celebrated with his disciples, and the bread and wine from that meal remain important symbols in Christian liturgy.

I can still remember the aromas and tastes of those Passover meals, with the entire family happy to be together, and the master of the house instructing us about the significance of each food on the holiday table. The Passover holiday occurs in the early spring, very close to Easter, and the warmer weather following the chill of winter, the brilliant colors from the blooming flowers and trees, contribute to the mood of rebirth and freedom.

In the Jewish tradition, the major holidays are celebrated on multiple days, so that one can enjoy the celebration with the maternal side of the family on one day, and the paternal side on the other day. My grandmothers, in keeping with their traditions, prepared the Passover meals making each food from basic ingredients, except for the grape wine and the matzoh (unleavened bread) which were purchased separately. As a young boy, I remember overhearing my paternal grandmother talking with her sisters on the phone about the size of the chickens she had purchased for the holiday. Both grandmothers made the traditional gefilte fish from pike, and the matzoh ball soup made from chicken, with the meat of the bird served as a separate dish. The aromas from the food remain in my memory. It was recently demonstrated that the odors from childhood are kept in our brain's long term memory, similar to words and visions. Our mood will change favorably or unfavorably later in life, being exposed to those familiar aromas we sensed as children.

The Passover wine is typically a very sweet Concord grape variety. I could never develop a taste for French red wine because it is not as sweet as the four cups of wine we would drink at our Passover meals.

With all the wonderful foods of the holiday, no Passover would be complete without matzoh, a flat, dry, unleavened bread that is both tasteless and very constipating. According to legend, the ancient Jews, in their haste to leave Egypt during the Exodus, ate matzoh instead of traditional bread because they didn't have time for the dough to rise. Matzoh is remarkable in many ways. You can keep an open box of matzoh on the shelf for years, and it will not spoil. Insects will never invade a box of matzohs; rodents would rather starve than eat it. Other traditional foods include eggs in salt water to commemorate spring and rebirth; salted parsley and horseradish which represent the bitterness of slavery, and finally the traditional meal consisting of meat, chicken and vegetables.

Our Passover meals were always attended by parents and siblings, grandparents, aunts and uncles, cousins and, often, strangers who had no family with whom to celebrate. We would read from a traditional prayer book (Hagaddah) to help to explain the meaning of Passover, and the significance of each traditional food and the four cups of wine we drink. The meal would conclude with festive songs and very sweet desserts. I can still hear the voices of my father and uncles explaining the Passover service, and can still envision my grandmothers bringing out the different plates of food. The great joy of being together with family at Passover, remain imbedded in my mind.

As my grandmothers aged and passed on, the Passover meals were prepared by my maternal Aunt Lillian on the first night, and my paternal Aunt Arlene on the second night. My aunts prepared the Passover foods in a fashion similar to my grandmothers. My aunts and uncles lived in private homes in the Bronx and New Jersey where twenty to thirty people would assemble for the holidays.

We lived in a small apartment, and my mother, who worked outside the home, never had the time or space to make the food preparations necessary for the Passover meal.

Fifty days after the end of Passover (Pentecost) is the holiday of the Shavuot which celebrates the day the Torah was given to Moses and the Jewish people on Mount Sinai commemorating the beginning of the Jewish Nation. Eating cheesecake is a custom of the holiday.

When I was eight and a half years-old and still living on Stratford Avenue in the South Bronx, I began my Hebrew school studies. Hebrew school was held for one-and-a-half to two hours after public school in a local synagogue, where I would learn to read and write Hebrew and learn about Jewish customs and history. My parents and grandmothers spoke Yiddish, usually to keep secrets from me. One of my grandmothers (my father's mother, Anna) could not read English, only Yiddish. She read *The Forward*, the Jewish-Yiddish newspaper to which I still subscribe to in an English version.

When I started Hebrew school my grandmother Anna, who lived in our apartment building, gave me two yarmulkes (Jewish head coverings) that she had saved for me. She told me to wear the black one during the week in Hebrew school and the white one on the Sabbath. I started to go to Saturday religious services which were called Junior Congregation, where we were separated from the adults. The majority of children who went to Hebrew schools were boys. Bat mitzvahs for girls would become more common in the next generation.

Going to Hebrew school was, in part, intended to prepare me for my bar mitzvah at age 13. Unlike my achievements in public school, I was not a good student. The school I attended after we moved was part of an orthodox synagogue, the Young Israel of Parkchester, which was around the corner from our apartment house on White Plains Road. The Young Israel Hebrew School curriculum was moving at an advanced pace, and I quickly fell behind in my studies and never caught up. My parents could not help me. Most of my Hebrew school classmates came from other neighborhoods and public schools, so I never made close friendships with them.

Although I did very well in learning Jewish history and customs, I often received D grades in Hebrew, especially in speaking and writing the language. I could read Hebrew, but never understood what I was reading, unless it was translated for me. Hebrew school provided a respite from the pressures of public school. I would often act as the class clown, which was especially annoying to the rabbi. In hindsight, I was the rebel of Hebrew school.

My second grade teacher in Hebrew school was an Israeli woman, Mrs. Weintraub, who never liked me, and gave me D grades. I tried to convince my mother that in Hebrew school, D stood for "dandy," but she didn't believe me. In third grade with Mr. Bronfman, a moonlighting public school teacher, I began to understand Hebrew a bit better, and my fourth grade teacher, Rabbi Maurice Schwartz, tried his best with me.

During the fourth grade of Hebrew school, I began my formal bar mitzvah lessons preparing to read and sing my haftorah portion. Haftorah literally translates as, "taking leave" and it is a blessing recitation which is central to the bar mitzvah ceremony. I recall that my cousin Robert, who had his bar mitzvah two years earlier, went blank when it was time to recite his haftorah in synagogue. Of course, I was worried about how I would perform at my own bar mitzvah. My haftorah lessons were taught to me one-on-one by Rabbi Schwartz, and I felt well prepared for the upcoming big day.

For a boy, a bar mitzvah is one of the most important days of his life (Fig. 5B). It is a puberty rite, at which he becomes a man of the faith who can now pray along with the adult men of the congregation. With the bar mitzvah, there is also the obligation to put on tefillin (also called phylacteries), a set of small black leather boxes containing scrolls of parchment inscribed with verses from the Torah, held by straps wrapped around the left arm and around the head during prayers. The idea of this ritual is to have the word of God wrapped around you.

Before my bar mitzvah ceremony, Rabbi Schwartz showed me how to put on tefillin, and he gave me a daily prayer book which I still have and treasure. My bar mitzvah was scheduled to be celebrated on Saturday, November 21, 1959. I was in the ninth grade in junior high school, and had turned 13 on November 9, 1959. The day of my bar mitzvah was cold and damp, and I woke up very excited. For the first time, my father and I went to synagogue together. Waiting at the corner of the street that morning were my father's younger brothers, Phil and Kenny. I never felt so proud in my life, walking to synagogue that day together with both my father and uncles.

During the synagogue service there was a Torah reading, followed by my haftorah recital. Many of our neighbors were there, sitting in the usual pattern with men separated from the women. My haftorah recital went very well, with maybe a few mistakes, and I recited my prayers as well as I could.

Following the Saturday morning service, there were three celebrations that weekend. The first in synagogue, was for the congregants who had attended the bar mitzvah service. The second was for neighbors and some relatives at our apartment. My father, who couldn't miss a Saturday business day, went to work after the service. The third party, and largest, was held the next day at the Paradeen Manor, a catering hall located off the Grand Concourse on Mount Eden Avenue. (At a height of 80 feet, Mount Eden, is the highest peak in the Bronx). The Cross Bronx Expressway, which was being constructed at the time, caused the Paradeen Manor to be demolished one year later since it was in the direct path of the road. The final bar mitzvah party involved much planning.

My parents looked at various venues for the party which included the Hotel Pierre, in Manhattan (one of Richard Nixon's daughters was married there) where the cost would have amounted to the combined salaries of my parents for two years. Another venue was Phil Gluckstern's, a Kosher restaurant in Manhattan, which was too modest. Other catering halls in the Bronx included the Imperial Gardens, the Park Terrace and the Concourse Plaza Hotel (across from Yankee Stadium, where the ballplayers stayed). My parents chose the Paradeen because the price was reasonable around $2,000 for 200 guests. The Master of Ceremonies, and the owner of the catering hall, was my orthodontist's brother. To save money my parents did not hire a photographer, so we have no pictures from the party. My father's friend, Sol Cohen, a nightclub photographer, did take individual posed photos of my sister and me in our apartment. We had a smorgasbord luncheon that did not include waiter service. For entertainment, we had a five-piece live band, whose leader was a childhood friend of my father, Hal Silvers.

The party was held on Sunday, November 22, 1959, in the afternoon. The large number of guests at the occasion was related to the large number of relatives I had living in the Bronx. My parents had 21 aunts and uncles who were the brothers and sisters of my grandparents. At the time, my grandmother, Regina, was my only living grandparent. My parents also invited 60 of their cousins along with their spouses and other family friends. My cousin Wendy (the mother of the Broadway star, Adam Pascal) was 16 that day and we acknowledged her "Sweet 16." I could only invite two friends from junior high school, Carl Buchman and Paul Trager. Today, most bar mitzvah and bat mitzvah parties include a predominance of school friends because families are smaller, and relatives don't live as close to one another. At the bar mitzvah party, there is a symbolic candle lighting ceremony which includes 13 candle lighters. If I recall, the candle lighters were my grandmother, my parents, my sister, four candle lighters representing my grandparents' families – the Frishman's, Schreiber's, Fishel's and Steiner's – my Uncle Phil and Aunt Lil Frishman, my Uncle Ken and his wife Arlene, my Uncle Mac Gayer and his wife Lillian, and my cousins from both my father's side and my mother's side of the family. I lit the last candle. This ceremony was followed up by a traditional Hora dance where all the guests danced around me, and I was lifted up on a chair.

That afternoon was indeed magical. Most of the guests are dead now, and again there are no pictures. The largest gift I received was $50 from my grandfather's brother, Izzy. Most of the gifts were $25 savings bonds, and the total gifts made up for the cost of the party and began my college fund.

Being 13 is a wonderful time in a Jewish boy's life. I was invited to go to other bar mitzvah parties of friends. There were two bar mitzvah services of friends that I remember distinctly. My friend, Stevie November, had a running nose while reciting his haftorah, with no tissue available. It was indeed a sight to behold, and not a pleasant one. I also remember going to my friend Gene's bar mitzvah at the Pleasantville School. Along with his parents, I was the only other person who attended.

What happened to my Hebrew school studies after the bar mitzvah? I was now in my fifth year of Hebrew school – now called Hebrew High School – and like many secular Jews my age, I dropped out. However, my ability to read Hebrew and my knowledge of Jewish history and culture provided me with a foundation for life. I know that God watches over me. There have been desperate times in my life that I'm not sure I could have survived without the support and comfort that my deep spiritual beliefs and traditions provide. Little did I know, one of those times was just around the corner.

CHAPTER

SUMMERS

"Summer will end soon enough, and childhood will as well."

- George R.R. Martin

Nw York City is particularly hot and humid in the summertime. This was certainly true 60 years ago, when few people had air conditioning in their homes and apartments. The only air conditioning available was in movie theaters or in a few places of business. Leaving the Bronx to escape the heat for the summer was a necessity, and our family often went to Rockaway Beach. The Bronx had its own beach, Orchard Beach at Pelham Bay Park, located on Long Island Sound and built by Robert Moses.

Rockaway Beach is located on the Rockaway Peninsula in New York City's borough of Queens (Fig. 6A). It is the largest urban beach in the U.S., stretching for miles along the Atlantic Ocean. The beach is public, and run by the New York City Department of Parks and Recreation. Woody Allen's movie *Radio Days* was filmed at Rockaway Beach.

In 1901, Rockaway's Playland, a famous amusement park, was built (Fig. 6B) and subsequently stores, hotels and summer bungalows were built near the shore where people from the city could spend the summer. A large wooden boardwalk ran parallel to the beach, and the hotels and bungalows were built on streets perpendicular to the boardwalk. Two bridges built in the 1930s spanned Jamaica Bay on the other side of Rockaway Beach, the Marine Parkway Bridge which connected the borough of Brooklyn to the peninsula, and the Cross Bay Memorial Bridge which connected Queens with the center of the peninsula.

In 1949 we spent our first summer in Rockaway, living in a rented bungalow on Beach 67th Street. My father would commute by car from his business in the Bronx every day, a hard drive since the cars had no air conditioning and the auto engines would often overheat, especially in bumper to bumper traffic on the Van Wyck Parkway (Made famous in a Seinfeld episode). Two auspicious events occurred that summer. The first occurred in a public parking lot near the beach. I had wandered off from my mother, and I thought I was lost. As I was only two and a half, and I went into a panic. My mother was actually watching me from behind a car and eventually responded to my crying. She told me she wanted to teach me a lesson about leaving her side. Although I was very young, I believe it instilled in me a deep fear of being lost and abandoned that I carry to this day.

The second event was my father's first heart attack. Dad was a great athlete. In fact, he was accomplished in every sport in which he participated. On a hot and humid Sunday, he was playing handball, a popular New York City sport, on a court off the boardwalk. My uncle, who was playing with him, would say later that it seemed like it was 100 degrees on the court with the sun beating down. My father, who was a heavy cigarette smoker, collapsed. He was brought to the hospital and was diagnosed with a heart attack. He was out of work 10 weeks, most of which he spent in Florida with my grandmother. My uncle ran my father's clothing store during his illness, so we were not left destitute. I was brought up with the knowledge that my father had a heart condition, and I was always concerned about him. He continued to smoke, as did my mother and many of his friends and family members.

Figure 6A: Rockaway Beach in the 1960s. The boardwalk in on the right. (Image courtesy of *The Wave*. Reprinted with permission.)

Figure 6B: Rockaway Playland in the 1960s. (Image courtesy of the New York City Municipal Archives. Reprinted with permission.)

I remember my father having yellow nicotine-stained fingernails and teeth from his cigarette habit, and I was always careful not to upset him, because of his heart condition.

During the summers of 1950-1952, we stayed in the Bronx in our new two-room apartment on Stratford Avenue. My parents, sister and I had passes for Castle Hill Pool, where there were swimming pools, ball fields and handball and shuffleboard courts. Castle Hill Pool was located in the northeast corner of the Bronx, (made famous in the DeNiro movie, *Raging Bull*), off Long Island Sound. We would travel there by two buses. The pool was the last stop on Castle Hill Avenue. Each family had a wooden locker to store beach chairs and towels. There were separate locker rooms for males and females, and the areas had outdoor shower stalls. Castle Hill Pool is no more. It was torn down and replaced by apartment buildings and condominiums. The best handball players in the world had competed at Castle Hill Pool.

During the summers of 1953-1955 we went back to Rockaway and stayed in a rooming house on Beach 62nd Street for two summers, and in another rooming house on Beach 61st for one summer. We shared a two-room apartment with my Uncle Mac, Aunt Lil and my two female cousins. We had a common bathroom. My father, mother, sister and I stayed in one room which included a kitchen. My sister and I slept on bunk-beds.

I remember these summers as being happy ones, although I had no male friends my age. I would play with the girls who lived in the rooming house. During the week, my mother stayed with my sister and me, and my father commuted every night back to the city for work, except Sunday, his day off. I loved swimming in the ocean and playing in the sand, digging holes or building sand castles. The women would sit on beach chairs, often using reflectors to increase the intensity of their sunburns, which would cause them to have great pain at night (Fig. 6C). At the time, vinegar was rubbed on the skin to relieve the pain of sunburn. Suntan lotions and sun blocks were not popular then.

When my father was at the beach, he would try to upend me in the ocean by swimming under-water between my legs or putting me on his shoulders to joust with another father and son, trying to knock one another off. As children, we were never allowed to swim in the water for too long. There was a constant fear of catching polio. Franklin Roosevelt had allegedly gotten polio after swimming in cold water.

The evenings were also very special when we would walk on the boardwalk. The boardwalk had multiple amusements and places to eat. It also had an outdoor movie theater where I remember seeing *Gone with the Wind*. What was exciting about the boardwalk was the penny arcade, where many of the games we enjoyed actually cost a penny to play. There were places where you could see old silent movies and cartoons. There was skee-ball where you would roll a ball into various holes to score points toward winning a prize. Poker-Reno was a game where you would roll a ball into holes representing different playing cards, as if you were playing poker. You would get points for prizes depending on what type of hand you achieved after rolling five balls. On the boardwalk you could snack on a Takee-cup chow mein served in a noodle dish where you ate the chow mein and then the dish. I had the best pizza I ever tasted on the boardwalk, and am still trying to find pizza that is made so well. Perhaps it was the salt air mixed with the pizza crust. On Thursday nights there were fireworks to watch, launched from a boat miles off the beach.

During these summers, because I didn't have many male friends my age, I became an avid reader. My favorite books were the *Dr. Doolittle* series by Hugh Lofting and the *Hardy Boys*. The rooming house we stayed in had a courtyard where the men played volleyball. I was never a good overall player, but I became an expert server, a special talent that I have maintained my entire life, being able to place the ball just in front of the back line.

Figure 6C: My Aunt Lil (left) and my mother at Rockaway Beach in the early 1950s.

There was one major event that occurred in Rockaway during the summer of 1953. We were playing in the street where I chased after a ball and was hit by a moving car. Luckily I was almost beyond the front of the car, so I was hit in the hip and knocked to the side. My Uncle Phil and Aunt Lil Frishman lived across the street from us, and my Aunt had a picture on a wall of her brother who had just died at the age of 38 from a heart attack. After I was hit and had fallen to the side, I saw my Aunt's brother's face. I thought I was dead. Maybe I was for a moment, but I recovered with no permanent injury.

The driver who hit me was driving a van carrying eggs. He had no auto insurance. I really wasn't hurt, but I was told to stay down by neighbors. I remember visiting a lawyer weeks after the accident. My parents settled for $300 with the driver because they didn't want to hurt him financially. The accident was really my fault because I didn't look. With the proceeds after the $75 legal fees, my parents bought U.S. savings bonds in my name.

Despite the accident, the lack of male friendships and the multiple episodes of poison ivy I contracted at the time (poison ivy was believed to be contagious like leprosy, and people would avoid you as if you were a leper), I look back at these three years at Padulsky's rooming house during the summers of 1953-54 and Charlie Levine's rooming house in 1955 as idyllic times.

Some of the happiest memories in Rockaway were the visits of my Uncle Sydney, my mother's older brother. He and his wife, my Aunt Dorothy, didn't get along very well, so he often came to visit us by himself. He died at the age of 41 from a heart attack, leaving two young children. Heart attack was a common occurrence in men between the age of 35 and 50 during the 1950s and 1960s, often related to cigarette smoking and a poor diet.

We didn't return to Rockaway in 1956. That winter we moved to Parkchester, and my parents decided to send my sister and me to day camp. My mother had returned to work as a bookkeeper at a ceramics factory located in the South Bronx. Very few married women with young children worked at the time. My father continued his struggles in his men's clothing store.

The camp was sponsored by the YMHA-YWHA (Young Men's Hebrew Association, Young Women's Hebrew Association), and was located in Pleasantville, New York. Today, the camp is a public school for wayward children. My sister and I would be picked up for camp by a bus in the Bronx, and the ride was about one hour each way. During the time on the bus we were kept busy by singing camp songs, especially "one hundred bottles of beer on the wall." It would take 20 minutes to sing the song, ending with "0 bottles of beer on the wall." I was in a group of nine-year-olds, most of us poor children from the East Bronx. Our counselor was Wally who was 18, and our junior counselor, Johnny, who was 15. I remember the pineapple juice we drank from a can, and the tinny taste of the juice. I had a terrible batting slump that summer, hardly able to hit a ball. However, I wasn't a bad batsman when my father would pitch to me. I was always a fast runner and remember participating in a game called "capture the white flag." I also recall swimming every day. I don't remember what we did when it rained. In the changing area where we put on our bathing suits, there was a peep hole where we could spy on the girls. Overall, I had a good time in camp, but I still had to sleep in our hot Bronx apartment every night.

During the summer of 1957 we returned to Charlie Levine's rooming house in Rockaway. Once again, I had no male friends my age. I used to spend my time reading and watching the ants at work. I became the Monopoly champion at the rooming house, defeating children and adults alike. I had my first "date" with Roberta Hirschfield, whose family also stayed in our rooming house. Her father owned a shoe store in Queens. Our family visited Rockaway Playland once that summer as well as the Steeplechase Park at Coney Island, Brooklyn.

I also learned an important lesson that summer. There was a baseball pool competition between the men in the rooming house and a scorecard was kept in the lobby. For some reason, I hid it. I was immediately under suspicion, but blamed another boy named Jerry. I ultimately was questioned about my crime and confessed. I received the worst beating of my life from my mother.

What I also recall about Rockaway were the parties the adults would have on Saturday nights, and hearing the laughter from our room. Although my parents argued every day, especially about money, they loved to celebrate with friends and relatives. I knew they loved each other, and that was reassuring to me growing up. I also remember a volleyball game where my father and one other man played against six men and my father's team won. I recall playing whiffle ball (a plastic ball with holes that you hit with a plastic bat) in the street. I wasn't bad at playing whiffle ball, and remember once making a terrific catch during a game with my eyes closed.

For the next three summers, 1958-1960, we went to the Catskill Mountains. That experience was an important component of a Jewish upbringing. With its many hotels and bungalow colonies, it also provided a true escape from the heat of the city. The Catskills were initially a place where people with tuberculosis or from crowded tenements would go for the cool mountain air. The Catskills were mentioned in Washington Irving's books. The thunderstorms were extremely loud, and Irving compared them to the noise of bowling.

We spent the three summers at a bungalow colony in Hurleyville, New York, nine miles from Monticello, the county seat of Sullivan County. Many of the bungalow colonies were built on farmland (Fig. 6D), and our colony was part of an area that was once a working farm owned by Polish Catholic immigrants, Pete and Annie Melchick. Annie ran the bungalow colony after her husband had died. She was a woman with old weathered skin, who dressed like a peasant and walked with a wooden stick, always followed by her two dogs, Brownie and Blackie.

Figure 6D: Catskills bungalow colony, 1955. (Image courtesy of the Catskills Institute. Reprinted with permission.)

My grandmother Regina, stayed with my sister and me in a divided bungalow where two families lived, on each side. There was a common porch, and each side of the bungalow had two bedrooms and a kitchen, and its own front and rear exits. Our neighbors for all three years were a Jewish Polish couple with one son. The mother was named Mindel. A Holocaust survivor, she had lost a leg during World War II. When she walked, she made a loud sound with her wooden prosthesis, which you could hear through the thin walls that separated the families. The first summer, in 1958, occurred just before I would start junior high school. Finally, I had two friends my age, Stanley Katinski and Richard Axel. Each of them had sisters who were my own sister's age so I didn't have to be responsible for her.

My parents would go into the city to work every Monday morning. My mother, who didn't drive, would arrive by bus on Friday night and we would meet her in town, which was about a mile away. My father would drive up from the city late Saturday night. We had no telephone or TV. The only pay phone was in a rooming house that was part of the colony, and we would call our parents in the city, at a scheduled time, once a week.

Our days were routine. We would walk to town every morning. The town was small, with one pharmacy-luncheonette, a grocery store and a kosher meat market. There was also the post office where our mail was delivered and I remember the criminal wanted posters on the wall. I told my sister the posters showed criminals who actually lived in Hurleyville. After the walk back and forth from town, we would play squash, using the handball court which was a common feature in all the bungalow colonies or we would play baseball with the handball court wall as the backstop. We would also go swimming in a pool that was filled with chlorinated swamp water, or we would just read books or play board games. It was wonderful when my parents were both there, because Dad would drive around the area so we could see the hotels or go to the larger towns. Monticello Raceway was being built, and the Catskill hotels were at their peak: Grossinger's, The Concord, Brown's and Kutchers. Many famous actors, musicians and comedians got their start as entertainers in the Catskill Mountains.

My grandmother was a saint. She walked to town every morning to shop, so she could prepare breakfast before we would awaken. One of our favorite pastimes was picking wild blueberries, and my grandmother would make them into a pie for my father each week. We drank buttermilk, a thick, sour tasting, high-cholesterol creamy dairy drink. We often ate blueberries mixed with sour cream. I especially liked to eat raw onions, which didn't make me a popular person.

Sometimes we would "hitch" a ride to Monticello or Loch Sheldrake, towns that had movie theaters. The grandfather of one of my friends had a car, and he once took us to the drive-in to see a Bridgette Bardot movie, *And God Created Woman*. In 1958 Bridgette Bardot was 25 and in her prime. Marilyn Monroe, Jayne Mansfield and Anita Ekberg were also popular glamour queens of the day.

During the summer of 1959, the Katinskis didn't return so Richie and I played ball together, and took long walks along the surrounding country roads, or went fishing with a hook strung to wooden sticks. During the fourth of July holiday, Richie and I bought some illegal firecrackers from one of the townspeople, and decided to set them off the next day after my parents had gone back to New York. We appropriated a black kerosene pot that was being used as an emergency flare for roadwork being done close by. Our brilliant plan was to use the lit kerosene pot as an ignition source to shoot off our firecrackers. The site we chose was a secluded verdant hill on the bungalow colony property.

During the lighting of the firecrackers, the flaming pot was knocked over, pouring burning kerosene down the hill, igniting the surrounding brush and trees in its path. We tried desperately to put out the flames with our feet, but to no avail. We ran down the hill and were confronted by Annie Melchick with her wooden walking stick. She had already seen the flames and had called the fire department. Initially denying responsibility, Richie and I ran to my bungalow where we confessed our crime to my grandmother. Although red in the face with anger, Grandma told Richie and me to leave the property and hide out in one of the local towns until darkness fell. Richie and I had our own master plan to escape beyond the town, and to begin a life on the run, but we returned home that night. We would ultimately find out that the fire was quickly extinguished, but about an acre of brush and woods had burned.

We would also learn that the fire marshal, who assesses the cause of fires, had suspected us as the perpetrators from whatever information he had. However, he never sought to arrest or prosecute us. My grandmother, in tears, had convinced him that we were good, studious boys, stupid yes, and that we would be punished. He had been both understanding and forgiving of our youthful folly. My grandmother told me that she would keep the fire a secret and not tell my parents, but she predicted that one day I would confess my crime to them. Ultimately, I did confess to my mother on my fiftieth birthday.

The fire was not the last time Grandma would provide cover for me. I would always revere her for her kindness, and her understanding and forgiving nature. Growing up in the Bronx, I had neighborhood friends who would be prosecuted by the juvenile courts for lesser crimes, and then sent off to military schools or to the dreaded public reform schools for discipline. One of my good friends was sent away for three years to reform school for shoplifting. He never was forgiven, but was instead branded for life as a criminal.

The fire of 1959 was not my only misadventure that summer. Richie and I used to walk to town every morning, a one mile distance, and we would frequent the local pharmacy which also served as a general store. We would look through newspapers, magazines and pocket books that were on display. This was the beginning of puberty for me, and I got the idea to buy a newspaper and then slip different magazines between the newspaper pages without paying for them. This went on for about two weeks until I was confronted by the wife of the pharmacist who had observed my activities. I was chastised by her, and banished from the store. In addition, I had to make restitution with my allowance money. "Never steal again," she warned me, "and I will forgive you for this indiscretion." She also told me that as long as she didn't hear about similar activities from other storekeepers in the town, she would not tell my grandmother or my parents.

When I returned to the Bronx after the summer, I became the most law-abiding teenager in my neighborhood, and have remained that way ever since. I was the best Boy Scout in our local troop. I also had recognized how close I had come to ruining my reputation and that of my family.

Over the years, I have also come to recognize how important the act of forgiveness is, especially with regard to children and adolescents. Clearly, young people need to be punished for their indiscretions, but ultimately they need forgiveness. When I look back at old friends who seemed to have their share of bad luck in their lives, I am convinced it was, in part, because they were not forgiven for minor crimes, a situation that ultimately destroyed their futures.

I am often asked to give graduation speeches, and during the ceremony I ask the graduates to publicly acknowledge their parents and grandparents. I also ask the students to thank those individuals, in absentia, who had forgiven them for petty indiscretions in the past.

In 1960, the year before I started high school, the Axel family did not return, but I had a new friend, Marty Roth, one of the best individuals I ever knew. Luckily, he had a sister my sister's age. Marty also had a cousin one year older, Carol Roth, who would visit periodically. She was my first infatuation. I never spoke to her about my feelings, and she never shared hers.

The three years in the Catskills were very special. Castle Hill Pool, Rockaway, the Catskills and day camp are all part of who I am today. I am grateful for these different experiences, and the sacrifice my parents and grandmother made so that my sister and I could enjoy the summers and escape the New York City heat and humidity. When we left the Catskills for the last time in 1960, I was about to begin high school. I would come to relish the long days of summer that shaped my imagination and gave me a deep appreciation of nature. Even as I said goodbye to my childhood and entered the tumultuous world of adolescence, I found a stillness and strength from those long summer days and balmy nights in the open air.

CHAPTER

DESTINY

"It was the best of times, it was the worst of times, it was the age of wisdom, it was the age of foolishness, it was the epoch of belief, it was the epoch of incredulity, it was the season of Light, it was the season of Darkness."

- Charles Dickens

For the first time in my life, I felt like I "fit in." During so many years of my early education, school had felt like a dangerous place, but the Bronx High School of Science (BHSS) was finally a safe place to be smart. BHSS is one of the most highly rated public high schools in the country and has eight Nobel laureates among its alumni, the most of any high school in the United States. Looking back, having the opportunity to attend BHSS solidified the early course I had set for myself to become a physician. Although high school is a very stressful period in every young person's life, and my experience was no different, my stress came in the form of academic challenges and the struggle to better myself rather than a struggle to simply survive.

In 1938, the BHSS was founded by the New York City Board of Education, under the influence of Dr. Morris Meister, and accepted academically-gifted students from all the New York City boroughs. BHSS was founded as a public, tuition-free school where qualified students could receive a specialized education that was usually reserved for the wealthy and privileged. In the search for talented students with a special aptitude for science, mathematics and overall intellectual acumen, the school required all applicants to take a written test in verbal ability and mathematical skill and reasoning. Students also needed to have strong academic records in junior high school, and to be recommended by their teachers and guidance counselors.

Most of the students came from the Bronx and Manhattan because of the school's location. Although BHSS started as an all boys' school in an antiquated, Gothic building (complete with gargoyles) on 184th Street and Creston Avenue in the west Bronx, the school started to accept girls in 1946, unlike the other specialized high schools Stuyvesant and Brooklyn Tech, which remained all male until many years later. A new BHSS building was erected in 1959 at 205th Street in the Bronx and houses the current school (Fig. 7A). I was in the first class that started high school in 1960 in the new building.

Ninety percent of the school's coursework was required, including four years of English, social studies and science, and three years of mathematics and a foreign language (I took a fourth year of French). In addition, all students were required to take courses in music, health education and hygiene, mechanical drawing and the dreaded science techniques laboratory. There were also advanced placement courses available where students could earn college credit.

I started BHSS in the tenth grade, having completed ninth grade in junior high school. The majority of my classmates were Jews, similar to me, descendants of immigrant parents and grandparents. I had a two-hour daily commute. Each morning I had to take the Pelham Bay subway line from Parkchester going toward Manhattan. The train was always full, and I never got a seat. I learned to read standing up, holding on to the overhead straps. At 125th Street, in Manhattan, I had to change to the Woodlawn-Jerome line past Yankee Stadium going uptown. I tried to do as much homework on

Figure 7A: The Bronx High School of Science. My class was one of the first to occupy the new building. Shown in the rear is a famous ceramic mural portraying some of history's greatest scientists. The school also has its own planetarium. Bronx Science alumni have won eight Nobel prizes, more than any other high school in the United States. (Image courtesy of the Bronx High School of Science. Reprinted with permission.)

the train as possible, despite the shaky ride. I always rode in the front train car so I could occasionally look out the front window, where I had the same view of the tracks as the motorman.

My sophomore year was eventful in many ways. First, a major hurricane struck the Bronx on the first day of school, and my train pass was blown out of my hand. I had to beg to get on the train. My academic subjects were geometry, world history (mostly European history with little discussion of anywhere else), biology, French and English, gym and mechanical drawing. My friend, Stevie November, who lived in my apartment building and was one year ahead of me, helped me to master the early concepts of geometry for which I will always be grateful to him. Mechanical drawing was a struggle, since I was never neat and had to do my drawings over and over until I got them right. I did well academically and had a 93 average. My English teacher, Mr. Canell, taught me how to read carefully, especially the assigned books by Dickens and Eliot.

One major event of 1960 was the presidential election with Vice President Nixon and Senator John Kennedy as candidates. Kennedy, a Democrat, was a hero to students my age. I had heard his late night nomination speech from a radio in our bungalow colony that previous summer. I always had an interest in the presidents and the election campaign was mesmerizing. The Bronx always voted with the Democratic Party (Franklin Roosevelt was a great hero for my parents and grandparents). What was of interest is that my father voted for Nixon, probably the only vote he received in the Bronx. Kennedy was the nation's president through my high school years. He wrote a letter to our high school graduating class in 1963. They say the 1950s ended with Kennedy's assassination later that year and, indeed, the world would never be the same after his passing.

A major personal event also occurred in 1960. Dad's business went bankrupt, and he lost everything, including his old Ford, which he cherished. He subsequently took on two jobs as a men's clothing salesman to pay back all his debts, requiring him to work seven days a week. He never took a vacation. Dad was always the stabilizing force in the family for my younger sister and me, and for his own widowed mother and younger brothers. Although he was not the "moneymaker" my mother wanted him to be, Dad remained cheerful, upbeat and was always supportive, helping my sister and me with schoolwork, including writing, science and math.

On December 9, 1961, when I was 15 and a junior at BHSS, we had a family celebration on a Saturday night on the last day of Hanukkah. Dad came home late, but in time to participate in some of the festivities. Although he appeared well that night, it would be the last time I would see him alive.

The next morning, on a Sunday, he left early while we were all sleeping to go to his second job in Brooklyn. That afternoon, I was watching a New York Giants vs. Philadelphia Eagles football game on TV, when my Uncle Mac knocked on the door. I heard my mother scream in anguish. She told us Dad was sick at Jacobi Hospital, and that I should stay home to watch my younger sister, while she and my uncle went to visit Dad. After one hour, she returned home and told us Dad was doing well in the hospital, and we would all go to see him. This was just a momentary denial on her part, for moments later she cried out that Dad was dead. We later found out he had felt ill at work that morning, and had tried to drive home. He made it to the Whitestone Bridge, approaching the Bronx, and pulled over. He was brought to the hospital in an ambulance. It was believed that he either died from his heart attack en route, or in the emergency room.

At that moment, my entire world crashed. My protector and best friend was gone. After the initial shock, my mind was full of questions. Who would support us? How would we eat? Would we be evicted from our apartment? How would my mother deal with the loss? Would she fall apart? What about my younger sister? I felt as if I had walked from one room into another, never to go back. Now I was an adolescent boy with no father, with no role model to guide him. What about the dream of college? Dad and I had just spoke about him taking some time off during the coming summer so we could visit schools. As the darkness fell that afternoon, the pain in my heart was unbearable. How would we ever get through this?

When I awoke the next day, I thought that maybe it was a dream. As a young child, I often had nightmares of people dying, and would be relieved to find out upon waking that those deaths were not real. Then I heard my mother crying in the next room. It was not a nightmare, but something real. My beloved father was dead. In an attempt to comfort me, neighbors and relatives would say, "You are now the man of house." This was not comforting; it was terrifying.

The funeral was a blur. It was my first. It was pouring rain that morning, and I was numb to everything. I don't even remember how we made it to the funeral home. When we arrived, I heard the screams of my uncle, my Dad's brother, and my grandmother sobbing in front of his casket. I remember only a few words of the rabbi's eulogy, "today the heavens are crying for Aaron Frishman." Hundreds of people, relatives and friends, had come to pay tribute to Dad. I never realized how profoundly he had impacted on the many people who attended. When we followed the casket to the hearse, my mother fainted. I believed she was dead, and I that I was now orphaned.

We arrived at the burial site in a New Jersey cemetery in the pouring rain. After my father's casket was lowered into the ground, close relatives shoveled dirt on the coffin. As is the custom in our faith, I recited the memorial prayer, the Kaddish, which a son always recites for a departed parent. Just then the rain stopped, the clouds parted and the chimes from the cemetery clock struck twelve times. Sunlight shined on Dad's grave. I realized that although Dad was gone, a greater force was watching over us, and perhaps, one day I would be able to discern a purpose for this tragedy.

After the untimely death of my father, my mother grieved deeply. For months I would hear her crying through the night, although she tried to be upbeat during the day so as not to upset my sister and me. Mom was only 43 years old when dad died, and she was left with two young teenage children. She became the sole supporter of the family with only the addition of a modest social security payment for orphaned children and my part-time job earnings as a delivery boy. The only money we had was from my father's small life insurance policy. There were no savings available because of my Dad's recent bankruptcy. During this time of loss, my mother did show great courage and determination, reassuring us that as a family we would persevere.

During the first days of mourning, I still felt great despair that was only heightened when I returned to school. In Dante's *The Divine Comedy* he called despair the greatest punishment that God could give; unlike physical pain, there is really nothing you can do to relieve it. I found solace during the first year of grieving by reciting the Kaddish prayer every day in synagogue during the early morning and evening services.

I tried to find meaning as to why such a profound loss would come to a family that was already suffering. It was as if a major earthquake had followed a hurricane. As the days and weeks went by, I started to discern a possible meaning to such a tragedy. As a result of my father's death, I had an even greater motivation to pursue a career in medicine to honor his memory and to help others. I would pay tribute to my father by trying to live each day by his high standards. I also felt that I now had an advocate in heaven that would never leave my side, and always watch over me. My dreams took on a new nobility and purpose; my father would not have died in vain.

I have since learned of a concept called "post-traumatic growth" or PTG. Although this concept is not new, Richard Tedeschi and Lawrence Calhoun coined the phrase and drew attention to the need to better understand the potentially positive outcomes that occur in the bereaved, even if the suffering and anguish over their loss persists. Some survivors will develop a new sense of purpose and, having endured the worst possible loss of someone they deeply cherish, can find new meaning and purpose in their lives and the strength to make positive changes within themselves and the world (*see Appendix B, #2*).

Although my junior year of high school was very challenging after losing my father, I also had a renewed sense of determination. In addition, I had received emotional support from my Uncle Mac and Aunt Lil, and from my rabbi. My uncle spent whatever time he had with me, knowing I had just lost my father. Uncle Mac was a man's man – a tall, lithe individual who owned a Sunoco gas station in the Bronx. He had four children of his own, but made sure I was comforted.

I was grateful that I had already had my bar mitzvah, so that I could honor my father by wearing tefillin and reciting the Kaddish for him in synagogue every morning and afternoon for 11 months. Saying Kaddish for your deceased parents ensures they will have a place in heaven. I would go to synagogue at 6:30 A.M., and could still make it to school on time because the rabbi arranged a car ride for me. In the afternoon, I would take the train home.

Looking back, I also realize that the insightfulness of my rabbi was a major influence both on me and on a teacher who was also grieving, Mr. Samuel Witkin. Mr. Witkin was 55 years old and had no children, but he had recently lost his mother. The rabbi sat us together in synagogue to recite the Kaddish, and we helped one another to cope during this very difficult time. I see now that pain, as awful as it is, makes us more connected and empathetic to others, especially those who are suffering. I will always be grateful to Mr. Witkin, and my rabbi, for their kindness and generosity of spirit.

My grades dropped somewhat, but I maintained over a 90 average. The hardest course I took that year was the science techniques lab, where we had to design and build a machine. I got through the course without the help of my father, and because I had the easiest teacher, Mr. Bonacci. I built an electronic metronome which actually worked. That year I was elected to Arista, the school's honor society, on my first try.

Socially I did not interact much with the girls in high school, some of whom were very attractive. With my academic demands and my father's death, I had no time for dating. In fact, most of my classmates had no time for dating. The girls I interacted with were my sister and female cousins. I did go on one date (a pseudo-prom) with Susan Fleckman, the smartest student in the class behind me. She wore a beautiful dress. A public bus was our mode of transport; there were no limousines to proms in those days.

One of the interesting parts of the school day was lunchtime in the cafeteria, where we were assigned a permanent seat. The student who sat across from me, Peter Lesser, was a San Francisco Giant baseball fan, and we argued for three years about who was the better player, Willie Mays or Mickey Mantle. Luckily, the Yankees beat the Giants in the World Series during my senior year, so I was able to win that argument. Mickey Mantle also won his third most valuable player award.

With my newfound resolve to pursue scientific research, I was awarded a National Science Foundation Student Grant during the summer between my junior and senior year. Both of my grandfathers, father and uncles all had heart attacks before the age of 60, so I was very motivated to explore the origins and potential cures for heart disease. As part of the grant, I did cardiovascular physiology research at Hunter College and Cornell Medical School on a project entitled, "Cardiac Manifestations of Hyperthyroidism." It was my initial foray into cardiac research, and I enjoyed every aspect of the experience. I had found my destiny. I knew then I would become a cardiologist, and I knew I would not stray from this path.

My Dad and I had always spoken about visiting colleges the summer after my junior year, but now he was gone. While thumbing through various college catalogues, I read that Boston University (BU) was offering an innovative six-year liberal arts-medicine program where one would save two years of undergraduate schooling while being guaranteed admission to medical school if all major courses were passed during the undergraduate portion of the program. Similar programs were started in 1961 at Northwestern and Johns Hopkins universities. Johns Hopkins gave up on the program very quickly, so the two programs being offered when I was applying were at BU and Northwestern.

Dr. Goodman, who had initially inspired me to consider becoming a physician at the age of seven (*see the Prologue*), advised me to pursue the BU program. Raised in Pennsylvania, Dr. Goodman remembered how difficult it was for him to be admitted to a medical school in the United States. Although I had felt I should go to college in New York City to be closer to my family following my father's death, I put in an application to the BU program, and received an immediate interview. Because I so desperately wanted to be a physician, I decided to visit BU on my own. I was only 15 when I interviewed for this prestigious program.

I had another fateful experience on the bus trip to Boston for my interview. During the initial part of the drive, I had a pleasant conversation with the man sitting next to me. He mentioned he was going home to his family. It was an overnight trip, so we both soon fell asleep. When the bus arrived at his stop in Worcester, Massachusetts, he remained motionless. It became apparent he had died in his sleep, most likely from a heart attack. When I realized what had happened, I couldn't help but relive my own experience, and my thoughts immediately went out to his family. Heart disease is a relentless enemy. For me, it was a further call to action and a reminder of the devastation of this horrible disease.

I took six major subjects in my senior year of high school, continued to say Kaddish for my father and had two jobs as a delivery-boy at a pharmacy and at a grocery store. My delivery vehicle was a bicycle with a big basket on the handlebars. Admittedly, the pharmacy deliveries were much more accommodating than the groceries. I also learned a great deal working in a pharmacy that would be helpful to me in later years.

The highlight of my senior year was being chosen co-editor-in-chief of the school's yearbook, *The Observatory* (Fig. 7B). The other co-editor was Richard Wind who would later became an obstetrician-gynecologist. This experience influenced all the writing and editorial work I would do in the years to come. In those early days of yearbook design, each page had to be laid out like a blueprint with photos and text. I had a deadline to be sure the yearbook was printed before graduation. I had to find the time and energy to put the book together in addition to the pressures and challenges of academic and home life. Fortunately, it was the 25th anniversary of BHSS, its "silver jubilee year," which gave us a theme for the yearbook. I had a wonderful faculty advisor, Nathan Glicksman, an English teacher, who would become my patient. I also had my own office, as did the editors of the school newspaper. This is the editorial I co-authored for the year book:

> The 25th anniversary of any institution is naturally a time of great celebration. Since this year is Science's Quarter Century Jubilee, we strove not to be an exception to this maximum. We recall that ours is a special school, created to meet the needs of more advanced students in the public school system.
>
> However, with all the celebrating and pounding one another in the back, we neglected two things. First, we looked back to 1938, the year of the school's creation and compared it directly with 1963. This is not essentially wrong. It is a good way of showing the vast improvements in the school between these years. However, we tend to forget that these changes did not occur overnight. It took 25 years, one quarter of a century of hard work and dedicated effort by scores of teachers, administrators, parents and students. If we compare each of the 25 years to its direct predecessor, we would not notice much change. Each year brought some innovation, some progress in making Science what it is today.
>
> Second, during these 25 years, many people have come to praise the school. They have praised the facilities, the faculty, the administration, the parents, and the curriculum. Whereas all these deserve much praise, the main factor contributing to its renown is too often neglected. This factor is Science's students. Given all these facilities, faculty and administration, without its students, Science would be merely another well-run school. Not only while in Science, but also as alumni, Science students have excelled. For each of the past 24 classes, there is a long list of hard-working achievers.
>
> However, we must not rest on our laurels. As each preceding year has added some piece to the entity that is Science, so we hope that in each of the next 25 years, Science will progress as much as it has in its first quarter century. It is up to us, the class of '63, as graduates and former students of Science, to continue to work toward the evolution of Science as not merely an excellent school, but as a widely known institution. Whereas, at Science, progress is not our most important product, it comes very close, and we should bear that in mind.
>
> The editors-in-chief of *Observatory* would like to extend, on behalf of the Class of '63, our congratulations to the Bronx High School of Science upon its 25th Anniversary Silver Jubilee Year, and our best wishes for the next 25 years.

I graduated BHSS with honors in 1963 (Fig. 7C), and the commencement was held in the Loews Paradise Theatre on the Grand Concourse. In looking back, BHSS was the most competitive school I ever attended and so some of the smartest people I ever met were my classmates. The school was a true meritocracy, where hard work and perseverance were rewarded, no matter how poor or disadvantaged you were. The school still remains a place for aspiring children of immigrant parents. I was disciplined at BHSS to make efficient use of time, and to compete with myself.

Figure 7B: I was the co-editor of the Bronx High School of Science yearbook, Observatory. I am seated on the right. My fellow co-editor, Richard Wind, is seated on the left. Richard later became an obstetrician/gynecologist. The yearbook faculty advisor was Mr. Nathan Glicksman (center), a demanding English teacher. He later wrote one of my letters of recommendation for college. Another member of the yearbook staff was Barbara Lewis (standing at left). Her son later became my student at Einstein. (Image courtesy of the Bronx High School of Science. Reprinted with permission.)

Figure 7C: My Bronx High School of Science yearbook picture, 1963. (Image courtesy of the Bronx High School of Science. Reprinted with permission.)

CHAPTER

ALL IN

"It is very difficult to slow down. The practice of medicine is like the heart's muscle contraction - it's all or none."

- Béla Schick

I left for Boston by bus to begin college in September, 1963. After my fateful trip to interview for the six-year program at BU, in the spring of 1963, I was accepted to both college and medical school at the age of 16. My mother, a recent widow, had also encouraged me to go to school in Boston, at a great personal sacrifice to her. I remember how sad I was to be leaving my mother and sister back in the Bronx.

I was the first member of my BU class to check into the dormitory, because I had been given a work scholarship award and had to start my employment as a part-time telephone switchboard operator and as a kitchen worker. I was the only member of my class to have a job. The dormitory I stayed in was Myles Standish Hall which had previously been a residential hotel made famous in Arthur Miller's play, *Death of a Salesman*. The dormitory was arranged into suites, and I was assigned to a five-room suite with four other roommates. We each had our own room.

There were 48 students in our program, 40 men and 8 women. The men were assigned to the same floor in the dormitory. We had our own classes, ate together and, for the most part, were separated from the other freshman students at the university. I had wonderful roommates. Three of us stayed together for the entire six-year program. My roommates were not only supportive of me; they were also peer role models. George Hines, a graduate of Stuyvesant High School in New York, would become a renowned cardiovascular surgeon, and another, Ed Forbes, a distinguished general surgeon. There was a high attrition rate in the program: of the 48 who started, 28 would finish. The high dropout rate was due, in part, to the realization of the students of the commitment required to be a physician, and, for some unfortunate students, psychiatric problems. One of my roommates dropped out because of academic issues, and he was replaced by another student, Jeffry Nurenberg, who would become a prominent psychiatrist and psychoanalyst.

The first year of the program was spent in the College of Liberal Arts located on Commonwealth Avenue (Fig. 8A). The course work included physics, physical chemistry, European history and English. During the first summer, I took courses in government, Spanish, sociology and English literature. Physical chemistry was the hardest course I have ever taken, but I received an A- and also made the Dean's List. My physical chemistry professor, Dr. Alfred Prock, would teach the course to BU six-year medical students for 40 years.

During our freshman year, John F. Kennedy was assassinated. We were told about it on Friday, November 22 at 1:00 P.M. by Dr. Prock as we entered his classroom. The United States has never been the same since Kennedy's assassination. Since Kennedy was from Massachusetts, the assassination and aftermath were even sadder.

I persevered through the freshman year, always keeping my nose to the grindstone. I did not want to disappoint myself or my family. That first summer I worked as a desk clerk in the dormitory

Figure 8A: The campus of Boston University in the late 1960s. The Charles River is in the foreground. I attended the undergraduate school of liberal arts for two years. (Image courtesy of Boston University. Reprinted with permission.)

while attending classes. My family was in Rockaway, but I only had three weeks of vacation before my sophomore year began, so I couldn't join them until mid-August.

I continued to do well in my sophomore and final college year (1964-65). The second year courses included organic chemistry, biology, psychology and anthropology. During the summer we took a course called Health and Society, and I was assigned to work at Bridgewater State Prison Hospital, a facility for the criminally insane. Bridgewater was a frightening place; at the time, some inmates were kept in cages. Our project, directed by the legal psychiatry department of BU, was to determine if any of the inmates were sane and could therefore be released. Albert DeSalvo, the Boston Strangler, was an inmate at Bridgewater at the time. He was killed during an attempted prison escape.

After two years of college, which included the summer coursework, I started medical school in September, 1965 at the age of 18 (Fig. 8B). The great Northeast blackout occurred two months later. Our class included 72 students, 40% of whom were from the program, and 60% who had been admitted by the traditional four-year college route. The program students were at a disadvantage during the first term. The initial course work was gross anatomy (six days a week), histology and neuroanatomy (Fig. 8C). We had to buy our own microscopes. Many of the conventional students had taken comparative anatomy in college courses, giving them an advantage. Our group struggled, and I worked very hard to pass the anatomy courses. However, by the second term, when we took physiology and biochemistry, there was little difference in how we performed compared to our older peers.

During the summer after my first year of medical school, I took additional liberal arts courses. It was the summer school coursework that had allowed us to accelerate and ultimately receive our undergraduate degrees. I also got a job as an emergency lab technician at the New England Deaconess

Figure 8B: The construction of the Boston University School of Medicine instructional building, finished during my senior year (1968-1969). At right are the old buildings where I took my basic science courses. The Pavilion Building at Boston City Hospital, where I completed my third and fourth year medicine rotations is in the foreground. In the rear is University Hospital where I completed my fourth year surgery rotation. (Image courtesy of Boston University. Reprinted with permission.)

Figure 8C: The Boston University School of Medicine's Building A where I took gross anatomy in the basement lab during my first year of medical school. (Image courtesy of Boston University. Reprinted with permission.)

Hospital and the Joslin Clinic (a famous diabetes facility), a job I kept part-time, throughout my final three years of medical school. Both the New England Deaconess and the Joslin Clinic were Harvard Medical School affiliates. I became an expert phlebotomist and could carry out lab tests in the clinical chemistry lab, the microbiology lab, the hematology lab and the blood bank. I learned to respect the hard work and precision necessary for a hospital lab to function. I also learned how best to order lab tests in my future clinical work, while also recognizing their limits.

My medical school academic performance really took off in my second year. I was first in my class in pharmacology, and did well in microbiology, pathology and pathophysiology. Our course director in pathology was Dr. Stanley Robbins, the editor and co-author of the famous textbook, *Pathologic Basis of Disease* (Fig. 8D). We also began physical diagnosis. Unlike the medical school curriculum of today, where students are exposed to patients early, we had no contact with patients until physical diagnosis. Also, the symbol of the physician at the time, was the black bag not the white coat (because physicians still made house calls). We did wear short white coats as second-year medical students, and wore civilian clothing as first-year students.

At the end of the second year we had to take part one of the National Board Exam, and over a three week period before the two day test, I never studied so hard. I passed with a highly satisfactory score, and celebrated afterwards by visiting the 1967 World's Fair in Montreal, Canada. Students who had failed the exam were left back to repeat the second year of medical school.

The summer after my second year of medical school, I worked at Boston State Hospital as a student psychiatry trainee supported by a grant. I have always enjoyed psychiatry and had already worked at Bridgewater State Hospital. I always felt that psychiatric disease in otherwise healthy individuals was such a tragedy. Although psychoanalysis was popular then, the medications that were being used were the first generation of antipsychotic drugs (phenothiazines) and antidepressants, which had numerous toxicities. When I tried to befriend a patient who was an engineer outside the hospital, the teaching attending warned me to keep my professional distance. I might have caused a psychotic relapse in my patient by not being readily available to help him when needed, because of the demands of my school work.

Third year began the major clinical clerkships. At age 20, I started surgery at the Boston Veterans Hospital. We were mixed with third year Tufts medical students who also rotated at the hospital. I liked the intellectual part of surgery, but didn't enjoy some of the duties assigned to medical students. We were required to scrub in to surgery in order to hold retractors, metal instruments that would hold back organs to allow the surgeon room to work; doing this for hours, without receiving any teaching. If I asked questions, I was often considered insubordinate. We had a great chief of surgery at the Veterans Administration hospital, Dr. Donald Nabseth. The chairman of surgery at the medical school was Dr. Richard Egdahl, (Fig. 8E) an endocrine surgeon who came to BU from the Medical College of Virginia, along with Dr. John Mannick, a vascular surgeon who would subsequently become chief of surgery at the Peter Bent Brigham Hospital and at Harvard. Dr. Egdahl edited a comprehensive textbook that included classical articles from the surgical literature. I also interacted with some surgical residents who had just come back from military duty in Vietnam. Many of them were very angry about their wartime experiences.

While I was in medical school (1965-69) the Vietnam War was at its height. The war started over the mistaken premise that the Communist Party was trying to spread its political influence over all of Southeast Asia (the domino theory), and Vietnam was the line drawn in the sand by the United States. Anger over the military draft and the war would cause major student protests on campuses all across the country (Fig. 8F). Many of my former high school classmates tried to avoid the draft by

Figure 8D: Dr. Stanley Robbins, our pathology professor, who edited the renowned textbook still used all over the world. (Image courtesy of Boston University. Reprinted with permission.)

Figure 8E: Dr. Richard Egdahl, then chairman of surgery at Boston University School of Medicine with actor Gregory Peck. (Image courtesy of Boston University. Reprinted with permission.)

going to Canada and other countries. During the time of the war, every male physician was eligible for the draft, but I was deferred while still in medical school. The military needed surgeons for combat duty, and would draft surgical residents in the middle of their training. Many of these draftees were upset about having their training interrupted. Although it was set in the Korean War, the television show *MASH* accurately depicted the frustrations, anger and stress experienced by surgeons in combat. Only humor could make the experience tolerable. After their military service was complete, these partially-trained surgeons returned to civilian hospitals to complete their residency.

During the 1960s while I was in college and medical school, not only were students protesting the war, but also great social changes were taking place, including the beginning of the civil rights movement, and equal rights for women and gays. The Medicare and Medicaid Programs were started in 1965, and major civil rights legislation was passed. For this reason, 1965 was a landmark year for great social change. Lyndon Johnson, one of my favorite presidents, was the political impetus behind these great government programs, (The Great Society) which also included the Head Start Program for disadvantaged children. Johnson believed that access to health care was a right and not a privilege, something that I, too, strongly believe in. Tragically, Johnson also supported the war in Vietnam, a position which would ultimately cause his political demise.

As a college and medical student enmeshed in my studies, I was not an active participant in the protests going on at the time (Fig. 8G), but a passive observer (at heart, I am a pacifist). I didn't truly support the war, but as a future physician felt it was my obligation to remain apolitical regarding the conflict, since I would one day be asked to take care of patients and not be an active combatant. One of my new roommates during medical school tried to protest the war by setting himself on fire in front of the University Chapel. He survived, but was thrown out of school. I never heard from him again.

The surgery rotation also included many of the surgical subspecialties such as ophthalmology, otolaryngology, orthopedics, neurosurgery, thoracic surgery, urology and anesthesia. These one-week experiences were not really sufficient. I was most impressed with the cardiothoracic surgeons who were the early pioneers of open heart surgery. I never saw a group of individuals who worked so hard in caring for patients; operating all day, and then staying up all night at the patient's bedsides to monitor their progress.

Surgery was followed by obstetrics/gynecology, which I took at the Framingham Union Hospital. Only two students were assigned at a time so we got to be present at many deliveries. We also worked at a gynecology clinic in a women's prison and, being a young student and rather naïve, I was extremely flustered after obtaining the sexual histories of the inmates.

The next clinical rotation was pediatrics. I was assigned to the Boston City Hospital, where I was overwhelmed by the extent of disease and social deprivation I found there (Fig. 8H). I watched children with cystic fibrosis suffocate in their own secretions, and saw the futility of treating children with leukemia and lymphoma, all conditions that are well managed today.

In addition to the suffering of the patients, I also witnessed a most tragic event involving my supervising intern. A three year old child was admitted to the pediatric ward from the emergency room with a high fever and lethargy. As students, we were responsible to do the basic lab work of all new patients, while the interns performed the initial history and physical exam. I drew blood from the child in order to perform a complete blood count and differential in the house staff lab. The white blood cell count of the patient was elevated, a sign of possible infection, and I prepared a Wright's stain

Figure 8F: The Boston University Student Union. There were daily rallies during the 1960s to protest the Vietnam War. (Image courtesy of Boston University. Reprinted with permission.)

Figure 8G: Students protesting the Vietnam War in Boston during the 1960s. (Image courtesy of Boston University. Reprinted with permission.)

of a blood smear. Under the microscope, I observed blue debris within the neutrophils. Thinking my blood smear was inadequate; I did repeated Wright stain preparations, but could not remove the debris. I thought there was a problem with the stain and went downstairs to tell my intern, Kathy Cocchiarella. Kathy was an effervescent blonde woman who had graduated in the first class of the Boston University six-year medical program. I was a member of the third class, two years behind her.

When I arrived on the ward, Kathy was performing mouth-to-mouth resuscitation on the child, who had just suffered a cardiac arrest. The child died without an initial diagnosis being made. However, on closer examination, the child had petechiae, red spots that appear on the skin as a result of bleeding, and the diagnosis of meningococcemia was suspected. Within the neutrophils, the gram-negative meningococcus diplococci will stain red with a Gram stain, but will stain blue with Wright's stain, and that was the debris I was seeing under the microscope. Inadvertently, I had made the diagnosis of meningococcemia, but didn't realize it initially.

That night after the child's death, Kathy developed a headache and high fever in her Boston apartment. Her husband, who was a pediatric resident, rushed her to Massachusetts General Hospital where she, too, died within an hour of arrival from meningococcemia. She had received no previous antibiotic prophylaxis.

The next morning, at conference, the Chief of Pediatrics, Dr. Horace Gezon, announced Kathy's death to the ward team, calling her "a saintly physician, a wonderful teacher, and a beloved human being who died trying to revive a child, putting herself in harm's way." Interns, residents and medical students can easily put themselves in grave danger when caring for patients. During the great influenza epidemic of 1918-1919, many interns and residents died in the line of duty from respiratory failure. The night float system was started at Boston City Hospital in the 1920s because some interns were diagnosed with cavitary tuberculosis, which was felt to be aggravated by fatigue and exhaustion. In more recent years, interns were exposed to hepatitis and HIV because of contaminated needle sticks. Health workers have also contracted Ebola virus infections in endemic areas.

I will always remember Kathy and her noble act. Had she been a member of the military, she would have won the Congressional Medal of Honor for her bravery. Subsequently, I have treated many patients with meningococcemia, and being experienced, have never lost a patient despite the severity of that illness. I enjoyed working in the field of pediatrics, but was always saddened by Kathy's death, which showed the risks we sometimes take when caring for patients.

Pediatrics was followed by my third psychiatric rotation located at Medford State Hospital in a Boston suburb. I was greatly affected by the large number of middle-class patients we treated with mental illness there, with family backgrounds similar to mine.

My final rotation for the year was internal medicine. My clerkship was at Boston City Hospital (Fig. 8I) where we were mixed with Harvard and Tufts students who also had clinical rotations at the same facility. Today, the only medical school affiliated with the hospital is BU. The medicine rotation was very exciting, and we were given a great deal of responsibility as students. Essentially, the house staff ran the hospital, with attending physicians (we called them visits) who were present only part of the day. Two of my attending physicians were Dr. Franz Ingelfinger, a gastroenterologist (Fig. 8J), and Dr. Arnold Relman (Fig. 8K), a nephrologist, who both would become editors-in-chief of the *New England Journal of Medicine*. Other notable attendings were Dr. Norman Levinsky, a nephrologist who would serve as chair of medicine at BU for 25 years, Dr. John Harrington, another nephrologist who would become dean at Tufts, and Dr. Aram Chobanian, a cardiologist, who would subsequently become dean of the medical school and president of BU (Fig. 8L).

Figure 8H: As a third-year medical student working at an inner-city pediatrics clinic. (Image courtesy of Boston University. Reprinted with permission.)

Figure 8I: A student ceremony on the Boston University School of Medicine campus. The backdrop is the old Boston City Hospital, one of the most famous clinical and research institutions in the U.S. (Image courtesy of Boston University. Reprinted with permission.)

Figure 8J: Dr. Franz Ingelfinger, a gastroenterologist, who was chief of medicine at Boston City Hospital during my early years of medical school. He would later become editor-in-chief of the *New England Journal of Medicine*, and both his son and daughter-in-law would become my students. (Image courtesy of Boston University. Reprinted with permission.)

Figure 8K: Dr. Arnold Relman, a nephrologist, who was chief of medicine at Boston City Hospital when I was a third year student. He, too, became editor-in-chief of the *New England Journal of Medicine*, where many of my papers have been published. (Image courtesy of Boston University. Reprinted with permission.)

At Boston City, we also spent a great deal of time caring for outpatients in the clinic, an important part of internal medicine training. We had lectures at the school every morning at eight o'clock before going to the hospital. I also continued to work one to two nights a week and on weekends as an emergency lab technician at the New England Deaconess Hospital and Joslin Clinic, the highest paying student job at $3.25 an hour. I learned to obtain a capillary blood specimen from an earlobe stick rather than a stabbing a finger.

Overall, the third year of medical school was quite a fulfilling experience. Though I had an interest in pediatrics and psychiatry, I was still poised to pursue a career in internal medicine and cardiology.

Notable historical events which occurred during the spring of 1968 were the assassinations of both Martin Luther King and Robert Kennedy. Dr. Martin Luther King had received his Ph.D from Boston University, and many of my teachers knew him. I consider him to be one of the four greatest individuals of the twentieth century (the other three on my list were Mahatma Gandhi, Anwar Sadat, and Nelson Mandela, all champions of peace). The student protests of the 1960s were also in full swing, but we were sheltered from the outside turbulence by being in medical school.

That year I was also hired to be a first-aid attendant at the Boston Garden sports arena, a job passed down by an upper classman, which gave me the opportunity to watch wrestling matches, hockey and basketball games, the circus and rock concerts for free. We were paid $10 an event, and were entitled to one free hotdog and could sit in the best seats. The job was one of the most exciting I ever had in medicine. Because of the rigid call schedules for residents, which prohibited any moonlighting, students were hired for this job and not house-staff. I'm still a big wrestling fan.

Fourth year began with an elective in pediatric research. For the first time medical students had four to five months of elective time instead of all required clinical rotations. In the past, all the third year clinical rotations were given again in the fourth year, albeit with more responsibility. My research project, under the supervision of Drs. Robert Klein and Horace Gezon, was trying to identify when the newborn colon was colonized with bacteria, and how the type of bacterial colonization, both aerobic and anaerobic, contributed to the presence or absence of neonatal diarrhea. The work was presented but never published, because I had difficulty with the anaerobic cultures. It illustrated for me the frustrations that researchers often experience in their investigations.

At BU we also had to write a mandatory doctoral thesis which could be based on original or library research. Because my pediatric research project had not really worked out, I did a library project on thyrocalcitonin, a newly discovered hormone. My faculty advisor was Dr. Isadore Rosenberg (Fig. 8M), a noted thyroid specialist from Boston City Hospital. In subsequent years I would mentor over 500 students, residents and fellows in thesis projects. I always felt this was an important part of undergraduate medical education, and also provided the opportunity for faculty to work one-on-one with students. However, I do feel the experience should be elective, and not mandatory, as we demonstrated in an article written about medical student theses (*see Appendix C #90*).

Following the pediatric rotation I had my fourth year medicine rotation, which was a cross between a clerkship and a sub-internship. Dr. Levinsky was my chief, and would write my main letter of recommendation for internship. These were the days before there was an intensive care unit (ICU). Following a heart attack, patients were treated in oxygen tents on busy hospital wards of 30-40 patients. There were few private rooms available except for quarantine purposes. We did not have the ethical dilemmas of keeping patients alive artificially, because there were few intensive care procedures available. For example, hemodialysis (or dialysis), a procedure in which a machine filters wastes, salts and fluid from the blood when the kidneys are no longer healthy enough, was reserved only for

Figure 8L: Dr. Aram Chobanian, my teacher at the Boston University School of Medicine, who ultimately became dean of the medical school and president of the university. One of the most effective individuals I ever met. He raised the medical school to national prominence, and helped found the Boston Medical Center. (Image courtesy of Boston University. Reprinted with permission.)

Figure 8M: Dr. Isadore Rosenberg, at left, a prominent thyroid specialist at Boston City Hospital who would serve as my medical school thesis advisor. From this experience, I went on to mentor over 500 students, from 1976 to the present, as a research thesis advisor at Einstein Medical School and New york Medical College. (Image courtesy of Boston University. Reprinted with permission.)

patients who were kidney transplant candidates. Everyone else died of kidney failure. I had a patient turned down for dialysis and kidney transplant because he was a homosexual. Homosexuality at the time was considered a mental illness; autism was considered a form of childhood schizophrenia, and these patients were often hospitalized in psychiatric hospitals.

Following fourth year medicine, I had a family medicine rotation called The Home Medical Service. This has been a BU rotation since the 1880s. We made house calls by ourselves, visiting patients with various medical problems. Carrying our black bag and wearing a business suit, each of us would visit patients in the housing projects and report to the family medicine attending at the home base, who would sign our prescription pads. I learned how important home visits are, especially in caring for patients with chronic illnesses. You really don't know a patient well until you know the family and home situation. I remember one house call where I was greeted by a naked woman at the door. I quickly turned around and ran down the stairs. If we had to draw blood from a patient at the home, especially one on furosemide (a medicine to treat fluid retention), you had to be good at it, because there was no one there to help you.

Following the Home Medical Service, I had a month of vacation in December, 1968, during which I also scheduled my interviews for house staff positions (internship). I applied predominantly to positions in New York and stayed with my mother and stepfather in their apartment that month. My mother had remarried in 1966 after a whirlwind courtship that I had helped along. My stepfather,

Irving (Izzy Zucker), was a wonderful man. Izzy had a son, who was a graduate of Hahnemann Medical College ('66), and Eli would serve as a mentor for me, and continues to be one today. He is now a retired family practitioner in Philadelphia.

The interview season was challenging, and I would eventually match at Montefiore Hospital in the Bronx for my house staff training. During that month of vacation, I also put together my class yearbook where I was once again the editor-in-chief.

Of importance, in late 1968 Nixon made his political comeback with his historic presidential election victory over Hubert Humphrey. In 1969, I started out with my second psychiatric rotation at Boston State Hospital, followed by my fourth year surgery rotation at Boston University Hospital (Fig. 8N). I had three months left after completing my mandatory fourth year rotations, and took three one-month electives in renal medicine, urology and cardiology. In the renal rotation, I learned how to really examine a urinary sediment. In urology, I learned to do a comprehensive genitalia exam and how to put in urinary catheters (which helped me as an intern), and in cardiology I learned the fundamentals of electrocardiography (EKG) from a great preceptor, Dr. Burton Polansky.

On May 18, 1969, I graduated simultaneously from both college and medical school (Fig. 8O). I received my Bachelor of Arts with a major in medical science, and my Doctor of Medicine (M.D.) degree. I had successfully completed the BU six-year program at age 22. Sadly, my stepfather could not attend the function because he had just had a heart attack a few weeks earlier at age 58. My surviving grandmother also could not attend as she had angina pectoris (chest pain) and could not travel. My sister, who had graduated that year from Lehman College of the City University if New York, and my mother attended the ceremony, as did my girlfriend at the time.

My mother and sister had seen me off when I started BU in 1963 and were there when I graduated in 1969. Twenty-eight of the 48 students who had initially started the program with me graduated. Senator Edmund Muskie, who had just run for Vice President, was the commencement speaker.

I have several important comments to make regarding my six years in Boston and on undergraduate medical education in general.

1. Was the BU six-year program a good idea? For me, it was, and I handled the work well. I was a bit awkward socially, but did have girlfriends. Because I was only 22 when I graduated, I decided to pursue an academic medicine career first, to see if I would like it. Had I been older, I might have gone right into private practice.

2. How does the medical school experience of the 1960s differ from what goes on now? Over time, there have been many changes for the better. Years ago we were taught by eminence not always by evidence, but we had spectacular teachers at the bedside who were great examples of clinical prowess. One role model was Dr. Louis Sullivan, a hematologist, who would become Health and Human Services Secretary under George H.W. Bush. He would write one of my letters of recommendation for house staff training (Fig. 8P).

In the 1960s we did not interact directly with patients until well into the second year of medical school, and never truly understood the relevance of basic science that was taught as a separate educational block. Today, students interact with patients early in their medical school studies. Students also have courses in ethics and the history of medicine, which were never offered to us.

3. What about working to support oneself in medical school? Extramural work puts a great additional burden on students. To even the playing field in school, it is far better that students don't work, and find other sources of financial support, such as scholarships and loans.

4. What advice would I give to medical students today? Find balance in your life. In medical school one has to work hard to succeed, but one needs to also find time to read novels, play sports (I

Figure 8N: University Hospital, a major teaching affiliate of the Boston University School of Medicine, where I took my fourth-year surgery rotation. (Image courtesy of Boston University. Reprinted with permission.)

Figure 8O: My graduation picture from medical school at age 22. As in high school, I was the editor-in-chief of the class yearbook. (Image courtesy of Boston University. Reprinted with permission.)

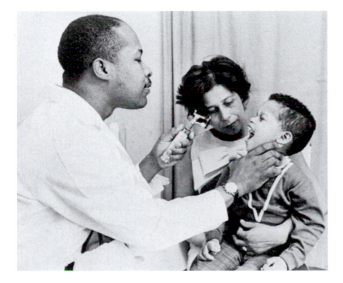

Figure 8P: Dr. Lous Sullivan, a prominent hematologist who was my instructor in pathophysiology. He subsequently became the first dean of the Morehouse School of Medicine in Atlanta and served as the Secretary of Health and Human Services under George H.W. Bush. (Image courtesy of Boston University. Reprinted with permission.)

Figure 8Q: Medical school wasn't all studying for exams. This is a photo of the medical school ice hockey team. I didn't know how to play, but I could skate. Two of my roommates were George Hines (center, wearing glasses) and Jeff Nurenberg (at right in glasses). I am in the back row, center next to Jeff. (Image courtesy of Boston University. Reprinted with permission.)

played on our medical school hockey team) and to socialize (Fig. 8Q). Medical school can be a wonderful experience, and I will always treasure that time of my life. I would also advise students to try to find a mentor, and adapt the habits of your good teachers and attending physicians in developing your own unique bedside style.

5. What would I recommend to improve the medical school experience? I would encourage individual students to participate in research or to prepare a thesis, but not make this a mandatory exercise. Students should also be encouraged to rotate through all the different clinical venues available, for training, and not concentrate their work in one hospital. I would make use of simulation labs where students can have standardized experiences. Ultimately, I would like to see the entire country utilize the same basic science curriculum, with some of the best teachers in the country providing instruction via the internet. This could also be a methodology for teaching some clinical subject matter. Students all have to take the same board examinations; therefore, the curriculum in different medical schools should be standardized. I also don't think there should be honors grades given during the first semester of medical school, since students enter with all different levels of preparation and varying study habits. A pass-fail system should be used initially.

CHAPTER

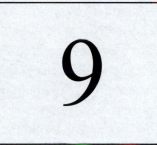

9

MATTERS OF
THE HEART

"The only way to do great work is to love what you do. If you haven't found it yet, keep looking. Don't settle. As with all matters of the heart, you'll know when you find it."

- Steve Jobs

Following graduation from medical school, I took a six-week vacation to Europe and Israel with my college and medical school roommate, Jeff Nurenberg, whose mother, at the time, worked for the U.S. State Department in Bucharest, Romania where he was born. The trip included visits to England, Austria, Switzerland, Romania, Turkey, Israel, Greece and Spain. At the time, Romania was a communist country under Nicolae Ceausescu, and I remember how apprehensive and frightened the population was under this totalitarian regime. I met a girl in Romania (Jeff's cousin) who asked me to send her a pair of blue jeans from the U.S., and not to write to her about politics. I sent the jeans to her when I returned home, but she never received my package.

We returned to the states on June 30, and I started my internship at Montefiore Hospital in the Bronx on July 1, 1969 (Fig. 9A). There was no hospital orientation for the trainees at that time, and I began working with patients right away. My first rotation was a two-month block at Morrisania Hospital, a public hospital affiliate of Montefiore, located near the lower Grand Concourse in a Bronx neighborhood that was undergoing great social change. At the time, the original Jewish population was all moving to the East Bronx development at Co-op City, a housing development even larger than Parkchester, and the vacated grand concourse apartments were being occupied by impoverished Puerto Rican and African-Americans families. There was a high crime rate, related in part to illegal drug use. I always felt that illicit drug use was a way for poor people to deal with hopelessness and spiritual and psychological pain. No person wants to be a drug addict or an alcoholic. No parents want to see this form of behavior from their children. Addiction is a great national tragedy.

Morrisania Hospital was in the area of the Bronx where the Morris family had lived during colonial times. One Morris descendent had signed the Declaration of Independence, and another (Gouverneur Morris) hand wrote the U.S. Constitution. The hospital had no air conditioning except in the new intensive care unit (ICU). There was no cardiac care unit (CCU), and most patients were hospitalized on 30 to 40 bed open male and female wards. The working schedule for interns was every other night and weekend. We worked 13 days every two weeks. One week you would be on 24-hour call Tuesday, Thursday and Friday and had to work Saturday morning. For the second week, you were on call on Monday, Wednesday and the entire weekend. The hardest shift was the weekend starting on Saturday morning where you would work through Monday without any time off (56 hours straight – I had never worked that hard before or since). The hospital was run by the house staff, and we had teaching rounds by attending physicians for just two hours a day. Otherwise, as interns we were often left alone, supervised by junior residents in their second postgraduate year (PGY-2). At one time I was following over 20 patients, including those in the ICU. During the summer heat I could watch swimmers at one of the private swim clubs across the street from the hospital (The Cascades).

Figure 9A: Montefiore Hospital in the Bronx which is, today, one of the best-known medical centers in the United States. (Image courtesy of Montefiore Hospital. Reprinted with permission.)

Luckily, I was 22, single and had enough resilience and tenacity to withstand the stress. Dr. Paul Spear was our chief at Morrisania, a soft-spoken hematologist. Unfortunately, the deputy chief was a terror. During the first two months of internship, we received no positive feedback from him, only negative criticisms. No matter how conscientious you were, the deputy chief would remind you of tasks you forgot to carry out, often not relevant to the patient. He made the internship at Morrisania Hospital like boot camp and combat rolled into one.

In September, I started my official training at Montefiore Hospital, which was founded in 1884 as a chronic disease hospital by a group of New York Jewish philanthropists in Manhattan. The hospital was named to commemorate the 100th birthday of Sir Moses Montefiore (1784-1885), a famous British philanthropist, who married into the British Rothschild family. In the early part of the twentieth century the hospital's initial Manhattan location was getting too crowded, and so it was relocated to the northwest Bronx where it stands today. In 1913, the new building opened. During the 1950s and 1960s Montefiore had evolved from a chronic disease hospital into an acute care facility, with the advent of anti-tuberculosis drugs.

My first rotation at Montefiore was oncology. My teaching attending was Dr. Leonard Essman, whose daughter was the comedienne Suzy Essman of *Curb Your Enthusiasm*. After the stress and strains of Morrisania, the oncology rotation was even more overwhelming since there was so little we could do for oncology patients at the time, and most of them were dying in the hospital. I remember one day when I obtained three autopsy permissions.

The on-call schedule at Montefiore on the wards was every third night, but we still worked over 100 hours a week. Montefiore had a new ICU and CCU, and the call on these units was 24 hours on, 24 hours off. We slept in the ICU if there was time to sleep, which was a rare occurrence. The emergency room rotation was also 24 hours on, 24 hours off. Again, the hospital was essentially run by the house staff at night and on weekends. In addition to patient care activities, we had to draw blood, start intravenous (IV) lines, perform EKGs, and transport patients to x-ray. We put in all the central IV lines, and inserted the catheters for peritoneal dialysis.

Later that year, I took a month of surgery as an elective at Morrisania, and had the opportunity to do an inguinal hernia repair, the only operation on a human I would ever carry out. However, I did perform a lot of suturing (stitching) during my different emergency room experiences.

During the internship year, one has the greatest learning curve in training. The experience was challenging, and I think I did a good job caring for the patients, but because of a lack of sleep a great deal of the year was a blur. One thing I clearly remember is watching Neil Armstrong and Buzz Aldrin on television as they landed on the moon on August 2, 1969 while I was on-call at Morrisania. In October, the Mets won the World Series. That first year I had two weeks of vacation, which I spent sleeping at my mother's house.

At Montefiore, I had a wonderful chief of medicine, Dr. David Hamerman, a prominent rheumatologist who would be my first real mentor (Fig. 9B). He is 92 now, and still active. He was also one of the early geriatricians. Dr. Sidney Gutstein, a gastroenterologist, was his deputy and was also very supportive.

Figure 9B: Dr. David Hamerman, a world-renowned rheumatologist and gerontologist, who was my chief of medicine at Montefiore Hospital in the Bronx where I completed my internship in medicine. He was my first clinical mentor. He encouraged me to pursue a career in academic medicine, eventually to become a chairman of medicine. (Image courtesy of Montefiore Alumni Association. Reprinted with permission.)

Figure 9C: The founding of the Albert Einstein College of Medicine. At left is Dr. Samuel Belkin, president of Yeshiva University; at right, Dr. Marcus Kogel, the school's first dean. Einstein himself looks quite pensive. (Image courtesy of Albert Einstein College of Medicine. Reprinted with permission.)

Montefiore was a special place to train. It was a trail-blazing institution in social medicine; the hospital and community linked together. It would merge with the Hospital of the Albert Einstein College of Medicine, becoming a two-campus greater Montefiore. The creation of Einstein Medical School had been inspired by the Jewish physicians on staff at Montefiore who were angered by the existing quota system that limited the number of Jewish applicants who were being accepted to medical school. Einstein was organized as part of Yeshiva University in 1955 and had no ethnic quotas (Fig. 9C). During my internship, the president of Montefiore was Dr. Martin Cherkasky, a pioneer in the social medicine movement. Today Montefiore is one of the largest academic medical centers on the east coast, and is now led by Dr. Stephen Safyer, who previously had been one of my students.

Unfortunately, in December 1969, during my internship, my last grandmother died. As described earlier, she had saved me on many occasions. She was in her late seventies, and had suffered from severe chest pain for a number of years. Her final illness was a probable stroke (cerebral hemorrhage), which she suffered in her apartment, and I rode to Montefiore Hospital with her in the ambulance. She was in the ICU, intubated for six days in a coma. I was asked by her attending physician, to give permission to turn off her respirator. I refused. I felt uncomfortable with having to make this decision, and could not give an end-of-life consent for her. I wish she had made a living will. She died while I was on-call in the hospital.

The highlight of my internship - I met my future wife, Esther, at Montefiore in April, 1970, and started to court her in June. She was, and still is, the most beautiful, intelligent and gracious woman I have ever known. Since my intern work schedule was so rigorous, our dates consisted of long walks at a local park where I would talk non-stop. I was always impressed with Esther as a listener. Esther lived with her mother in the Bronx, and when I would visit her house after work I often fell asleep on the floor from exhaustion.

Esther was born in Israel, the oldest daughter of Polish Holocaust survivors, and she, like me, was raised in the Bronx. She attended public school and learned to speak English from watching television and listening to records. Similar to our family, she had spent summer vacations with her family at Rockaway Beach and in the Catskills, although our paths never crossed. She went on to become a registered nurse and earned an additional degree in psychology. She attended the City University of New York and the Columbia University School of Graduate Nursing.

I proposed to Esther in September, 1970, at Point Lookout, Long Island, after we had taken a long bike ride along the Atlantic Coast. She accepted right away, and our engagement took place over a six month period. I was now a medical resident with a slightly easier work schedule. We had an engagement party at her house in October, 1970 (Fig. 9D). That November, she planned a surprise 24th birthday party for me (something Esther often does).

We were married on Thursday evening, March 11, 1971, around the Jewish Holiday of Purim (Queen Esther of Persia is the heroine of that holiday). Our modest wedding took place at the Lincoln Park Synagogue in Yonkers, New York, which still exists (Fig. 9E). We were married by Rabbi Sternstein, my wife's maid of honor was her sister, Muriel and my best man was Gene Kohen, a friend since my childhood days. Esther and I would have two "honeymoons" (one at the Fallsview Hotel and the other at the Nevele Hotel). Both are in the Catskills, where we had spent our summer vacations as children.

As a medicine resident, the on-call schedule was more reasonable, every third to fourth night, and the rotations included general ward medicine, CCU-ICU and the emergency room. Now I was in a decision-making leadership role. First year residents take care of twice as many patients as compared to the internship year, but have a bit more time for a personal life as well as academics. I worked at

Figure 9D: Our engagement party at Esther's home in the Bronx (1970).

Figure 9E: Our wedding at the Lincoln Park Jewish Center, Yonkers, New York in March, 1971.

both Montefiore and Morrisania hospitals. I made an academic presentation on prostaglandins that was a required part of the training program.

I was now head of a ward team that consisted of two interns, and two to three Einstein third and fourth year students. One of my interns, Dr. David Greenblatt, a Harvard graduate, was the best intern I ever worked with. His father, Dr. Milton Greenblatt, a psychiatrist, was the head of Boston State Hospital where I had worked as a medical student. David would become a leading clinical pharmacologist at Massachusetts General Hospital. Dr. Hamerman was our ward teacher that July.

Montefiore was one of the leading hospitals in the implantation of pacemakers, and ultimately in cardiac electrophysiology. Dr. Seymour Furman would put in the world's first transvenous pacer at Montefiore, working with Dr. Doris Escher.

I thoroughly enjoyed my second year at Montefiore. I lived with my new wife in campus housing which was attached by tunnel to the hospital, so I could be on-call at the apartment. This was not the case at Morrisania where one had to sleep in the hospital when on-call. Again, the residents ran the hospital at night and on the weekends. I had a large family living in the Bronx, and they used the physicians affiliated with Montefiore as their caregivers. It was said that at any one time, "one to two percent" of the inpatient census were "Frishman's relatives."

During these years it was not uncommon to complete the required three year internal medicine training period at more than one hospital. For my second year of medicine residency, my final year, I transferred to Bronx Municipal Hospital, a large public hospital (compromising Jacobi and Van Etten hospitals) in the east Bronx (Fig. 9F). At Bronx Municipal, we also rotated as chief medical residents through the Einstein College Hospital that was on the medical school campus. Jacobi Hospital began receiving patients in 1955 just at the time the Albert Einstein College of Medicine opened. Van Etten Hospital was a tuberculosis facility that opened in the early 1950s, but became more of a general pulmonary care center after tuberculosis became less of an in-patient disease.

At Jacobi, I worked with an extremely bright group of residents and interns and at times served as the chief medical resident on night call. The second year residency curriculum consists of many subspecialty electives that included cardiology, renal, infectious diseases, endocrine, gastroenterology, hepatology, pulmonary, general internal medicine and hematology/oncology. Our teachers at Jacobi were almost all basic science researchers who taught at the hospital for a few hours each day before returning to their labs at the medical school. I gave a resident seminar that year on the hematological complications of alcoholism.

At age 24, I was responsible for an entire medicine ward service. Our chief of medicine was Milford Fulop (Fig. 9G), a Columbia trained internist who was brilliant, but didn't always believe in providing positive feedback. We were all intimidated by him, but also highly respectful of his clinical acumen. His associate was Dr. Harold Adel. The house staff union was just being formed. Previously an intern or resident could never complain about working conditions. We were all afraid of being fired from our jobs if we showed any outward signs of weakness. Many of us fought off serious depression and exhaustion to get through our medicine training.

Figure 9F: Bronx Municipal Hospital which includes Jacobi Hospital (right), a public institution, where I served as a resident and later as an attending physician. (Image courtesy of Albert Einstein College of Medicine. Reprinted with permission.)

Figure 9G: Dr. Milford Fulop, hospital chief at Bronx Municipal during my residency and who later became the chairman of medicine at Einstein. He was a brilliant clinician-researcher and one of my role models. (Image courtesy of Albert Einstein College of Medicine. Reprinted with permission.)

The internal medicine training program ended with the certification exam, a two-day multiple-choice test. As with the National Board exams, I studied extremely hard and, at 25, became a board certified internist after successfully passing the exam. My internal medicine textbook, *Cecil-Loeb*, was worn from wear.

Internal medicine training is a very intense experience, caring for both inpatients and outpatients while trying to master procedures and absorbing a tremendous body of knowledge. Overall I think I was successful in achieving what was necessary. My criticisms of the experience at the time were:

1. The intense on-call coverage without senior physician supervision. These issues would be rectified at Einstein 20 years later by the Bell Commission guidelines. Ultimately, the work week would be reduced to 80 hours, with no on-call shift lasting more than 16 consecutive hours, and required in-hospital 24-hour supervision by an attending physician. I remember being so exhausted during my training that I would immediately fall asleep in teaching conferences. Whatever I learned came from my own reading and patient interactions.

2. There was little to no positive feedback given by our superiors. I always felt there was only criticism, which didn't foster confidence in young trainees. As residents, we clearly knew our patients well, and even with our knowledge limitations, tried to do a good job caring for them. I worked with wonderful chiefs, Drs. Hamerman and Fulop, and I would adapt many of their better qualities into my own leadership style; perseverance, job knowledge, honesty, transparency, meticulousness and accepting the responsibility to teach, while serving as a role model for junior trainees.

On a personal level, a major event that occurred during my senior residency year was the birth of our first child, Sheryl Renee, in 1972, at the Einstein College Hospital (Fig. 9H). I now had the responsibilities of fatherhood, marriage and a demanding job.

During my last year of training, my wife, daughter and I had moved back to the Parkchester neighborhood in the east Bronx. I was now ready for subspecialty training (fellowship) in cardiology. I completed a two-year fellowship in cardiology (1972-1974) at New York Hospital-Cornell Medical Center. I always knew I wanted to go into cardiology and had previously applied for subspecialty training in Boston and in New York. My top three choices had been Montefiore, the Harvard Service at Boston City Hospital and New York Hospital-Cornell. My wife did not want to leave New York, so I was limited to two choices. Heeding my wife's counsel, I decided to go to Cornell, even though it involved a difficult daily commute to the city from the Bronx where we continued to live.

New York Hospital is the oldest hospital in the city, chartered by King George III of England in 1773. The hospital is affiliated with the Cornell Medical School, and in 1972 was clearly a premier site for both cardiology training and research. New York Hospital had one of the first CCUs in the country. I was one of four first year fellows, and our chief was Dr. Thomas Killip, often called "the father of acute coronary care" (Fig. 9I). Cornell was a recipient of a Myocardial Infarction Research Unit Grant from the National Institute of Health, one of eight sites in the U.S. The Swan-Ganz catheter came out of this program, as well as other major research discoveries regarding the treatment of myocardial infarctions (heart attacks).

In 1972, coronary angiography was being performed by radiologists at Cornell, not cardiologists. Echocardiography (echo) was first introduced. We had no technicians, and taught ourselves how to use the echo machine from pictures in an early textbook. We would record the image off an oscilloscope using a Polaroid Land camera. We learned basic bedside cardiology, and used phonocardiography and vectorcardiography techniques. We read resting ECGS, stress ECGS and 24-hour Holter ECGs every day. Cardiac catheterization was done predominantly for valve disease, but within a year

Figure 9H: With Esther and our first child Sheryl, while I was in my medicine residency at Bronx Municipal Hospital.

Figure 9I: Dr. Thomas Killip, III, known as "the father of acute coronary care." He was the chief of cardiology at New York Hospital-Cornell Medical Center, where I completed my fellowship and worked at my first academic job. (Image courtesy of Weill Cornell Medical College. Reprinted with permission.)

the cardiologists started to do their own coronary angiograms.

We also had spectacular pediatric cardiologists at New York Hospital. Dr. Mary Allen Engle was the first disciple of Dr. Helen Taussig, the founder of pediatric cardiology at Johns Hopkins. I had the opportunity to work with Dr. Engle and with two of the great cardiothoracic surgeons of the time, Dr. C. Walton Lillehei, a heart surgery pioneer, and Dr. Paul Ebert. Coronary bypass surgery was a relatively new procedure, and there were many valve replacement operations being performed, as well as innovative corrections of various congenial heart disease lesions.

My junior attendings were Dr. Stephen Scheidt (Fig. 9J), one of my mentors, who would replace Dr. Killip as chief of cardiology after I left Cornell. He was also the fellowship director. Dr. Scheidt was a brilliant clinician and I modeled much of my teaching style after him; which was to make the educational experience for students enjoyable and fun. Dr. Michael Wolk, another young attending, would later become president of the American College of Cardiology. Dr. Joseph Hayes ran the ECG Lab and Dr. Susan Kline directed the catheterization lab. A senior attending, Dr. Isadore Rosenfeld, was the cardiologist for Aristotle Onassis, Danny Kaye and many other celebrities.

My research career really began at New York Hospital (Fig. 9K). Dr. Killip was given the opportunity by industry to test a new cardiovascular drug from England, a beta-adrenergic blocker called propranolol, for the treatment of angina pectoris. While I was a first year fellow, he asked me to run

Figure 9J: A holiday party at New York Hospital-Cornell Medical Center, where I was a cardiology fellow (second from right). Dr. Stephen Scheidt is at right. He was one of the best teachers with whom I have ever worked. We wrote an entire paper during a flight from Dallas to New York.

Figure 9K: New York Hospital, facing Manhattan's East River (1972). (Courtesy of Historic American Buildings Survey.   Used under Creative Commons Attribution 4.0 License.)

one of the first placebo-controlled studies of a new cardiovascular drug. The study was sponsored by the drug manufacturer, Ayerst Laboratories, and as a fellow I had my own research office and a full-time technician. Our study showed the safety and efficacy of using propranolol for the treatment of angina pectoris (chest pain caused from reduced blood flow to the heart muscle), a revolutionary advance in cardiac care. The study led to two major publications in *Circulation* and in *The American Journal of Cardiology* (see *Appendix C #2,3*).

At New York Hospital, I also participated in basic cardiology research involving thrombosis (clotting) in coronary artery disease. I presented my research findings at the National Scientific meetings of the American Heart Association and the American College of Cardiology.

In 1972, during my fellowship, I was sitting on a plane at LaGuardia Airport waiting to leave for Dallas to attend the annual American Heart Association Scientific Session. I was called off the plane just before take-off. My stepfather, Izzy Zucker, had a sudden death at the age of 61, dying in the street. He had previously suffered a heart attack just before my graduation from medical school in 1969, and had suffered angina pectoris for three years thereafter. We had been considering coronary angiography and possible coronary bypass for him, but the procedures were never carried out. He was a good man, like a second father, and the second to die from premature coronary artery disease.

My chief, Dr. Killip, would always be my model for the clinician-scientist and after 40 years I still interact with him. The Myocardial Infarction Research Unit Program at New York Hospital also gave me exposure to the current and future leaders of academic cardiology from other leading centers, such as Johns Hopkins, the University of Chicago, Massachusetts General, the University of Alabama, the University of Rochester, Cedars-Sinai (home of the Swan-Ganz catheter) and Duke.

Early in my internship, I had joined the U.S. Army's Berry Plan where, as a reserve officer, future training would be done in civilian hospitals followed by my entry into the military as a cardiologist. As I was finishing my fellowship, Dr. Killip didn't want me to go into the Army, but rather to continue with my research. But I had an obligation to serve, so after completing my fellowship I went into the military. I was offered a position in the U.S. Army Research and Development Command Unit to work on coronary blood flow physiology under Dr. Thomas Gregg, but because I didn't want to make the extended time commitment of three to four years that was required for that assignment, I went into the regular Army Medical Corps instead.

At this point, after medical school at Boston University, three years at Einstein Medical School affiliated hospitals, Montefiore and Bronx Municipal Hospitals, and two years at New York Hospital-Cornell, I felt I had been extremely well trained. I was now ready to put another notch on my belt, a military hospital experience.

CHAPTER

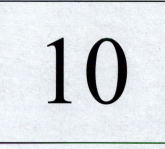

GUARDIANS

"We must never forget why we have, and why we need our military. Our armed forces exist solely to ensure our nation is safe, so that each and every one of us can sleep soundly at night, knowing we have 'guardians at the gate.'"

- Allen West

I had grown up in a family where both my father and all of my uncles had served in the military during World War II. My father was drafted into the Army, had completed his basic training at Fort Dix, New Jersey and was then assigned to the last horse cavalry regiment which was based at Fort Sill, Oklahoma, an artillery facility. My Dad, who achieved the rank of corporal, also spent some time at Fort Ord in California, but never saw action overseas. His brother, Phil, was assigned to an armored infantry unit in Europe, and was wounded in action multiple times, receiving the Purple Heart. My father's youngest brother, Ken, served in the Philippines in 1945. My mother's brother, Sydney, served in the Navy. My parents were married while my father was on active duty and on furlough. I had always had an interest in military history, was a Boy Scout, and an avid reader of military comic books as a youth. I attended medical school (1965-1969) during the heart of the Vietnam War, when the military was drafting almost all male physicians into active service after graduation. At that time, males could get an educational deferral to complete medical school. As a student, I saw many resident physicians going off to the military in the midst of their training, while many others were returning to complete their residency. During medical school, I did an orthopedics rotation at the Chelsea Naval Hospital in Boston, which at the time was packed with young Marine combat victims who had been evacuated back to the U.S. following the North Vietnamese Tet Offensive of 1968.

Because of my young age at graduation from medical school (22), I was certain to be drafted. To avoid being assigned the role of a general medical officer, I had joined the Berry Plan, which allowed a graduating physician to complete his residency (women were not eligible for the draft) and fellowship training in a civilian hospital and then to report for active duty as a specialist. I was deferred as a cardiologist, and entered the Army as a medical officer in July, 1974, in my specialty (Fig. 10A).

At the time, the war in Vietnam was beginning to wind down, and the draft was over. I was excited to serve, although my wife was unhappy about it. Luckily I was assigned close to home at the U.S. Walson Army Hospital, a large military hospital at Fort Dix, New Jersey, that also served McGuire Air Force Base (Fig. 10B). Our commanding officer was Colonel Leon Dixon, an African-American internist-cardiologist who was very popular with the medical staff because of his fairness and wisdom (Fig. 10C). I was assigned a small house in the officers' bachelor's quarters across from the hospital, and we kept our residence in the Bronx where my wife and daughter stayed. I would commute to the Bronx two or three times a week, and my wife and daughter would often visit the base. In my second year, my wife moved down to the area permanently, and my daughter started nursery school on the base. While on active duty, I was also appointed to the faculty of Cornell Medical School as an instructor, and would return periodically to New York Hospital to complete my research projects.

After I completed basic officer training, I was assigned to the cardiology section with the rank

Figure 10A: My official Army photo (1974). At age 27, I was a major in the Army Medical Corps. Ultimately I would be promoted to the rank of lieutenant-colonel as a reservist during Desert Storm.

Figure 10B: Walson Army Hospital Fort Dix, New Jersey. I was assigned here as chief of cardiology for most of my active duty tour from 1974 to 1976. At this 500-bed hospital, we took care of active duty personnel and retirees from the Army and Air Force. McGuire Air Force Base can be seen in the rear. It was a privilege for me to serve in the military, an experience that aided me in all my future leadership positions.

Figure 10C: My hospital commander, Colonel Leon Dixon of the U.S. Army Medical Corps, Fort Dix, New Jersey. He was one of the most impressive leaders with whom I have had the pleasure of working. He was fair, honest and extremely devoted to the medical officers under his command.

of Major. I had a clinical practice in the Army that was similar to what one would have in civilian life, taking care of retired military veterans and active duty personnel and their dependents with heart disease. I helped design a new coronary care unit at the hospital, and introduced echocardiography as a diagnostic test. My other assignments included being on night and weekend call as an internist (medical officer of the day) and as an emergency room physician (physician of the day). I also saw patients in the Fort Dix stockade, including hundreds of soldiers who had been caught after being absent without leave (AWOL) and were about to be dishonorably discharged.

Being an Army medical officer was a privilege. Having clinical responsibility for active duty soldiers, their dependents and the retired veterans was a great experience, and I was truly blessed to have had this opportunity.

While on active duty, I also helped set up a cardiology rehabilitation program for victims of myocardial infarction, for which I received the U.S. Army Commendation Medal from the Secretary of the Army, Martin Hoffmann. In recognition of my military service, I would ultimately receive the New York State Distinguished Service Cross from Governor Mario Cuomo.

In the medical corps there is a lot of support from medics, nurses and administrators, and a physician's hospital order is indeed an order. In contrast to today, the military hospitals at the time were run very well. During my two years in the military, I was an eye witness to three major historical events:

1. I was in the emergency room on August 9, 1974, when Richard Nixon resigned as president. It was depressing to see our Commander in Chief brought down. Within minutes, Gerald Ford's photograph replaced Nixon's in the chain of command table of organization which was posted outside the hospital commander's office.

2. The war in Vietnam officially ended on April 30, 1975, with the emergency evacuation of the American embassy in Saigon. To be part of a defeated army, no matter what your political position on the war, was extremely disheartening.

3. I was discharged from active duty on July 7, 1976, three days after the Bicentennial, essentially a spiritual rebirth of the nation, after the defeat in Vietnam.

I was also a witness to one of the great medical fiascos, the swine flu epidemic that never was. The sole victim of the so-called "epidemic" was a Fort Dix soldier, who died on the base in February, 1976. Gerald Ford's decision to make a vaccination mandatory across the country, based on this one case, may have cost him the election to Jimmy Carter later that year. I saw how an irresponsible press could whip the population into a frenzy.

I also spent a month at the war games held at Fort Bragg, North Carolina, with the 82nd Airborne Division, where I was assigned as a medical officer to one of the last army field hospital units (36th Medical Clearing Company) (Fig. 10D). After the Vietnam War ended, the military had to have a morale boost so these massive inter-service war games (Solid Shield) were organized. That year, 1975, I slept in a tent from Memorial Day until the end of June, camped at Pink Hill, North Carolina. I would also fly on medical evacuation helicopters to Camp Lejeune, a marine base on the coast (Fig. 10E). The experience was just like the movie and TV show *MASH*, living with the mosquitos and heat, eating combat rations left over from previous wars and ending with a combat landing on a beach in a C-130 transport plane (Fig. 10F). Fortunately, as a physician, I never had to jump out of airplanes. Our side, the blue team, defeated the red team (101st Airborne Division) from Fort Campbell, Kentucky, which had invaded North Carolina (Fig. 10G).

I am very grateful to the Army, and feel proud that I could serve, with distinction, both my country and the soldiers and their families who had made such a major sacrifice.

Figure 10D: With the 82nd Airborne Division, Fort Bragg, North Carolina during war games (1975).

Figure 10E: Exiting an Army medical evacuation helicopter during Army war games with the 82nd Airborne Division, Fort Bragg, North Carolina. The war in Vietnam had just ended (1975).

Figure 10F: At the war games in Fort Bragg, North Carolina (1975). Making the world safe for democracy.

Figure 10G: As a physician commander of the 36th Medical Clearing Company, 82nd Airborne Division, Fort Bragg, North Carolina, during war games.

In the military, I also had the opportunity to serve as a chief of cardiology at the age of 28, an experience that would help me in my future administrative roles in medicine. I had thought about staying on active duty after completing my required two years of service, but my wife said, "that's it" and she's the boss. My assignment would have been the cardiology catheterization laboratory at Landstuhl, Germany. I returned to reserve duty during Desert Storm as a lieutenant-colonel, but ultimately would resign my commission after the Gulf War ended because of family and work pressures. I was grateful to the elder George Bush for not extending the war, and allowing me to leave the Army. Today, I remain an active member of two veterans' organizations, The American Legion and The Jewish War Veterans, and march each year with these units at the Memorial Day and Veterans Day celebrations in my hometown of Scarsdale, and in White Plains.

Today, I write letters of recommendation issued from our school for medical students with military scholarships who are applying for residency. My letters always end with "as a former medical officer who served during the Vietnam and Desert Storm eras, I am pleased to recommend this student, devoted to his/her profession, and to his/her country."

CHAPTER

PRACTICE

"Use your gifts faithfully, and they shall be enlarged; practice what you know and you shall attain to a higher knowledge."

- Matthew Arnold

During the early part of 1976, I began to look for civilian cardiology positions in both academic settings and in private practice. I was 29 years-old, now board certified in both internal medicine and cardiology, and was serving as a chief of cardiology of a large army hospital while maintaining a part-time academic appointment at Cornell Medical School.

I was certain I wanted to pursue a career in academic medicine. However, almost all of my Army colleagues and fellow house staff were going into private practice. I did look at some cardiology group practices in southern New Jersey and in New York, but they were lacking the intellectual and scientific attributes that were important to me.

I had four academic job opportunities. I could stay at Cornell working under Drs. Stephen Scheidt and Dr. John Laragh, a famous hypertension researcher who had become the new chief of cardiology. My previous chief, Dr. Thomas Killip, had left Cornell to become the chairman of medicine at Evanston Hospital in Illinois. I had an offer from the Deborah Heart and Lung Center located in Brown Mills, New Jersey. Deborah was located right outside the confines of Fort Dix where I was stationed, and I attended conferences there and occasionally referred them patients from the army hospital. Their chief, Dr. Alden Gooch, offered me a position in non-invasive cardiology with no specific administrative role. I was offered a position at Montefiore by Dr. James Scheuer, their new chief of cardiology, with major responsibilities in the exercise cardiology unit. Finally, I was offered a position at the Albert Einstein College of Medicine and the Einstein College Hospital (Fig. 11A), which had now merged with Montefiore as an academic campus. Dr. Edmund Sonnenblick, a world-famous cardiac physiologist, had just come from Harvard and the Peter Bent Brigham Hospital to be the chief of cardiology at Einstein (Fig. 11B). I was offered the position of director of the non-invasive lab, a role that would include clinical oversight for electrocardiography, exercise testing and echocardiography. This position offered me the opportunity to return to the Bronx, to work under a renowned physician-scientist and to resume my research in cardiovascular pharmacology. On July 8, 1976, the day after my Army discharge, I assumed this new position, with the academic rank of assistant professor of medicine at Einstein. My chairman of medicine would be Dr. Milford Fulop, my former residency director at Bronx Municipal Hospital.

My new position was multi-faceted, which I thoroughly enjoyed. I had a private practice, I ran the non-invasive cardiac lab, I taught medical students, residents and fellows and I was involved in innovative curricula development. I resumed my cardiovascular drug trials. It was also important to be located on the medical school campus where I could interact with my basic science colleagues.

My family was also growing. Before I left the Army, Esther and I had our second child, Amy Helene, who was born May 2, 1976, at the Einstein College Hospital. Dr. Irwin Kaiser delivered Amy, as he would all of our children (Fig. 11C). We now lived in a 7-room apartment in my in-law's two

Figure 11A: The Albert Einstein College of Medicine, a great source of pride for the Bronx. It was the first American medical school established under Jewish auspices. I served on the full-time faculty for 21 years (1976-1997), and still serve as a visiting professor, for a total of 40 years of service to the school. (Image courtesy of Albert Einstein College of Medicine. Reprinted with permission.).

Figure 11B: Dr. Edward Sonnenblick, one of the great cardiovascular scientists. He hired me in 1976 to run the non-invasive cardiology lab at the Einstein College Hospital. He was one of my mentors, and together we co-authored many articles and books. (Image courtesy of Albert Einstein College of Medicine. Reprinted with permission.).

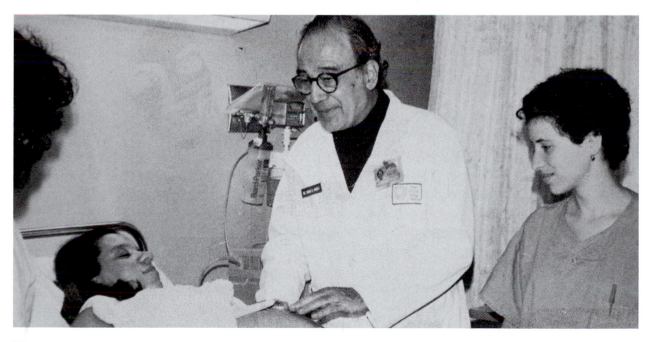

Figure 11C: We are all interrelated. Dr. Irwin Kaiser, at left, delivered our three children at the Einstein College Hospital. I subsequently taught two of his children. At right is Dr. Elizabeth Leggatt, the resident, who ultimately delivered my daughter Amy's three children. I also taught Dr. Leggatt's husband.

family house on Rochambeau Avenue, just down the street from Montefiore.

In 1976, Jimmy Carter would be elected President. Soon after that, in 1977, New York City would be in the middle of its financial crisis. The South Bronx was deteriorating, and the summer of 1977 in New York City would be known as the "Summer of Sam," related to the Son of Sam killings that were happening at the time. The North Bronx community where we lived was fairly stable. Our oldest daughter began kindergarten, and then first grade, at a Jewish day school, Salanter Riverdale Academy.

Everything at work was going well. This time period marked the peak of the revolution in cardiac pharmacology in which entirely new classes of drugs were being tested and then introduced into clinical practice: the beta-adrenergic blockers (*see Appendix J, Appendix C #321*), the alpha-adrenergic blockers, calcium blockers, angiotensin receptor blockers, angiotensin converting enzyme inhibitors, thrombolytics, new anticoagulants, new inotropes and the statins. I was a part of this endeavor right from the beginning, and have continued to be involved throughout my entire academic career. I was always among the first investigators chosen to test a newly developed cardiovascular drug. My reputation in this area was, in part, related to my early success in evaluating propranolol at Cornell in 1972, and to my working with Dr. Sonnenblick, to whom industry often turned to with their recent discoveries. I never discovered the drugs, but demonstrated to the world how to use them.

In clinical research, a great deal of the success comes from the ability to recruit suitable patients for the drug trials. Being in the Bronx, gave me a great advantage. First, there was a shortage of practicing physicians, and patients were eager to come under our care. Second, our patients had easy access to our research clinic, which had been endowed by a generous philanthropist.

Almost all of our studies were placebo-controlled. I never had an intellectual or ethical issue with putting patients on placebo. In every study in which I participated (over 300 trials from 1972 to the present), patients (research subjects) always did better on placebo than would be expected (*see Appendix C #319*). The placebo effect is real, allowing the body's own healing powers to come forth especially when one is under the care of a giving and compassionate health professional. I also made an ethical decision for myself - if I ever put a patient on placebo where he/she would be at risk, and a complication occurred, I would stop doing research. I am still participating in clinical trials after 43 years, having studied thousands of subjects on innovative drug therapies.

I am grateful to all my study subjects, many of whom also became my patients in private practice. I always offered my services as a primary care physician to research subjects who completed trials, so they never would feel that I had used them as a "guinea pig" during the study. I never paid a patient for his or her research participation, but I did offer free medical care related to the trial. Through the years I may have saved Medicare, Medicaid and private insurance carriers many millions of dollars in patient care reimbursements.

Although the majority of the studies I conducted were supported by industry, I never had any ethical conflict. I interacted with some outstanding people in industry, and have written about the important role of industry in drug development (*see Appendix K, Appendix C #336*). I was always careful to avoid any conflict of interest with any drugs I recommended in practice and in my teaching. If I spoke about a new drug in a lecture, I always made it a practice to discuss competitive agents from a neutral position. I am uncomfortable with giving pharmaceutical industry-sponsored lectures today because we have to follow a script. As a result, I give very few industry-sponsored presentations.

I became a world expert on the beta-adrenergic blocking drugs and adrenergic pharmacology. In 1979, Dr. Edward Sonnenblick and I had an article on dobutamine published in the *New England Journal of Medicine* (*see Appendix D, Appendix C #6*). I also wrote a 13-part series on beta blockers in the late 1970s for the *American Heart Journal,* and a series of articles on these drugs that were published in the *New England Journal of Medicine* (1981-1998) (*see Appendix C #18, #24, #34, #38, #83, Appendices E-G*). I had my first book published in 1980, *Clinical Pharmacology of the Beta-Adrenoceptor Blocking Drugs* (Appleton-Century-Crofts); a second edition was published in 1984 (*see Appendix C #123*).

The beta-adrenergic blockers have also served as pharmacology probes to understand the mechanisms of agonist and antagonist adrenergic receptor action, leading to the awarding of multiple Nobel Prizes (*see Appendix J*), the most recent was awarded to Dr. Robert Lefkowitz, originally from the Bronx, and my old neighborhood.

Despite my research productivity as a faculty member at Einstein, I can recall that the basic science faculty would often look down on patient oriented clinical researchers like myself as being second-class academicians.

During these years I worked with several chairmen of medicine including Dr. Fulop who was Acting Chairman at Einstein from 1975-1980. Drs. Fulop and Sonnenblick competed for the permanent position which in 1980, was awarded to Dr. Louis Sherwood, an endocrinologist from Michael Reese Hospital and the University of Chicago (Fig. 11D). Dr. Sherwood had edited the Seminars from the Beth Israel Hospital section in the *New England Journal of Medicine.*

Dr. Sherwood would give me one of my big breaks, as will be discussed later. The Dean at Einstein was Dr. Ephraim Friedman, an ophthalmologist, who had also been my teacher at BU (Fig. 11E). He would ultimately leave Einstein to become president of the Massachusetts Eye & Ear Infirmary. The President of Yeshiva University, Einstein's University sponsor, was Dr. Norman Lamm, a famous rabbinical scholar. I would take care of Dr. Lamm's father, and Dr. Lamm himself would also become one of my patients.

Dr. Sonnenblick was a chief who let me "do my own thing." As a result, I had a great deal of autonomy. He had his own research interests that were different from mine, and there was never any competition between us, only mutual respect. I also had an excellent working relationship with Dr. Robert Frater, the chief of cardiothoracic surgery, a pioneer in the field, and a world expert on the workings of the mitral valve. It is important for optimal patient care that cardiothoracic surgeons and cardiologists work closely together.

I had a major role in teaching and curriculum development, interests I would maintain throughout my career. My teaching style was modeled after my interactions with Dr. Stephen Scheidt at Cornell and Dr. Martin Cohen (Fig. 11F) at Einstein. Teaching is like acting, in that you hope to convey information in an entertaining way, capturing the attention of the audience. During each year, I served as a teaching attending at both Bronx Municipal Hospital and the Einstein College Hospital, and my activities, as a ward teacher were described in a book titled *Residents* (*see Appendix B #5*),. A ward team that we supervised consisted of a resident, two or three interns and three medical students. I was also an attending physician in the coronary care units of both hospitals, and for the cardiology consult service. In 1980, I would also assume the role of chief of the cardiology service at the Einstein College Hospital under Dr. Sonnenblick.

As a teacher, I was involved in the development of a unique course entitled, "the Return to Basic Science." In medical school, there is always the issue for students of how basic science teaching relates to clinical training. A decision was made at the school to shorten the time for basic science by three months in the first two years of medical school, and add three months of basic science teaching at the end of the third year. Those of us who taught the course tried to teach subjects that students could better appreciate after they had been on the wards (such as clinical pharmacology and preventive medicine). As the director of the course I did a great deal of the lecturing. The course was highly rated, but the students complained they were under too much pressure with such an abbreviated time for basic science instruction in the first two years. Students also have difficulty going back to the lecture halls once they have been on the patient wards. After many years, the course was discontinued and the basic science teaching time was expanded. However, even now as a visiting professor I continue to give my course lectures in clinical pharmacology to the Einstein students (1977-present).

Based on the Return to Basic Science Course, and other teaching activities, I would receive two career development awards in medical education. The first was the Teaching Scholar Award from the American Heart Association, one of two grants given annually. The second was the Preventive Cardiology Academic Award from the cardiorenal section of the National Institutes of Health, also one of two awards given annually. I would maintain close friendships with the other awardees and, as a group; many of us would become the future leaders in medical education.

After a few years on the Einstein faculty, I had become one of the most popular and respected teachers in the school. In the late 1970s, students had been affected by the turbulent times of the 1960s and early 1970s following the Kennedy assassination and the unpopularity of the Vietnam War. Across the country, the students in medical school became politically active, and made their concerns known, unlike during my medical school years when we seemed far more passive. Students wanted to abolish grades and exams and to dismantle the school's Alpha Omega Alpha (AOA) chapter of the National Honor Medical Society. Dr. Friedman, the Dean, called me in to stem the tide of protest regarding AOA, and asked me to speak to the students. I mentioned to them that recognition for excellence was not something to be ashamed of; the military does it all the time. The students promised to keep the chapter if I would become the faculty advisor, and they also elected me into the society (Fig. 11G). In 1978, at the age of 31, I became the Councilor (faculty advisor) for the AOA chapter at Einstein and would remain a Councilor for the next 38 years (*see Appendix T, Appendix C, #375*). I would also become the Councilor at New York Medical College (NYMC), making me the only person, since the founding of AOA in 1902, to serve as Councilor at two medical schools. I may also hold the all-time Councilor longevity record.

I have also been active in AOA on a national level, elected to the board of directors and also serving as the regional Councilor for all the Northeastern medical schools. In 1997 I would receive the AOA-AAMC (Association of American Medical Colleges) Distinguished Teaching Award in 1997, given to the best medical educators in North America (medical education's "Nobel Prize").

Many medical schools also have their own local faculty honor societies. At Einstein it was the Davidoff Society, named after a renowned neurosurgeon from the original Einstein faculty. Dr. Davidoff had trained under Dr. Harvey Cushing. I was elected to the society at an early point of my faculty tenure, and would become the third president, replacing Dr. Dominick Purpura, a neuroscientist, who had left Einstein to become the dean at Stanford. He would return to serve as Einstein's dean (Fig. 11H), replacing Dr. Ephraim Friedman.

I also began a student thesis program at Einstein. As mentioned previously, I had written a thesis in medical school as it was a graduation requirement. BU no longer requires a graduation thesis. However, based on my own experience as a student, I had a favorable feeling about student theses, and from 1976 until the present I have mentored 12-15 students a year in either an original research project or in preparation of a review article. Almost all of the 520 students I have mentored have had their theses published in a peer-review journal, and one student was a book co-author (*see Appendix C #129*). Many have chosen careers in academic medicine based on their student thesis experiences. After I left Einstein in 1997, the thesis did become a requirement for graduation at that school.

Figure 11D: Dr. Louis Sherwood, the chairman of medicine at the Einstein College of Medicine who appointed me as chief of medicine at the Einstein College Hospital in 1982 when I was 35. He was an oustanding scientist and clinical leader. (Image courtesy of Albert Einstein College of Medicine. Reprinted with permission.).

Figure 11E: Dr. Ephraim Friedman, who was my ophthalmology professor in medical school and would become my first dean when I worked at Einstein. A remarkable individual, he subsequently became president of the Massachusetts Eye and Ear Infirmary in Boston. (Image courtesy of Boston University Medical School. Reprinted with permission.).

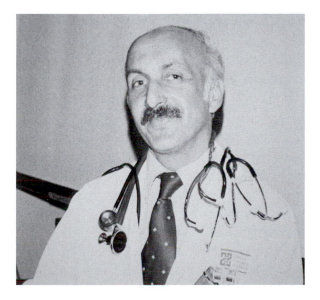

Figure 11F: Dr. Martin Cohen, a model of what a clinical teacher should be. He was ward attending during my residency years, and I become his colleague in the cardiology section at Einstein where he is still active in practice and teaching. (Image courtesy of Albert Einstein College of Medicine. Reprinted with permission.)

In a survey research project, we found that a student thesis should be an option provided by a school but not a requirement (*see Appendix C #90*). The success of the student thesis program was also one of the factors contributing to my winning the AOA-AAMC Distinguished Teacher Award, and ultimately becoming a Master of the American College of Physicians.

The current President of New York Medical College (NYMC) and Touro University, Dr. Alan Kadish, completed two student theses with me. Both were original projects completed in 1980. The first was a clinical demonstration that chronic beta blocker treatment be maintained right up to the time of coronary bypass surgery. This research observation has probably done more to reduce the rate of perioperative myocardial infarction worldwide than any other pharmacologic intervention. The second project was the first published report in the United States on the use of transesophageal echocardiography (*see Appendix C #15*).

In addition to my work in cardiovascular pharmacology, I also became involved in cardiovascular epidemiology. I had come from Boston University, the school responsible for the Framingham Heart Study, which is still ongoing. The results of Framingham showed the significance of hypertension, male gender, hypercholesterolemia, cigarette smoking, obesity and diabetes as risk factors for cardio-vascular disease. The study reported findings in middle-aged individuals but initially did not provide information on risk factors in individuals over the age of 75. Along with the chairman of neurol-ogy, Dr. Robert Katzman, a noted expert on dementia, and Dr. Miriam Aronson, a gerontologist, we launched the Bronx Longitudinal Aging Study in 1978, funded by the National Institutes of Health, to help identify potential risk factors for cardiovascular disease and dementia in the well elderly. The study is now complete. We made two major observations. First, that most of the cardiovascular risk factors in middle age still operate in old age, except for gender and body weight (*see Appendix C #213*), and second, that the presence of cardiovascular disease is associated with a higher risk of all-cause dementia (*see Appendix C #51*). These findings suggest possible interventions that would prevent or postpone both cardiovascular disease and dementia. I was able to get board certified in geriatrics based on my work in this study.

One negative factor in beginning an academic medicine career in the 1970s was the poor salary support that was provided to young faculty. I started out with a total salary for 1976-77 of $34,000 and we were discouraged from moonlighting. Dr. Fulop would say, "If you were full time, you were all time." To encourage us to do research, we had little opportunity for earning money in private practice. Faculty were allowed to keep honoraria earned by speaking and writing, but one had to first develop a scholarly reputation. In the past, academic medicine was often a career path only for independently wealthy individuals.

I did moonlight in three different jobs during these early years in order to support my family. First, I performed histories and physical exams at the homes of Metropolitan Life Insurance clients in the Bronx, a lowly job for a budding professor. Second, I became the cardiologist for the Martin Luther King Health Center in the South Bronx, an early "Great Society" health facility that was part of the Montefiore Family and Social Medicine Program. I ran one evening clinic and read all their electrocardiograms (ECGs). As a native of the Bronx, I was never fearful about working in any neigh-borhood, but was always alert to the dangers of the city. Finally, I was the director of the emergency room (ER) at Queens General Hospital, a large public institution. I worked one overnight weekday shift and every Saturday, a 24-hour shift that lasted until Sunday morning. My office was next to the psychiatry patient holding area, so sleeping was often difficult. Emergency medicine was not yet an established specialty, so most emergency rooms were run by house staff often supervised by moon-lighting internists, pediatricians and surgeons. I was able to hold onto this job because the interns and

Figure 11G: In 1978 I was chosen as faculty advisor for the national medical honor society, Alpha Omega Alpha (AOA) chapter at Einstein. I would hold this position at two medical schools, Einstein and New York Medical College. Beside me is the Einstein student AOA President.

Figure 11H: Dr. Dominick Purpura, a neuroscientist who served as dean of Stanford University Medical School and later at Einstein for 25 years. (Image courtesy of Albert Einstein College of Medicine. Reprinted with permission.)

residents saw most of the patients, and I was only there to supervise. I did a tremendous amount of my academic writing during my ER shifts, including my first textbooks and my *New England Journal of Medicine* articles. I will always be grateful to the house staff who worked so hard caring for patients in the emergency room during these years. In 1982, it became impossible to continue my work at Queens General, and I was doing better financially in my regular job. At the same time I was now getting many offers to lecture all over the country. Reflecting on the past, moonlighting never interfered with my academic work, but it kept me away from family.

The salary issue is still what keeps many qualified individuals from pursuing academic careers. Starting salaries are better now, but academic medicine also involves a major private practice commitment for the faculty member that competes with research time and teaching.

In 1980, I was promoted to the rank of associate professor at Einstein. Achieving this rank used to be an important milestone at Einstein because with the promotion came faculty tenure, but this is no longer the case. In early 1982, Dr. Sherwood, the chairman, called me into his office to offer me the position of chief of medicine at the Einstein College Hospital with a major increase in my salary. I would also have an office next to his in the chairman's suite. I accepted the offer right away.

At the age of 35, my academic career would now include leadership of a major hospital department of medicine, an administrative role which I would dovetail successfully with my research, teaching and practice functions. I would always be thankful to Dr. Sherwood for giving me this major opportunity to now prove myself as an academic leader.

CHAPTER

12

PROGRESS

"Men make history, and not the other way around. In periods where there is no leadership, society stands still. Progress occurs when courageous, skillfull leaders seize the opportunity to change thisngs for the better."

- Harry S. Truman

In 1982, a few months after my thirty-fifth birthday, Dr. Sherwood, the chairman of medicine at the Albert Einstein School of Medicine and Montefiore Hospital, called me into his office. He told me that Dr. Saul Moroff, the chief of medicine at the Einstein College Hospital, the school's on-campus university hospital, that was also part of Montefiore (Fig. 12A), would be taking a terminal sabbatical, and Dr. Sherwood asked me if I could replace Dr. Moroff as of July 1. My great career ambition was to be an internist and cardiologist, but I had secondary aspirations to be a chief of medicine, and I accepted the offer immediately (Fig. 12B). I had wonderful role models in medical school who exemplified the type of person a chief of medicine should be: Robert Wilkins (Fig. 12C), who would win the Lasker Prize for his work in the pharmacologic treatment of hypertension, was my chairman of medicine at BU and the chief of medicine at the University Hospital in Boston; and Chester Keefer (Fig. 12D), who controlled the nation's penicillin supply during World War II, was chairman emeritus at BU. Other notables were Dr. Arnold Relman, a nephrologist, who was my chief of medicine at Boston City Hospital and would become chair of medicine at the University of Pennsylvania and subsequently editor-in-chief of the *New England Journal of Medicine*; Dr. Franz Ingelfinger, a gastroenterologist, another chief of medicine at Boston City Hospital, who would also become editor-in-chief of the *New England Journal of Medicine* and Dr. Norman Levinsky (Fig. 12E), a nephrologist, who was also a chief of medicine at Boston City who would in time also replace Dr. Wilkins as chairman of medicine at Boston University (he would serve in this capacity for 25 years).

My role models from my residency and fellowship years were Dr. David Hamerman who was the chief of medicine at Montefiore, Dr. Milford Fulop , chief of medicine at Bronx Municipal Hospital Center, Dr. John Sandson, chief of medicine at the Einstein College Hospital and acting Chairman at Einstein when I was a resident (he would later become dean of medicine at Boston University) and finally, my predecessor, Dr. Saul Moroff. I did not know the chairman well at New York Hospital-Cornell, Dr. Alexander Bearn, who had come from Rockefeller University. I was influenced more by my cardiology chief at Cornell, Dr. Thomas Killip, who would become chief of medicine at Evanston Hospital in Illinois, an affiliate of Northwestern, and then the chief at The Henry Ford Hospital in Detroit.

The departments of medicine at Einstein and Montefiore were unified for the first time under Dr. Sherwood. There was a hospital chief at the Einstein College Hospital (me), a chief of medicine at Bronx Municipal (Dr. Fulop), and a chief of medicine at Montefiore (Dr. James Scheuer) who had replaced Dr. Hamerman. Dr. Hamerman, a rheumatologist, went on to establish a new section of geriatrics at Einstein and Montefiore. All of us reported to Dr. Sherwood. I also reported to Dr. Fulop regarding the house staff program, since he was the residency program director. The subspecialty section chiefs who worked at the College Hospital all reported to me. The private practice of the faculty

Figure 12A: The Jack Weiler Hospital (part of Montefiore Hospital) of the Albert Einstein College of Medicine, where I was chief of medicine. (Image courtesy of Albert Einstein College of Medicine. Reprinted with permission.)

Figure 12B: A formal photo of me as chief of medicine, Einstein College Hospital, 1982.

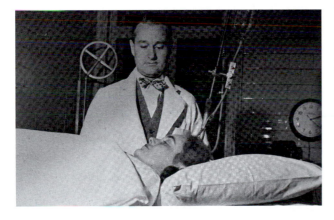

Figure 12C: Dr. Robert Wilkins was chairman of medicine at Boston University when I was a medical student. He later introduced the first effective treatments for hypertension (high blood pressure), a subject that would become a major clinical and research interest for me. (Image courtesy of Boston University School of Medicine. Reprinted with permission.)

Figure 12D: Dr. Chester Keefer was chairman emeritus of medicine at Boston University while I was a student. During World War II, he controlled the American supply of penicillin. (Image courtesy of Boston University School of Medicine. Reprinted with permission.)

was under the control of the medical school, but it was losing money, despite the high income from sections like cardiology. Ultimately, Montefiore Hospital would take over the faculty practice, and did a much better job in its management. Currently, Montefiore Hospital is in the process of taking over the Einstein Medical School.

The hospital presidents I worked under during my time on the Einstein-Montefiore faculty were Dr. Martin Cherkasky, Dr. Carl Eisdorfer, a psychiatrist, Dr. Michael Cohen, a pediatrician and, finally, Dr. Spencer Foreman, a pulmonary medicine specialist. Dr. Foreman was recruited from Mount Sinai Hospital of Baltimore (I served on his search committee). Like Dr. Cherkasky, he would become one of the most effective hospital administrators in the U.S. (Fig. 12F). My hospital site administrators were James Roemer and Patrick Wardell, both highly effective people, and our medical director was Dr. David Kessler, a pediatrician and attorney who would ultimately become the most famous commissioner of the U.S. Food and Drug Administration (FDA)(Fig. 12G), and who later became the dean of the schools of medicine of Yale and the University of California, San Francisco. David is a remarkable individual who attended both Harvard Medical School and the University of Chicago Law School at the same time.

I had three wonderful deputy directors at the college hospital including Dr. Edward "Woody" Eisenberg, an infectious disease specialist, Dr. Elliot Lazar, a cardiologist who would become head of quality at New York-Presbyterian Hospital and Dr. Matthew Berger, who would ultimately replace me as chief of medicine after I left for New York Medical College. All three of them had been residents under me at Einstein, and were familiar with my leadership style. My subspecialty section chiefs were all superb and included Dr. Ed Sonnenblick and Dr. Robert Forman in cardiology, Dr. Joseph Reichel and Dr. Jay Dobkin in pulmonary-critical care, Dr. Jan Dutcher and Dr. Peter Wiernik (a former Director of the National Cancer Institute) in hematology-oncology, Dr. Donald Feinfeld and Dr. Vaughn Folkert in nephrology, Dr. Steven Baum and Dr. Ruy Soiero in infectious disease, Dr. Norman Fleischer (Director of the NIH- funded Diabetes Center) and Dr. Joel Zonszein in endocrinology, Dr. Leslie Bernstein in gastroenterology, Dr. Alan Wolkoff in hepatology (Head of the NIH funded Liver Center) and Dr. Harold Keiser in rheumatology,   Dr. Steven Baum, chief of infectious diseases, would become chief of medicine at Beth Israel Hospital in New York and subsequently the dean of Students at Einstein.

Other administrative people I worked with at the medical school included Dr. Harry Gordon, a pediatrician who was an acting dean, and Dr. Dominick Purpura, a neurosurgeon and neuroscientist who served as dean of Einstein for 25 years. The parent University of Einstein, Yeshiva University, was headed by Dr. (Rabbi) Norman Lamm and Rabbi Israel Miller, who was a major figure in the reparations negotiations with Germany for holocaust survivors of World War II (Fig. 12H). For years, Rabbi Lamm and I have exchanged the many books we have each written.

The Einstein College Hospital, which ultimately became the Weiler Hospital Division of Montefiore, was a 450-bed tertiary care hospital. The chief of cardiothoracic surgery did most of his operative work at the facility. The hospital at the time had no emergency room of its own, but used the Bronx Municipal (Jacobi) Hospital for this purpose. Patients were transferred for advanced care to our facility. Today, the hospital has its own functioning emergency room.

My administrative office was located on the eighth floor of the hospital on a medicine ward. I had two wonderful secretaries, Evelyn Ponzio and Anne Palladino. Carol Ruggerio replaced Eve and Ann when they retired, and Carol later moved with me to New York Medical College.

For a chief of medicine, the best place to be located is on a patient ward. My door was closed only when I met with someone for a scheduled appointment. Faculty members, residents, students,

Figure 12E: Dr. Norman Levinsky, a nephrologist, was chief of medicine at Boston City Hospital during my fourth year of medical school. He later served as chairman of medicine at Boston University for over 25 years. (Image courtesy of Boston University School of Medicine. Reprinted with permission.)

Figure 12F: Two giants Dr. Dominick Purpura (at left), was dean of medicine at Einstein for 25 years; Dr. Spencer Foreman (second from right), was president of Montefiore. I was privileged to work for both of them. Second from left is Montefiore's Dr. Harold Rifkin, a renowned diabetes specialist and one of the best bedside teachers I ever had. In the rear, second from left, is Dr. Ira Rubin, a cardiologist who taught electrocardiography while I was an intern.

Figure 12G: Dr. David Aaron Kessler, a pediatrician by training. David and I worked together at the Einstein College Hospital for several years, and he later became a very effective director of the U.S. Food and Drug Administration (FDA). Under his leadership food labels became easier to understand, and he led a strong national anti-smoking campaign.

Figure 12H: With Dr. Norman Lamm, president of Yeshiva University of which Albert Einstein College Medicine was a part, and Yeshiva's Dr. Israel Miller, who was a leader in the negotiations with Germany to make reparations to victims of the Holocaust.

patients, nurses and patient family members could simply walk in to the office to discuss any topic with me. In this way, I felt the constant pulse of the hospital, and I knew first-hand what was going on. From this experience I learned that, for a chief of medicine, the further one's office is from the wards the less you get to know what is happening in the hospital.

I had two other offices including a research office where Joanne Cioffi-Pryor sat. She would become my editorial assistant and together we would put together fifteen books, over a thousand papers and chapters, all while running three journals (*Heart Disease, Cardiology in Review* and *The American Journal of Medicine*). Joanne, who has worked with me for 32 years, is the best in what she does. I also had an office in the chairman's suite at the medical school.

In 1982, when I took over as chief, there were no Medicare diagnosis related groups (DRGs), no quality assurance programs, and medical house staff still worked up to 120 hours a week. Among my major early accomplishments was the implementation of DRGs at the hospital, an important government mandate that, over time, shortened hospital length of stay and encouraged the institution to be more efficient. We began the quality assurance program which enabled us to improve medical care in the hospital on an ongoing basis, and made physicians and nurses more accountable for clinical outcomes. Einstein formed one of the first emergency medicine residencies in the U.S.

The major reform in house staff training in almost 100 years began at Einstein in response to the death of Libby Zion, a patient who died at New York Hospital in Manhattan, allegedly because of the actions of an unsupervised, overworked and sleep deprived resident physician. A New York State policy was put in place to shorten resident work hours and require closer house staff supervision. This movement was led by Dr. Bertram Bell, a faculty colleague at Einstein and former teacher of mine, who led (and gave his name to) the "Bell Commission" that helped establish these reforms. In anticipation of the changes, which were to go into place on July 1, 1989, we recognized that we could no longer cover all the patients in the hospital with house staff. In early 1989 we opened a 60-bed hospital inpatient unit, the first of its kind in the U.S., where physician assistants (PAs) would replace house staff in providing coverage. There was initially great resistance to this change, especially among the attending staff, who wanted interns and residents and not PAs to help cover their patients. Fortunately, we hired the right group of PAs to help launch the ward, and the attendings quickly recognized the skill of these individuals in providing care. Subsequently, many of the attendings would demand that their patients be placed on the PA ward, rather than on the house staff wards. This endeavor was a great success for which I am very proud, and has served as a model for the country, with both the use of PAs and nurse practitioners as physician extenders. The original PAs I had hired in 1989 are still working in the hospital.

Since we were the home of the Bell Commission, our hospital had to be at the forefront of house staff reform. We made up the first 80-hour work week schedule in the country, which went into effect on July 1, 1989. As an individual committed to educational research, I helped evaluate the effects of the change on the house staff, the attending staff and on patient outcomes *(see Appendix C #65)*. Although there was great anxiety regarding what would happen with the shortened work hours, the transition was uneventful. In our first published assessment, the house staff reported being very happy with the change, however, the attending staff felt that with more patient sign-outs, the house staff did not know their patients as well as they should. In reality, patient outcomes really were not affected adversely. In the end, the change, on balance, was the right thing to do, because we saw a dramatic drop in the numbers of mental depression episodes among house staff related to work fatigue. Ultimately, the Bell Commission work hour requirements would be adopted nationally *(see Appendix L, Appendix C #354)*. Clearly, there are more patient sign-outs when more house staff are involved, but at the same time, supervision of trainees is mandated (*see Appendix N, Appendix C #368*). During my own house staff years, especially in the public hospitals where I worked, the residents were directly responsible for almost all patient care and were, often unsupervised, which is now no longer the case.

I was able to address the future effects of the Bell Commission reforms in a graduation speech I gave at Einstein in 1989, (Fig. 12I) just before the changes took place (*see Appendix C #168*). My warning regarding the changes was that future physicians should not learn to practice using a time clock mentality.

As chief of medicine I had to deal with hospital worker and house staff union strikes. I have always been a supporter of labor unions, coming from a garment worker family. There were a total of three house staff strikes organized by the union. Two of the strikes were regarding salary and benefits, and the third was for improved ancillary support for patients. These strikes were not very disruptive, and were settled quickly. However, the 1199 hospital workers union strike in 1984 posed a much greater challenge. During the summer of that year the workers went on strike for eight weeks in an attempt to achieve an increase in salaries and fringe benefits. In the hospital, the only individuals left, who were not on strike, were the attending physician staff, nurses, non-union administrative staff, house staff and the medical students. The hospital was kept open, and it was decided that nurses, house staff and students would continue in their usual work roles. The attending physician staff and the administrators would fill those jobs of the union workers. To lead by example, I served food in the cafeteria for eight weeks. The advantage of this assignment was that, each day, I was able to both see and speak with the house staff and nurses as they came through the food line. Some of my colleagues worked in the kitchen washing dishes, some worked as messengers. Some members of my research staff were union members, but out of loyalty to me and to our patients, they came to work before the pickets went up. The individuals who marched outside our hospital on the picket lines were workers from other unionized hospitals. There was a real siege mentality with the constant shouting of the strikers outside, but we persevered over the eight weeks. The hospital did not close, the patients were well provided for, and some people said that the hospital care was never so good.

I truly feel this was one of my "finest hours." As a leader of the attending staff, I maintained morale and saw to it that we persevered through the crisis. I worked seven days a week (days and nights) during the strike, and I have to acknowledge my family for sacrificing their summer vacation that year. The strike was ultimately resolved. I still really don't know if it ended because of the agreements that were made, or because the strikers were just exhausted from picketing all summer in the heat.

Along with my administrative responsibilities, my research continued to thrive. Our clinical research space ultimately was endowed by a benefactor as the Rousso Clinical Pharmacology Unit. At Einstein, I had been the first investigator to set up a clinical research program on the medical school campus since the emphasis previously there had been on basic science. From 1976-1997, we tested every single cardiovascular drug that had been under investigation during this period in over 200 trials, including many agents that became great clinical successes. As principal investigator of these studies, I helped to generate millions of dollars in overhead for the school and hospital, while providing free care for thousands of patients, which in turn, saved millions of dollars in health insurance costs. I will always be grateful to my research staff, which included 20 nurses and research technicians, some of whom went on to other health care careers to become leaders in their fields. I am also appreciative of the efforts of countless Einstein medical students and fellows who worked with us, many of whom went on to successful academic careers of their own.

We were involved in the first study showing the potential benefit of angiotensin converting enzyme (ACE) inhibitors in heart failure and were funded to participate in two large National Institute of Health (NIH) studies confirming these early findings. The studies of left ventricular dysfunction (SOLVD) demonstrated the long-term benefit of ACE inhibition treatment in patients with heart failure, now a standard treatment worldwide (*see Appendix C #58, #64*). I also was a co-investigator in the Systolic Hypertension in the Elderly Program (SHEP), also funded by the NIH, which showed the utility of treating isolated systolic hypertension in the elderly, dispelling many myths regarding this common cardiovascular condition (*see Appendix C #57*).

I continued as co-principal investigator of the Bronx Longitudinal Aging Study funded by the NIH, which established risk factors for cardiovascular disease and dementia in the well elderly (*see Appendix C #51, #213*). I also served as co-investigator in the NIH-sponsored Asymptomatic Coronary Ischemia Pilot trial (ACIP) which showed the significance of silent myocardial ischemia in patients with coronary artery disease (*see Appendix C #76*). I completed all the objectives of the NIH-sponsored Preventive Cardiology Academic Award teaching grant. Finally I became the co-principal investigator of the largest-ever clinical trial, the Women's Health Initiative (WHI). My wife, Esther, was a co-investigator (Fig. 12J). Einstein was the New York City center for this national study which was designed to determine whether hormone replacement therapy with estrogen or estrogen plus progesterone in post-menopausal women would prolong life when compared to placebo treatment. The surprising negative findings of the study clearly showed the importance of performing placebo-controlled clinical trials in medicine (*see Appendix C #93*). In recognition of my research work in epidemiology and in clinical trials, I was given a secondary appointment at the medical school as professor of epidemiology and social medicine. I had already been appointed professor of medicine at the school in 1985, nine years after I had assumed my faculty position at Einstein.

I also continued my student thesis program, mentoring 10-15 students a year. One project led to a full-length textbook entitled, *Beta3-Adrenergic Agonism* (Futura Publishing) (*see Appendix C #129*). I

Figure 12I: Moments after delivering my commencement address to the Einstein Medical School Class of 1989. Judging from my smile, I think the speech went well. This was an important address, in which I discussed house staff working reforms that were soon to take effect in New York State.

Figure 12J: My wife, Esther, and I were both co-investigators for over 10 years in the Women's Health Initiative study, the largest clinical trial in U.S. history. I was the co-principal investigator of the New York City center, and Esther was the nurse manager of a satellite site.

Figure 12K: Receiving the Albert Einstein College of Medicine honorary alumnus award at graduation (1993). Dean Purpura is to my right.

Figure 12L: Albert Einstein College of Medicine graduation (1989). I was the commencement speaker (seated second from right, first row)

I also continued to be active in clinical practice, and had a prominent patient following. I took care of many school and hospital benefactors, along with administrators, faculty and their families. In addition, I continued to take care of many underserved patients from our area.

I continued my heavy teaching schedule which included chief of service rounds, medicine and cardiology attending rounds, and giving lectures to the students, residents, and fellows. In 1991, I was appointed associate chairman of the department, at the medical school assuming the responsibilities for all of the student teaching programs in medicine, which included the clerkships and sub-internship rotations in our affiliated hospitals, and I also played an important role in establishing the Sabbath-observing programs for orthodox Jewish students.

In recognition of my teaching efforts at Einstein, I was given both the Gordon and Rosen awards as the best teacher in the school. I also was made an honorary alumnus of Einstein (Fig. 12K), and in 1995 was recognized as the best teacher since the school's inception 40 years prior. I was chosen as a commencement speaker (Fig. 12L), and I also received the Montefiore Hospital Alumni Association Distinguished Alumnus Award. The 1996 school yearbook was dedicated to me. During this time, Boston University, my alma mater, elected me into their Collegium of Distinguished Alumni (Fig. 12M), and the BU medical school chose me as their Distinguished Alumnus in 1994 (Fig. 12N). In 1997, I received the nation's Distinguished Teacher Award from the Association of American Medical Colleges (AAMC) and Alpha Omega Alpha (AOA). I continued to serve as the local faculty advisor to AOA. When I received the AOA-AAMC award I had already agreed to move on to New York Medical College (NYMC) and, at the AAMC awards ceremony in Washington D.C., both the deans of Einstein and NYMC (Fig. 12O) were present, as well as Dr. Foreman, the president of Montefiore and the AAMC.

During my time as hospital chief, I was involved in two major extramural continuing education activities. The first was a 40 day trip with my family to the Far East where I served as a visiting professor in Korea, the Philippines, Thailand, Taiwan, Singapore, Malaysia and Japan. I have always enjoyed visiting other medical schools as a teacher, both in North America, South America, and overseas. From these visits, I learned a great deal about the universal way we practice medicine, and how local culture can affect patient care. During my academic career, I have had the opportunity to visit almost every North American medical school, and have recognized, just as Voltaire did in Candide, that at the end of every journey "there is no place like home" (*see Chapter 13*).

The second activity was a program sponsored by industry and the National Aerospace Agency (NASA) in 1990 in which all the U.S. astronauts and Russian cosmonauts were brought together with their respective medical support teams. The meeting was held in Florida, and I co-chaired the proceedings with Eugene Cernan, the last man to walk on the moon during the Apollo 17 mission. President George H.W. Bush congratulated and recognized us for our efforts in bringing this meeting together (I have his letter of thanks framed in my office) (Fig. 12P).

I was also involved in meetings with other former U.S. Presidents (Figs. 12Q, 12R). I started my first journal with Dr. Walter Flamenbaum, the *Journal of Clinical Hypertension*, published by Elsevier. Ultimately the journal was taken over by the newly-formed American Society of Hypertension to be their official journal, and renamed the *American Journal of Hypertension*.

During the 15 years as an academic leader at Einstein, I have enjoyed great success as an administrator, teacher, clinician, researcher, writer and editor. As mentioned previously, I have co-authored and co-edited multiple books including *Current Cardiovascular Drugs* (Fig. 12S), and my magnum opus, *Cardiovascular Pharmacotherapeutics* (*see Appendix C #132*). Because of my academic and clinical efforts, I was able to lift the reputations of both the medical school and hospital.

Figure 12M: Esther joined me at my 25th medical school reunion on the campus of Boston University (1994).

Figure 12N: At the reunion with my stepfather, Herbert Granick, my mother, Frances, and Esther.

Figure 12O: Receiving the Distinguished Teacher Award from Alpha Omega Alpha, the national medical honor society, and the Association of American Medical Colleges (1997). On my right is Dr. David Dale, president of Alpha Omega Alpha and dean of the University of Washington School of Medicine.

In 1997, after turning 50, I felt I had accomplished everything I wanted to do at Einstein and at Montefiore. However, I was not the department chairman. After seven years in the position of chairman, Dr. Sherwood had resigned in 1987. He then went to work for Merck and Company, the pharmaceutical firm. At the time of his resignation, the dean wanted me to pursue the chairmanship. I was only 40 years old at the time with three young children; and felt the need to be available for my family. Dr. James Scheuer became the chairman. I did not know whether I would replace him in the future when he would decide to step down (Fig. 12T).

So it was not until my late forties that I began looking at outside chairman of medicine positions. My wife and children did not want to move from the New York City area, so my search was limited in scope. There was a chairman search going on at New York Medical College, just 15 miles north of Einstein. I pursued the position and was ultimately selected by the search committee and the school and hospital administration to be both chairman of medicine at New York Medical College and director of medicine at Westchester Medical Center in Valhalla, New York. I accepted the position in the spring of 1997, and started my new job in November just after my 51st birthday.

It was very hard for me to leave Einstein/Montefiore and the Bronx. I had been a house officer and attending physician there for 24 years and now would be moving my office to Westchester, which is still attached to the Bronx by land (the Bronx was part of Westchester until 1900 when the area joined New York City, and is the only borough that is not an island). Although I had thoroughly enjoyed my positions at Einstein and Montefiore and left on top, I always felt some tension as a hospital chief and associate chairman related to working both for a hospital and a hospital president, and for a medical school and its dean. Everything went smoothly as long as the school and hospital were on the same wavelength. However, I was able to work well within these boundaries and helped to resolve some of the conflicts between institutions. I would face a similar situation when I moved to Westchester, working again for both a new dean and hospital president. However, I was ready for this challenge, and felt well prepared by my Einstein-Montefiore experiences (Fig. 12U).

Figure 12P: With President George H.W. Bush. During his presidency, I co-chaired a medical meeting with Eugene Cernan (the last man to walk on the moon, Apollo 17) which brought together members of the U.S. and Soviet space programs and included physicians, astronauts and cosmonauts.

Figure 12Q: At a meeting with President Ronald Reagan, one of the most pleasant individuals I ever met.

Figure 12R: With President Gerald Ford.

Figure 12S: One of my books on display at an American Heart Association annual meeting.

Figure 12T: Dr. James Scheuer, a chairman of medicine at Einstein who appointed me as his associate chairman, my last administrative position at the medical school.

Figure 12U: At an Einstein graduation with Dr. Howard Dean (left), a student of mine (Einstein '78), who later became Governor of Vermont and a presidential contender. Fernando Ferrer, Bronx Borough President, is at right.

CHAPTER

HOME

"Love begins by taking care of the closest ones - the ones at home."

- Mother Theresa

My home has truly been at the heart of everything I do, from my childhood to this very moment. Although I have achieved much in my life on a professional level, my greatest personal satisfaction and joy has come from my family (Fig. 13A).

This chapter could have been titled simply, "Esther," because throughout our many years together (as of this writing, we have been married for 45 years) she has been the center of my life (Fig. 13B). She is my best friend, and a source of great strength for our family. We are extremely devoted to each other, and to our children and grandchildren.

We have three children and six grandchildren who all live close to us. After a hot New York City summer in 1977, and a severe winter in 1977-78, we moved out of the Bronx to a house in Scarsdale, New York, a far cry from the old two-room apartment of my youth. We moved on June 24, 1978, my wife's birthday, and have lived in the same five bedroom, colonial style house, which sits on one level acre, bordering a nature preserve. Our children would complete their education through high school in the Scarsdale public school system, where they were all very happy. We made parenting a priority. Although work was very important, I was always very active in my children's lives. My children and grandchildren say, "I never missed one of their team games, a play or a musical performance." Of this particular achievement, I am very proud. Sometimes I couldn't stay for the entire event because of a hospital emergency, but the children always saw me there, even if it was for an abbreviated time.

My oldest daughter, Sheryl, was born when I was a medical resident at the Einstein Hospital. (Fig. 13C). She started pre-school at Fort Dix when I was in the Army, and was always a good student in both her secular and religious studies. Sheryl is empathetic and socially responsive. She completed her undergraduate studies at Union College (Chester A. Arthur's alma mater as well as William Seward's.) Union was the 2015 Division I National Champion in collegiate ice hockey. Sheryl is an elder law attorney who worked for one of the original specialty firms in this specialty. As a teenager, she had worked with me on my geriatric research projects, where her interests in elder law developed. She also does child advocacy law, and is a national figure in this branch of legal practice.

Sheryl graduated from The Benjamin Cardozo Law School of Yeshiva University in 1996, where she met her future husband Robert Rosman. Rob is a native of Philadelphia, and attended George Washington University as an undergraduate. Sheryl and Rob married just after graduation from law school. I had the privilege of hooding both of them for their Juris Doctor (J.D.) degree at Lincoln Center in New York since I was still a Yeshiva faculty member (as a member of the Einstein Faculty) Rob, a rabid "Grateful Dead" fan, has attended all of their concerts nationwide including their last one. He has his own real estate law firm in Manhattan.

Sheryl and Rob live in Irvington, New York (near the historical home of Washington Irving) and have three children, Aaron (named for my father), Rebekah, his twin, and Zachary. Aaron has

Figure 13A: With Esther and our children in front of our house (1982).

Figure 13B: With Esther in our backyard (1984).

Figure 13C: My oldest daughter, Sheryl, at her high school graduation.

Figure 13D: My daughter, Amy, in her senior prom dress.

autism which has been a challenge, but the family has risen to the occasion, and he is doing very well in a residential school. He has a pure heart and soul, and serves as an inspiration to other children with developmental disabilities. One of the great family events was Aaron's bar mitzvah where he recited his prayers in front of the entire congregation. His sister Rebekah is in high school where she is a top student and a champion soccer goalie. Zack, 13, the youngest, is in middle school where he has won multiple scholastic competitions and is a curling champion. He recently celebrated his bar mitzvah.

Our second child, Amy was born while I was on active duty in the Army (Fig. 13D). We like to say that is why, even today, she is always ordering everyone around. During Amy's early years, when she went to sleep-away camp in the Pocono Mountains, I worked as a camp physician, usually for two-week periods during the summer, which were great respites for me. Amy graduated from New York University and Columbia Teachers College with a concentration in special education. She teaches third grade in a local public school, and is one of the best known educators in the region. She is married to Jacob Amir, of Israeli descent, who is a litigation attorney. He works in the law practice of the former NY lieutenant-governor and Westchester County Executive. Jacob was a classmate of my daughter Sheryl and her husband. Amy and Jacob live in Ardsley, New York, which borders Irvington with their three children Joshua, 14, Mikayla, 12, and Samantha, 8. Joshua is an accomplished student, a talented musician and a black belt in karate. Mikayla is an excellent student and athlete as is her sister, Samantha.

Michael, our son, was born in 1981 (Fig. 13E), a strong student and the great athlete his father never was (Fig. 13F). However, I did receive my tae kwon do karate black belt at age 60 (Fig. 13G). Michael played varsity football, basketball and baseball. As a youngster, he attended a New York Yankee Training Camp at the stadium. He graduated from Muhlenberg College in Pennsylvania (named for the first speaker of the House of Representatives) and from the University of Miami School of Law. Michael is a distinguished medical malpractice defense lawyer. He is now an attorney for the New York State Supreme Court working under Judge Barry Salman. He recently coached an inner city public school team in a regional mock law trial competition, which they won. Michael and his championship team were honored by the Yankees on the field at the new Stadium. Michael recently married Courtney Dastis, a graduate of the University of Delaware, and a Director of Computer Programming for a non-for-profit organization. It was a Hasidic Wedding held on an upstate farm (Fig. 13H). Michael and Courtney are major outdoors people. She comes from an old Greek-Jewish family that can date their origins back 2000 years to ancient Israel. Michael and Courtney live in Manhattan, across from the Museum of Natural History.

I also have a plethora of nieces and nephews, cousins and a favorite Uncle Ken, my dad's youngest brother, who is 88. He has been a major influence in my life and in many ways, served as a surrogate father and mentor. I also have a stepbrother, a physician in Philadelphia, who has also served as a role model for me since our widowed parents married 50 years ago when I was attending medical school and he was an intern (Fig. 13I).

Throughout my career, I was very sensitive about protecting the time I spent at home with my family (Fig. 13J). When the children were growing up, and I had to travel to meetings, if possible, I tried to bring the whole family along. It was an opportunity for the children to see what kind of work I was involved with, and I was reminded of the time spent, which was so precious, with my father at his place of work. When our children got older, and my wife could not travel with me, I would take at least one of the children with me, so we could have a one-on-one experience together. When I could not bring the family on work trips, I tried to get tasks done, so that when I returned home, I could spend more time with them. I would prepare talks and manuscripts, and review and correct papers while on a plane or in a hotel room. I never played golf because of my family commitments (although

Figure 13E: Esther and our son Michael.

Figure 13F: My son Michael, the athlete I never was.

Figure 13G: Receiving my tae kwando black belt in karate, at age 60 with my teachers, Grand Master Shin and Henry Weber.

Figure 13H: My son, Michael, awaiting his bride at their Hasidic wedding with Rabbi Benjamin Silverman.

I did work as a caddy in my youth), and my major source of exercise is taking long walks with my wife, children and grandchildren.

Our family winter vacations are spent in Hallandale on the Southeast Coast of Florida, where we have a home. I have always liked being at the beach and swimming in the ocean, since it reminds me of my youth and the summer vacations spent at Rockaway Beach in New York.

My wife loves to plan parties. Her favorite expression is, "It is good to make a party to celebrate an occasion." Every year since our children born, Esther has prepared the first Passover meal in our house. We usually host a large number of guests, which often include Christian friends and strangers. Esther works for weeks in preparation for this event. My role, as always, has been that of the food tester, to make sure her recipes are on the mark. The tastes I acquired from my grandmothers' foods are the standards I use to judge her cooking. I am then banned from the kitchen after my taste testing job is done.

For the Passover meal, friends and family sit around a long table. Our dining room table, when extended, can accommodate at least twenty adults and children. My wife and I always sit at opposite ends of the table with our guests between us. I sit next to our three grandsons and my wife sits next to our three granddaughters. My wife and daughters serve the various Passover ritual foods with the dinner, and I provide the explanations, as my father and uncles did before me, regarding the significance of the holiday to our guests, while recounting the story of the Exodus of the Jewish people from ancient Egypt. Dinner can take three to four hours, but I must say, that in my experience, the guests all leave satisfied with the large amounts of wine and food that are consumed. What is most remarkable is that my wife, Esther is always able to duplicate what my grandmothers did, reproducing aromas and tastes of previous generations, dating back 3000 years.

Guests never forget these meals at our house and my wife's gracious hospitality. It is part of a long tradition that she continues to carry forth. I hope my daughters and daughter-in-law will continue the tradition in years to come , which has meant so much to my wife and I. Although we need food for sustenance, it is so much more than that. With food, we celebrate life, our heritage, and the true meaning of family and friends.

These days, as I did for my children, I now attend one school sporting event for my grandchildren almost every day. And as a former Bronxite, I am also the biggest Yankee fan there is and can often be found at the stadium with my family and friends. I have taken my children and grandchildren to hundreds of Yankee games. We have reserved seats at Yankee Stadium that are right behind the opponent team's dugout. In these seats, we always get souvenir baseballs, either thrown by from the ball boy, or by the opponent catcher returning to the dugout with a third strike ball that he would then toss to the children.

In terms of my favorite travel destinations, my wife and I love to visit San Francisco and the Pacific Northwest. Overseas, it's Paris, Rome, London and Israel (Figs. 13K, 13L). Our favorite restaurant is The Kittle House in Chappaqua, New York, which has an all-Americana menu, and an excellent wine cellar. It is also the favorite restaurant of Bill and Hillary Clinton, who, live close by. In fact, Bill Clinton was a patient in our hospital (it's not a HIPAA violation to mention this, since it was reported in the national newspapers).

Losing a parent as a teenager was devastating, but for the short time I had my father he was a devoted, caring, amazing man who was an excellent role model for me. After more than 50 years since Dad's sudden and unexpected death, I have tried to find meaning from such a loss. It solidified my desire to pursue a career in medicine where I would help others in anguish. I also became involved in scientific research to develop new treatments for heart disease. My mother would live until the age

Figure 13I: With my stepbrother, Dr. Eli Zucker, my sister-in-law, Nancy and my wife, Esther.

Figure 13J: Skating with Michael and Amy.

Figure 13K: With Esther in Rome.

Figure 13L: Frishman Street in Tel Aviv, Israel, named for our family. I am standing under the street sign with my daugther, Sheryl, in the late 1970's. There is also a Frishman Beach in Tel Aviv.

of 88 and when she died, I recited the mourner's Kaddish for her, over eleven months, as I did for my father 45 years earlier when I was 15. She married twice after my father's death, to two good men, Irving "Izzy" Zucker, a widower, and Herbert Granick, an elderly bachelor, and was widowed each time. As I said previously, I am immensely proud of all my achievements, but none of it would have been possible without a stable, loving home at the center (Fig. 13M). One should never underestimate the importance of family, especially the blessing of a devoted spouse.

Figure 13M: My pride and joy. Front row from left: grandson Aaron, daughter-in-law, Courtney, granddaughters, Mikayla, Samantha and Rebekah, and grandson Zachary. Back row from left: son Michael, son-in-law Rob, daughters Sheryl and Amy, grandson, Joshua, son-in-law Jacob, Esther and me.

CHAPTER

14

LEADERSHIP

"If your actions inspire others to dream more, learn more, do more, and become more, you are a leader."

- John Quincy Adams

Two of the most rewarding, yet challenging, positions in academic medicine are those of chairman of the department of medicine at the medical school and chief of medicine at the affiliated university hospital. In these capacities, one has the responsibility for the faculty, primary and subspecialty clinical care, research (basic science and clinical) and the education of medical students, residents, fellows and colleagues. Indirectly, through his/her students and trainees, the chairman has an impact on the care of thousands of patients every day, but as an individual practitioner, he/she still takes care of patients one at a time. I have held both positions for over 18 years now at New York Medical College and Westchester Medical Center, one of the longest tenures in the nation.

I was identified as the lead candidate for the positions of chairman of medicine at New York Medical College (NYMC) and director of medicine at Westchester Medical Center (WMC) by a search committee made up of basic scientists and clinicians from the school and affiliated hospitals (Fig. 14A). I was then appointed to these positions by Monsignor Harry Barrett, president and CEO of NYMC, who was also a priest from the Archdiocese of New York with a public health background, Dean Ralph O'Connell, a psychiatrist, and Edward Stolzenberg, the hospital's commissioner of health for WMC (Fig. 14B). The salary I would receive in my new positions was twice that paid to me by Einstein-Montefiore, and I was given a magnificent office in an old medical school building, the Munger Pavilion. My wife, working with the school's architects, designed my office suite, which included my office, a large ante-room, three bathrooms, a conference room and a library for my bound journals and textbooks that were previously stored on shelves in the basement of my house. My wife threatened the school, that if the books weren't moved from our basement, she wouldn't let me show up to take the job. The office also had a large terrace. Munger Pavilion was previously a county tuberculosis hospital that had been taken over by the medical school (Fig. 14C). My office was the former solarium, a very light room, with multiple windows, where in the past, the tuberculosis patients would be exposed to sunlight during the cold months and the terrace was where they sat during the warmer months. My practice office was also in the building. I no longer had a hospital office, as I had at Einstein.

The department of medicine at NYMC is one of the largest in the country, encompassing multiple affiliated hospitals, 800 teaching physicians and researchers, 300 residents and fellows and 2,500 support staff including nurse practitioners and physician assistants. The hospital and medical school buildings sit on 600 verdant acres, probably the largest and most beautiful academic medical center campus in North America (Figs. 14D-F). NYMC, one of the oldest private schools in the U.S., was founded as a homeopathic medical school in 1860 in Manhattan. As a health practice, homeopathy was very popular in the U.S. at that time, and among of the nineteenth century homeopathic medical schools included Hahnemann (named after the founder of homeopathy) in Philadelphia, and Boston University (my alma mater). NYMC ultimately evolved into an allopathic medical school, although

Figure 14B: Taking part in the Medicine at the Millennium conference at NYMC in 2000. Dr. Arnold Relman (second from left), who was visiting professor had been my chief of medicine at Boston City Hospital during my student days. Monsignor Harry Barrett, president of NYMC, is standing far left, and Dean Ralph O'Connell is second from right. I am standing in the rear to the right of Dr. Relman.

Figure 14A: My formal photo at the time of my appointment as chairman of medicine at New York Medical College (NYMC) and director of medicine at Westchester Medical Center (1997).

Figure 14C: The Munger Pavilion at NYMC, is a former tuberculosis sanatorium, housed my administrative office for 15 years.

Figure 14D: The shared campus of Westchester Medical Center and New York Medical College campus in Valhalla, New York. (Image courtesy of New York Medical College. Reprinted with permission.).

homeopathy courses were still being taught through the 1950s. NYMC was one of the first medical schools to own its own hospital (Flower Hospital which then became Flower-Fifth Avenue Hospital). Because of financial problems in the 1970s, mostly involving the hospital, NYMC was taken over by the Archdiocese of New York, at which time was led by Cardinal Terence Cooke, a Bronx native. There are other Catholic medical schools in the U.S., including Georgetown and Loyola of Chicago, but NYMC was the only school run by an archdiocese. The school also moved to Westchester County on the campus of the Westchester County Medical Center which would become a primary hospital affiliate. Other school affiliates of NYMC at the time of my appointment included Metropolitan Hospital, a public hospital in Manhattan, representing the longest affiliation between one medical school and a hospital, dating back to 1883 (Fig. 14G), the Catholic Health Care System of New York City with its flagship hospital, St. Vincent's Hospital (Fig. 14H), The New York Eye & Ear infirmary, the oldest specialty hospital in the U.S., Stamford Hospital in Connecticut and Calvary Hospital in the Bronx. In 2010, the 150th anniversary of the school, I became the historian for the occasion (*see Appendix W*), although I didn't attend NYMC as a student.

WMC (when I started it was known as Westchester County Hospital) is the only tertiary- quaternary care hospital in the Southern Hudson Valley, serving a population of three million residents in eight neighboring counties. At the time, the hospital had 600 beds, including a psychiatric facility, and is a major transplant, trauma and cardiovascular treatment center. As a major referral hospital, it has the highest level of patient disease severity in the U.S.

Having previously worked at a Jewish medical school with Jewish hospital affiliates, I was now in a Catholic school with many religious and non-sectarian affiliations. As chairman and director, I was again affected by the tensions that often exist between a medical school and its affiliated university hospital, as I was at Einstein-Montefiore. However, I was prepared to deal with it. A medical school has major responsibilities for student education (Fig. 14I) and research, the hospital for clinical care, clinical research and residency training.

I started at NYMC and WMC in November 1997, having been appointed as a professor of both medicine and pharmacology. I had never obtained a pharmacology appointment at Einstein because my research was considered clinical (patient focused) and not basic, even though I was a major teacher in the medical school's pharmacology course at Einstein, and have remained so. Before starting in my position in November, as chairman, I met with all my section heads during the previous summer to discuss what expectations we had for one another. My administrative secretary, Carol Ruggiero, and my editorial assistant, Joanne Cioffi-Pryor, had moved with me from Einstein, so I had familiar figures working with me in the office (Fig. 14J). About a quarter of my department faculty at WMC had been former students and residents of mine from Einstein and at Montefiore, so I had a basis of support, right from the beginning.

I made no administrative changes at the onset. My department administrator at NYMC, Connie Cacciopa, had been appointed by my predecessor Dr. Richard Levere. I initially appointed three new vice chairmen. The vice chairman for medical education, Dr. Robert Lerner, had been the acting chairman prior to my arrival. Dr. Lerner is also a classic hematologist, and is director of both the hematology section and the hematology-oncology fellowship program. He is one of the few current faculty members who had worked for the school when it was located in Manhattan. Dr. Lerner has been helpful to me through the years, especially with letter of recommendation letter writing for faculty and students. I appreciate his wisdom and candor. He is now 80 years old and still working with me as vice chairman. Dr. Gary Wormser, a world-renowned expert on tick-borne diseases, and head of the infectious disease section, was appointed as vice chairman for research. The third vice chairman was

Figure 14E: New York Medical College, one of the basic science buildings. The anatomy lab is on the top floor in a sunlit area, an improvement over the dark basement labs of the past.

Figure 14F: New York Medical College, the "Sunshine Cottage" administration building. (Image courtesy of New York Medical College. Reprinted with permission.).

Figure 14G: Metropolitan Hospital in Manhattan enjoys the oldest continous affiliation (since 1883) between a public hospital and a single medical school, New York Medical College.

Figure 14H: St. Vincent's Hospital in Manhattan. Founded in 1849 by the Sisters of Charity, it was the receiving hospital for survivors of the Titanic and from 9/11.

Dr. Eric Rackow followed by Dr. Dennis Greenbaum, both critical care specialists who were hospital chiefs at St. Vincent's Hospital until it closed. Ultimately I selected an administrative vice chairman, Dr. Stephen Peterson, who was head of the general internal medicine section and the residency program director at WMC. He would serve as my right-hand person regarding our department's private practice.

My other section heads were Dr. Alvin Goodman, a nationally-renowned nephrologist, who started the dialysis program in Westchester. Alvin was the only section head who was Westchester-based from the start, being in place before the medical school moved from Manhattan. He ultimately retired but endowed a chair in nephrology in his name, and also left an endowment at the school for renal education and research. I then appointed Dr. Renee Garrick (Fig. 14K) as section chief. Renee had been my resident at Einstein. She is a highly effective person who would ultimately be chosen to be president of the medical staff at the hospital, chief medical officer and vice dean at the school. My director of geriatrics is Dr. Krishan Gupta, an English-trained physician who was also director of the hospital's affiliated nursing home facility and head of the geriatrics fellowship. The head of endocrinology and metabolism was Dr. Louis Southren, a prominent researcher who trained many of the endocrinology leaders in New York. When I started, he was at the end of his career, but I kept him on. After his death, he was then succeeded by Dr. Irene Weiss who had come to us from Metropolian Hospital. The head of pulmonary, sleep medicine and critical care is Dr. George Maguire who has now been in that position for 30 years (Fig. 14L). Dr. Edward Lebovics was the acting chief for the section of gastroenterology and hepatology when I arrived. Here I would face my first administrative challenge within the gastroenterology section; there was another physician who felt he deserved the position. He ultimately left our full-time group for private practice at another hospital, and I then appointed Dr. Lebovics as the permanent chief, and he still serves in this capacity (Fig. 14M).

When I arrived, Dr. Melvin Weiss was the acting chief of cardiology and director of the cardiac catheterization laboratory at the hospital. Dr. Weiss had been trained at Columbia, and was one of the leading interventional cardiologists in the region. I eventually appointed him to the permanent chief position. He would ultimately resign his position, and was replaced by Dr. Julio Panza, recruited from Georgetown Medical School and the Washington Hospital Center. Julio has been an outstanding addition to the department.

I also recruited Drs. Raymond Dattwyler from Stony Brook University School of Medicine. Ray, a nationally renowned allergist, was appointed Chief of Allergy, Immunology and Rheumatology to replace Dr. Arthur Weinstein, who had left for Georgetown. Dr. Julia Ash has served as director of the rheumatology sub-section since my arrival. The oncology section is led by Dr. Tauseef Ahmed, a regional leader in the management of cancers of the blood. Dr. Ahmed has also been in place as section chief since my arrival at NYMC.

I have worked with dedicated directors of our medical student programs, including Drs. Merville Marshall, John Raffalli, Stephen Moshman, and Gary Stallings, who is now an assistant dean. Dr. Christine Carosella and Dr. Kausik Kar have served as directors of the medicine sub-internship program, Dr. Carol Karmen, as director of the student outpatient program.

The directors of our medicine residency (Fig. 14N) are another outstanding group of academic leaders and include Drs. Stephen Peterson, Andrew Gutwein, Sachin Sule and Christopher Nabors.

I also have had a very good relationship with my first hospital administrators, then President, Edward Stolzenberg, and the hospital medical director, Dr. George Reed, one of the pioneers of heart surgery, who also served as chief of cardiothoracic surgery. Upon Dr. Reed's retirement, he was replaced in cardiac surgery by Dr. Stephen Lansman and Dr. David Spielvogel, who had been recruited from Mount Sinai Hospital in New York. I also had the good fortune to work with Dr. Louis Del Guercio, the chairman of surgery who was the "father" of surgical critical care, and his disciple, Dr. John Savino, who ultimately replaced him.

I have always had excellent relationships with Monsignor Barrett and Dean O'Connell when they were the top administrators from the medical school. Dean O'Connell, an extremely effective person, would be my dean for 15 years. He is one of the most knowledgeable individuals I know on all subjects, and a scion of a distinguished New York Irish family. I always enjoyed my interactions with him, and had great respect for his wisdom. Since I worked well with the hospital and school administrations, I often served as the bridge for relieving tensions between them.

I was able to make a relatively smooth transition to the chairmanship at New York Medical College because I respected the work culture and environment. I have learned to appreciate that in all

Figure 14I: The Chairmen of Medicine Interest Group of New York City, 1998. We had a handshake agreement never to steal faculty from one another. Standing at left is Dr. Stephen Kamholz from the State University of New York, Downstate. Seated to my left is Dr. Saul Farber, who was both chairman and dean of New York University School of Medicine for over 30 years, and to my right Dr. Barry Coller from Mount Sinai. Back row, standing from left, are Dr. James Scheuer, my last chairman at Einstein, Dr. Myron Weisfeldt from Columbia, and Dr. Ralph Nachman from Cornell.

Figure 14J: At an Alpha Omega Alpha (AOA) National Medical Honor Society reception with Dr. Edward Harris Jr., the AOA National Executive Secretary and Carol Ruggiero, my secretary and office administrator for 25 years, both at Einstein and New York Medical College (NYMC). Carol and I are both South Bronx natives.

Figure 14K: Dr. Renee Garrick, chief of nephrology and chief medical officer of Westchester Medical Center. Renee was my trainee at Einstein.

aspects of academic medicine and leadership, if change must be made, it must be executed after careful thought and deliberation. I also learned from my previous positions at Einstein and Montefiore that one should lead by personal example and not by intimidation or threats.

The greatest challenge I faced as chairman, however, was how best to run the private practice of the department. This is an issue faced by all medicine chairmen. When I first came to NYMC, there was an attempt to unite the faculty into a multi-specialty practice group. An organization had already been set up to serve as the foundation for the group, the Medical Faculty Health Alliance, which handled managed care contracting for the practice. The faculty practice was governed by a loose agreement of clinical directors called the Federated Faculty Practice Plan. Essentially, the academic departments had their own independent private practices, including the department of medicine. Other than the obligatory dean's tax to the school, NYMC had no real control over the practices. I had come from Einstein-Montefiore where I had worked under a school-run practice plan that was ultimately replaced by a successful hospital-run practice.

The department of medicine practice plan at NYMC was a professional corporation that had been set up by the previous chairman. The chairman was the major shareholder, although each section had to manage its own academic and clinical programs with a small tax paid to the chairman. I found this structure to be ideal, especially if the chairman is benevolent, which I have always tried to be, and ensures that all the sections are productive and solvent, and that individual faculty member are rewarded and recognized for the job that they do,

Over the past 18 years, I have learned that a pure private for-profit practice has no real place in an academic department. The mission of a pure private practice is often mercenary, and usually not scholarly. The only practice models that might work are those controlled by the school, hospital or a hybrid practice like we had (Medical Research Associates) attached to the school. The academic practice at the Einstein medical school is still controlled and managed by Montefiore Hospital as a unified entity. Similarly, the practice at the new Hofstra medical school on Long Island is controlled and managed by the North Shore-Long Island Jewish Healthcare System. In each situation, the chairman of medicine can pursue research and other academic programs with the private practice earnings that are allotted to him/her.

I have continued in my private practice during my years as chairman, first through our practice corporation and now as an employee of the hospital. I believe that a chairman of medicine must continue to practice so as to set an example for his/her clinical departments. My practice is 50 percent general internal medicine and 50 percent cardiology. Ultimately, my last job in medicine will be that of a practitioner, the main reason I became a physician.

Despite some challenges with the private practice, I have helped to guide the department in its gaining a national reputation as a strong educational and clinical research entity. Our students match in the most prestigious medicine residency programs in the country, which was not the case with NYMC students in the distant past. Residency directors from other institutions write to tell us that our students are not only bright, but the most humanistic. I get to know almost every student, and personally write at least 100 letters of recommendation each year for students applying in categorical medicine or for those who need one year of medicine training before pursuing other specialties. Across the nation, my letters are considered "gold," and are honest straightforward appraisals of our students (Fig. 14O). Each summer is dedicated to letter writing and student advisement (*see Appendix U*).

In recognition of my continued dedication to medical education; the students at NYMC have chosen me as their outstanding teacher, each year. I am a member of the NYMC faculty honor society (Goldstein Society). I was given the Humanism in Medicine Award by the AAMC. I received the

Figure 14M: Dr. Edward Lebovics, director of gastroenterology and hepatobiliary diseases at NYMC. His predecessor, Dr. William Rosenthal, endowed the professorship that gave me the title of Rosenthal Professor at NYMC.

Figure 14L: Dr. George Maguire, chief of pulmonary medicine and critical care at NYMC and WMC for over 30 years.

Figure 14N: Graduating residents from Westchester Medical Center in 1998. I am standing in front (right). At left are two of my vice-chairmen, Dr. Robert Lerner and Dr. Stephen Peterson. To my right is Dr. Karen Seiter, who was my resident at Einstein, and is now a leading leukemia specialist.

Distinguished Service Award from the NYMC Alumni Association, and have had the school yearbook dedicated to me. I am the faculty advisor (Councilor) for the school's Alpha Omega Alpha (AOA) Honor Society Chapter, a position I also held at Einstein. My greatest legacy as a medical academician is that I have taught over 7,500 medical students at Einstein and NYMC, inducted 1200 students into AOA, supervised over 500 students in preparation of their honors theses with most of them published, and helped to train 1500 residents and fellows. I was able to accomplish all of this successfully at two separate New York medical schools and academic medical centers.

I am also a front-line teacher of the residents. I make morning report and chief of service rounds, in medicine and cardiology, run grand rounds, and supervise the residency recruitment. We enjoy a wonderful house staff year after year, people who have risen to the challenge of helping to take care of the sickest patients in the country, while serving as teachers and role models for our students.

The department of medicine has responsibility for teaching students in all four years of the medical school. One of the strongest academic programs in the school is the second year pathophysiology course, which our department co-directs with pathology. In the past, I had served as the course co-director (Fig. 14P). Dr. Stephen Moshman from our department, coordinates the course now. Other department faculty instruct students in physiology, biochemistry, microbiology, pharmacology, physical diagnosis, ethics and the history of medicine.

The many innovative changes we have made in our student and house staff programs have brought us national recognition. We send all our students to Calvary Hospital in the Bronx, the only acute care hospital in the country for the terminally ill. I made this a requirement of the medicine clerkship, and we have documented an increased appreciation by our students for compassionate end-of-life care without the need for physician-assisted suicide (*see Appendix C #100*). We have successfully managed student clerkships and sub-internships at six different clinical sites which have their own individual residency programs. I have been the leader on campus in making sure we have enough clinical sites for our students, including the addition of Lenox Hill Hospital in Manhattan and three hospitals in Western Connecticut, (Greenwich, Norwalk and Danbury Hospitals), which are also Yale affiliates. The Achilles heel of a medical school are its clinical affiliates.

Regarding house staff innovations at WMC, our hospital is the only New York site to be part of the Educational Innovations Project (EIP) of the Accreditation Council for Graduate Medical Education (ACGME), the internal medicine residency accrediting agency. We were last inspected by the accrediting organization in 2003, and our next inspection is scheduled in 2021 (18 years) at at time when the maximum accreditation period is now 10 years. Being part of EIP, we are expected to be a model residency program for the country. With the Bell Commission reforms in place, there are now many more resident/patient hand-offs with the potential for misinformation being given.

With the help of Dr. Christopher Nabors in our department, we have developed a computer-based hand-off system, which allows attending input and supervision of house staff to avoid errors (*see Appendix C #107*). This approach to hand-offs has received national recognition. We have also been pioneers in the implementation of the Milestone Evaluation Program that has now become the standard means for assessing residents and fellows in the U.S. (*see Appendix N, Appendix C #116*).

I have continued to be active in research, focusing on cardiovascular drug trials. Most recently we have been looking at various anti-inflammatory drugs to prevent second myocardial infarctions in survivors of a myocardial infarction using an interleukin-1 inhibitor and methotrexate. During my time at NYMC, because of its close proximity to Einstein, I was also able to also continue some of my research activity at that institution, including the Bronx Aging Study and the Women's Health Initiative, and seeing these long-term projects through from beginning to end.

Figure 14O: One of the joys of being chairman is celebrating with the students on Match Day, when the assignments for hospital internships and residencies are announced. Note the students on their cell phones in the background, calling their families with their match results.

Figure 14P: Lecturing to the NYMC students in pathophysiology.

Figure 14Q: With Dr. Sachin Sule (left), Residency Program Director at WMC and Dr. Leanne Forman, Co-Chief of General Internal Medicine.

Our department includes a Cardiovascular Research Institute that has done pioneer work in the area of cardiac apoptosis and stem cell biology. Under the leadership of Dr. Piero Anversa, a cardiac pathologist, the concept of myocardial regeneration was born. Dr. Edmund Sonnenblick, my former chief of cardiology at Einstein, would attend Dr. Anversa's research meetings and provide his input as a physiologist. Dr. Sonnenblick died of cancer in 2006, and was attending the research meetings until the last week of his life (*see Appendix V*). Dr. Anversa and his group ultimately left NYMC. He and I co-edited one of the first books on cardiac stem cells and myocardial regeneration (*see Appendix C #135*).

Regarding other research programs, we were able to recruit Dr. Michael Goligorsky, a renowned nephrology researcher, to become the first Alvin Goodman Professor of Medicine and leader of the Nephrology Institute. Dr. Goligorsky has been a highly successful funded investigator.

In organizing a research program in the department, I have tried to create an institute in each section. In this way, the clinicians and researchers could interact, yet have some independence from one another. I don't believe in independent research centers, because this detracts from the authority of the chairman and section heads Centers and center directors may wander off on their own, which can reduce their loyalty to the department as a whole. The department at New York Medical College now has institutes as part of the cardiology, nephrology and oncology sections. We are trying to develop an institute within infectious diseases for tick-borne diseases. I have not been able to develop funded research programs in every section, although each section remains strong in its clinical care and education missions.

Within departments of medicine across the U.S., one usually finds the most research-intensive clinical faculty, which was the case at Einstein, and now, under our administration, it is also true for NYMC. An important role of the chairman is to also recruit new talent. Overtime, I made new appointments of section chiefs in cardiology, endocrinology, allergy-immunology-rheumatology, gastroenterology and hepatobiliary, nephrology, general internal medicine and palliative care. I never fired a chief, but allowed resignation and retirement to create vacancies. I am convinced that this approach contributed to the stability of the department. I recently appointed Drs. Leanne Forman and Arif Mumtaz to replace Dr. Stephen Peterson as chief of general internal medicine (Fig. 14Q). Dr. Peterson had gone on to become chief of medicine at the New York Methodist Hospital in Brooklyn and I have subsequently divided general internal medicine into two sub-sections: an in-patient hospitalist section (we were at the forefront of the hospitalist movement dating back to 1997) and an outpatient section, responsible for the medical clinic and the outpatient private practice. We also created a Palliative Care Section, a necessary service in our hospital with such a high level of patient illness. We were able to recruit Dr. Michael Frankenthaler, a regional leader in this area of practice. Palliative care has recently received considerable attention regarding the reimbursement for this activity by the federal Medicare program.

The director of the residency program reports both to me, and to the directors of the general internal medicine section. I have had four residency program directors during my tenure. The most common reason for change was faculty burnout, since this is a very demanding position. I have also had four department administrators, the last of whom having been with me for 10 years. The current section heads of hematology, pulmonary, oncology, infectious diseases and geriatrics are individuals who had these positions when I arrived at NYMC 18 years ago. They have provided a source of continuity and strength. I do not believe one should make change for the sake of making change; experience and history go a long way. Of course, there is always turnover in a large enterprise like a department of medicine. If I know that an individual is offered a better position, I have always encouraged him/her to take it. It is a source of pride for me to have my faculty advance in their careers, whether here or elsewhere.

Along with my research activities, I have continued my writing and editorial projects. To date I have published over 1100 original articles, editorials, reviews and book chapters and have published approximately 250 abstracts related to oral and poster research presentations. I have never let up on my writing. During my time at NYMC, I started a new journal, *Heart Disease*, published by Lippincott. This was the second journal I started. The challenge one faces in the first years of a journal is to get it accepted for indexing in in various databases. Authors won't contribute to a journal unless it is indexed in the first year of publication. *Heart Disease* ultimately merged with *Cardiology in Review*, now published by Wolters Kluwer. My co-editor is Patrick O'Gara, Chief of Cardiology at the Peter Bent Brigham Hospital and Harvard Medical School, and the immediate past president of the American College of Cardiology. *Cardiology in Review* is one of two institutionally-based peer review cardiovascular journals in North America not supported by a professional society. However, the journal is an unofficial affiliated publication of the American Heart Association. The journal is published six times a year, has an impact factor that puts it in the top third of cardiovascular journals in the world, and has been a forum for our medical students, residents and fellows to publish their research work. Joanne Cioffi-Pryor, my capable editorial assistant, serves as the journal's managing editor.

During the last ten years, I was also appointed supplements editor for the *American Journal of Medicine*, the official journal of the Alliance for Academic Internal Medicine, a national organization which includes the Association of Professors of Medicine (all the medicine chairpersons in North America including Canada and Puerto Rico), the Association of Program Directors in Internal Medicine, the Association of Subspecialty Professors and the Medicine Clerkship Directors of North America. The *American Journal of Medicine*, with a readership of 150,000 physicians, is one of the three major internal medicine journals published in North America.

I have also co-authored and co-edited multiple textbooks (*see Appendix C #123-136*) including three editions of *Cardiovascular Pharmacotherapeutics*, four editions of *Current Cardiovascular Drugs* and the volumes *Cardiovascular Regeneration and Stem Cell Therapy* and *Complementary and Integrative Therapies for Cardiovascular Disease*. I edited the *Year Book of Medicine* (*see Appendix C #137-147*) for 10 years, and currently serve on multiple editorial boards and as a journal reviewer. Much of my skills in editorial work and writing can be dated back to the editorships of both my high school and medical school yearbooks where I learned to discipline myself regarding deadlines and manuscript organization.

When writing, one has to have an idea in one's mind what the final manuscript will look like, and then go for it. It is also important to constantly recheck and rewrite. When writing and editing sentences for scientific publications, one has to be able to say what one itends, using the fewest amount of words, and to make use of figures and tables when necessary to summarize and explain concepts in a clear manner. I learned this from writing multiple articles in the *New England Journal of Medicine*. Finally, one has to enjoy writing. I still compose my first drafts on a legal writing pad and then give my handwritten text to Joanne and to my other administrative assistants, Charlene, Donna and Barbara to type. Then I work off a triple-spaced typed text in preparing my next version, I am not yet comfortable writing with a computer but recognize that this is the future. I still enjoy having a book or journal in my hands to read. Right now I think better with a legal pad, and I keep it close by to record my ideas before I forget them. In medicine, one has an obligation both in writing and speaking to convey observations and discoveries to colleagues and the larger audience, which includes patients. Writing is more difficult than public speaking for most physicians, and I have continued to spend a good deal of my time mentoring colleagues and trainees on how to publish their work. There is a great joy in seeing your work in print, and once you are successful, it feeds on itself so much that you want to do more.

A chairman must be in constant communication with his department to convey information, to discuss new ideas and to dispel rumors. I meet with my section chiefs and institute heads once a month, and with each individual on the faculty at least once a year, to set priorities and goals. There are many impromptu meetings to attend, especially those that are unexpected when problems arise. I write a comprehensive departmental newsletter, and am constantly writing memos and congratulation letters to the faculty in recognition of their accomplishments. I try to meet at least quarterly with the chiefs of medicine in our affiliated hospitals, and with many of their section chiefs. I have an outstanding support staff that helps in the dissemination of information and new policies to both our faculty and trainees

I meet with the chief medical residents at WMC daily and with the entire house staff at least once a month. I get to know every house officer very well, and am able to write letters of recommendation for each of them from personal knowledge. I am very active in the house staff recruitment process, meet with all the candidates in groups, and do personal interviews with many of them (Fig. 14R).

As chairman I am also involved in multiple school activities beyond my role as a teacher. I frequently meet, one-on-one, with the new chancellor and dean. I served as a member of the executive committee for the school curriculum, and on various liaison committees for medical education accreditation visits. I also serve on the school's graduate medical education oversight committee where I am kept informed about local and national residency education issues. I have headed the search committees for various chairpersons (surgery, pathology) and for our current chancellor, Dr. Edward Halperin (Fig. 14S) and our current dean, Dr. D. Donald Miller (Fig. 14T).

One of my most challenging school positions was serving as chairman of the promotions and tenure committee, where I often needed to make Solomonesque decisions. I served in this capacity for 15 years, and feel I was successful in representing both the interests of the faculty and the school. Another challenging part of my daily existence is the required school meetings I must attend while trying to make time for all the other necessary activities, including teaching, research, practice, writing, editing and everyday administrative work.

As director of medicine of WMC, I also have multiple non-school meetings to attend. I am a member of the executive committee of the hospital medical staff and represent our department. I serve as co-chairman of the hospital's medical operations committee. Another time-consuming job is my role as chairman of the hospital's credentials committee where again careful and thoughtful decision making is often necessary. There are also countless unscheduled meetings of ad hoc committees. For example, I recently had to help credential new medical staff from a satellite hospital acquisition, and also was part of an Ebola task force at our institution.

I meet with hospital administration frequently, but not always on a scheduled basis. I serve on the hospital's board of directors as an appointee of both the Westchester County Legislature and the County Executive. I am one of three physicians on the board, and have served for almost seven years under different political administrations. In addition, I currently serve on the board of directors of our state approved malpractice insurance carrier, Academic Health Physicians, a company which only insures full-time academic physicians. With its unique insurance model, it is one of the best malpractice insurance companies in the country, regarding claims and settlements. One of the great challenges I have faced as Chairman, is working for two administrations, both at the school and at the hospital. My ultimate responsibility is to see that the academic medical center thrives as a successful clinical, educational and research unit. During my 34 years of leadership at two medical schools and their affiliated hospitals, I think I have been quite successful in this effort.

Figure 14R: Westchester Medical Center's medicine house staff (2015). I am in the center with arms crossed.

Figure 14S: The chancellor and former dean of New York Medical College, Dr. Edward Halperin, a true Renaissance man. We teach a course on the history of medicine together.

Figure 14T: My wife, Esther, and I with the current dean, Dr. D. Donald Miller.

A chairman also has to be active on the national scene as a representative of the school and hospital. I have been active in the American Heart Association (AHA) and the American College of Cardiology (ACC), our national cardiology organizations. I served on the AHA Board of Directors of Burlington County, New Jersey when I was in the Army and on the board of the Westchester-Putnam County New York chapter where I was recognized with the "Heart of Distinction" award. I will always be grateful to the AHA for the Teaching Scholar Award that helped to support my early endeavors in medical education. Since 1972, I have been an active speaker and presented at many local and national AHA-sponsored meetings, and have served on guideline committees (*see Appendix C #108*). I could not be more active regarding national leadership positions, in the AHA because of time constraints.

Regarding the ACC, I was elected New York State Governor and co-authored the constitution of the new New York State Regional Chapter with my father's cousin, Dr. Leonard Steinfeld, a pediatric cardiologist from Mt. Sinai Hospital in New York. What a thrill to have two Frishman cousins serve as founders of the chapter. I was subsequently elected the first president of the state chapter, which has continued to thrive.

We were able to link the ACC chapter with the New York Cardiological Society, the oldest ongoing cardiology interest group in the western hemisphere, whose origin dates back to 1926. The New York Cardiological Society served as the stimulus to organize the ACC. I was president of the New York Cardiological Society when it aligned with the ACC New York state chapter forming a professional organization that flourishes today with over 1500 members. I have also served as a New York State Regional Councilor for the American College of Physicians, the largest specialty society in the U.S., and was elected a Master of the College.

I also belong to other societies including the Association of University Cardiologists, the Association of Professors of Cardiology and others, although I am not as active in these organizations. In addition, I am a member of the Critical Care Society, having in the past been board-certified in critical care medicine, and a member of multiple pharmacology societies, having been board-certified in clinical pharmacology. I am also a member of multiple geriatric societies, having been board certified and recertified in geriatrics. In addition, I was board certified in medical management, after having taken graduate business courses at New York University in organizational management. I also have a certificate in management from the Wharton School of Business of the University of Pennsylvania (the alma mater of Donald Trump).

Finally, as department chairman I represent NYMC as a member of the Association of Professors of Medicine, part of the Alliance for Academic Internal Medicine. I have served on both the research and publication committee of the organization, recognition reflective of the excellence of our department, and the respect we now receive on a national level from our peers.

During my time as a chairman, I have had some unique experiences. First, we had former President Bill Clinton as a patient at WMC in 2004 (Fig. 14U). He and his wife Hillary have a home in Chappaqua (Fig. 14V), just north of the hospital, and he had his cardiac catheterization and coronary angiogram here. He was found to have triple vessel coronary artery disease and he ultimately underwent coronary artery bypass surgery. I had the opportunity to interact with him on multiple occasions, as I have had with four other presidents: Richard Nixon, Gerald Ford, Ronald Reagan and George H.W. Bush. I have written articles on presidential medical history, and am working on a book related to this topic (*see Appendix Q, Appendix C #369*).

My wife also co-hosted one of the first political fund-raising dinners on March 22, 2000, when Hillary Clinton began her run for the New York Senate. Hilary was still the first lady, and many of

Figure 14U: With former President Bill Clinton at Westchester Medical Center, where he had been a patient.

Figure 14V: With Senator Hillary Clinton on a visit to Westchester Medical Center.

my relatives, who are not big donors, attended the event. She is a remarkable individual, as is former President Bill Clinton. Hillary is a wonderful listener, and makes you feel that she is absorbing every word you say.

I also have had the opportunity to interact with Cardinal Edward Egan (Fig. 14W) who was the Archbishop of New York and the head of the New York archdiocese during 9/11. Through the Cardinal, who was my patient, I was able to meet Pope Benedict XVI when he visited the old Yankee Stadium to celebrate mass during its last year of existence As I mentioned earlier, I tried to get the Pope's autograph on a baseball, but to no avail.

What defines the qualities of a chairman is how he/she deals with crises and challenges. Financial pressures are a constant for any chairman, especially in the current economic environment. During the time our practice was a separate organization, we never missed a payroll, paid our faculty competitive salaries, supported education and research and never had to dismiss anyone, faculty or staff over money issues. However, for financial reasons and to strengthen our group for the future and to maintain financial stability, we recently aligned our practice with the hospital. This was a very difficult decision, and not all the faculty were comfortable joining the hospital, with many wanting to keep their independence. However, I had seen the success of an academic hospital-run faculty practice at Montefiore and Einstein, and felt comfortable with my decision. I subsequently became the first director of medicine of Advanced Physician Services, the hospital run private practice, while continuing to serve in my role as director of medicine for the hospital.

WMC went through a major financial crisis in the early 2000s. The hospital had gone from a county facility to a public benefit corporation, and now had to function, independent of government support. The hospital was operating now as a private facility, yet carrying all the expenses of state unions and pensions. A cash flow problem developed, and cuts in the hospital budget had to be made. At the time, I was the president of our managed care organization representing the entire clinical faculty, and I had recommended that our department take an eight percent reduction in hospital salary support. This move demonstrated to the local and state government officials that we physicians were sincere about helping the hospital. The state subsequently provided aid that saw us through the crisis. My ability to convince the faculty to trust me, and to take this cut, turned out to be my one of my greatest achievements at WMC. Not one physician or nurse left the hospital during this crisis. Ultimately, the overall financial situation improved under a new hospital administration led by Mary Brown, Michael Israel (Fig. 14X), Gary Brudnicki and Marsha Casey, and the previous cuts were reversed. Mary Brown had come from the Ochsner Clinic in New Orleans, Michael Israel from Duke, Gary Brudnicki from St. Raphael's Hospital-Yale, and Marsha Casey from Vanderbilt. The latter three make up the current senior hospital administration at WMC.

NYMC was the school most affected by the terrorist attack on 9/11/2001. One of our major teaching affiliates, St. Vincent's Hospital in Manhattan, was the closest hospital to the World Trade Center. When the planes struck the twin towers in the morning, 150 of our students on site watched the towers fall from the hospital windows, and were available to help with some of the injured patients who were initially brought to the emergency room (E.R.). The students were also there that night when ambulances went passing by the hospital with no casualties being brought in, because there would be no more survivors. The picture of the teams waiting for patients at the St. Vincent's E.R. was transmitted all over the world. I was on call at WMC awaiting casualties which also never arrived. Twenty four hours later, I travelled down to St. Vincent's with the school chaplain, Deacon O'Toole, to speak with the students and residents. The hospital building was covered with photographs of missing people, all victims of the attack. I had asked the students to chronicle the event and experience, but no one could do it. Subsequently, I wrote one of the only articles on 9/11 from the medical perspective (*see Appendix I, Appendix C #268*).

The Catholic Health Care System was a major affiliate of NYMC, where many of our students rotated for their clinical clerkships and sub-internships. But rather than having the success of the financial turnaround at WMC, St. Vincent's Hospital in Manhattan would close forever because of its financial situation. On April 2013, the hospital suddenly shut its doors after being the flagship hospital for the Archdiocese of New York since 1849. The house staff suddenly had no jobs, and we needed to find a place to send our students. Again the department of medicine rose to the occasion and we absorbed the students into our clerkships in our other affiliates, including WMC. At the same time, the 200 St. Vincent residents were absorbed by our affiliates and other surrounding hospitals. A closure of a house staff program of this size had never occurred in the U.S., and we were able to pull through.

I chronicled the St. Vincent closing and its aftermath (*see Appendix M, Appendix C #359*). It is a great tragedy when a hospital, a house of healing, closes its doors; it is similar to a mosque, church or synagogue closing. I witnessed the closure of these great Catholic hospitals, St. Vincent's in Manhattan, St. Agnes in White Plains, St. Clare's in Manhattan, (where Babe Ruth died) Mother Cabrini in Manhattan, St. John's and Mary Immaculate Hospitals in Queens, and St. Mary's Hospital in Brooklyn. Two other hospitals, Our Lady of Mercy Hospital in the Bronx and St. Vincent's Hospital on Staten Island would be taken over by other health care systems. The great Catholic health care system of

Figure 14W: Marching as the Grand Marshall at a NYMC commencement. Cardinal Edward Egan is standing to my left.

Figure 14X: Michael Israel, president and chief executive officer of Westchester Medical Center and The Westchester Health Care System. The system services the New York's Hudson Valley, which includes eight counties with a total population of three million. One of the most effective hospital administrators I have ever worked for, Israel is credited with turning around a hospital in distress.

New York, which provided such excellent care for millions of patients for over 150 years, would never be the same.

Because of the financial stresses facing the Archdiocese of New York, a decision had been made whether to sell the medical school. Dr. Karl Adler who had replaced Father Barrett as President of NYMC was leading the charge; Dean Ralph O'Connell was ambivalent about the move. I enjoyed working for both of them, but there was great anxiety among the faculty and students regarding the sale. Touro University, an orthodox Jewish school, and the largest Jewish university in the world, would take over the school in 2011. Touro also has four osteopathic medical schools under its jurisdiction, and many other health professional schools located all over the country. It is the first time NYMC would have a parent university. With NYMC and the osteopathic medical schools, Touro would now graduate 760 medical students each year, approximately three percent of the nation's graduates; the largest number from one university.

For me, Touro's takeover of NYMC was a remarkable occurrence. I had worked at Einstein, another orthodox Jewish medical school for almost 25 years as a house officer and a teacher. I would now be working at a second orthodox Jewish school that had previously been a Catholic institution.

Figure 14Y: I have served on the board of the Westchester Institute for Human Development (WIHD) for 10 years. In photo, the nationally renowned institution for patients with developmental disabilities was being recognized by State Senator Nicholas Spano (third from left) and Westchester County Executive, Andrew Spano (center). Between them is Dr. Ansley Bacon, WIHD's director for 30 years. I am standing third from right.

The president of Touro and the medical school is Dr. Alan Kadish, a cardiologist who was a student of mine at Einstein in the class of 1980. We had done research together. On the day that Touro took over the school, Alan asked me to witness putting up the first mezuzah on the doorpost of the medical school administration building, ushering in the fifth era for NYMC. The first NYMC era was the homeopathic period from 1860-1895, the second era was the Flower Hospital period from 1895-1939 (NYMC would be one of the first medical schools in the U.S. to own its own hospital); the third era was the NYMC-Flower Fifth Avenue Hospital period from 1939-1974. The Catholic archdiocese era would go on from 1974-2011. Now with Touro, we are in the orthodox Jewish era. Currently, I am the only faculty member to be a professor at both orthodox Jewish medical schools, Einstein and NYMC. The school seems to be thriving under Touro. Four times in the past 150 years, NYMC was threatened with closure, only to rise again under new management.

I was also part of another turnaround. The Westchester Institute for Human Development (WIHD) is a not-for-profit institute dedicated to the care of the developmentally disabled in the lower Hudson River Valley. The institute had been part of the medical school and then part of WMC. Our grandson Aaron, who has disabilities, has received services from the institute. The facility had been losing money while it was part of WMC, and the hospital spun it off as an independent entity. I joined the original three member board of directors as an officer 10 years ago (Fig. 14Y). We started without having any money, and, through political lobbying, and excellent management, the institute is now a great success. WIHD is one of the leading facilities of its kind in the U.S. (University Center for Excellence in Disabilities (USED). It is a major site for clinical care, child advocacy, teaching and research. I have remained on the board of directors, and continue to serve as a board officer. From this experience, and the experience at WMC, I have learned that with vision and leadership, one can turn a money-losing academic organization into a successful enterprise.

The cardiology section of the department has always put great demands on me. When I joined NYMC, cardiology was an independent private practice group that I was trying to repatriate into the departmental practice. In 2011, most of the group left WMC to join the Columbia Medical School practice. Essentially we were left with few cardiologists at the hospital, which also threatened the cardiothoracic program and the hospital in general. To help deal with the threat, I assumed the role of acting chief of cardiology. The remaining cardiologists became employees of the hospital and a group was founded called Westchester Heart and Vascular, which included our outstanding cardiothoracic and vascular surgeons. I was the founding chief of cardiology, working closely with Alan Bey, a highly capable hospital administrator of this new practice entity. We then went on to hire 11 new cardiologists within two months, to replace the group that had left, including new interventional and non-invasive practitioners from major academic medical centers. We also recruited a new group from Orange County (a northern region), and by this action I was able to make up for the loss of cardiothoracic and vascular surgery referrals that had been caused by the Columbia group's departure. Together, we rebuilt a stronger cardiology section, now linked to the hospital and department. During my tenure, the hospital started a catheter-based valve replacement program, built a new hybrid cardiovascular lab and we strengthened the fellowship and research program. I also assumed responsibility for the school's pathophysiology course which had been run by a member of the previous cardiology group. I served as acting chief for two and a half years and led the search for my permanent replacement, Dr. Julio Panza, from Georgetown. The cardiology crisis was one I handled very well, and I am very proud of what I had accomplished, rising to help save both the cardiovascular program and the hospital. Remarkably, I was able to run the cardiology section and the department of medicine together without a problem, although I postponed taking a vacation for two years.

I have witnessed many hospital closures, but now I am part of a rescue. St. Francis Hospital, a 100-year old facility in Poughkeepsie, New York, was failing and Westchester Medical Center purchased the hospital, changing its name to Mid-Hudson Hospital. As chief of medicine at both WMC and Mid-Hudson, I have worked to bring both attending staffs together as one clinical unit, and in this effort, we have been successful. It is gratifying to be part of a rebirth, not a closure of an important community hospital.

Most recently, WMC has grown exponentially from a 600 bed Valhalla based campus to a 2000 bed Health Care System (Westchester Health), responsible for the care of patients in a catchment area of three million residents covering an area the size of Connecticut. Our system now includes nine hospitals, with 12,000 employees and WMC remaining the main tertiary care facility. When I came to WMC and NYMC from the Bronx in 1997, my vision in line with that of administration was to create a care system that was as good as, or better than any healthcare system or hospital facility in New York City. We envisioned that any resident of the Hudson River Valley, adult or child, would never have to go to the city for their health care. With our able administration and clinical staff we have accomplished that goal. I am so proud to have been a part of this effort. To further recognize the accomplishments of our academic medical center, we joined with the Philips Corporation, one of the three largest medical equipment companies in the world, to be their clinical partner in testing new technologies, a unique arrangement that has received international recognition. Through this partnership, we have also begun a state-of-the-art telemedicine program that will allow us to help better manage patients located in our northern hospital affiliates, especially those individuals with critical care problems.

The medical center was also an awardee of one of the largest federally funded Delivery System Reform Incentive Payment (DSRIP) grants to create an innovative health care program for both out-patient and in-patient care in our region. At this stage of my career, I have seen just what effective leadership can accomplish in clinical care, medical education and research. What an experience it has been.

On another note, I have been exposed to four interesting disease epidemics during my 50 years as a medical student, resident and attending physician. The first was the epidemic of serum hepatitis brought on by contaminated blood transfusions and needle sticks. One of my co-residents at Montefiore died from serum hepatitis and liver failure caused by a contaminated needle stick. With better surveillance of the blood supply, and strict needle and syringe precautions, this is no longer a major problem.

The second was the "swine flu" epidemic of 1976 (*see Chapter 10*). I was stationed at Fort Dix in February 1976 when the only fatality from swine flu occurred in a basic trainee. Since the virus was felt to be similar to the one brought on in the 1918-19 world influenza epidemic, a national panic set in that was fanned by the press. However, there was no actual swine flu epidemic in 1976. President Gerald Ford did order a national swine flu vaccination program that led to a paralyzing illness in some patients from the vaccine (Guillain-Barre syndrome). This decision, based on inadequate information and bad advice, may have cost Ford the election in November, 1976, to Jimmy Carter.

Third, I lived through the acquired immunodeficiency syndrome (AIDS) plague that began to emerge in 1981-82. When I became the chief of medicine at the Einstein College Hospital at, AIDS was not yet recognized as a disease entity. On morning report the residents would present cases to me of homosexual patients having a diarrheal illness which was labeled "gay-bowel disease." Subsequently, unusual pneumonias were seen that previously only occurred in immunocompromised patients. It was then that AIDS was described as a new clinical entity, and in the Bronx we were one of its epicenters.

Before an effective therapy was developed, almost all the patients with AIDS died, and our Bronx hospital wards were full of these terminally-ill patients. I knew physicians who had died from AIDs, related to contaminated needle sticks or their own homosexuality. A report we published described a difference in AIDS-related illness due to the mode of infection. We showed that the drug-addicted patients had more heart involvement with the disease, while the homosexual patients had more Kaposi's sarcomas (*see Appendix C #196*).

One of the great pharmacologic advances that occurred in my lifetime was the rapid development of anti-HIV drugs by the pharmaceutical industry, a feat that has taken AIDS from being a fatal disease to a chronic outpatient condition, with a very low mortality; indeed, a miracle.

Fourth, as Director of Medicine at WMC, I have recently been on the frontline in helping to develop Ebola virus precautions and treatment protocols for our hospital, a designated center for treating the disease.

In my final reflections, what have I learned as a chairman of medicine, having served in this capacity for a longer term than most? I am fond of lists, and have developed my top seven attributes for being an effective chairman:

1. A chair needs to be resilient, and demonstrate an aura of equanimity at all times.
2. A chair needs to be honest, transparent, professional, discreet and loyal to his/her faculty.
3. A chair should first respect his students, researchers, nurses, support staff and faculty in the hope of then earning their respect.
4. A chair should do everything he/she expects from the faculty, and lead by personal example. (He/she should practice, teach, write, edit and perform research.)
5. A chair should have an ongoing vision for the department, linked to that of the hospital and the medical school.
6. A chair should be a champion of quality improvement and performance enhancement.
7. A chair should be a champion of diversity and inclusiveness in the department.

I have also learned from both experience and observation what defines the best organizational model for a modern academic department of medicine. The chairman should be the chief of medicine for both the school and hospital, and should have oversight of all the training programs, research, and practice, using leadership and faculty consensus. The overall department should be divided into sections with research institutes, all reporting to the chair. Each section and section chief should be empowered to run their own academic activities (teaching, research, practice) with the direct oversight of the chair. The chair should have the means to help sections that have financial problems either through an academic tax of all the sections, or from garnering additional support from the hospital and medical school. The chair also needs to be a visionary, and have the means to implement his/her programs hiring excellent managers to carry out the departmental goals and objectives with appropriate resources provided. The private practice of the department should be run by the hospital as a multi-specialty group, tied to an academic mission with the chair responsible and accountable for the clinical activities and quality of care provided by the faculty and trainees. A pure private practice outside of the hospital's control, even if affiliated with the medical school, will not perform as an academic unit.

I have now been chairman of medicine over 18 years (Fig. 14Z), which some might think is too long a term. Being in my positions, one always hears threats from different constituencies (individual faculty, disgruntled section heads), but one should always be true to one's self and always look out for the entire enterprise. One of my favorite poems that inspired me since I was a young boy was *If* by Rudyard Kipling (*see page ix*).

As I mentioned earlier, being chairman and hospital chief are the best jobs in academic medicine. At NYMC and WMC, I have led a strong department that is highly respected nationwide. I had aspired to become a chairman since I was a medical student, and during my lifetime was able to achieve my dream (*see Appendix H*). It has been said that what you learn and the character you build while achieving your goal are more important than achieving the goal itself, and I must agree.

Figure 14Z: In 2016, beginning my nineteenth year as chairman of medicine.

I would like to close with several aphorisms I've written over the years that relate to the topics discussed in this chapter:

On Being a Chairman of Medicine

"The life of a Chairman of Medicine is similar to that of a baseball player. If 30 percent of the time you accomplish what you want to do, you're a .300 hitter, a star. Sometimes you hit a homerun, but more often you strike out. There are also people out there who want to send you down to the minor leagues. However, always give it your best every day when you come up to bat."

"Unlike administration and batting, taking care of patients is similar to playing the outfield. You have to avoid making errors when the ball is hit to you."

"A Chair of Medicine leads by his/her personal example, and not by intimidation."

"The success of a chairman is measured not by his/her personal accomplishments, but by the accomplishments of the departmental faculty and trainees."

On Leadership

"Always remember that smart people preceded you, and have confronted many of the same problems you face. Learn from history, so as to avoid making the same mistakes of your predecessors."

"The four major qualities of a leader are that of being honest, loyal, discreet and transparent. These are the same qualities that you should look for in other people."

"A leader must have vision of where he/she wants to go, and the ability to move people in that direction."

Students and Teaching

"The best teachers of medicine respect their students.

Health Care

"Medicine is a ministry, not an industry."

"In health care, everyone's job is important, and each person is deserving of respect for what they do."

"A physician's major role is to relieve pain; physical pain, psychological pain, and spiritual pain."

Taking Care of Patients at the Bedside

"Always find some point of commonality with a patient when you go to the bedside. It fosters the therapeutic bond."

Nurses

"Always honor the nurses. They are the individuals who spend the most time with patients in the hospital."

The Placebo Effect

"The good physician gets a positive placebo effect from patients by touching, kindness and just being there. This is an important part of the therapeutic response."

On Mentoring

"Try to find a mentor; he/she will make your professional career and personal life easier to manage."

Commuting to Work

"You should always work on the side of the bridge where you live."

On 9/11

"In the aftermath of this national tragedy, we must rededicate ourselves to doing good in our clinics and hospitals where we care for the sick and infirm, in our laboratories where we search for the cures of human ailments and in our pursuit for world peace. Our affiliated institutions and their staffs were examples for the world in demonstrating the capacity of the human spirit, and their actions will forever be enshrined with the memories of those who were lost." (*see Appendix I, Appendix C, #268*)

On Research

"The joy of research comes from the privilege of being the first person to uncover a truth that God already knows."

On the Existence of God

"One only needs to observe the remarkable ultrastructure of a human cell, and the miracles one sees as a physician-cardiologist, to know that a gracious loving God exists."

EPILOGUE

OPPORTUNITY

"The future is not an inheritance; it is an opportunity and an obligation."

- Bill Clinton

I feel that my life to date has been comparable to that of the main character in the book and movie, *Forrest Gump.* Like him, I was both an eyewitness to, and a participant in, many historical events that occurred over the last half century – Vietnam, civil rights, 9/11, Desert Storm, massive advances in medicine, (especially in cardiovascular pharmacology), and so much more. It has been quite a ride.

I was raised by parents from the "Greatest Generation," products of the Great Depression and World War II, who were descendants of immigrant garment workers. I survived my youth in the Bronx, but was affected by an epidemic of premature coronary heart disease that took the lives of so many, including cherished members of my own family. I lived through the 1960s as a student during war protests, the revolutions in civil rights, health care and the feminist and gay rights movements. Autism and homosexuality were considered mental illnesses then, which is no longer the case. Today, great strides have been made to address many of the country's social problems, exemplified by the recent Supreme Court decision to recognize gay marriage, and the passing of the Affordable Care Act. Health care should be a right, and not a privilege, in a country as prosperous as ours.

Regarding cardiac disease, there was little available to treat patients when I was a medical student. However, over the past 45 years, it has been a privilege for me to participate in many of the breakthroughs that have occurred in the medical treatment of heart attack, heart failure, high blood pressure, arrhythmia (irregular heartbeats) and high cholesterol. I was involved, as an early clinical investigator, in the studies of the beta-adrenergic blockers, the blockers of the renin-angiotensin system, the calcium blockers and the statins that have favorably changed the natural history of heart disease and stroke. In the U.S., fewer patients now have heart attacks, and those that do, have them later in life, and usually survive. Patients with heart failure, who used to die within months of the diagnosis, can live for 25-30 years on current medical therapy. With the treatment of hypertension there are fewer strokes, especially those related to bleeding in the head (cerebral hemorrhage).

I foresee that in the near future, heart attack will disappear as a cause of death with the use of statins and more potent cholesterol lowering drugs that are now becoming available due to advances in molecular pharmacology. Individuals will be living longer, and aging and its consequences will be the major health care concern for the nation Our federally-funded Bronx-Aging study suggested that senile Alzheimer's disease may have a vascular cause and therefore might be preventable with the therapies that we now use to treat heart disease and stroke (*see Appendix C #51*).

We are reaching a point now that humans will soon be living to their natural lifespans. For the first time in the U.S., more individuals are reaching the age of 85 than children being born. The goal of future preventative therapy is to help allow individuals to live as well as possible, right up to the point of their natural death from old age. Advances in cell therapy may even increase lifespan, but this must occur with preserved quality of life.

I am grateful to my teachers and mentors who have helped guide me throughout my research career, and to the thousands of patients who participated in our clinical trials. From these experiences I have learned to also appreciate the power of placebo, and how important the physician-patient relationship is in healing. As a teacher myself, I have been privileged to train over 7,500 medical students and 1,500 residents, and fellows to become successful physicians, researchers and teachers.

I truly believe I have been successful as an academic physician and chairman because of the blessings and support both family and friends, while learning to overcome obstacles and tragedies throughout my life with the perseverance and resilience I obtained from my forbears. Of course, I will be forever grateful to my first mentor, the man who inspired me to become a physician, Dr. Albert Goodman. He was a model of grace, kindness and conduct. He was also true to his word, Dr. Goodman would never charge me in the years to come, and while I received professional courtesy, my parents and grandmother were billed regularly.

Dr. Goodman followed my progress in school and in my later subsequent residency training with great interest. With his encouragement, my widowed mother let me attend an accelerated college-medical school program in Boston, which was a life-changing decision. Dr. Goodman found great joy in my accomplishments. I borrowed his bedside style in my own interactions with patients.

Like mere mortals, angels, too, have their own problems. Dr. Goodman was not spared. He had lost his beloved wife from cancer, leaving him with two young children. He never remarried, but always had an array of "lady friends." In his eighties, he retired and moved to Florida. I would visit with him whenever our family vacationed there. He grew extremely hard of hearing, and his thick brown hair turned white. However, he never lost the sparkle in his face and his genuine interest in people.

At the age of 90, he had a heart attack. His daughter called me in New York, and I quickly left work to board a flight to Miami to visit with him in the hospital. When I approached his bed in the intensive care unit, he acknowledged me with his big smile and the usual sparkle in his eyes, and asked me, "Billy, why are you here?" I answered loudly so I knew he would hear me, "Professional courtesy, Dr. Goodman, professional courtesy."

What to do next as I approach 70 years of age? I remain in good health, although I could lose 20 pounds. I will always be a practicing physician as long as I am mentally and physically able. It is a great privilege to help in God's work to heal the sick. It is also most rewarding to prevent premature illness, especially with the effective therapies that are now available, and which will only continue to improve in the near and distant future.

As long as I am able, I will also be a teacher. It has been a great privilege for almost 35 years, half my life, to have served as a hospital chief and chairman of a department of medicine. I do see myself continuing in these capacities, at least for the near future, while grooming my successors. I am excited about the changes in healthcare and want to see how we will progress. Hopefully, we will one day have a single-payer health care system. I will continue with my writing and journal editing. Having completed multiple medical texts and now a scientific memoir, I am ready to write a novel (a medical mystery).

My research continues to thrive as we continue to look for additional treatments to combat heart disease, and I also continue with my efforts to improve the medical education processes. What about the possibility of a higher-academic position such as a dean or university president, or even being commissioner of the FDA? Although I have explored these possibilities over the past ten years, I always come back to my roots as a clinician, teacher and researcher where I still enjoy being on the frontline. However, if duty calls, I will serve.

At the end, I remain true to myself and my principles (Fig.15A). I would like to spend time travelling with my wife, children and grandchildren, and just being around them. Life is a balance, and one should always have his/her priorities focused in the right direction - happy home, happy job.

After these many years, one of my greatest joys comes from running down to the hospital emergency room, to reassure a frightened young wife and her children that Dad will make it after his heart attack. At the center of everything I have accomplished, is my father's memory. Although he left this world too soon, his life is honored each time another one is saved through the work I have had the pleasure to pursue. My father's premature and tragic death was not in vain. Dad, we triumphed over tragedy.

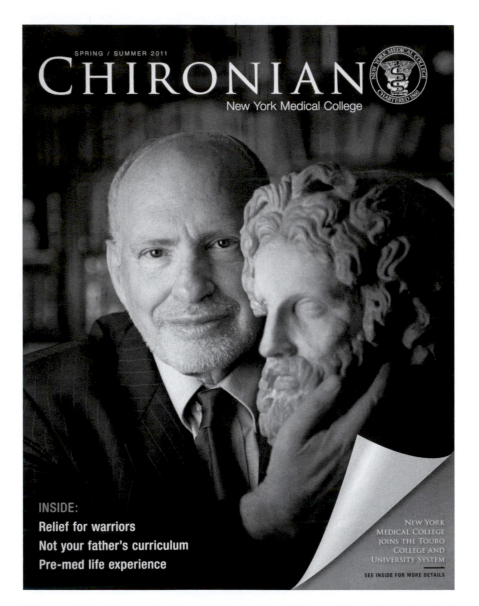

Figure 15A: A recent photo taken in my office at New York Medical College. It appeared on the cover of an issue of the university magazine, *Chironian*. (Image courtesy of the *Chironian*. Reprinted with permission.)

ACKNOWLEDGMENTS

Having co-authored and co-edited multiple textbooks in the past, which described research endeavors and scientific advances, exploring one's self and own academic career requires a completely different approach to written expression. Also, placing an individual within the historical context of his/her time, and what role they played as both a participant and observer of events, adds another dimension and complexity when telling the story.

I lived through the Vietnam and Desert Storm eras as an Army Medical Officer. As a physician and administrator, I was in the frontline for the swine flu, AIDS and Ebola epidemics. As a researcher, I played an active role during the golden era of cardiovascular drug development. As a teacher, I was at the epicenter of house staff duty reforms and a student thesis program. As a hospital department chief I have been an active participant in the physician assistant and nurse practitioner movements, and most recently in the use of telemedicine with the most modern technology available.

New York Medical College (NYMC) and its hospital affiliates were at the center of 9/11 and tropical storm Sandy. As chairman of medicine at NYMC, I was a witness to these, and other historical events. A childhood friend won the Nobel Prize in Medicine. I was influenced by my teachers in medical school who included Drs. Franz Ingelfinger and Arnold Relman who both became editors of the *New England Journal of Medicine*; Dr. Louis Sullivan, a hematologist, who became Secretary of Health and Human Services under George H.W. Bush, Dr. Thomas Dawber, who was head of the Framingham Heart Study, Dr. Robert Wilkens who won the Albert Lasker Award for Clinical Medicine Research for the drug treatment of hypertension, Dr. Stanley Robbins who edited the definitive pathology textbook still used today and Dr. Gregory Pincus, a steroid chemist, who discovered the oral contraceptive.

As a resident and fellow, I worked under Drs. Doris Escher and Seymour Furman, the pioneers of transvenous pacing and cardiac electrophysiology, and Dr. Thomas Killip, the "father of acute coronary care." As a hospital chief at Einstein, I worked closely with Dr. David Kessler, Einstein's medical director, who would become the most proactive and effective commissioner of the Food and Drug Administration (FDA). During my professional career, I have interacted with five US Presidents including Richard M. Nixon, Gerald Ford, Ronald Reagan, George H.W. Bush, and Bill Clinton. At Montefiore-Einstein and Westchester Medical Center, I worked under four great hospital and medical center presidents: Dr. Martin Cherkasky, Dr. Spencer Foreman, Mr. Edward Stolzenberg, and Mr. Michael Israel; five formidable medical school deans: Drs. Ephraim Friedman, Dominick Purpura, Ralph O'Connell, Edward Halperin and D. Douglas Miller, and four university presidents: Dr. Norman Lamm, Msgr. Harry Barrett, Dr. Karl Adler and Dr. Alan Kadish (a former student).

I am also grateful to many other individuals who have influenced my academic life. Drs. David

Hamerman, Louis Sherwood and Edmund Sonnenblick at Montefiore-Einstein saw in me the potential to be an academic leader. Dr. Ralph O'Connell, Dean at NYMC, and Mr. Edward Stolzenberg, President at WMC, gave me the opportunity to fulfill my lifelong professional dream to be a Chairman of Medicine and Hospital Chief, positions I have held now for over 18 years. I am the only individual to have served both as a professor of medicine at the only two orthodox Jewish medical schools (Albert Einstein College of Medicine and New York Medical College).

I am grateful to the thousands of medical students and residents I have trained, who have inspired me to do my best as a teacher and as a role model, and to the thousands of patients I have treated in practice and in research, who have inspired me to be the best physician I could be.

As a leader, I have had the opportunity to enjoy success at two civilian academic medical centers (Montefiore/Einstein and Westchester Medical Center/New York Medical College) for over 34 years and for two years at a military hospital. Working at these institutions, I am appreciative of the hard work and dedication of my professional colleagues, my research coordinators, the nurses, and all the support staff. In my department, everyone has an important role to play.

I am grateful to the National Institutes of Health, the American Heart Association and the pharmaceutical industry for supporting my research efforts for over 40 years.

I was fortunate to always have an outstanding office staff around me: Evelyn Ponzio, Anne Palladino, Carol Ruggiero, Barbara Donnadio, Charlene Benincasa, Donna James, Maryanne Russo and the many wives of medical students who worked as my secretaries over the years. Joanne Cioffi-Pryor has served as my editorial assistant for over 30 years, helping me with my journals, manuscripts, books and lectures. Joanne and Carol have only recently retired, and I wish them only the best in the years to come. Joanne was instrumental in helping me put together the original manuscript for this book, and Charlene and Barbara helped with the revised version, submitted for publication. Donna Moriarity provided additional editorial assistance.

I want to acknowledge my cousin Dr. Alan Frishman, of Hobart University, who provided many family documents that were used in the book, and my Uncle Conrad (Ken) Frishman, my father's youngest brother, for providing me with an oral history of our family.

I wish to thank my publisher, Steven Korn, and Science International for having faith in this project and helping to see it through to its successful completion. Steven has published many books of mine through the years, and he is clearly one of the leading scientific editors, as well as a good friend. I am also very grateful to him for introducing me to my creative and proficient developmental editor for the project, Shireen Dunwoody. She not only helped me to polish the manuscript, but also helped me to appreciate my life story in a completely new way. Sadness from a tragedy has a shelf-life, but the grief endures and either expands you and gives you a greater capacity for empathy and achievement, or it diminishes you. While working with Shireen, I had an opportunity to step back and truly appreciate the overall narrative of my life and choices. At times, finalizing this memoir was a very emotional journey. I am truly thankful to have had a trustworthy, kind writing companion on the path of self-discovery.

Finally, I wish to acknowledge my immediate family for all their support. First, my parents, of blessed memory, who provided a loving, home for me as well as their personal examples of perseverance, integrity and hard work. Esther, my wife of 45 years, has been through it all during my professional career, and I am eternally grateful for her unselfish love, support, courage, sage advice and for providing such a gracious and spiritual home life. With God's help, I look forward to our spending many more years together. My children, Sheryl, Amy and Michael, and their spouses Rob, Jacob and Courtney, are a great source of pride for me, as are my grandchildren Aaron, Rebekah, Zachary, Joshua, Mikayla and Samantha.

This book depicts almost 70 years of my life. Remaining vital, I hope to prepare an update during the next 70 years to come.

APPENDICES

INDEX OF APPENDICES

APPENDIX A: TIMELINE OF KEY EVENTS

1946: Born on November 9

1948: Moved to Stratford Avenue, the Bronx

1951: Began elementary school

1954: (February) Dr. Goodman visit - inspiration to become a physician

1955: Began Hebrew school

1956: Mother returns to work; move to White Plains Rd. (Parkchester); began new elementary school, PS 102

1958: Began junior high school (JHS 127)

1959: (November) Bar Mitzvah; fire incident in the Catskills

1960: Graduates from JHS; father's bankruptcy

1961: Father's death; National Science Foundation Program; Ford Future Scientist Award; decision to become a cardiologist

1963: High school graduation; began Boston University (BU) (six-year liberal arts-medicine program)

1965: Began medical school at BU

1966: Mother remarries stepfather, Irving "Izzy" Zucker

1969: Graduates from college/medical school; began internship at Montefiore; mother moved to Atlantic Beach in Long Island

1970: (April) Met wife, Esther (Sandowsky), and began dating in June

1971: Married Esther

1972: Board-certification as an internist; birth of first daughter, Sheryl Renee; began cardiology fellowship; death of stepfather

1974: Completed fellowship; began active duty in the Army Medical Corps as a cardiologist

1976: Discharged from active duty; became Assistant Professor of Medicine at Albert Einstein School of Medicine and Director of the Non-Invasive Cardiology Lab; birth of second daughter, Amy Helene

1978: Move to Scarsdale, New York

1980: Publication of *Clinical Pharmacology of the Beta-Adrenoceptor Blocking Drugs*

1981: Son, Michael Aaron is born

1982: Became Chief of Medicine at the Hospital of the Albert Einstein College of Medicine, Montefiore Medical Center

1997: Became Chairman of Medicine at New York Medical College and Director of Medicine at Westchester Medical Center; publication of *Cardiovascular Pharmacotherapeutics*

APPENDIX B: ADDITIONAL READINGS

1. Alda, Arlene. *Just Kids from the Bronx.* New York: Henry Holt and Company, 2015.

2. Calhoun, Lawrence, Tedeschi, Richard, Cann, Arnie and Hanks, Emily. Positive outcomes following bereavement: paths to posttraumatic growth. *Psychologica Belgica.* 2010;50:125-143.

3. Carter, Vivian Rattay. *Images of America: Rockaway Beach.* Charleston: Arcadia Publishing, 2012.

4. Corman, Avery. *My Old Neighborhood Remembered.* Fort Lee: Barricade Books, 2014.

5. Duncan, David Ewing. *Residents: The Perils and Promise of Educating Young Doctors.* New York: Scribner, 1996.

6. Kanner, Stefan. *A Summer World.* New York: Farrar, Straus and Giroux, 1989.

7. Levenson, Dorothy. *Montefiore: The Hospital as a Social Instrument.* New York: Farrar, Straus and Giroux, 1984.

8. Twomey, Bill. *The Bronx in Bits and Pieces.* Bloomington: Rooftop Publishing, 2007.

9. Ultan, Lloyd and Hermalyn, Gary. *The Bronx: It Was Only Yesterday, 1935-1965.* New York: The Bronx Historical Society, 1992.

10. Ultan, Lloyd. *The Northern Borough. A History of the Bronx.* New York: The Bronx Historical Society, 2009.

11. Vogler, Christopher. *The Writer's Journey: Mythic Structure for Writers, Third Edition.* Studio City: California, Michael Wiese Productions, 2007.

APPENDIX C: PRINCIPAL PUBLICATIONS

Original Articles

1. Frishman WH, Epstein A, Kulick S, Killip T. Heart failure sixty-three years following traumatic arteriovenous fistula. *Am J Cardiol* 1974;34:733-736.
2. Frishman W, Weksler B, Christodoulou J, Smithen C, Killip T. Reversal of abnormal platelet aggregability and change in exercise tolerance in patients with angina pectoris following oral propranolol. *Circulation* 1974;50:887-896.
3. Frishman W, Smithen C, Befler B, Kligfield P, Killip T. Non-invasive assessment of clinical response to oral propranolol. *Am J Cardiol* 1975;35:635-644.
4. Frishman W, Christodoulou J, Weksler B, Smithen C, Killip T, Scheidt S. Aspirin therapy in angina pectoris: effects on platelet aggregation, exercise tolerance and electrocardiographic manifestations of ischemia. *Am Heart J* 1976;92:3-10.
5. Frishman WH, Christodoulou J, Weksler B, Smithen C, Killip T, Scheidt S. Abrupt propranolol withdrawal in angina pectoris. Effects on platelet aggregation and exercise tolerance. *Am Heart J* 1978;95:169-179.
6. Sonnenblick EH, Frishman WH, LeJemtel TH. Dobutamine: a new synthetic cardioactive sympathetic amine. *N Engl J Med* 1979;300:17-22.
7. Frishman WH, Ribner H. Anticoagulation in myocardial infarction: a modern approach to an old problem. *Am J Cardiol* 1979;43:1207-1213.
8. Frishman WH, Kostis J, Strom J, Hosler M, Elkayam U, Davis R, Weinstein J, Sonnenblick EH. Clinical pharmacology of the new beta blocking drugs. Part 9. A comparison of pindolol and propranolol in treatment of patients with angina pectoris. The role of intrinsic sympathomimetic activity. *Am Heart J* 1979;98:526-535.
9. Frishman W, Factor S, Jordan A, Hellman C, Elkayam U, LeJemtel T, Strom J, Unschuld H, Becker R. *Circulation* 1979;59:1070-1075.
10. Elkayam U, LeJemtel T, Mathur M, Frishman W, Ribner H, Strom J, Sonnenblick EH. Prazosin therapy in congestive heart failure: importance of prolonged hemodynamic evaluation of vasodilator agents. *Am J Cardiol* 1979;441:540-545.
11. Becker R, Frishman W, Frater RWM. Surgical management of mitral valve endocarditis: a review of 26 patients. *Chest* 1979;75:314-319.
12. Ribner H, Isaacs E, Frishman W. Lidocaine prophylaxis against ventricular fibrillation in acute myocardial infarction. *Prog Cardiovasc Dis* 1979;21:287-313.
13. Elkayam U, Halprin SL, Frishman W, Strom J, Cohen MN. Echocardiographic findings in right ventricular infarction. *Cath Cardiovasc Diag* 1979;5:289-294.
14. Davis R, Strom J, Frishman W. Echographic findings of vegetations in bacterial endocarditis: an indication for urgent valvular replacement. *Am J Med* 1980;69:57-63.
15. Matsumoto M, Oka Y, Strom J, Frishman W, Kadish A, Becker RM, Frater RWM, Sonnenblick EH. Application of transesophageal echocardiography to continuous intraoperative monitoring of left ventricular performance. *Am J Cardiol* 1980;46:95-105.
16. Strom J, Frishman W, Davis R, Matsumoto M, Becker R, Frater RWM. Echocardiographic and surgical correlations in bacterial endocarditis. *Circulation* 1980;62:164-167.
17. Frishman W. β-adrenoceptor antagonists. New drugs and new indications. *N Engl J Med* 1981;305:505-506.
18. Frishman W. Nadolol: a new beta-adrenoceptor blocking drug. *N Engl J Med* 1981;305:678-682.
19. Frishman WH, Strom J, Kirschner M, Poland M, Klein N, Halprin S, LeJemtel T, Kram M, Sonnenblick EH. Labetalol therapy in patients with systemic hypertension and angina pectoris: effects of combined alpha and beta adrenoceptor blockade. *Am J Cardiol* 1981;48:917-928.
20. Klein N, Siskind S, Frishman W, Sonnenblick E, LeJemtel T. Hemodynamic comparisons of intravenous amrinone and dobutamine in patients with severe congestive heart failure. *Am J Cardiol* 1981;48:170-175.
21. Fein S, Klein N, Frishman W. Exercise testing soon after uncomplicated myocardial infarction. *JAMA* 1981;245:1863-1868.
22. LeJemtel TH, Keung E, Frishman WH, Ribner HS, Sonnenblick EH. Hemodynamic effects of captopril in patients with severe chronic heart failure. *Am J Cardiol* 1982;49:1484-1488.
23. Frishman WH, Klein NA, Strom JA, Willens H, LeJemtel TH, Jentzer J, Siegel L, Klein P, Kirschen N, Silverman R, Doyle R, Kirsten E, Sonnenblick EH. Superiority of verapamil to propranolol in stable angina pectoris: a double blind randomized crossover trial. *Circulation* 1982;65 (suppl I):I-51-59.
24. Frishman WH. Atenolol and timolol: two new systemic beta-adrenoceptor antagonists. *N Engl J Med* 1982;306:1456-1462.
25. Packer M, Frishman WH. Verapamil therapy for stable and unstable angina pectoris: calcium channel antagonists in perspective. *Am J Cardiol* 1982;50:881-885.
26. Frishman WH, Klein N, Klein P, Strom JA, Tawil R, Strair R, Wong B, Roth S, LeJemtel T, Pollack S, Sonnenblick EH. Comparison of oral propranolol and verapamil for combined systemic hypertension and angina pectoris: a placebo controlled, double-blind, randomized, crossover trial. *Am J Cardiol* 1982;50: 1164-1172.
27. Kugler J, Maskin CS, Frishman WH, Sonnenblick EH, LeJemtel TH. Variable clinical response to long-term angiotensin inhibition in severe heart failure: demonstration of additive benefits of alpha-receptor blockade. *Am Heart J* 1982;104:1154-1159.

28. Frishman WH, Klein N, Strom J, Cohen MN, Shamoon H, Willens H, Klein P, Roth S, Iorio L, LeJemtel T, Pollack S, Sonnenblick EH. Comparative effects of abrupt withdrawal of propranolol and verapamil in angina pectoris. *Am J Cardiol* 1982;50:1191-1195.

29. Frishman WH, Kirsten E, Kates R. Clinical relevance of verapamil plasma levels in stable angina pectoris. *Am J Cardiol* 1982;50:1180-1184.

30. Kostis JB, Frishman W, Hosler MH, Thorsen NL, Gonasun L, Weinstein J. The treatment of angina pectoris with pindolol: the significance of intrinsic sympathomimetic activity of β-blockers. *Am Heart J* 1982;104:496-504.

31. Kugler J, Maskin C, Laragh J, Sealy J, Frishman WH, Sonnenblick EH, LeJemtel T. Regional and systemic metabolic effects of angiotensin converting enzyme inhibition during exercise in patients with severe heart failure. *Circulation* 1982;66:1256-1261.

32. Maskin, C, Forman R, Frishman W, Sonnenblick E, LeJemtel TH. Failure of dobutamine to increase exercise capacity despite hemodynamic improvement in severe chronic heart failure. *Am J Cardiol* 1983;51:177-182.

33. Frishman WH. Multifactorial actions of β-adrenergic blocking drugs in ischemic heart disease. *Circulation* 1983;67(Suppl 1):111-118.

34. Frishman WH. Pindolol: a new β-adrenoceptor antagonist with partial agonist activity. *N Engl J Med* 1983;308:940-944.

35. Michelson EL, Frishman WH, Lewis JE, Edwards WT, Flanigan WJ, Bloomfield SS, Johnson BF, Lucas C, Freis ED, Finnerty FA. Multicenter clinical evaluation of the long-term efficacy and safety of labetalol in the treatment of hypertension. *Am J Med* 1983;75(4A):68-80.

36. Jacob H, Brandt L, Farkas P, Frishman WH. Beta-adrenergic blockade and the gastrointestinal system. *Am J Med* 1983;74:1042-1051.

37. Frishman WH, Weinberg P, Peled HB, Kimmel B, Charlap S, Beer N. Calcium-entry blockers for the treatment of severe hypertension and hypertensive crisis. *Am J Med* 1984;77(2B):35-45.

38. Frishman WH, Furberg CD, Friedewalk WT. β-Adrenergic blockade in survivors of acute myocardial infarction. *N Engl J Med* 1984;310:830-837.

39. Frishman WH, Crawford MH, DiBianco R, Farnham DJ, Katz RJ, Kostis JB, Mohiuddin SM, Sawin HS, Thadani U, Zellner S. Combination propranolol and bepridil therapy in angina pectoris. *Am J Cardiol* 1985;55:43C-49C.

40. Frishman WH, Kirkendall W, Lunn J, McCarron D, Moser M, Schnaper H, Smith LK, Sowers J, Swartz S, Zawada E. Diuretics versus calcium entry blockers in systemic hypertension: a preliminary multicenter experience with hydrochlorothiazide and sustained-release diltiazem. *Am J Cardiol* 1985;56:92H-96H.

41. Frishman WH, Kimmel B, Charlap S, Saltzberg S, Stroh J, Weinberg P, Moniszko E, Wiezner J, Dorsa F, Pollack S, Strom J. Twice daily administration of oral verapamil in the treatment of essential hypertension. *Arch Intern Med* 1986;146:561-565.

42. Robbins MJ, Frater RWM, Soeiro R, Frishman WH, Strom JA. Influence of vegetation size on the clinical outcome of right-sided infective endocarditis. (Recipient of Grand Prize Award ACP Associates Competition). *Am J Med* 1986;80:165-171.

43. Goldberger J, Stroh J, Peled H, Cohen M, Frishman WH. Prognostic factors in acute pulmonary edema. *Arch Intern Med* 1986;146:489-493.

44. Frishman WH, Zawada ET, Smith LK, Sowers J, Swartz SL, Kirkendall W, Lunn J, McCarron D, Moser M, Schnaper H. A comparative study of diltiazem and hydrochlorothiazide as initial medical therapy for mild to moderate hypertension. *Am J Cardiol* 1987;59:615-625.

45. Frishman WH, Garofalo JL, Rothschild A, Rothschild M, Greenberg SM, Soberman J. Multicenter comparison of the nifedipine gastrointestinal system and long-acting propranolol in patients with mild to moderate systemic hypertension receiving diuretics: a preliminary experience. *Am J Med* 1987;83(6B):15-19.

46. Frishman W, Charlap S, Kimmel B, Teicher M, Cinnamon J, Allen L, Strom J. Diltiazem compared to nifedipine and combination treatment in patients with stable angina: effects on angina, exercise tolerance and the ambulatory ECG. *Circulation* 1988;77:774-786.

47. Frishman WH, Charlap S. Calcium-channel blockers for combined systemic hypertension and myocardial ischemia. *Circulation* 1988;75(6 Pt 2):V154-162.

48. Frishman WH, Glasser SP, Strom JA, Schoenberger J, Liebson P, Poland M. Effects of dilevalol on left ventricular mass and function in non-elderly and elderly hypertensive patients: double-blind comparisons with atenolol and metoprolol. *Am J Cardiol* 1989;63:69I-74I.

49. Frishman WH, Flamenbaum W, Schoenberger J, Schwartz GL, Vidt DG, Neri GS, Greenberg S, Lazar E, Godrey JC, Stevenson A, Lamon KD, Chang Y, Magner DJ. Celiprolol in systemic hypertension: results of a placebo-controlled double-blind titration study. *Am J Cardiol* 1989;63:839-842.

50. Frishman WH, Giles T, Greenberg S, Heiman M, Raffidal L, Soberman J, Laifer L, Nadelmann J, Lazar E, Strom J. Sustained high-dose nitroglycerin transcutaneous patch therapy in angina pectoris: evidence of attenuation of effect over time. *J Clin Pharmacol* 1989;29:1097-1105.

51. Aronson MK, Ooi WL, Morgenstern PH, Hafner A, Masur D, Crystal H, Frishman W, Fisher D, Katzman R. Women, myocardial infarction and dementia in the very old. *Neurology* 1990;40:1102-1106.

52. Nadelmann J, Frishman WH, Ooi WL, Tepper D, Greenberg S, Guzik H, Lazar EJ, Heiman M, Aronson M. Prevalence, incidence and prognosis of recognized and unrecognized myocardial infarction in persons aged 75 years or older: The Bronx Aging Study. *Am J Cardiol* 1990;66:533-537.

53. Frishman WH, Lazar EJ. Reduction in mortality, sudden death, and nonfatal reinfarction with beta-adrenergic blockers in survivors of acute myocardial infarction: a new hypothesis regarding the cardioprotective action of beta-adrenergic blockade. *Am J Cardiol* 1990;66:66G-70G.

54. Frishman WH, Heiman M, Soberman J, Greenberg S, Eff J, for the Celiprolol International Angina Study Group. Comparison of celiprolol and propranolol in stable angina pectoris. *Am J Cardiol* 1991;67:665-670.

55. Aronson MK, Ooi WL, Geva D, Masur D, Blau A, Frishman WH. Dementia: age-dependent incidence, prevalence and mortality in the old. *Arch Intern Med* 1991;151:989-992.

56. Frishman WH, Heiman M, for the Nisoldipine Multicenter Angina Study Group. Usefulness of nisoldipine for stable angina pectoris. *Am J Cardiol* 1991;68:1004-1009.

57. The SHEP Cooperative Research Group. Prevention of stroke by antihypertensive drug treatment in older persons with isolated systolic hypertension: final results of Systolic Hypertension in the Elderly Program (SHEP). *JAMA* 1991;265:3255-3264.

58. SOLVD Investigators. Effects of angiotensin converting enzyme inhibition with enalapril on survival in patients with reduced left ventricular ejection fraction and congestive heart failure. *N Engl J Med* 1991;325:293-302.

59. Zimetbaum P, Frishman WH, Ooi WL, Derman MP, Aronson M, Gidez LI, Eder HA. Plasma lipid and lipoproteins and the incidence of cardiovascular disease in the old: The Bronx Longitudinal Aging Study. *Arterioscler Thromb* 1992;12:416-423.

60. Guzik H, Ooi WL, Frishman WH, Greenberg S, Aronson MK. Hypertension: Cardiovascular implications in a cohort of old old. *J Am Geriatr Soc* 1992;40:348-353.

61. Frishman WH, Nadelmann J, Ooi WL, Greenberg S, Heiman M, Kahn S, Guzik H, Lazar E, Aronson M. Cardiomegaly on chest x-ray: prognostic implications in a 10 year study of an old old cohort. A report from the BAS. *Am Heart J* 1992;124:1026-1030.

62. Frishman WH. Comparative efficacy and concomitant use of bepridil and beta blockers in the management of angina pectoris. *Am J Cardiol* 1992;69:50D-60D.

63. Gradman AH, Frishman WH, Kaihlanen PM, Wong SC, Friday KJ. Comparison of sustained-release formulations of nicardipine and verapamil for mild to moderate systemic hypertension. *Am J Cardiol* 1992;70:1571-1575.

64. SOLVD Investigators. Effect of enalapril on mortality and the development of heart failure in asymptomatic patients with reduce left ventricular ejection fractions. *N Engl J Med* 1992;327:685-691.

65. Conigliaro J, Frishman WH, Lazar EJ, Croen L. Internal medicine housestaff and attending physician perceptions of the impact of New York State 405 regulations on working conditions and supervision of residents in two training programs. *J Gen Med* 1993;8:502-507.

66. Landau A, Frishman WH, Alturk N, Adjei-Poku M, Fornasier-Bongo M, Furia S. Improvement in exercise tolerance and immediate β-adrenergic blockade with intranasal propranolol in patients with angina pectoris. *Am J Cardiol* 1993;72:995-998.

67. Frishman WH, Bryzinski BS, Coulson LR, DeQuattro VL, Vlachakis ND, Mroczek WJ, Dukart G, Alemayehu D, Koury K. A multifactorial trial design to assess combination therapy in hypertension: treatment with bisoprolol and hydrochlorothiazide. *Arch Intern Med* 1994;154:1461-1468.

68. Frishman WH, Brobyn W, Brown RD, Johnson BF, Reeves RL, Wombolt DG. Amlodipine versus atenolol in essential hypertension. *Am J Cardiol* 1994;73:50A-54A.

69. Crystal HA, Ortof E, Frishman WH, Gruber A, Hershman D, Aronson M. Serum vitamin B12 levels and incidence of dementia in a healthy elderly population: a report from the Bronx Longitudinal Aging Study. *J Am Geriatr Soc* 1994;42:933-936.

70. Hershman DL, Simonoff PA, Frishman WH, Paston F, Aronson MK. Drug utilization in the old old, and how it relates to self-perceived health and all cause mortality. Results from The Bronx Aging Study. *J Am Geriatr Soc* 1995;43:356-360.

71. Feinfeld DA, Guzik H, Carvounis CP, Lynn RI, Somer B, Aronson M, Frishman WH. Sequential changes in renal function tests in the old old: results from The Bronx Longitudinal Aging Study. *J Am Geriatr Soc* 1995;43:412-414.

72. Frishman W, Pepine CJ, Weiss R, Baiker WM, for the Zatebradine Study Group. Addition of zatebradine, a direct sinus node inhibitor, provides no greater exercise tolerance benefit in patients with angina pectoris taking extended-release nifedipine: results of a multicenter, randomized, double-blind, placebo-controlled, parallel group study. *J Am Coll Cardiol* 1995;26:305-312.

73. Frishman WH, Ram CVS, McMahon FG, Chrysant SG, Graff A, Kupiec JW, Hsu H, for the Benazepril/Amlodipine Study Group. Comparison of amlodipine and benazepril monotherapy to combination therapy in patients with systemic hypertension: a randomized, double-blind, placebo-controlled parallel group study. *J Clin Pharmacol* 1995;35:1060-1066.

74. Pratt CVM, McMahon RP, Goldstein S, Pepine CJ, Andrews TC, Dyrda I, Frishman WH, Geller NL, Hill JA, Morgan NA, Stone PH, Knatterud GL, Sopko G, Conti CR, for the ACIP Investigators. Comparison of subgroups assigned to medical regimens used to suppress cardiac ischemia (The Asymptomatic CardiacIschemia Pilot (ACIP) Study. *Am J Cardiol* 1996;77:1302-1309.

75. Kahn S, Frishman WH, Weissman S, Ooi WL, Aronson M. Left ventricular hypertrophy on electrocardiogram: prognostic implications from a 10 year cohort study of older subjects. A report from the Bronx Longitudinal Aging Study. *J Am Geriatr Soc* 1996;44:524-529.

76. Stone PH, Chaitman B, McMahon RP, Andrews TC, MacCallum G, Sharaf B, Frishman W, Deanfield JE, Sopko G, Pratt C, Goldberg AD, Rogerts WJ, Hill J, Proschan M, Pepine CJ, Bourassa MG, Conti CR, for the ACIP Investigators. Relationship between exercise-induced and ambulatory ischemia in patients with stable coronary disease. The Asymptomatic Cardiac Ischemia Pilot (ACIP) Study. *Circulation* 1996;94:1537-1544.

77. Frishman WH, Heiman M, Karpenos A, Ooi WL, Mitzner A, Goldkorn R, Greenberg S. Twenty-four hour ambulatory electrocardiography in elderly subjects: prevalence of various arrhythmias and prognostic implications. A report from the Bronx Longitudinal Aging Study. *Am Heart J* 1996;132:297-302.

78. Bernstein JM, Frishman WH, Chang CJ. Value of ECG PR and QTc interval prolongation and heart rate variability for predicting cardiovascular morbidity and mortality in the elderly: the Bronx Aging Study. *Cardiol in Elderly* 1997;5:31-41.

79. Frishman WH. Mibefradil. a new selective T-channel calcium antagonist for hypertension and angina pectoris. *J Cardiovasc Pharmacol Ther* 1997;2:321-330.

80. Messerli FH, Frishman WH, Elliott WJ, for the Trandolapril Study Group. Effects of verapamil and trandolapril in the treatment of hypertension. *Am J Hypertens* 1998;11(3 Pt 1):322-327.

81. Frishman WH, Bittar N, Glasser S, Habib G, Smith W. Additional anti-anginal and anti-ischemic efficacy of mibefradil in patients concomitantly treated with long-acting nitrates for chronic stable angina pectoris. *Clin Cardiol* 1998;21:483-490.

82. Davis BR, Vogt T, Frost PH, Burlando A, Cohen J, Wilson A, Brass LM, Frishman W, Price T, Stamler J for the Systolic Hypertension in the Elderly Program Cooperative Research Group. Risk factors for stroke and type of stroke in persons with isolated systolic hypertension. *Stroke* 1998;29:1333-1340.

83. Frishman WH: Carvedilol. *N Engl J Med* 1998;339:1759-1765.

84. Levitsky J, Frishman WH. Sodium ion/hydrogen ion exchange inhibition: a new pharmacologic approach to myocardial ischemia and reperfusion injury. *J Clin Pharmacol* 1998;38:887-897.

85. Frishman WH, Glasser S, Stone P, Deedwania P, Johnson M, Fakouhi D. Comparison of controlled-onset extended-release verapamil to amlodipine and amlodipine plus atenolol on exercise performance and ambulatory ischemia in patients with chronic stable angina pectoris. *Am J Cardiol* 1999;83:507-514.

86. Feinfeld DA, Keller S, Somer B, Wassertheil-Smoller S, Carvounis CP, Aronson M, Frishman WH. Falling serum creatinine and blood urea nitrogen over a 6 year period in the very old. *Geriatr Nephrol Urol* 1999;8:131-135.

87. Neutel J, Frishman WH, Oparail S, Papademitriou V, Guthrie G. A comparison of telmisartan with lisinopril in patients with mild-to-moderate hypertension. *Am J Therap* 1999;6:161-166.

88. Warshafsky S, Packard D, Marks SJ, Sachdeva N, Terashita DM, Kaufman G, Sang K, DeLuca AJ, Peterson SJ, Frishman WH. Efficacy of 3-hydroxy-3-methylglutaryl coenzyme A reductase inhibitors for prevention of stroke. *J Genl Intern Med* 1999;14:763-74.

89. Glasser S, Frishman W, White W, Stone P, Johnson M. Circadian heart rate response to chronotherapy versus conventional therapy in patients with hypertension or myocardial ischemia. *Clin Cardiol* 2000;23:524-529.

90. Frishman WH. Student research projects and theses. Should they be a requirement for medical school graduation? *Heart Dis* 2001;3(3):140-144

91. Black HR, Elliott WJ, Weber MA, Frishman WH, Strom JA, Liebson PR, Hwang CT, Ruff DA, Montoro R, DeQuattro V, Zhang D, Schleman MM, Klibaner MI, for the Stage 1 Systolic Hypertension (SISH) Study Group. One-year study of felodipine or placebo for stage 1 isolated systolic hypertension. *Hypertension* 2001;38:1118-1123.

92. Hsia J, Rodabough R, Rosal MC, Cochrane B, Howard BV, Snetselaar L, Frishman WH, Stefanick ML. Compliance with National Cholesterol Education Program Dietary and Lifestyle Guidelines among older women with self-reported hypercholesterolemia: The Women's Health Initiative. *Am J Med* 2002;113:384-392.

93. Writing Group for the Women's Health Initiative Investigators (William H. Frishman MD, Co-principal investigator of NYC clinical center). Risks and benefits of estrogen plus progestin in healthy postmenopausal women. Principal results from the Women's Health Initiative Randomized Controlled Trial. *JAMA* 2002;288:321-33.

94. Messina CR, Lane DS, Glanz K, Smith West D, Taylor V, Frishman WH, Powell L for the WHI Investigators. The relationship of social support and social burden to breast cancer screening in the Women's Health Initiative. *Health Psychol* 2004;23:582-594.

95. Kadish AH, Greenland P, Limacher MC, Frishman WH, Daugherty SA, Schwartz JB. Estrogen and progestin use and the QT interval in postmenopausal women. *Ann Noninvas Electrocardiol* 2004;9:366-374.

96. Sukhija R, Aronow WS, Yalamanchili K, Peterson SJ, Frishman WH, Babu S. Association of ankle-brachial index with severity of angiographic coronary artery disease in patients with peripheral arterial disease and coronary artery disease. *Cardiology* 2005;103(3):158-160.

97. Frishman WH, Hainer JW, Sugg J for the M-FACT Study Group. A factorial study of combination hypertension treatment with metoprolol succinate extended release and felodipine extended release. Results of the Metoprolol Succinate-Felodipine Antihypertensive Combination Trial (M-FACT). *Am J Hypertens* 2006;19:388-395.

98. Messerli F, Frishman WH, Elliott WJ, Bacher PH, Pepine CJ. Antihypertensive properties of a high-dose combination of trandolapril and verapamil-SR. *Blood Pressure Suppl* 2007;1: 6-9.

99. Sukhija R, Aronow WS, Sorbera C, Peterson SJ, Frishman WH, Cohen M. Mortality, left ventricular ejection fraction, and prevalence of new left ventricular wall motion abnormality at long-term follow-up in patients with implantable cardioverter defibrillators treated with biventricular pacing versus right ventricular pacing. *Am J Therap* 2007;14:328-330.

100. Sulmasy DP, Cimino JE, He MK, Frishman WH. U.S. medical students' perceptions of the adequacy of their schools' curricular attention to care at the end of life: 1998-2006. *J Palliative Med* 2008;11:707-716.

101. Huang J, Kaminski PM, Edwards JG, Wolin MS, Frishman WH, Gewitz MH, Mathew R. Pyrrolidine dithiocarbamata restores endothelial cell membrane integrity and attenuates monocrotaline-induced pulmonary artery hypertension. *Am J Physiol: Lung Cell Molec Physiol* 2008;294:L1250-1259.

102. Lai HM, Aronow WS, Kruger A, Desai H, Amin H, Frishman WH, Cohen M, Sorbera C. Effect of beta blockers, angiotensin-converting enzyme inhibitors or angiotensin receptor blockers, and statins on mortality in patients with implantable cardioverter-defibrillators. *Am J Cardiol* 2008;102:77-78.

103. Cavusoglu E, Chopra V, Gupta A, Choksi PU, Ruwende C, Yanamadala S, Frishman WH, Pinsky DJ, Marmur JD. Relation of baseline serum potassium levels to angiographic findings in patients with known or suspected coronary artery disease. *Am J Hypertens* 2009;22:754-762.

104. Kruger A, Aronow WS, Lai HM, Desai H, Singla A, Frishman WH, Cohen M, Sorbera C. Prevalence of appropriate cardioverter defibrillator shocks in 1,038 consecutive patients with implantable cardioverter defibrillators. *Am J Therap* 2009;16:323-325.

105. Cavusoglu E, Ruwende C, Chopra V, Poludasu S, Yanamadala S, Frishman WH, Eng C, Pinsky DJ, Marmur JD. Relation of baseline plasma ADMA levels to cardiovascular morbidity and mortality at two years in men with diabetes mellitus referred for coronary angiography. A*therosclerosis* 2010;210:226-231.

106. Desai H, Aronow WS, Ahn C, Gandhi K, Hussain S, Lai HM, Sharma M, Frishman WH, Cohen M, Sorbera C. Risk factors for appropriate cardioverter-defibrillator shocks, inappropriate cardioverter-defibrillator shocks, and mortality in 549 patients with heart failure. *Am J Cardiol* 2010;105:1336-1338.

107. Nabors C, Peterson SJ, Lee W-N, Mumtaz A, Shah T, Sule S, Gutwein AH, Forman L, Eskridge E, Wold E, Stallings GW, Burak KK, Karmen C, Behar CF, Carosella C, Yu S, Kar K, Gennarelli M, Bailey-Wallace G, Goldberg R, Guo G, Frishman WH. Experience with faculty supervision of an electronic resident sign-out system. APM Perspectives. *Am J Med* 2010;123:376-381.

108. Aronow WS, Fleg JL, Pepine CJ, Artinian ND, Bakris G, Brown AS, Ferdinand KC, Forcia MA, Frishman WH, Jaigobin C, Kostis JB, Mancia G, Oparil S, Ortiz E, Reisin E, Rich MW, Schocken DD, Weber MA, Wesley DJ. ACCF/AHA 2011 Expert Consensus Document on Hypertension in the Elderly. A Report of the American College of Cardiology Foundation Task Force on Expert Consensus Documents developed in collaboration with the American Academy of Neurology, Association of Black Cardiologists, American Geriatrics Society, American Society of Hypertension, American Society of Nephrology, American Society for Preventive Cardiology, and the European Society of Hypertension. *J Am Coll Cardiol* 2011;57:2037-2114.

109. Nabors C, Peterson SJ, Weems R, Forman L, Mumtaz A, Goldberg R, Borges JA, Doctor I, Luben O, Frishman WH. A multidisciplinary approach for teaching systems-based practice to internal medicine residents. *J Grad Med Ed* 2011;3:75-80.

110. Nabors C, Peterson SJ, Forman L, Stallings GW, Mumtaz A, Sule S, Shah T, Aronow W, DeLorenzo L, Chandy D, Lehrman S, Frishman WH, Holmboe E. Operationalizing the internal medicine milestones - an early status report. *J Grad Med Ed* 2013;5:130-137.

111. Balasubramaniyam H, Kolte D, Palaniswamy C, Yalamanchili K, Aronow WS, McClung JA, Khera S, Sule S, Peterson SJ, Frishman WH. Predictors of in-hospital mortality and acute myocardial infarction in hospitalized patients with thrombotic thrombocytopenic purpura. *Am J Med* 2013;126:1016.e1-7.

112. Khera S, Kolte D, Palaniswamy C, Mujib MU, Aronow WS, Singh T, Gotsis W, Silverman G, Frishman WH. ST-elevation myocardial infarction in the elderly: temporal trends in incidence, utilization of percutaneous coronary interventions, and outcomes in the United States. *Intl J Cardiol* 2013;168: 3683-3690.

113. Khera S, Kolte D, Aronow WS, Palaniswamy C, Mujib M, Ahmed A, Chugh SS, Balasubramaniyam N, Edupuganti M, Frishman WH, Fonarow G. Trends in acute kidney injury and outcomes after early percutaneous coronary intervention in the elderly. *Am J Cardiol* 2013;112:1279-1286.

114. Peterson SJ, Nabors C, Frishman WH. Milestones: Direct observation may be the key to accelerated training. *Am J Med* 2013;126:1031-1032.

115. Kolte D, Khera S, Palaniswamy C, Mujib M, Fonarow GC, Ahmed A, Jain D, Frishman WH, Aronow WS. Early invasive versus initial conservative treatment strategies in octogenarians with UA/NSTEMI. *Am J Med* 2013;126:1076-1083.

116. Nabors C, Peterson SJ, Forman L, Stallings GW, Mumtaz A, Sule S, Shah T, Aronow W, Delorenzo L, Chandy D, Lehrman SG, Frishman WH, Holmboe E. Operationalizing the internal medicine milestones-an early status report. *J Grad Med Educ* 2013;5:130-137.

117. Kolte D, Khera S, Aronow WS, Mujib M, Palaniswamy C, Sule S, Jain D, Gotsis W, Ahmed A, Frishman WH, Fonarow GC. Trends in incidence, management, and outcomes of cardiogenic shock complicating ST-elevation myocardial infarction in the United States. *J Am Heart Assoc* 2014;13;3:0000590.

118. Khera S, Kolte D, Aronow WS, Palaniswamy C, Subramanian KS, Hashim T, Mujib M, Jain D, Paudel R, Ahmed A, Frishman WH, Bhatt DL, Panza JA, Fonarow GC. Non-ST elevation myocardial infarction in the United States: contemporary trends in incidence, utilization of the early invasive strategy, and in hospital outcomes. *J Am Heart Assoc* 2014;28:3.

119. Gupta T, Garg J, Sharma M, Khera S, Kolte D, Aronow WS, Frishman WH, Lanier GM. Non-ischemic cardiomyopathy in a patient with multiple myeloma without amyloidosis. *Am J Med* 2014;127:1063-1066.

120. Kolte D, Khera S, Aronow WS, Palaniswamy C, Mujib M, Ahn C, Iwai S, Jain D, Sule S, Ahmed A, Cooper HA, Frishman WH, Bhatt DL, Panza JA, Fonarow GC. Regional variation in incidence and outcomes of in-hospital cardiac arrest in the United States. *Circulation* 2014;131:1415-1425.

121. Gupta T, Paul N, Kolte D, Harikrishnan P, Khera S, Aronow WS, Mujib M, Palaniswamy C, Sule S, Jain D, Ahmed A, Cooper HA, Frishman WH, Bhatt DL, Fonarow GC, Panza JA. Association of chronic renal insufficiency with in-hospital outcomes after percutaneous coronary intervention. *J Am Heart Assoc* 2015;4:e002069.

122. Gupta T, Harikrishan P, Kolte D, Khera S, Subramanian KS, Mujib M, Masud A, Chandraseker P, Sule S, Diwakar J, Ahmed A, Lanier GM, Cooper HA, Frishman WH, Bhatt DL, Fonarow GC, Panza JA. Trends in management and outcomes of ST-Elevation mycocardial infarction in patients with end stage renal disease in the United States. *Am J Cardiol* 2015; 115:1033-1041.

Books

123. Frishman WH, ed. *Clinical Pharmacology of the Beta-Adrenoceptor Blocking Drugs.* New York: Appleton-Century-Crofts l980; 2nd ed. Norwalk: Appleton-Century-Crofts, l984.
124. Packer M, Frishman WH, eds. *Calcium Channel Antagonists in Cardiovascular Disease.* Norwalk: Appleton-Century-Crofts l984.
125. Morganroth J, Frishman WH, Horowitz L, Likoff M, Lowenthal D, eds. *Cardiovascular Drug Therapy.* Chicago: Yearbook Medical Publishers, l986.
126. Frishman WH, Weiner D, eds. *Therapy of Angina Pectoris.* New York: Marcel Dekker l986.
127. Frishman WH, ed. *Medical Management of Lipid Disorders: Focus on Prevention of Coronary Artery Disease.* Mt. Kisco: Futura Publishing Co.,l992.
128. Cruickshank JM, Dollery C, Frishman WH, eds. *Current Cardiovascular Drugs.* London: Current Science; International edition, l993. Frishman WH, Dollery CT, Cruickshank JM, eds. *Current Cardiovascular Drugs.* Philadelphia: Current Science, North American edition, l994. Frishman WH, ed. *Current Cardiovascular Drugs, 2nd Ed.* Philadelphia: Current Science, North American edition, l995. Frishman WH, ed. *Current Cardiovascular Drugs, 3ʳᵈ Ed.* Philadelphia: Current Medicine, 2000. Frishman WH, Cheng-Lai A, Nawarskas J, eds. *Current Cardiovascular Drugs 4ᵗʰ Ed.* Philadelphia: Current Medicine, 2005.
129. Goldberg DE, Frishman WH. *Beta3-Adrenergic Agonism: A New Concept in Human Pharmacotherapy.* New York: Futura Publishing Co. Inc., l995.
130. Opie LH, Chatterjee K, Frishman W, Gersh BJ, Kaplan NM, Marcos FI, Poole-Wilson PA, Sonnenblick EH, Thadani U, eds. *Drugs for the Heart, 4th Ed.* Philadelphia: Saunders, 1995.
131. Messerli FH, ed, Frishman WH, section ed. *Cardiovascular Drug Therapy, 2nd Ed.* Philadelphia: W.B. Saunders, 1996.
132. Frishman WH, Sonnenblick EH, eds. *Cardiovascular Pharmacotherapeutics.* New York: McGraw Hill Inc., 1997 (reprinted and updated 2002). Frishman WH, Sonnenblick EH, Sica D, eds. *Cardiovascular Pharmacotherapeutics, 2ⁿᵈ Ed.* New York: McGraw Hill, 2003. Frishman WH, Sica DA, eds. *Cardiovascular Pharmacotherapeutics 3rd Ed.* Minneapolis: Cardiotext Inc., 2011.
133. Frishman WH, Sonnenblick EH, eds. *Cardiovascular Pharmacotherapeutics Companion Handbook.* New York: McGraw Hill Inc., 1998. Frishman WH, Sonnenblick EH, Sica D, eds. *Cardiovascular Pharmacotherapeutics Manual 2ⁿᵈ Ed.* New York: McGraw Hill, 2004. Frishman WH, Sica DA, eds. *Cardiovascular Pharmacotherapeutics Abridged and Updated 3rd Ed.* Minneapolis: Cardiotext,2012.
134. Frishman WH, Weintraub MI, Micozzi M, eds. *Complementary and Integrative Therapies for Cardiovascular Disease.* St. Louis: Elsevier, 2005.
135. Leri A, Anversa P, Frishman WH, eds. *Cardiovascular Regeneration and Stem Cell Therapy.* UK/New York: Blackwell/Futura, 2007.
136. Cheng-Lai A, Nawarskas J, Frishman WH. *Hypertension: A Clinical Guide.* Philadelphia: Wolters Kluwer, 2007.

Year Book of Medicine

137. Cline MJ, Frishman WH, Greenberg NJ, Klahr S, Malawista SE, Mandell GL, Petty TL, Utiger RD, eds. *Year Book of Medicine, 1997.* Chicago: Mosby Year Book Inc.
138. Cline M, Frishman W, Jett J, Klahr S, Malawista S, Mandell G, McCallum RW, Utiger RD, eds. *Year Book of Medicine 1998.* Chicago: Mosby Year Book Inc.
139. Bagdade JD, Barkin JS, Frishman W, Jett J, Klahr S, Malawista SE, Mandell GL, Young NS, eds. *Year Book of Medicine 1999.* St. Louis: Mosby.
140. Barkin JS, Frishman WH, Jett JR, Klahr S, Loehrer PJ Sr., Malawista SE, Mandel GL, Mazzaferri EL, eds. *Year Book of Medicine 2000.* St. Louis: Mosby.
141. Mandell G, Frishman W, Barkin JS, Klahr S, Malawista SE, eds. *Year Book of Medicine 2001.* St. Louis: Mosby.
142. Barkin JS, Frishman WH, Jett JR, Klahr S, Loehrer PJ Sr., Mazzaferri EL, Pillinger MH, eds. *Year Book of Medicine 2002.* St. Louis: Mosby.
143. Barkin JS, Frishman WH, Klahr S, Loehrer PJ, Mazzaferri EL, Phillips BA, Pillinger MH, Snydman DR, eds. *Year Book of Medicine 2003.* St. Louis: Mosby.
144. Barkin JS, Frishman WH, Klahr S, Loehrer PJ, Mazzaferri EL, Phillips BA, Pillinger MH, Snydman DR, eds. *Year Book of Medicine 2004*: Philadelphia: Elsevier.
145. Barkin JS , Frishman WH, Klahr S, Loehrer P, Sr., Mazzaferri EL, Phillips BA, Pillinger M, Snydman DR, eds. *Year Book of Medicine 2005*: Philadelphia: Elsevier.
146. Barkin JS, Frishman WH, Garrick R, Loehrer P, Sr., Mazzaferri EL, Phillips BA, Pillinger M, Snydman DR, eds. *Year Book of Medicine 2006*: Philadelphia: Elsevier.
147. Barkin JS, Berney SM, Frishman WH, Garrick R, Loehrer PJ, Mazzaferri EL, Phillips BA, Snydman DR, eds. *Year Book of Medicine 2007*: Philadelphia: Elsevier.

Medical Clinics

148. Frishman WH, ed. Special Topics in Cardiovascular Pharmacotherapy. *Cardiology Clinics* 1987;5:.
149. Frishman WH, ed. Cardiovascular Pharmacotherapy (3 parts). *Medical Clinics of North America* Jan 1988, March 1998, May 1998.

Consumer Books

150. Frishman WH, Shields R. *What you Need to Know and Do About Your High Cholest*erol. Real Information You Can Use. Pocket Doc™ Library Patient Guide. Massachusetts: Consumer Education Publishing, 1996.
151. Frishman WH, Shields R. *Hypertension.* Massachusetts: Consumer Education Publishing, 1996.

Monographs, Chapters in Books and Review Articles

152. Frishman WH. Clinical pharmacology of the new beta-adrenergic blocking agents. part I: pharmacodynamic and pharmacokinetic properties. *Am Heart J* 1979;97:663-670.

153. Spivack C, Ocken S, Frishman WH. Calcium antagonists: clinical use in treatment of systemic hypertension. *Drugs* 1983;25:154-177.

154. Frishman WH, Charlap S. Verapamil in treatment of chronic stable angina. *Arch Intern Med* 1983;143:1407-1415.

155. Michelson EL, Frishman WH. Labetalol: an alpha- and beta adrenoceptor blocking drug. *Ann Intern Med* 1983;99:553-555.

156. Frishman WH, Furberg CD, Friedewald WT. The use of beta-adrenergic blocking drugs in patients with myocardial infarction. *Curr Probl Cardiol* 1984;9:1-50.

157. Frishman WH. Beta-adrenergic blocker withdrawal. *Am J Cardiol* 1987;59:26F-32F.

158. Maza SR, Frishman WH. Therapeutic options to minimize free radical damage and thrombogenicity in ischemic/reperfused myocardium. *Am Heart J* 1987;114:1206-1215.

159. Kralstein J, Frishman WH. Malignant pericardial disease: diagnosis and treatment. *Cardiol Clin* 1987;5:583-589.

160. Schoen RE, Frishman WH, Shamoon H. Hormonal and metabolic effects of calcium-channel antagonists in man. *Am J Med* 1988;84:492-504.

161. Hachamovitch R, Strom JA, Sonnenblick EH, Frishman WH. Left ventricular hypertrophy in hypertension and the effects of antihypertensive drug therapy. *Curr Probl Cardiol* 1988;13:371-421.

162. Frishman WH, Skolnick AE, Strom JA. Effects of calcium-entry blockade on hypertension-induced left ventricular hypertrophy. *Circulation* 1989;80(suppl):IV151-IV161.

163. Skolnick AE, Frishman WH. Calcium channel blockers in myocardial infarction. *Arch Intern Med* 1989;149:1669-1677.

164. Charlap S, Lichstein E, Frishman WH. Electromechanical disassociation: diagnosis, pathophysiology, and management. *Am Heart J* 1989;118:355-360.

165. Frishman WH, Garofalo JL, Rothschild A, Rothschild M, Greenberg SM, Soberman J. The nifedipine gastrointestinal therapeutic system in the treatment of hypertension. *Am J Cardiol* 1989;64:65F-69F.

166. Frishman WH, Sokol S, Aronson MK, Wassertheil-Smoller S, Katzman R. Risk factors for cardiovascular and cerebrovascular diseases and dementia in the elderly (monograph). *Curr Probl Cardiol* 1998;23:1-68.

167. Frishman WH, Charlap S. The alpha- and beta-adrenergic blocking drugs. In: Parmley WW, ed. *Cardiology.* Philadelphia: Lippincott, 1990;1-18.

168. Frishman WH. Something Special. Valedictory Address to the 1989 Graduating Classes of the Albert Einstein College of Medicine and the Sue Golding Graduate Division of Yeshiva University. *Einstein Quarter J Biol Med* 1990;8:31-33.

169. Nadelmann J, Frishman WH. Clinical use of β-adrenoceptor blockade in systemic hypertension. *Drugs* 1990;39:862-876.

170. Zimetbaum P, Frishman W, Aronson M. Hyperlipidemia, vascular diseases, and dementia with advancing age: epidemiologic considerations. *Arch Intern Med* 1991;151:240-244.

171. Frishman WH, Lazar EJ, Gorodokin G. Pharmacokinetic optimization of therapy with beta-adrenergic blocking agents. *Clin Pharmacokin* 1991;20:311-318

172. Frishman WH, Skolnick AE, Miller KP. Secondary prevention post infarction: the role of β-adrenergic blockers, calcium-channel blockers and aspirin. In: Gersh BJ, Rahimtoola SH, eds. *Management of Myocardial Infarction.* New York: Elsevier Science, 1991:469-492.

173. Dustan HP, Caplan LR, Curry CL, DeLeon AC, Douglas FL, Frishman W, Hill MN, Washington RL, Steigerwalt S, Shulman N, Taubert K, Champagne B. Report of the Task Force on the Availability of Cardiovascular Drugs to the Medically Indigent. *Circulation* 1992;85:849-860.

174. Frishman WH. Comparative pharmacokinetic and clinical profiles of angiotensin converting enzyme inhibitors and calcium antagonists in systemic hypertension. *Am J Cardiol* 1992;69:17C-25C.

175. Frishman WH. Tolerance, rebound and time-zero effect of nitrate therapy. *Am J Cardiol* 1992;70:43G-48G.

176. Frishman WH. β-Adrenergic blockers. In: Izzo JL, Jr, Black HR, eds. *Hypertension Primer of the American Heart Assoc* 1993;297-300.

177. Frishman WH, Sonnenblick EH. β-adrenergic blocking drugs and calcium blockers. In: Alexander RW, Schlant RC, Fuster V, eds. *The Heart, 9th ed.* New York: McGraw Hill 1998:1583-1618.

178. Landau AJ, Gentilucci M, Cavusoglu E, Frishman WH. Calcium antagonists for the treatment of congestive heart failure. *Coron Artery Dis* 1994;5:37-50.

179. Kang PM, Landau AJ, Eberhardt RT, Frishman WH. Angiotensin II receptor antagonists: a new approach to blockade of the renin-angiotensin system. *Am Heart J* 1994;127:1388-1401.

180. Loskove J, Frishman WH. Nitric oxide donors in the treatment of cardiovascular and pulmonary diseases. *Am Heart J* 1995;129:604-613.

181. Schwartz J, Freeman R, Frishman W. Clinical pharmacology of estrogens: focus on their cardiovascular actions and cardioprotective benefits of replacement therapy in postmenopausal women. *J Clin Pharmacol* 1995;35:314-329.

182. Frishman WH, Huberfeld S, Okin S, Wang Y-H, Kumar A, Shareef B. Serotonin and serotonin antagonism in cardiovascular and non-cardiovascular disease. *J Clin Pharmacol* 1995;35:541-572.

183. Katz B, Rosenberg A, Frishman WH. Controlled release drug delivery systems in cardiovascular medicine. *Am Heart J* 1995;19:359-368.

184. Frishman WH, Cavusoglu E. β-Adrenergic blockers and their role in the therapy of arrhythmias. In: Podrid PJ, Kowey PR, eds. *Cardiac Arrhythmias—Mechanisms, Diagnosis and Management.* Baltimore: Williams & Wilkins, 1995:421-433.

185. Opie LH, Sonnenblick EH, Frishman WH, Thadani U. β-Blocking drugs. In: Opie LH, Gersh BJ, eds. *Drugs for the Heart, 4th Ed.* Philadelphia: WB Saunders 1995:1-30.

186. Opie LH, Frishman WH, Thadani U. Calcium channel antagonists. In: Opie LH, Gersh BJ, eds. *Drugs for the Heart, 4th Ed.* Philadelphia: WB Saunders 1995:50-82.

187. Opie LH, Frishman WH. Lipid-lowering and antiatherosclerotic drugs. In: Opie LH, Gersh BJ, eds. *Drugs for the Heart, 4th Ed.* Philadelphia: WB Saunders, 1995:288-307.

188. Patel RC, Frishman WH. AIDS and the Heart: Clinicopathologic assessment. *Cardiovasc Pathol* 1995;4:173-183.

189. Cavusoglu E, Frishman WH. Sotalol: a new β-adrenergic blocker for ventricular arrhythmias. *Prog Cardiovasc Dis* 1995;37:423-440.

190. Tamirisa P, Frishman WH, Kumar A. Endothelin and endothelin antagonism: roles in cardiovascular disease and health. *Am Heart J* 1995;130:601-610.

191. Frishman WH, Burns B, Atac B, Alturk N, Altajar B, Lerrick K. Novel antiplatelet therapies for treatment of patients with ischemic heart disease. Inhibitors of platelet glycoprotein IIb/IIa integrin receptor. *Am Heart J* 1995;130:877-892.

192. Frishman WH. Postinfarction survival: role of β-adrenergic blockade. In: Fuster V, Ross R, Topol EJ, eds. *Atherosclerosis and Coronary Artery Disease.* Philadelphia: Lippincott-Raven, 1996:1205-1214.

193. Frishman WH, Sung HM, Yee HCM, Liu LL, Keefe D, Einzig A, Dutcher J. Cardiovascular toxicity with cancer chemotherapy. *Curr Probl Cardiol* 1996;21:225-288.

194. Frishman WH, Hotchkiss H. Selective and non-selective dopamine receptor agonists: an innovative approach to cardiovascular disease treatment. *Am Heart J* 1996;132:861-870.

195. Gomberg-Maitland M, Frishman WH. Recombinant growth hormone: a new cardiovascular drug therapy. *Am Heart J* 1996;132:1244-1262.

196. Patel RC, Frishman WH. Cardiac involvement in human immunodeficiency virus infection. *Med Clin N Amer* 1996;80:1493-1512.

197. Frishman WH, Murthy VS, Strom JA, Hershman DL. Ultrashort-acting ß-adrenoreceptor blocking drug: esmolol. In, Messerli FH, ed. *Cardiovascular Drug Therapy, 2nd ed.* Philadelphia: Saunders 1996: 507-516.

198. Frishman WH, Hershman D. Amlodipine. In, Messerli FH, ed. *Cardiovascular Drug Therapy, 2nd ed.* Philadelphia: Saunders 1996: 1024-1040.

199. Frishman WH, Hershman D. ß-Adrenergic blocking drugs in cardiac disorders. In, Messerli FH, ed. *Cardiovascular Drug Therapy, 2nd Ed.* Philadelphia: Saunders 1996:465-474.

200. Frishman WH, Sonnenblick EH. Cardiovascular uses of calcium-antagonists. In, Messerli FH, ed. *Cardiovascular Drug Therapy, 2nd Ed.* Philadelphia: Saunders 1996:891-901.

201. Goldschmidt M, Landzberg BR, Frishman WH. Nicorandil: a potassium-channel opening drug for the treatment of ischemic heart disease. *J Clin Pharm* 1996;36:559-572.

202. Frishman WH, Skolnick AE. Secondary prevention postinfarction: the role of ß-adrenergic blockers, calcium channel blockers, and aspirin. In, Gersh BJ, Rahimtoola SH, eds. *Acute Myocardial Infarction, 2nd ed.* New York: Chapman & Hall 1996:766-96.

203. Frishman WH, Gabor R, Pepine C, Cavusoglu E. Heart rate reduction in the treatment of chronic stable angina pectoris: experience with the sinus node inhibitor. *Am Heart J* 1996;131:204-210.

204. Frishman WH. Faculty practice plan governance and management. *Faculty Practice Plans.* Florida: Am Coll Phys Exec, 1997.

205. Frishman WH, Weiser M, Michaelson MD, Abdeen MA. The pharmacologic approach to the treatment of obesity. J Clin Pharm 1997;37:453-473.

206. Frishman WH. Fixed-dose combinations with ß-adrenergic blockers and diuretics: conventional dose and very low dose formulations. In, Opie LH, Messerli F, eds. *Combination Drug Therapy for Hypertension.* New York/Philadelphia: Authors Publishing House/Lippincott-Raven Publishers 1997: 25-34.

207. Frishman WH. Results of hypertension treatment with low dose combinations of a ß-adrenergic blocker and a diuretic. *Am J Hypertens* 1997;10(3):17s-23s.

208. Frishman WH, Michaelson MD. Use of calcium antagonists in patients with ischemic heart disease and systemic hypertension. Symposium Issue. *Am J Cardiol* 1997;79:33-38.

209. Frishman WH. Alpha- and beta-adrenergic blocking drugs (Chapter 20). In, Parmley WW, Chatterjee K, eds. *Cardiology.* Philadelphia: Lippincott-Raven Publ., 1997.

210. Celentano DC, Frishman WH: Matrix metalloproteinases and coronary artery disease: a novel therapeutic target. *J Clin Pharm* 1997;37:991-1000.

211. Burns B, Frishman WH. Calcium antagonists in elderly patients with systemic hypertension: In, Epstein M, ed. *Calcium Antagonists in Clinical Medicine, 2nd Ed.* Philadelphia: Hanley & Belfus 1998; 307-320.

212. Gomberg-Maitland M, Frishman WH. Thyroid hormone and cardiovascular disease. *Am Heart J* 1998; 135:187-196.

213. Frishman WH, Sokol S, Aronson M, Wassertheil-Smoller S, Katzman R. Risk factors for cardiovascular and cerebrovascular diseases and dementia in the elderly: Findings from the Bronx Longitudinal Aging Study (monograph). *Curr Probl Cardiol* 1998;23:1-68.

214. Post JB IV, Frishman WH. Fenoldopam. a new dopamine agonist for the treatment of hypertensive urgencies and emergencies. *J Clin Pharm* 1998;38:2-13.

215. Frishman WH, Sonnenblick EH. ß-Adrenergic blocking drugs and calcium channel blockers. In, Alexander RW, Schlant RC, Fuster V: *Hurst's the Heart, 9th Ed.* New York: McGraw Hill 1998;1583-1618.

216. LeJemtel TH, Sonnenblick EH, Frishman WH. The diagnosis and management of heart failure. In, Alexander RW, Schlant RC, Fuster V, eds. *Hurst's the Heart, 9th Ed.* New York: McGraw Hill 1998;745-81.

217. Yashar PR, Fransua M, Frishman WH. The sodium-calcium ion membrane exchanger: physiologic significance and pharmacologic implications. *J Clin Pharm* 1998;38:393-401.

218. Hurst AK, Hoffman K, Frishman WH, Elkayam U. The use of β-adrenergic blocking agents in pregnancy and lactation. In, Elkayam U, Gleicher N, eds. *Cardiac Problems in Pregnancy, 3ʳᵈ Ed.* New York: Wiley Liss, 1998: 357-372.

219. Frishman WH, Chiu R, Landzberg BR, Weiss M. Medical therapies for the prevention of restenosis following percutaneous coronary interventions. *Curr Probl Cardiol* 1998;23:533-640.

220. Frishman WH, Anandasbapathy S. Innovative drug treatments for viral and autoimmune myocarditis. *J Clin Pharmacol* 1998;38:295-308.

221. Frishman WH. ß-Adrenergic blockers. In, Izzo JL Jr., Black HR, Sr. eds. *Hypertension Primer, 2nd Ed.* Dallas: American Heart Assoc 1998;362-365.

222. Mashour NH, Lin GI, Frishman WH. Herbal medicine in the treatment of cardiovascular disease: clinical considerations. *Arch Intern Med* 1998;158:2225-2234.

223. Sinha S, Frishman WH. Matrix metalloproteinase and abdominal aortic aneurysm: a potential therapeutic target. *J Clin Pharmacol* 1998;38:1077-1088.

224. Frishman WH. 40ᵗʰ Annual AOA Induction Address: An Odyssey of a Clinical Researcher. *Einstein Quarter J Biol Med* 1998;15:121-125.

225. Frishman WH, Cheng A, Aronow WS. Cardiovascular drug therapy in the elderly. In, Tresch DD, Aronow WS, eds. *Cardiovascular Disease in the Elderly Patient.* New York: Marcel Dekker, 1999:739-768.

226. Frishman WH: Beta-adrenergic blocking drugs. In, Alexander RW, Schlant RC, Fuster V, eds. *Handbook of the Heart, 9th ed.* New York: McGraw Hill 1999;693-710.

227. Frishman WH. Calcium channel antagonists. In, Alexander RW, Schlant RC, Fuster V, eds. *Handbook of the Heart, 9th ed.* New York: McGraw Hill 1999;711-723.

228. Goldfrank D, Haytoglu T, Frishman WH, Zalt Mohammad. Raloxifene, a new selective estrogen receptor modulator. *J Clin Pharmacol* 1999;39:767-774.

229. Frishman WH, Levine WG. Pharmacology. *ACC Self-Assessment Program Drug Database (ACCSAP 2000),* 1999.

230. Moser M, Frishman WH. Beta blockers with vasodilating activity: focus on carvedilol: In Messerli FH, ed. *The ABCs of Antihypertensive Therapy.* New York: Authors Publishing House, 2000: 78-92.

231. Sokol SI, Cheng-Lai A, Frishman WH, Kaza CS. Cardiovascular drug therapy in patients with hepatic diseases and patients with congestive heart failure. *J Clin Pharmacol* 2000;40:11-30.

232. Frishman WH. Recent advances in cardiovascular pharmacology. *Curr Probl Cardiol* 2000;25:221-296.

233. Frishman WH, Grewall P. Serotonin and the heart: pathophysiologic and therapeutic considerations. *Ann Med* 2000;32:195-209.

234. Perlmutter JB, Frishman W, Feinstein RE. Major depression as a risk factor for cardiovascular disease: therapeutic implications. *Heart Dis* 2000;2:75-82.

235. Palkhiwala SA, Yu A, Frishman WH. Imidazoline receptor agonist drugs for treatment of systemic hypertension and congestive heart failure. *Heart Dis* 2000;2:83-92.

236. Aronow WS, Frishman WH, Cheng-Lai A. Cardiovascular drug therapy in the elderly. *Heart Dis* 2000; 2;151-167.

237. Lah J, Frishman WH. Adrenomedullin: a vasoactive and natriuretic peptide with therapeutic potential. *Heart Dis* 2000;2:259-265.

238. Brosnan BD, Frishman WH, Sun DK, Grossman C. Adverse dermatologic effects of cardiovascular drug therapy. *Heart Dis* 2000;2:220-247.

239. Nelson M, Passeri J, Frishman WH. Therapeutic angiogenesis: a new treatment modality for ischemic heart disease. *Heart Dis* 2000;2:314-325.

240. Frishman WH. Increased vascular compliance/decreased cardiovascular risk: what the studies tell us. *Heart Dis* 2000;2:384-88.

241. Dervan S, Frishman WH. Hormone replacement therapy use in elderly women: a literature review. *Cardiovasc Rev & Rep* 2000;21:205-214.

242. Aronow WS, Frishman WH. Risk factors for atherosclerosis in the elderly. In, Rosenthal RA, Zenilman ME, Katlic MR, eds. *Principles and Practice of Geriatric Surgery.* New York: Springer-Verlag 2001; 448- 459.

243. Aronow WS, Frishman WH. Physiologic changes in cardiac function with aging. In, Rosenthal RA, Zenilman ME, Katlic MR, eds. *Principles and Practice of Geriatric Surgery.* New York: Springer-Verlag 2001;437-447.

244. Opie LH, Frishman WH. Drug interactions. In, Fuster V, Alexander RW, O'Rourke RA, Roberts R, King SB III, Wellens HJJ, eds. *Hurst's The Heart, 10ᵗʰ Ed.* New York: McGraw Hill 2001;2251-2270.

245. LeJemtel TH, Sonnenblick EH, Frishman WH. Diagnosis and management of heart failure. In, Fuster V, Alexander RW, O'Rourke RA, Roberts R, King SB III, Wellens HJJ, eds. *Hurst's The Heart, 10ᵗʰ Ed.* New York: McGraw Hill 2001;687-724.

246. Abrams J, Frishman W, Bates SM, Weitz J, Opie L. Pharmacologic options for treatment of ischemic disease. In, Antman EM, ed. *Cardiovascular Therapeutics. A Companion to Braunwald's Heart Disease, 2ⁿᵈ Ed.* Philadelphia: Saunders, 2001:97-153.

247. Kelsch T, Kikuchi K, Vahdat S, Frishman WH. Innovative pharmacologic approaches to cardiopulmonary resuscitation. *Heart Dis* 2001;3:46-54.

248. Kaur S, Frishman WH, Singh I, Tamirisa P, Kumar A. Endothelin as a therapeutic target in the treatment of cardiovascular disease. *Heart Dis* 2001;3:176-188.

249. LeJemtel TH, Sonnenblick EH, Frishman WH. Diagnosis and management of heart failure. In, O'Rourke RA, Fuster V, Alexander RW, eds. *Hurst's The Heart Manual of Cardiology 10ᵗʰ Ed.* New York: McGraw Hill 2001:49-59.

250. Opie LH, Frishman WH. Adverse cardiovascular drug interactions and complications. In, O'Rourke RA, Fuster V, Alexander RW, eds. *Hurst's The Heart Manual of Cardiology 10ᵗʰ Ed.* New York: McGraw Hill 2001: 647-666.

251. Kaplan RC, Frishman WH. Systemic inflammation as a cardiovascular disease risk factor and as a potential target for drug therapy. *Heart Dis* 2001;3:326-332.

252. Guttenplan N, Lee C, Frishman WH. Inhibition of myocardial apoptosis as a therapeutic target in cardiovascular disease prevention: focus on caspase inhibition. *Heart Dis* 2001;3:313-318.

253. Frishman WH. Update in Cardiology. *Ann Intern Med* 2001;135:439-446.

254. Frishman WH, Ky T, Ismail A. Tobacco smoking, nicotine, and nicotine and non-nicotine replacement therapies. *Heart Dis* 2001;3:365-377.

255. Nawarskas J, Rajan V, Frishman WH. Vasopeptidase inhibitors, neutral endopeptidase inhibitors, and dual inhibitors of angiotensin-converting enzyme and neutral endopeptidase. *Heart Dis* 2001;3: 378-85.

256. Frishman WH, Kowalski M, Nagnur S, Warshafsky S, Sica D. Cardiovascular considerations in using topical, oral, and intravenous drugs for the treatment of glaucoma and ocular hypertension: focus on β-adrenergic blockade. *Heart Dis* 2001;3:386-397.

257. Frishman WH. Chelation therapy for coronary artery disease: panacea or quackery? (editorial). *Am J Med* 2001;111:729-730.

258. Frishman WH. Angina pectoris. In, Rakel RE, Bope ET: *Conn's Current Therapy.* Philadelphia: W.B. Saunders 2002:256-261.

259. Chien PC, Frishman WH. Lipid disorders. In, Crawford MH: *Current Diagnosis & Treatment in Cardiology* 2ⁿᵈ ed. New York: McGraw Hill 2003:15-30.

260. Marks SJ, Batra RR, Frishman WH. Estrogen replacement therapy for cognitive benefits: viable treatment or forgettable "senior moment"? *Heart Dis* 2002;4:26-32.

261. Monchamp T, Frishman WH. Exercise as a treatment modality for congestive heart failure. *Heart Dis* 2002;4:110-116.

262. Frishman WH. Effects of non-steroidal antiinflammatory drug therapy on blood pressure and peripheral edema. *Am J Cardiol* 2002;89:18D-25D.

263. Frishman WH, O'Brien M, Naseer N, Anandasabapathy S. Innovative drug treatments for viral and autoimmune myocarditis. *Heart Dis* 2002;4:171-183.

264. Frishman WH, Brosnan BD, Grossman M, Dasgupta D, Sun DK. Adverse dermatologic effects of cardiovascular drug therapy (Parts 1,2,3). *Cardiol Rev* 2002;10(4):230-246;10(5):285-300;10(6):337-348.

265. Frishman WH, Ismail A. The role of infection in atherosclerosis and coronary artery disease: a new therapeutic target. *Cardiol Rev* 2002;10:199-210.

266. Tabriziani H, Shieu A, Frishman WH, Brandt LJ. Drug therapies for mesenteric vascular disease. *Heart Dis* 2002;4:306-314.

267. Ragucci E, Zonszein J, Frishman WH. Pharmacotherapy of diabetes mellitus: implications for the prevention and treatment of cardiovascular disease. *Heart Dis* 2003;5:18-33.

268. Frishman WH. A day of remembrance: given on the September 11, 2002 memorial service at New York Medical College (editorial). *Heart Dis* 2003;5:1.

269. Stier CT Jr., Koenig S, Lee DY, Chawla M, Frishman WH. Aldosterone and aldosterone antagonism in cardiovascular disease: focus on eplerenone (INSPRA). *Heart Dis* 2003;5:102-118.

270. Weinberger J, Frishman WH, Terashita D. Drug therapy of neurovascular disease. *Cardiol Rev* 2003;11: 122-146.

271. Frishman WH. Beta-adrenergic blockers (Cardiology Patient Page). *Circulation* 2003;107;e117-119.

272. Frishman WH. Advances in positive inotropic therapy: Levosimendan (editorial). *Crit Care Med* 2003; 31:2408-2409.

273. Frishman WH, DelVecchio A, Sanal S, Ismail A. Cardiovascular manifestations of substance abuse. Part 1: Cocaine *Heart Dis* 2003;5:187-201. Part 2: Alcohol, amphetamines, heroin, cannabis, caffeine. *Heart Dis* 2003;5:253-271.

274. Frishman W, Arshad A, Bansal A. Cardiac manifestations in human immunodeficiency virus infection. In, Wormser G, eds. *AIDS and Other Manifestations of HIV Infections.* Amsterdam, Elsevier/Academic Press 2004:635-649.

275. Frishman WH, Aronow WS, Cheng-Lai A. Cardiovascular drug therapy in the elderly. In Aronow WS, Fleg JL, eds. *Cardiovascular Diseases in the Elderly Patient 3ʳᵈ Ed.* New York: Marcel Dekker 2004:95-130.

276. Aronow WS, Frishman WH. Angina in the elderly. In Aronow WS, Fleg JL, eds. *Cardiovascular Diseases in the Elderly Patient 3ʳᵈ Ed.* New York: Marcel Dekker 2004:273-295.

277. Frishman WH, Yesenski G, Iqbal M. Systemic hypertension in the elderly. In Aronow WS, Fleg JL, eds. *Cardiovascular Diseases in the Elderly Patient 3ʳᵈ Ed.* New York: Marcel Dekker 2004:131-151.

278. Gupta M, Vavasis C, Frishman WH. Heat shock proteins in cardiovascular disease: a new therapeutic target. *Cardiol Rev* 2004;12:26-30.

279. Nguyen Y, Naseer N, Frishman WH. Sauna as a therapeutic option for cardiovascular disease. *Cardiol Rev* 2004;12:321-324.

280. Frishman WH, Sinatra ST, Moizuddin M. The use of herbs for treating cardiovascular disease. *Sem Integr Med* 2004;2:23-35.

281. Wolff AI, Frishman WH. Animal-assisted therapy in cardiovascular disease. *Sem Integ Med* 2004;2: 131-134.

282. Park D, Huang T, Frishman WH. Phytoestrogens as cardioprotective agents. *Cardiol Rev* 2005;13:13-17.

283. Murphy S, Frishman WH. Protein kinase C in cardiac disease and as a potential therapeutic target. *Cardiol Rev* 2005;13:3-12.

284. Goldberg RF, Fass AE, Frishman WH. Transmyocardial revascularization: defining its role. *Cardiol Rev* 2005;13:52-55.

285. Varma R, Garrick R, McClung J, Frishman WH. Chronic renal dysfunction as an independent risk factor for the development of cardiovascular disease. *Cardiol Rev* 2005;13:98-107.

286. Taur Y, Frishman WH. The cardiac ryanodine receptor (RyR2) and its role in heart disease. *Cardiol Rev* 2005;13:142-46.

287. Frishman WH, Sonnenblick EH, Anversa P. Environmental factors in cardiac hypertrophy and failure. In Walsh RA, ed. *Molecular Mechanisms of Cardiac Hypertrophy and Failure.* London: Taylor & Francis 2005:341-365.

288. Kermani T, Frishman WH. Nonpharmacologic approaches for the treatment of hyperlipidemia. *Cardiol Rev* 2005;13:247-255.

289. Frishman WH, Schlocker SJ, Awad K, Tejani N. Pathophysiology and medical management of systemic hypertension in pregnancy. *Cardiol Rev* 2005;13:274-284.

290. Lai A, Frishman WH. Rho-kinase inhibition in the therapy of cardiovascular disease. *Cardiol Rev* 2005;13:285-292.

291. Hanjis C, Frishman WH, Lerner RG: Aspirin resistance: mechanisms and clinical implications. *Cardiol Rev* 2006;14:18-25.

292. Ro A, Frishman WH. Peripartum cardiomyopathy. *Cardiol Rev* 2006;14:35-42.

293. Kalala S, Krishna M, Shah R, Lebovics E, Frishman WH. Postmenopausal hormone replacement therapy and the risks of calculous gallbladder disease. *Clin Geriatr* 2006;4:25-29.

294. Frishman WH, Mitta W, Kupersmith A, Ky T. Nicotine and non-nicotine smoking cessation pharmacotherapies. *Cardiol Rev* 2006;14:57-73.

295. Nguyen T, Frishman WH, Nawarskas J, Lerner RG. Clopidogrel variability of response: possible mechanisms and clinical implications. *Cardiol Rev* 2006;14:136-142.

296. Bacani C, Frishman WH. Chymase: a new pharmacologic target in cardiovascular disease. *Cardiol Rev* 2006;14:187-193.

297. Casiero D, Frishman WH. Cardiovascular complications of eating disorders. *Cardiol Rev* 2006;14:227-31.

298. Palamara KL, Mogul HR, Peterson SJ, Frishman WH. Obesity. New perspectives and pharmacotherapies. *Cardiol Rev* 2006;14:238-258.

299. Sule SS, Frishman WH. Nebivolol. New therapy update. *Cardiol Rev* 2006;14:259-264.

300. Sahakian A, Frishman WH. Humor and the cardiovascular system. *Alt Therap Health & Med* 2007;13: 56-58.

301. Frishman WH. β-Blockers in hypertension. In Black H, Elliott W, eds. *Clinical Hypertension: A Companion to Braunwald's Heart Dis 1st Ed.* Philadelphia: Elsevier 2007:231-238.

302. Abrams J, Frishman WH, Freedman J. Pharmacologic options for treatment of ischemic disease. In Antman EM, ed. *Cardiovascular Therapeutics 3rd Ed.* Philadelphia: Elsevier 2007:77-120.

303. Gandelman G, Frishman WH, Wiese C, Green Gastwirth V, Aronow WS, Horowitz HW. Intravascular device infections: epidemiology, diagnosis and management. *Cardiol Rev* 2007;15:13-23.

304. Ravipati G, McClung JA, Aronow WS, Peterson SJ, Frishman WH. Type 5 phosphodiesterase inhibitors in the treatment of erectile dysfunction and cardiovascular disease. *Cardiol Rev* 2007;15;76-86.

305. Sica DA, Gehr TWB, Frishman WH. Use of diuretics in the treatment of heart failure in the elderly. *Clinics Geriatr Med* 2007;23: 07-121.

306. Petchetti L, Frishman WH, Petrillo R, Kolanuvada R. Nutriceuticals in cardiovascular disease: psyllium. *Cardiol Rev* 2007;15:116-122.

307. Frishman WH. Importance of medication adherence in cardiovascular disease and the value of once-daily treatment regimens. *Cardiol Rev* 2007;15:257-263.

308. Sepehrdad R, Frishman WH, Stier CT Jr., Sica DA. Direct inhibition of renin as a cardiovascular pharmacotherapy: focus on aliskiren. *Cardiol Rev* 2007;15:242-256.

309. Leri A, Kajstura J, Anversa P, Frishman WH. Myocardial regeneration and stem cell repair (monograph). *Current Probl Cardiol* 2008;33:85-154.

310. Frishman WH, Sica DA. Beta-adrenergic blockers. In Izzo JL Jr., Sica D, Black HR, eds. *Hypertension Primer 4th Edition: The Essentials of High Blood Pressure.* Philadelphia: Wolters Kluwer/Lippincott Williams & Wilkins 2008;446-450.

311. Frishman WH. A tribute to Edmund H. Sonnenblick 1932-2007 (editorial). *Cardiol Rev* 2008;16:1-3.

312. Frishman WH, Novak S, Brandt LJ, Spiegel A, Gutwein A, Kohi M, Rozenblit G, Hines G. Pharmacologic management of mesenteric ischemia. *Cardiol Rev* 2008;16:59-68.

313. Desai N, Sajjad J, Frishman WH. Urotensin II: a new pharmacologic target in the treatment of cardiovascular disease. *Cardiol Rev* 2008;16:142-153.

314. Mehrinfar R, Frishman WH. Flavanol-rich cocoa: a cardioprotective nutriceutical. *Cardiol Rev* 2008;16: 109-115.

315. Mamtani R, Frishman WH. Medical acupuncture: an evidence-guided approach. In Weintraub MI, Mamtani R, Micozzi MS, eds. *Complementary and Integrative Medicine in Pain Management.* New York: Springer Publishing Co. 2008:215-227.

316. Mamtani R, Frishman WH. Ayurveda & yoga. In Weintraub MI, Mamtani R, Micozzi MS, eds. *Complementary and Integrative Medicine in Pain Management.* New York: Springer Publishing Co. 2008:245-266.

317. Ahn A, Frishman WH, Gutwein A, Passeri J, Nelson M. Therapeutic angiogenesis: a new treatment approach for ischemic heart disease (Parts 1 & 2). *Cardiol Rev* 2008;16:163-171 and 219-229.

318. Frishman WH, Barkowski RS. Cholesteryl ester transfer protein inhibition for coronary heart disease prevention: real hope or despair? (commentary) *Am J Med* 2008;121:644-646.

319. Glasser SP, Frishman WH. The placebo and nocebo effect. In Glasser SP: *Essentials of Clinical Research.* Springer 2008:111-140.

320. Frishman WH, Aronow WS, Cheng-Lai A. Cardiovascular drug therapy in the elderly. In Aronow WS, Fleg JL, Rich MW, eds. *Cardiovascular Disease in the Elderly 4th Ed.* New York: Informa Healthcare 2008:99-135.

321. Frishman WH. Fifty years of beta-adrenergic blockade (1958-2008): A golden era in clinical medicine and molecular pharmacology (commentary). *Am J Med* 2008;121:933-934.

322. Frishman WH. β-Adrenergic blockers: A 50 year historical perspective. *Am J Therap* 2008;15:565-576.

323. Erickson B, Sperber K, Frishman WH. Toll-like receptors: new therapeutic targets for the treatment of atherosclerosis, acute coronary syndromes and myocardial failure. *Cardiol Rev* 2008;16:273-279.

324. Riley E, Dasari V, Frishman WH, Sperber K. Vaccines in development to prevent and treat atherosclerotic disease. *Cardiol Rev* 2008;16:288-300.

325. Koo MH, Nawarskas JJ, Frishman WH. Prasugrel: a new antiplatelet drug for the prevention and treatment of cardiovascular disease. *Cardiol Rev* 2008;16:314-318.

326. Srinivas G, Anversa P, Frishman WH. Cytokines and myocardial regeneration: a novel treatment option for acute myocardial infarction. *Cardiol Rev* 2008;17:1-9.

327. Pierre-Louis B, Kumar A, Frishman WH. Fabry disease: cardiac manifestations and therapeutic options. *Cardiol Rev* 2009;17:31-35.

328. Seiki S, Frishman WH. Pharmacologic inhibition of squalene synthase and other down-stream enzymes of the cholesterol synthesis pathway: a new therapeutic approach to treatment of hypercholesterolemia. *Cardiol Rev* 2009;17:70-76.

329. Frishman WH, Beravol P, Carosella C. Alternative and complementary medicine for preventing and treating cardiovascular disease. *Disease-a-Month* 2009;55:115-192.

330. Peterson SJ, Abraham NG, Frishman WH. Targeting heme oxygenase: therapeutic implications for diseases of the cardiovascular system. *Cardiol Rev* 2009;17:99-111.

331. Shah RH, Frishman WH. Adenosine A1 receptor antagonism: a new therapeutic approach for the treatment of decompensated heart failure. *Cardiol Rev* 2009;17:125-131.

332. Pierre-Louis B, Prasad A, Frishman WH. Sarcoidosis. Cardiac manifestations and therapeutic options. *Cardiol Rev* 2009;17:153-158.

333. Zubko R, Frishman WH. Stem cell therapy for the kidney? *Am J Therap* 2009;6:247-256.

334. Khakpour H, Frishman WH. Lipoprotein-associated phospholipase A$_2$. An independent predictor of cardiovascular risk and a novel target for immunomodulation therapy. *Cardiol Rev* 2009;17:222-229.

335. Quazi R, Palaniswamy C, Frishman WH. The emerging role of apelin in cardiovascular disease and health. *Cardiol Rev* 2009;17:283-286.

336. Frishman WH. The patient-physician-industry-government partnership. A societal good (commentary). *Am J Med* 2009;122:886-887.

337. Desai HV, Aronow WS, Peterson SJ, Frishman WH. Cardiac amyloidosis: new approaches to diagnosis and management. *Cardiol Rev* 2010;18:1-11.

338. Sherman CB, Peterson SJ, Frishman WH. Apolipoprotein A-1 mimetic peptides: a potential new therapy for the prevention of atherosclerosis. *Cardiol Rev* 2010;18:141-147.

339. Frishman WH. 150 years of excellence (1860-2010). *Fleur-o-scope* (New York Medical College Year Book) 2010:52-59.

340. Cheng JWM, Frishman WH, Aronow WS. Updates on cytochrome P450 mediated cardiovascular drug interactions. *Disease a Month* 2010;56:163-179.

341. Somberg J, Cherubini A, Lowenthal DT, Paran E, Mecocci P, Williams LS, Senin U, Hahr AJ, Molitch ME, Cheng JWM, Frishman WH, Aronow WS. Topics in clinical pharmacology: cardiovascular and diabetes mellitus. *Disease a Month* 2010;56:101-180.

342. Schwarcz MD, Frishman WH. Testosterone and cardiovascular disease. *Cardiol Rev* 2010;18:251-257.

343. Parikh N, Frishman WH. Liver X receptors: a potential therapeutic target for modulating the atherosclerotic process. *Cardiol Rev* 2010;18:269-274.

344. Grossman J, Frishman WH. Relaxin: a new approach for the treatment of acute congestive heart failure. *Cardiol Rev* 2010;18:305-312.

345. Hingorany S, Frishman WH. Soluble guanylate cyclase activation with cinaciguat. A new approach to the treatment of decompensated heart failure. *Cardiol Rev* 2011;19:23-29.

346. Tian D, Frishman WH. Vernakalant: a new drug to treat patients with acute onset atrial fibrillation. *Cardiol Rev* 2011;19:41-44.

347. Sharma M, Frishman WH, Gandhi K. RESPeRATE: Non-pharmacological treatment of hypertension. *Cardiol Rev* 2011;19:47-51.

348. Ng MM, Sica DA, Frishman WH. Rheos: an implantable carotid sinus stimulation device for the non-pharmacologic treatment of resistant hypertension. *Cardiol Rev* 2011;19:52-57.

349. Azmoon S, Demarest C, Pucillo AL, Hjemdahl-Monsen C, Kay R, Ahmadi N, Aronow WS, Frishman WH. Neurologic and cardiac benefits of therapeutic hypothermia. *Cardiol Rev* 2011;19:108-114.

350. Weiss IA, Bloomgarden N, Frishman WH. Subclinical hypothyroidism and cardiovascular risk: recommendation for treatment. *Cardiol Rev* 2011;19:291-299.

351. Kelkar A, Kuo A, Frishman WH. Allopurinol as a cardiovascular drug. *Cardiol Rev* 2011;19:265-271.

352. Liss Y, Frishman WH. Vitamin D: a cardioprotective agent? *Cardiol Rev* 2012;20:38-44.

353. Beridze N, Frishman WH. Vascular Ehlers-Danlos syndrome: pathophysiology, diagnosis and prevention and treatment of its complications. *Cardiol Rev* 2012;20:4-7.

354. Alpert J, Frishman WH. A bridge too far (editorial). *Am J Med* 2012;125:1-2.

355. Capone C, Buyon JP, Friedman DM, Frishman WH. Cardiac manifestations of neonatal lupus: a review of autoantibody associated congenital heart block and its impact in an adult population. *Cardiol Rev* 2012;20:72-76.

356. Ricotta D, Frishman WH. Mipomersen: a safe and effective antisense therapy adjunct to statins in patients with hypercholesterolemia. *Cardiol Rev* 2012;20:90-95.

357. Hauck C, Frishman WH. Systemic hypertension: the roles of salt, vascular Na+/K+ ATPase and the endogenous glycosides, ouabain and marinobufagenin. *Cardiol Rev* 2012;20:130-138.

358. Frishman WH, Pallerla K. Cardiovascular pharmacologic therapies under investigation: 2012. *Cardiol Rev* 2012;20:102-110.

359. Zheng E, Frishman WH. The closing of St. Vincent's Hospital in New York City: what happened to the House Staff Orphans? (commentary). *Am J Med* 2012;125: e5-6.

360. Filopei J, Frishman W. Radiation-induced heart disease. *Cardiol Rev* 2012;20:184-188.

361. Palaniswamy C, Frishman WH, Aronow WS. Carcinoid heart disease. *Cardiol Rev* 20: 167-176, 2012

362. Kim AJ, Frishman WH. Laughter-induced syncope. *Cardiol Rev* 2012;20:194-196.

363. Lamba G, Frishman WH. Cardiac and pericardial tumors. *Cardiol Rev* 2012;20:237-252.

364. Burke GM, Sica DA, Frishman WH. Renal sympathetic denervation for the treatment of systemic hypertension. *Cardiol Rev* 2012;20:274-278.

365. Frishman WH. Forty years in academic cardiology (commentary). *Cardiol Rev* 2012;20:265-267.

366. Frishman WH, Aronow WS. Pharmacology of anti-arrhythmic drugs in the elderly. In Rich MW, Shen W-K, eds. *Cardiac Rhythm Disorders in Older Adults. Clin Geriatr Med* 2012;28: 575-615.

367. Frishman WH, Elkayam U, Aronow WS. Cardiovascular drugs in pregnancy. *Cardiol Clin* 2012;30:463-491.

368. Frishman WH, Nabors C, Peterson SJ. Faculty supervision of the house staff handoff process: the time has come (commentary). *Am J Med* 2013;126:e1-2.

369. Frishman WH, Zimmerman FH, Lerner RG. Vascular and heart diseases in the incumbent presidents and vice presidents of the United States of America: A medical-historical perspective. *Cardiol Rev* 2013;21: 1-8.

370. Dunbar A, Gotsis W, Frishman W. Second-hand tobacco smoke and cardiovascular disease risk: an epidemiological review. *Cardiol Rev* 2013;21:94-100.

371. Papolos A, Frishman W. SERCA2a, a potential gene therapy target for heart failure. *Cardiol Rev* 2013;21:151-154.

372. Garg V, Frishman WH. A new approach to inotropic therapy in the treatment of heart failure. Cardiac myosin activators. *Cardiol Rev* 2013;21:155-159.

373. Garg V, Frishman WH. A new approach to inotropic therapy in the treatment of heart failure. Urocortin. *Cardiol Rev* 2013;21:160-165.

374. Palaniswamy C, Mishkin A, Aronow WS, Kalra A, Frishman WH. Remote patient monitoring in chronic heart failure. *Cardiol Rev* 2013;21:141-150.

375. Frishman WH. A thirty-five year odyssey of an AOA chapter councilor. *Pharos* 2013;76:4-6.

376. Frishman WH, Alpert J. Reducing hospital readmissions for cardiovascular disease: is it feasible? Commentary. *Am J Med* 2013;126:753-754.

377. Palmeiro C, Davila MI, Bhat M, Frishman WH, Weiss IA. Subclinical hyperthyroidism and cardiovascular risk: recommendations for treatment. *Cardiol Rev* 2013;21:300-308.

378. Espana-Schmidt C, Ong EC, Frishman W, Bergasa NV, Chaudhari S. Medical residency training and hospital care during and after a natural disaster: Hurricane Sandy and its effects. *Am J Med* 2013;126: 944-45.

379. Mund RA, Frishman WH. Brown adipose tissue thermogenesis: β$_3$-adrenoreceptors , a potential target for the treatment of obesity in humans. *Cardiol Rev* 2013;21:265-269.

380. Peterson SJ, Nabors C, Frishman WH. Milestones: direct observation may be the key to accelerated training (commentary). *Am J Med* 2013;126:1031-1032.

381. Wang C, Lerner RG, Frishman WH. Statins and venous thromboembolic disease prophylaxis. *Cardiol Rev* 2013;21:295-299.

382. Bosch N, Frishman WH. Newer therapeutic strategies to alter HDL level and function. *Cardiol Rev* 2014;22: 17-24.

383. Koulova A, Frishman WH. Air pollution exposure as a risk factor for cardiovascular disease morbidity and mortality. *Cardiol Rev* 2014;22: 30-36.

384. Thaker AM, Frishman WH. Sortilin: the mechanistic link between genes, cholesterol and coronary artery disease. Cardiol Rev 2014;22:91-96.

385. Frishman WH, Glicklich D. The role of non-pharmacologic device interventions in the management of drug-resistant hypertension. *Curr Atherosclerosis Reports* 2014;16:405.

386. Weinreich M, Frishman WH. Antihyperlipidemia therapies targeting PCSK9. Cardiol Rev 2014;22:140-146.

387. Gulati V, Harikrishnan P, Palaniswamy C, Aronow SA, Jain D, Frishman WH. Cardiac involvement in hemochromatosis. *Cardiol Rev* 2014;22:56-68.

388. Hartman J, Frishman WH. Inflammation and atherosclerosis: a review of the role of interleukin-6 in the development of atherosclerosis and the potential for targeted therapy. Cardiol Rev 2014;22:147-151.

389. Kolte D, Vijayaraghavan K, Khera S, Sica DA, Frishman WH. Role of magnesium in cardiovascular disease. *Cardiol Rev* 2014;22:182-192.

390. McCarty S, Frishman WH. Interleukin 1β: an anti-inflammatory target against atherosclerotic disease. *Cardiol Rev* 2014;22:176-181.

391. Coburn E, Frishman W. A comprehensive review of the prognostic value of galectin-3 in heart failure. *Cardiol Rev* 2014;22:171-175.

392. Robinson LB, Frishman WH. Anacetrapib: a potential new therapy for dyslipidemia. *Cardiol Rev* 2014;22:253-261.

393. Frishman WH. The placebo and nocebo effect. In Glasser SP, ed. *Essentials of Clinical Research 2nd Ed.* The Netherlands: Springer 2014:145-176.

394. Sharma M, Pinnamaneni S, Aronow WS, Jozwik B, Frishman WH. Existing drug under investigation for pulmonary arterial hypertension. *Cardiol Rev* 2014;22:297-305.

395. Kosmas CE, Frishman WH. New and emerging LDL-cholesterol lowering drugs. *Am J Therap* 2015; 22:234-241.

396. Gulati V, Harikrishnan P, Palaniswamy C, Aronow WS, Jain D, Frishman WH. Cardiac involvement in hemochromatosis. *Cardiol Rev.* 2014;22:56-68.

397. Doshi JV, Agrawal S, Garg J, Paudel R, Palaniswamy C, Doshi TV, Gotsis W, Frishman WH. Percutaneous mitral heart valve repair: MitraCiip. *Cardiol Rev* 2014;22:289-296.

398. Segraves J, Frishman WH. Highly sensitive cardiac troponin assays: a comprehensive review. *Cardiol Rev* 2015;23:282-289.

399. Frishman WH. Pharmacists in primary care (editorial). *Am J Med* 2015;128:443-444.

400. Frishman WH. Is the stethoscope becoming an outdated diagnostic tool? *Am J Med* 2015;127:668-669.

401. Glicklich D, Frishman WH. Drug therapy of apparent treatment-resistant hypertension: focus on mineralocorticoid receptor antagonists. *Drugs* 2015;75:473-485.

402. Pashun RA, Frishman WH. Therapeutic role of innovative anti-inflammatory medications in the prevention of acute coronary syndrome. *Cardiol Rev* 2015;23:252-260.

403. Frishman WH. Reflections on the Physicians Payment Sunshine Act. *Am J Med* 2016;129:3-4.

Interviews

Roberts W. William Howard Frishman, M.D., *Am J Cardiol* 1998:81:1323-1338.

Editorships of Medical Journals

<u>Founding Co-Editor</u>: *Journal of Clinical Hypertension,* Elsevier (1985-1987) became the *American Journal of Hypertension*

<u>Founding Editor in Chief</u>: *Heart Disease,* Lippincott: Williams and Wilkins, (1999-2003)

<u>Co-Editor in Chief</u>: *Cardiology in Review,* Wolters Kluwer, (an affiliated journal of the American Heart Assoc) (2004-)

<u>Editor (Supplements)</u>: *American Journal of Medicine,* Elsevier, (official journal of the Alliance for Academic Internal Medicine) (2005-)

MEDICAL INTELLIGENCE

DRUG THERAPY

JAN KOCH-WESER, M.D., *Editor*

Dobutamine: A New Synthetic Cardioactive Sympathetic Amine

EDMUND H. SONNENBLICK, M.D.,
WILLIAM H. FRISHMAN, M.D.,
AND THIERRY H. LEJEMTEL, M.D.

DOBUTAMINE* is a new, synthetic, intravenously administered catecholamine that acts directly to increase myocardial contractility without inducing marked tachycardia or greatly changing peripheral arterial resistance.[1] These features make it useful for treating acute cardiac failure characterized by low cardiac output and elevated diastolic filling pressures, and in July, 1978, it was approved for clinical use in this country.

Norepinephrine is the endogenous catecholamine that is synthesized and stored in granules in adrenergic nerve endings in the myocardium. When sympathetic nerves to the heart are activated, norepinephrine is released from its stores and stimulates specific sites on the myocardial cell surface, termed β_1-adrenergic receptors. Stimulation of these receptors in-

creases the rate of discharge of the sinoatrial node, thereby augmenting heart rate, enhances atrioventricular conduction and increases the force and speed of contraction of atrial and ventricular myocardium. Most released norepinephrine is subsequently taken up by the same adrenergic nerve endings and stored for renewed release. Smaller amounts are metabolized. Drugs created by changes in the structure of norepinephrine also activate cardiac β-adrenergic receptors. Some of these synthetic sympathomimetic amines also act by releasing endogenous norepinephrine.[2]

Depending on their structure (Fig. 1), catecholamines activate receptors other than cardiac β_1-adrenergic receptors (Table 1). β_2-adrenergic receptors mediate vasodilatation in the peripheral vasculature and bronchodilatation in the lungs. α-adrenergic receptors in peripheral vessels mediate arterial vasoconstriction in opposition to the effects of the β_2-adrenergic receptors. The net action of any of the amines shown in Figure 1 depends on their dominant receptor activity (Table 2).

Appropriate treatment of heart failure depends on the exact hemodynamic disturbances associated with the specific clinical problem. In general, chronic congestive heart failure is present when cardiac output is insufficient to meet the metabolic demands of the body because of inadequate myocardial contractility, loss of myocardial tissue, excessive work load or a combination of these factors. The hemodynamic picture is commonly characterized by an elevated ventricular filling pressure and a decrease in stroke volume. Some increase in heart rate may help to compensate for a decreased stroke volume, and peripheral resistance rises to maintain arterial pressure. When the process occurs slowly, digitalis glycosides have long been used as an inotropic agent to augment ventricular contractility, and diuretics are administered to reduce excess fluid accumulation and thus to lower filling pressures (preload) in the heart. More recently, vasodilators have also been employed to decrease preload by reducing venous return and to decrease

From the Division of Cardiology, Department of Medicine, Albert Einstein College of Medicine, 1300 Morris Park Ave., Bronx, NY 10461, where reprint requests should be addressed to Dr. Sonnenblick.

Supported in part by a training grant (HL 07071-02) from the U.S. Public Health Service.

*Dobutamine hydrochloride (Dobutrex, Lilly).

18   THE NEW ENGLAND JOURNAL OF MEDICINE   Jan. 4, 1979

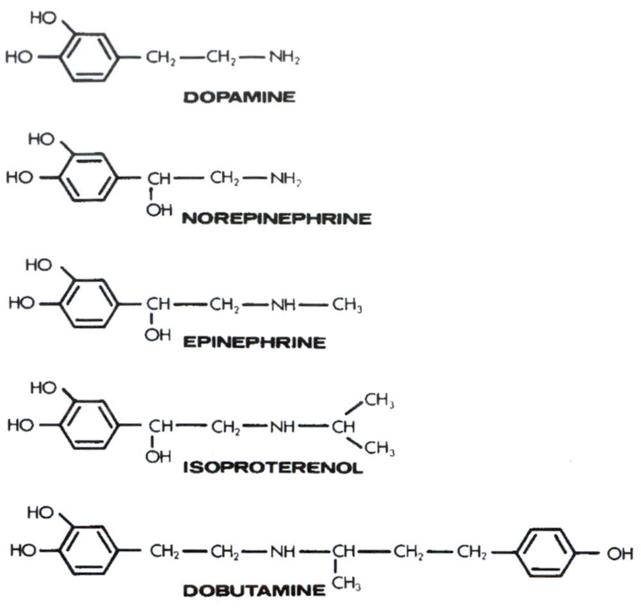

Figure 1.

cardiac work (afterload) by lowering peripheral resistance.

Acute left ventricular failure is commonly seen after a large myocardial infarction or after cardiopulmonary bypass, when myocardial function may be severely depressed. When acute pump failure is so severe that an adequate cardiac output cannot be maintained, hypotension may ensue despite an elevated peripheral resistance, presenting the picture of cardiogenic shock. Catecholamines or other sympathomimetic amines may be required in this setting.

Sympathomimetic amines such as norepinephrine, epinephrine and isoproterenol augment myocardial contractility by stimulating β_1-adrenergic receptor sites in the myocardium directly or, as metaraminol (Aramine) does, by releasing endogenous norepinephrine as well.[2] However, their clinical application has generally been limited by their positive chronotropic effects, which cause tachycardia and by their action either to increase or to decrease peripheral resistance and thus to change arterial pressure. For example, isoproterenol markedly increases myocardial contractility and cardiac output but also causes tachycardia and may produce ventricular arrhythmias.[3] Furthermore, the stimulation of β_2-adrenergic receptors in the peripheral arterial system can decrease peripheral resistance and thus in arterial pressure, which may not be desirable when myocardial ischemia is a potential problem. In contrast, norepinephrine stimulates α-adrenergic receptors in the periphery and thus causes arterial pressure to rise substantially.[4] Although this effect may be beneficial in the presence of severe hypotension, the increase in peripheral resistance can produce undesirable arterial hypertension when starting from adequate pressures. Peripheral vasoconstriction can also vitiate the rise in cardiac output that an increase in myocardial contractility would otherwise produce, and thus reduce tissue perfusion.

Dopamine, a precursor in the endogenous synthesis of norepinephrine, stimulates the myocardium directly and also indirectly through release of norepinephrine stores. It has demonstrated less prominent chronotropic effects than isoproterenol and less vasoconstrictive effects than norepinephrine. It has the

Table 2. Adrenergic-Receptor Activity of Sympathomimetic Amines.

	α	β_1	β_2
	PERIPHERAL	CARDIAC	PERIPHERAL
Norepinephrine	++++	++++	0
Epinephrine	++++	++++	++
Dopamine*	++++	++++	++
Isoproterenol	0	++++	++++
Dobutamine	+	++++	++
Methoxamine	++++	0	0

*Causes renal & mesenteric dilatation by stimulating dopaminergic receptors.

unique property of stimulating vasodilatory dopaminergic receptors in the kidney. In large doses dopamine exerts vasoconstrictive effects that may not be desirable in the absence of hypotension. Accordingly, the effect of high doses of dopamine on cardiac-output response is variable.[5]

Dobutamine is the result of systematic modification of the chemical structure of isoproterenol (Fig. 1). Tuttle and Mills[1] demonstrated that dobutamine produces positive inotropic effects in the intact dog, with relatively little change in peripheral vascular resistance, heart rate, or rhythm.

PHARMACOLOGIC ACTIONS OF DOBUTAMINE

Dobutamine acts directly on β_1-adrenergic receptors in the myocardium. Unlike dopamine, it does not also stimulate the heart indirectly by releasing norepinephrine from nerve endings.[1] In isolated myocardial preparations, dobutamine produces positive inotropic and chronotropic effects similar to those observed with isoproterenol.[6,7] In laboratory animals, dobutamine (2.5 to 15 μg per kilogram per minute) causes dose-related increments in cardiac contractil-

Table 1. Some Receptor Actions of Catecholamines.

ADRENERGIC RECEPTOR	SITE	ACTION
β_1	Myocardium	Increase atrial & ventricular contractility
	Sinoatrial node	Increase heart rate
	Atrioventricular conduction	Enhance conduction
β_2	Arterioles	Vasodilatation
	Lungs	Bronchodilatation
α	Peripheral arterioles	Vasoconstriction

ity.[1,8,9] Cardiac output rises, and ventricular diastolic pressure tends to fall. Total peripheral arterial resistance is slightly reduced, and arterial pressure is not greatly changed, tending to increase slightly with lower doses and decreasing slightly with higher doses. Only minor increases in heart rate occur as long as the dose is less than 20 μg per kilogram per minute. After administration of β-adrenergic blocking agents, dobutamine decreases cardiac output and increases total peripheral resistance, demonstrating the residual action of dobutamine on α-adrenergic receptors that is uncovered when the more dominant β_2-adrenergic action is inhibited.

In the intact animal, dobutamine exerts a more prominent inotropic than chronotropic action as compared to isoproterenol.[1] The reason for this difference in response has not been explained, but dobutamine appears to exert a relatively less pronounced effect on the sinoatrial node than on ventricular contractile tissue.[10] Reflex tachycardia resulting from isoproterenol's hypotensive action only partially explains this difference, since neither vagotomy nor sympatholytic drugs affect the result.[1,7]

Dobutamine increases sinus-node automaticity and enhances atrioventricular nodal and intraventricular conduction.[11] However, when given in amounts having similar inotropic effects, dobutamine, like dopamine, increases the sinus-node rate to a lesser extent than isoproterenol, while enhancing atrioventricular and intraventricular conduction to a similar extent.[1,10]

Injection of dobutamine into the femoral arterial bed causes slight vasoconstriction at low doses and a biphasic action of initial vasoconstriction and subsequent vasodilatation at higher doses.[12] Phenoxybenzamine, which blocks α-adrenergic receptors, inhibits the vasoconstrictor component, and propranolol, which blocks adrenergic β_1 and β_2 receptors, prevents the vasodilator component. Dobutamine is less potent than norepinephrine as a peripheral vasoconstrictor[12] and does not act on the specific dopamine receptors in the kidney that produce renal vasodilatation.[13]

Dobutamine, like dopamine, requires continuous intravenous administration. Its half-life in the plasma of man is two minutes. The drug is eliminated in the body by biotransformation in the liver to inactive glucuronide conjugates and 3-0-methyldobutamine. Most of these metabolites are excreted in the urine, and a small percentage in the feces. Biliary excretion with subsequent reabsorption may occur, but has not yet been demonstrated in man.[14]

In summary, dobutamine acts primarily on adrenergic β_1 receptors, whereas β_2 and α receptors are only stimulated to a slight degree (Table 2). With doses producing similar increments in cardiac contractile force, dobutamine exerts a much weaker β_2-adrenergic action than isoproterenol and a much weaker α-adrenergic action than norepinephrine. Thus, at moderate dose levels, augmentation of myocardial contractility is the most prominent action of dobutamine without major changes in arterial pres-sure or heart rate. At very high doses, tachycardia and a lowering of peripheral resistance may become evident, to produce actions resembling those of isoproterenol.

USE IN CONGESTIVE HEART FAILURE

Dobutamine has been shown to cause dose-related increases of cardiac output in patients with varying degrees of heart failure.[15-18] Intravenous infusions at rates ranging from approximately 2.5 to 15.0 μg per kilogram per minute induced a progressive increase in cardiac output. Pulmonary wedge pressure decreased, reflecting a fall in diastolic filling pressure in the left ventricle. At lower doses, the increase in output occurred with little or no change in mean arterial pressure or heart rate. The more severe the state of failure, the greater the improvement observed.[16] However, at higher dose levels substantial increments in heart rate also occurred.

When dobutamine was administered for periods as long as 72 hours to patients with left ventricular failure, at rates ranging from 2.5 to 15.0 μg per kilogram per minute, a sustained improvement in cardiac output occurred accompanied by a reduction in mean pulmonary-capillary wedge pressure.[18] Urine output and sodium excretion increased during the period of infusion. Of note was the fact that cardiac and renal function improved without the undesirable side effects of tachycardia, premature ventricular contractions, increased pulmonary or systemic vascular resistance, or tachyphylaxis. The improvement in renal function is probably secondary to improved cardiac output because studies in animals fail to show any noteworthy effect on renal vascular receptors.

COMPARISON WITH OTHER DRUGS

The effects of infusions of dobutamine (2.5, 5 and 10 μg per minute) have been compared with those of isoproterenol (0.02, 0.04 and 0.08 μg per minute) in patients with aortic ball-valve prostheses. Both drugs caused comparable increments in the rate of left ventricular ejection, indicating an increase in myocardial contractility. However, isoproterenol caused markedly greater increases in heart rate than dobutamine.[19] In another study of patients with chronic low-output cardiac failure, isoproterenol and dobutamine produced similar increments in cardiac output. Changes in mean arterial pressure, mean pulmonary-artery pressure, left ventricular filling pressure and systemic resistance were not appreciably different. Again, the heart rate was increased more by isoproterenol than by dobutamine.[20]

In yet another study of patients with low-output cardiac failure the dosages of dobutamine and dopamine were adjusted to produce similar increments in cardiac output.[21] Heart rate increased similarly with both drugs, but, although dobutamine decreased mean arterial and pulmonary-capillary wedge pressures, dopamine did not change arterial pressure and increased wedge pressure.

Similar findings were demonstrated in a crossover study of dopamine and dobutamine (2.5 to 10 μg per kilogram per minute) in patients with congestive heart failure.[22] Dobutamine produced a progressive rise in cardiac output by increasing stroke volume, while simultaneously decreasing both systemic and pulmonary vascular resistances and pulmonary-capillary wedge pressure. There was no increment in heart rate or premature ventricular contractions at this dose level. As arterial pressure rose with increased doses of dopamine, pulmonary wedge pressure also rose, and the incidence of premature ventricular contractions per minute increased. At a dose greater than 6 μg per kilogram per minute, dopamine augmented heart rate. During a 24-hour infusion of each drug, only dobutamine produced a sustained increase of stroke volume, cardiac output, urine flow, urine sodium concentration, creatinine clearance and peripheral blood flow. Renal and hepatic blood flow was not significantly altered by either drug.

In patients who had undergone cardiopulmonary bypass, dobutamine was a potent inotropic drug.[23,24] In general, tachycardia was less prominent, and fewer arrhythmias were observed than with the use of isoproterenol. This effect may prove an advantage of dobutamine when it is used during emergence from cardiopulmonary bypass, in which augmentation of cardiac contractility may be necessary for adequate pump function.

Recently, sodium nitroprusside has been used to augment left ventricular function by reducing peripheral arterial resistance (afterload reduction).[25,26] In heart failure, dobutamine (10 μg per kilogram per minute) and nitroprusside produced similar increments in cardiac output.[27,28] However, as compared to nitroprusside, dobutamine caused a higher arterial pressure and heart rate and less reduction in pulmonary-capillary wedge pressure. When the two drugs were infused together, the combination resulted in a higher cardiac output and lower pulmonary vascular resistance than was observed with either drug alone.[27] The ability of dobutamine to increase contractility and of vasodilators to reduce peripheral resistance are additive in improving ventricular performance. With both types of drugs the salutary effects are greatest when failure is present.[26]

APPLICATION IN MYOCARDIAL INFARCTION WITH PUMP FAILURE

Nearly all nutritive coronary blood flow occurs during diastole. In the presence of obstructed coronary arteries, coronary blood flow is determined primarily by the pressure gradient between the diastolic aortic pressure and the filling pressure in the left ventricle, and the time in diastole at which flow can occur. Tachycardia reduces this diastolic time. Hypotension or an increase in left ventricular diastolic pressure decreases the gradient for flow. These factors will reduce coronary blood flow through a narrowed large coronary artery or from collateral vessels, and myocardial ischemia may be produced.[29,30] Both initial development of ischemia and the extent of subsequent ultimate myocardial infarction depend on a balance between oxygen demands and coronary blood supply.[31] To the degree that an inotropic agent like dobutamine can improve very depressed pump function without worsening the degree and extent of myocardial ischemia, it should be useful in the setting of myocardial infarction.

In one study of anesthetized dogs with experimental acute myocardial ischemia but no failure (i.e., normal left ventricular diastolic pressures), dobutamine increased heart rate and enhanced myocardial contractility. Regional myocardial blood flow increased to all areas of the heart although electrophysiologic evidence of ischemia persisted.[32] The mean systemic pressure and left ventricular end-diastolic pressure did not change significantly. In another group of conscious dogs with acute myocardial infarction, the same dose of dobutamine increased myocardial blood flow to all areas of the heart without causing noteworthy changes in mean systemic arterial pressure, left ventricular end-diastolic pressure and heart rate. In the instrumented dog with severe global ischemia, neither isoproterenol nor dobutamine improved myocardial contractility. In contrast, the increased perfusion pressure induced by norepinephrine increased myocardial blood flow while augmenting contractility.[33]

Studies such as these may be interpreted as follows. Dobutamine, like other catecholamines,[34] increases myocardial oxygen consumption (MV_{O_2}) by augmenting contractility. Other actions that augment MV_{O_2}, such as increased heart rate or systolic pressure (ventricular-wall tension), occur to a much lesser degree. In the failing heart, in which left ventricular diastolic pressure is high, dobutamine increases contractility, reduces left ventricular filling pressure and thus augments the gradient for diastolic coronary blood flow. When a coronary vessel is obstructed, this improved gradient will also augment collateral blood flow into an ischemic area. The overall effect of potentially increasing coronary collateral blood flow due to increased perfusion gradient while reducing MV_{O_2} by making the heart smaller will be to ameliorate ischemia.[30,35,36] The decrease in heart size also reduces wall tension for any systolic pressure that also tends to reduce oxygen needs. If tachycardia or hypotension occurs, as is seen after the use of isoproterenol, ischemia will be worsened. By raising arterial diastolic pressure, norepinephrine might also be beneficial. On balance, the net effect on ischemia of a catecholamine administered to increase contractility and ventricular performance will depend on its ability to alter the balance between oxygen requirements and the determinants of coronary flow.[30] Because dobutamine tends not to produce tachycardia, and preserves diastolic aortic pressure while decreasing diastolic ventricular pressure, it will tend to improve coronary blood flow. At the same time the reduction in heart size should compensate for the effect of increased contractility to augment oxygen needs.[37] When dobutamine is used in the absence of heart failure, the increase in contractility that increases oxygen requirements is not offset by a large reduction in filling pressure that would have reduced oxygen requirements. Since coronary obstruction may limit a rise in coronary flow, ischemia may result or be worsened if it is present. This situation is especially noticeable when isoproterenol is given in the presence of a non-failing ischemic heart since hypotension and tachycardia may substantially reduce coronary flow at the same time that oxygen needs are increased. Because of these considerations, studies in animals are often difficult to interpret since experimental ischemia is generally not accompanied by heart failure and the relative detrimental effects of tachycardia or hypotension are not usually considered. Myocardial ischemia and infarction in man are subject to the same considerations.

The ability of dobutamine to increase cardiac output in failure, without increasing oxygen needs or reducing coronary flow through tachycardia, has recommended its use in "pump failure" associated with an acute myocardial infarction.[30] However, data on this subject are very limited. In a recent investigation of patients with acute myocardial infarction,[38] dobutamine was administered at rates ranging from 1 to 40 μg per kilogram per minute for 24 hours. To evaluate the effects of dobutamine on cardiac performance and myocardial injury, the treated group was compared to control patients matched for anticipated infarct size and to other control patients matched for early ventricular arrhythmias. Dobutamine significantly increased cardiac output and decreased pulmonary-capillary wedge pressure without significantly altering heart rate or systemic blood pressure. The extent of myocardial infarction in relation to what was predicted, the frequency of reinfarctions and extension of infarction were similar in control and treated patients. These investigators concluded that dobutamine in doses sufficient to augment ventricular performance after myocardial infarction did not exacerbate myocardial injury or the frequency of ventricular dysrhythmias. If ventricular failure had been present in all cases, reductions in ischemia might have resulted, as discussed above. Thus, dobutamine should be useful in acute infarction when "pump failure" characterized by low cardiac outputs and elevated ventricular filling pressures is present.

When mild hypotension is present, dobutamine may increase the arterial pressure by augmenting cardiac output. However, in cardiogenic shock characterized by severe hypotension and left ventricular failure, an increase in peripheral resistance may also be required to increase arterial pressure to adequate levels. Measurements of arterial and pulmonary wedge pressure should be obtained, and adequate volume expanders administered to correct relative hypovolemia. If hypotension still persists, either dopamine in high doses or norepinephrine (Levophed) may be required, rather than dobutamine. It should be recalled that high doses of dopamine resemble norepinephrine in its vasoconstrictive action. Indeed, when moderate to high doses of dopamine have been required to sustain cardiac contractility, nitroprusside has been used simultaneously to offset excessive peripheral vasoconstriction, which may raise the arterial pressure beyond required levels, creating an added load for an already burdened heart. In this latter circumstance, dobutamine may substitute for the drug combination of dopamine and nitroprusside. The drug is approved for intravenous use, the usual dose being 2.5 to 10 μg per kilogram per minute. Dosages as high as 40 μg per kilogram per minute have been used.

ADVERSE EFFECTS

The most serious adverse effect of all the sympathomimetic amines is the precipitation of arrhythmias. The electrophysiologic properties of dobutamine are similar to those of isoproterenol, and ventricular arrhythmias have followed the use of both drugs. However, it is claimed that dobutamine causes a lower incidence of arrhythmias as compared with isoproterenol[24] and dopamine.[22] If rapid ventricular rates occur in the presence of obstructive coronary-artery disease, ischemia can be induced or worsened, as noted above.

Dobutamine may cause a marked increase in heart rate or systolic blood pressure. Approximately 10 per cent of patients in clinical studies have had rate increases of 30 beats per minute or more, and about 7.5 per cent have had an increase in systolic blood pressure of 50 mm Hg or higher. Reduction of dosage usually reverses these effects promptly. Because dobutamine facilitates atrioventricular conduction, patients with atrial fibrillation may be at risk of development of a rapid ventricular response.

Other side effects reported in 1 to 3 per cent of patients include nausea, headache, anginal pain, palpitation and shortness of breath.

No abnormal laboratory values have been attributable to dobutamine. Infusions of up to 72 hours have revealed no adverse effects other than those seen with shorter infusions.

CONCLUSIONS

Dobutamine, a synthetic derivative of isoproterenol, directly increases myocardial contractility with less peripheral arterial effects or tachycardia than is seen with other sympathomimetic agents at dose levels causing similar increases in contractility. Administered intravenously, it should be useful for the treatment of relatively acute heart failure uncomplicated by severe hypotension.

22   THE NEW ENGLAND JOURNAL OF MEDICINE   Jan. 4, 1979

REFERENCES

1. Tuttle RR, Mills J: Dobutamine: development of a new catecholamine to selectively increase cardiac contractility. Circ Res 36:185-196, 1975
2. Harrison DC, Chidsey CA, Braunwald E: Studies on the mechanism of action of metaraminol (Aramine). Ann Intern Med 59:297-305, 1963
3. Gunnar RM, Loeb HS, Pietras RJ, et al: Ineffectiveness of isoproterenol in shock due to acute myocardial infarction. JAMA 202:1124-1128, 1967
4. Vatner SF, Higgins CB, Braunwald E: Effects of norepinephrrine on coronary circulation and left ventricular dynamics in the conscious dog. Circ Res 34:812-823, 1974
5. Higgins CB, Millard RW, Braunwald E: Effects and mechanisms of action of dopamine on regional hemodynamics in the conscious dog. Am J Physiol 225:432-443, 1973
6. Bodem R, Skelton CL, Sonnenblick EH: Inotropic and chronotropic effects of dobutamine on isolated cardiac muscle. Eur J Cardiol 2:181-189, 1974
7. Lumley P, Broadley KJ, Levy GP: Analysis of the inotropic: chronotropic selectivity of dobutamine and dopamine in anaesthetised dogs and guinea-pig isolated atria. Cardiovasc Res 11:17-25, 1977
8. Robie NW, Goldberg LI: Comparative systemic and regional hemodynamic effects of dopamine and dobutamine. Am Heart J 90:340-345, 1975
9. Vatner SF, McRitchie RJ, Braunwald E: Effects of dobutamine on left ventricular performance, coronary dynamics, and distribution of cardiac output in conscious dogs. J Clin Invest 53:1265-1273, 1974
10. Tuttle RR, Hillman CC, Toomey RE: Differential β adrenergic sensitivity of atrial and ventricular tissue assessed by chronotropic, inotropic, and cyclic AMP responses to isoprenaline and dobutamine. Cardiovasc Res 10:452-458, 1976
11. Loeb HS, Sinno MZ, Saudye AI, et al: Electrophysiologic properties of dobutamine. Circ Shock 1:217-220, 1974
12. Robie NW, Nutter DO, Moody CI, et al: In vivo analysis of adrenergic receptor activity of dobutamine. Circ Res 34:663-671, 1974
13. Goldberg LI, Hsieh Y-Y, Resnekov L: Newer catecholamines for treatment of heart failure and shock: an update on dopamine and a first look at dobutamine. Prog Cardiovasc Dis 19:327-340, 1977
14. Murphy PJ, Williams TL, Kau DLK: Disposition of dobutamine in the dog. J Pharmacol Exp Ther 199:423-431, 1976
15. Loeb HS, Khan M, Klodnycky ML, et al: Hemodynamic effects of dobutamine in man. Circ Shock 2:29-35, 1975
16. Beregovich J, Bianchi C, D'Angelo R, et al: Haemodynamic effects of a new inotropic agent (dobutamine) in chronic cardiac failure. Br Heart J 37:629-634, 1975
17. Akhtar N, Mikulic E, Cohn JN, et al: Hemodynamic effect of dobutamine in patients with severe heart failure. Am J Cardiol 36:202-205, 1975
18. Leier CV, Webel J, Bush CA: The cardiovascular effects of the continuous infusion of dobutamine in patients with severe cardiac failure. Circulation 56:468-472, 1977
19. Jewitt D, Birkhead J, Mitchell A, et al: Clinical cardiovascular pharmacology of dobutamine; a selective inotropic catecholamine. Lancet 2:363-367, 1974
20. Loeb HS, Khan M, Saudye A, et al: Acute hemodynamic effects of dobutamine and isoproterenol in patients with low output cardiac failure. Circ Shock 3:55-63, 1976
21. Loeb HS, Bredakis J, Gunnar RM: Superiority of dobutamine over dopamine for augmentation of cardiac output in patients with chronic low output cardiac failure. Circulation 55:375-381, 1977
22. Leier CV, Heban PT, Huss P, et al: Comparative systemic and regional hemodynamic effects of dopamine and dobutamine in patients with cardiomyopathic heart failure. Circulation 58:466-475, 1978
23. Tinker JH, Tarhan S, White RD, et al: Dobutamine for inotropic support during emergence from cardiopulmonary bypass. Anesthesiology 44:281-286, 1976
24. Sakamoto T, Yamada T: Hemodynamic effects of dobutamine in patients following open heart surgery. Circulation 55:525-533, 1977
25. Guiha NH, Cohn JN, Mikulic E, et al: Treatment of refractory heart failure with infusion of nitroprusside. N Engl J Med 291:587-592, 1974
26. Chatterjee K, Parmley WW: The role of vasodilation therapy in heart failure. Prog Cardiovasc Dis 19:301-325, 1977
27. Mikulic E, Cohn JN, Franciosa JA: Comparative hemodynamic effects of inotropic and vasodilator drugs in severe heart failure. Circulation 56:528-533, 1977
28. Berkowitz C, McKeever L, Croke RP, et al: Comparative responses to dobutamine and nitroprusside in patients with chronic low output cardiac failure. Circulation 56:918-924, 1977
29. Buckberg GD, Fixler DE, Archie JP, et al: Experimental subendocardial ischemia in dogs with normal coronary arteries. Circ Res 30:67-81, 1972
30. Kirk ES, LeJemtel TH, Nelson GR, et al: Mechanisms of beneficial effects of vasodilators and inotropic stimulation in the experimental failing ischemic heart. Am J Med 65:189-196, 1978
31. Braunwald E, Ross J Jr, Sonnenblick EH: Mechanisms of Contraction of the Normal and Failing Heart. Second edition. Boston, Little, Brown, 1976
32. Willerson JT, Hutton I, Watson JT, et al: Influence of dobutamine on regional myocardial blood flow and ventricular performance during acute and chronic myocardial ischemia in dogs. Circulation 53:828-833, 1976
33. Vatner SF, McRitchie RJ, Maroko PR, et al: Effects of catecholamines, exercise, and nitroglycerin on the normal and ischemic myocardium in conscious dogs. J Clin Invest 54:563-575, 1974
34. Vasu MA, O'Keefe DD, Kapellakis GZ, et al: Myocardial oxygen consumption and hemodynamic effects of dobutamine, epinephrine and isoproterenol. Fed Proc 34:435, 1975
35. Kirk ES, Hirzel HO, Sonnenblick EH: The relative role of supply and demand in the effect of isoproterenol on infarct size. Circulation 55, 56:Suppl 3:III-149, 1977
36. Kirk ES, Nelson GR, Sonnenblick EH: Digitalis: mechanisms of action in ischemic heart failure. Circulation 51, 52:Suppl 2:II-24, 1975
37. Tuttle RR, Pollack GD, Todd G, et al: The effect of dobutamine on cardiac oxygen balance, regional blood flow, and infarction severity after coronary artery narrowing in dogs. Circ Res 41:357-364, 1977
38. Gillespie TA, Ambos HD, Sobel BE, et al: Effects of dobutamine in patients with acute myocardial infarction. Am J Cardiol 39:588-594, 1977

500   THE NEW ENGLAND JOURNAL OF MEDICINE   August 27, 1981

DRUG THERAPY

JAN KOCH-WESER, M.D., *Editor*

β-Adrenoceptor Antagonists: New Drugs and New Indications

WILLIAM H. FRISHMAN, M.D.

THE finding that the relative potency of a series of sympathomimetic amines varied with the effector organs or systems led Ahlquist in 1948 to conclude that there were two distinct types of adrenergic receptors, which he classified as α and β.[1] The discovery of β-adrenoceptor antagonists 10 years later[2] gave strong support to Ahlquist's hypothesis and initiated

From the Division of Cardiology, Department of Medicine, Albert Einstein College of Medicine, 1825 Eastchester Rd., Bronx, NY 10461, where reprint requests should be addressed to Dr. Frishman.

Supported in part by a grant (HL 00653-1) from the National Institutes of Health. Dr. Frishman is a Teaching Scholar of the American Heart Association.

one of the most important advances in cardiovascular pharmacotherapy.

Although β-blockers were initially intended as treatment for angina pectoris, it soon became clear that they had much to offer as therapy for other clinical disorders: hypertension, arrhythmia, thyrotoxicosis, hypertrophic cardiomyopathy, migraine, and glaucoma.[3,4] As a class, the β-adrenergic blockers have been so successful that scores of them have been synthesized. Six are available or in the process of being released for use in the United States (Fig. 1). The application of these agents has been accelerated by the development of drugs possessing a degree of selectivity for two subgroups of the β-adrenoceptor population: β_1 receptors in the heart, and β_2 receptors in the peripheral circulation and bronchi. More controversial has been the introduction of β-blocking agents with α-adrenergic blocking properties, varying degrees of intrinsic sympathomimetic activity (partial agonist effect), and nonspecific membrane stabilizing action (Table 1).[4-7] There are also major pharmacokinetic differences between these drugs.[5,7,8]

Four β-adrenergic blockers are now marketed in the United States: propranolol for angina pectoris, arrhythmia, systemic hypertension, and migraine prophylaxis; metoprolol for hypertension[8]; timolol for glaucoma; and nadolol for angina pectoris and hypertension (nadolol will be discussed in the next Drug Therapy article). Pindolol and atenolol will be marketed shortly and discussed thereafter.

Despite extensive experience with these and other β-blockers inside and outside the United States, there are no studies suggesting that one of these drugs has major advantages or disadvantages in relation to another in the treatment of cardiovascular disease.[3,4,7,8] When any β-blocker developed since the synthesis of propranolol is titrated to the proper dose, it can be effective in patients with arrhythmia, hyper-

Table 1. Pharmacodynamic Properties of Some β-Adrenoceptor Blocking Drugs.[5,6]

DRUG	β_1-BLOCKADE POTENCY RATIO (PROPRANOLOL = 1.0)	RELATIVE β-1 SELECTIVITY	INTRINSIC SYMPATHOMIMETIC ACTIVITY	MEMBRANE STABILIZING ACTIVITY
Atenolol	1.0	+	0	0
Metoprolol	1.0	+	0	0
Nadolol	1.0	0	0	0
Pindolol	6.0	0	+	+
Propranolol	1.0	0	0	++
Timolol	6.0	0	0	0

tension, or angina pectoris.[3,7,9] However, one drug may be better than another in decreasing side effects in certain patients and in specific clinical situations.[5-8,10] To judge the value of different β-adrenoceptor blockers, one must compare the pharmacodynamic and pharmacokinetic properties that may provide an added margin of safety for the patient, alter any propensity toward undesirable side effects, reduce the incidence of drug interactions, or influence the ease of effective dosing.[7,8,11,12] One must also compare the efficacy of these drugs in therapeutic situations in which beneficial effects may not be entirely related to their ability to block β-adrenergic receptors.[8]

BASIC PHARMACOLOGIC DIFFERENCES

Potency

β-Adrenergic blockers are competitive inhibitors of catecholamine binding at β-adrenoceptor sites. They reduce the effect of any concentration of a catecholamine agonist on a sensitive tissue.[5] The dose-response curve of the agonist is shifted to the right; a given tissue response then requires a higher concentration of the agonist in the presence of a β-blocking drug. β_1-Blocking potency can be judged by the inhibition of tachycardia produced by isoproterenol; potency varies from compound to compound (Table 1).[5] Although differences in potency are of no therapeutic relevance, they do explain the different drug concentrations needed to achieve effective β-adrenergic blockade.

Most β-blocking drugs exist as pairs of optical isomers and are marketed as the racemic mixtures. Almost all the blocking activity is found in the negative (−) levorotatory stereoisomer.[5,13] The two stereoisomers of β-adrenergic blocking drugs are useful for differentiating between the pharmacologic effects of β-adrenergic blockade and membrane stabilizing activity (possessed by both optical forms). The (+) dextrorotatory stereoisomers are of no recognized therapeutic value.[4,5]

Membrane Stabilizing Activity

In high concentrations well above therapeutic levels, certain β-blockers have a quinidine-like or "local-anesthetic" membrane stabilizing effect on the

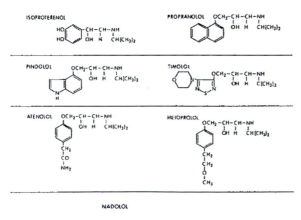

Figure 1. Molecular Structures of the β-Adrenergic Agonist Isoproterenol and Some β-Adrenergic Blocking Drugs.

cardiac action potential.[4,5] This property is unrelated to β-adrenergic blockade and is not relevant to clinical management of arrhythmias.[14] There is no evidence that membrane stabilizing activity is responsible for any negative hemodynamic effects of β-blocking drugs in patients. For example, propranolol (which has membrane stabilizing activity) and timolol and nadolol (which lack this property) equally depress left ventricular function.[7] However, membrane stabilizing activity can manifest itself clinically during massive intoxication with a β-blocker.[15]

Selectivity

Lands et al. suggested that β-adrenoceptors could be classified into distinct types.[16] They were designated β_1 (lipolysis and cardiostimulation) and β_2 (bronchodilatation and vasodilatation).[16] The subclassification of β-adrenoreceptors is an important advance that has led to the development of agonist and antagonist drugs that are relatively selective at either β_1-receptor or β_2-receptor sites.[17]

The β-adrenoceptor blockers may be classified as selective or nonselective,[7] according to their relative abilities to antagonize the actions of sympathomimetic amines in some tissues at lower doses than those required in other tissues.[5,8] When employed in low doses, β_1-selective blocking agents such as metoprolol inhibit cardiac β_1-receptors but have less influence on bronchial and vascular β-adrenoceptors (β_2). In higher doses, however, β_1-selective agents will also block β_2-receptors.[8] Because selective β_1-blockers have less of an inhibitory effect on the β_2-receptors, they have two theoretical advantages. The first is that selective agents may be safer than nonselective agents in patients with acute or chronic obstructive pulmonary disease, since β_2-receptors remain available to mediate adrenergic bronchodilatation. In some clinical trials in patients with asthma, relatively low doses of β_1-selective agents caused a lower incidence of side effects than did similar doses of propranolol.[5,8,18] However, even selective β-blockers may aggravate bronchospasm in certain patients,[4] so that these drugs should generally not be used in bronchospastic disease. The second theoretical advantage is that unlike propranolol, β_1-selective blockers in low doses may not block the β_2-receptors that mediate dilatation of arterioles.[19] This property might be an advantage in treatment of hypertension with relatively low doses of β_1-adrenergic blockers,[8] but this possibility has not been demonstrated. During infusion of epinephrine, nonselective β-blockers can cause a pressor response by blocking β_2-receptor-mediated vasodilatation, since α-adrenergic vasoconstrictor receptors are still operative.[20] Selective β_1-antagonists may not induce this pressor effect in the presence of epinephrine and may lessen the impairment of peripheral-blood flow. It is possible that leaving the β_2-receptors unblocked and responsive to epinephrine may be functionally important in some patients with asthma, hypoglycemia, hypertension, or peripheral vascular disease treated with β-adrenergic blocking drugs.[10]

Intrinsic Sympathomimetic Activity (Partial Agonist Activity)

Certain β-adrenoceptor blocking drugs have intrinsic sympathomimetic activity (partial agonist activity), but none of these agents has been approved for clinical use in the United States. In a β-blocker this property is identified as a slight cardiac stimulation, which can be blocked by propranolol.[21] The β-blocking drugs with this property slightly activate the β-receptor, in addition to preventing the access of natural or synthetic catecholamines to the receptor. Dichloroisoprenaline, the first β-adrenoceptor blocking drug, exerted such marked partial agonist activity that it was unsuitable for clinical use.[4] However, compounds with less partial agonist activity are effective β-blocking drugs. Of the six drugs listed in Table 1, only pindolol has this property. A quantitative assessment of partial agonist activity in a β-blocker can be made in animals with no resting sympathetic tone whose mechanisms for control of the autonomic nervous system have been abolished by adrenalectomy or pretreatment with reserpine.[21] The partial agonist effects of β-adrenoceptor-blocking drugs differ from those of the agonist epinephrine or isoproterenol, in that the maximum pharmacologic response that can be obtained is less, although the affinity for the receptor is high.[5] In the treatment of patients with arrhythmia,[22] angina pectoris of effort,[23] or hypertension,[24] drugs with mild to moderate partial agonist activity appear to be as efficacious as β-blockers lacking this property. It is still debated whether the presence of partial agonist activity in a β-blocker constitutes an overall advantage or disadvantage in cardiac therapy.[4,7,8] Drugs with partial agonist activity cause less slowing of the heart rate at rest than propranolol or metoprolol, although the increments in heart rate with exercise are similarly blunted.[23] They may also depress atrioventricular conduction less than agents lacking this property.[25] It has been claimed by some investigators that partial agonist activity in a β-blocker protects against myocardial depression, bronchial asthma, and peripheral vascular complications.[3,4] The evidence supporting this claim is certainly not clear-cut, and more definitive clinical trials are necessary to decide these questions.[4,7]

Pharmacokinetic Properties

Although the β-adrenergic blocking drugs as a group have similar pharmacologic effects in cardiovascular diseases, their pharmacokinetics are markedly different (Table 2).[5-7,26-28] Differences in completeness of gastrointestinal absorption, amount of first-pass hepatic metabolism, lipid solubility, protein binding, extent of distribution in the body, penetration into the brain, concentration in the heart, rate of hepatic biotransformation, pharmacologic activity of metabolites, and renal clearance of a drug and its metabolites may influence the clinical usefulness of these drugs in some patients.[5,7,8,25] The desirable pharmacokinetic characteristics in this group of com-

Despite the lack of correlation between plasma levels and therapeutic effect, there is some evidence that a relation does exist between the logarithm of the plasma level and the β-blocking effect (blockade of exercise or isoproterenol-induced tachycardia).[5,8,26,27]

Clinical Implications

The β-adrenoceptor blockers appear to have a similar spectrum of therapeutic cardiovascular effects despite the presence or absence of selectivity or partial agonist activity.[25] Generally, if one agent in adequate doses does not work, neither will another. It is also not helpful to add one β-blocker to another in the hope of improving the therapeutic response. A similar profile of side effects is seen in about 5 to 10 per cent of patients receiving β-blocking drugs. Most of these effects are mild and transient; they include dizziness, fatigue, paresthesias, depression, and gastrointestinal disturbances.[10,30] When mild side effects are encountered, they can sometimes be counteracted by lowering the dose of β-blocker or by changing from one β-blocker to another. The more important cardiovascular side effects are rare in patients with normal left ventricular function. These reactions, which include pulmonary edema, hypotension, and heart block, accompany the use of any β-blocker and appear most often in patients who are dependent on stimulation of the sympathetic nervous system for preservation of myocardial function.[10,30] In bronchospastic disease, the β-blockers with β_1 selectivity or partial agonist activity may be of use in some patients.[7,10] The value of peripheral vascular sparing effects with β_1-selective agents and of decreased brain uptake with hydrophilic β-blocking compounds is less well established.

There are major differences among β-blockers in regard to side effects that appear unrelated to β-adrenergic blockade.[4,10] The Food and Drug Administration has made extraordinary safety demands for these drugs. Close scrutiny is needed because of the possible tumorigenicity of certain compounds in animals and because the oculomucocutaneous syndrome had been observed after practolol in patients.[4,10] The long-term safety of many β-blockers has been well established, but as the new drugs are marketed, they should be carefully monitored for unanticipated adverse effects.

NEW INDICATIONS FOR β-ADRENERGIC BLOCKERS

Open-Angle Glaucoma

In treating systemic hypertension with β-adrenoceptor blocking drugs, it was fortuitously discovered that these agents reduced intraocular pressure in patients with concomitant glaucoma.[31] As early as 1968, topical application of propranolol was shown to reduce intraocular pressure[32]; however, its mild local-anesthetic properties made investigators reluctant to use it for treatment of glaucoma. Topical application of timolol — a nonselective β-blocker without this local-anesthetic property or partial agonist activity —

also reduced intraocular pressure.[33] The mechanism of its ocular hypotensive effect has not been firmly established, but it may reduce the pressure by decreasing the production of aqueous humor.[33] Timolol maleate (Timoptic) was approved by the FDA in 1978 for the topical treatment of increased intraocular pressure in patients with chronic open-angle glaucoma. It is also approved for patients with aphakia and glaucoma, for some patients with secondary glaucoma, and for patients with elevated intraocular pressure who are at sufficient risk to require lowering of this pressure. The oral and intravenous forms of this drug have been shown to be effective in angina pectoris, hypertension, and arrhythmia, but it has not been approved in the United States for these indications.

Timolol maleate has been studied primarily in comparative trials with topical epinephrine or pilocarpine in patients with open-angle glaucoma.[33,34] Its use in acute closed-angle glaucoma has not been reported in published studies. Timolol is at least as effective as pilocarpine and epinephrine in reducing intraocular pressure by 25 to 30 per cent in up to 90 per cent of patients.[33] Timolol does not affect pupil motility or accommodation, and for these reasons may be better tolerated than miotics. Although a slight reduction in the magnitude of the ocular hypotensive effect of timolol occurs during the first one to two weeks of treatment, serious tachyphylaxis has apparently not been a problem in long-term (one year) studies.[33]

There is little published information on the pharmacokinetic actions of timolol during ocular administration.[33] Such studies are needed to determine the extent of systemic absorption. That systemic absorption does occur through conjunctival and nasal mucosa has been suggested by lowered pressure in both treated and untreated eyes and by the presence of small amounts of the drug in the plasma and urine.[33] In single-dose studies in rabbits, peak levels occur in blood and aqueous humor 30 minutes after administration of a 0.5 per cent solution. In human beings the start of the reduction in pressure can be detected within half an hour after a single dose. The maximal effect usually occurs in one to two hours, and appreciable lowering of pressure can be maintained for as long as 24 hours after a single dose. Systemically absorbed timolol is biotransformed in the liver, and its metabolites are excreted primarily in the urine.[33]

Timolol ophthalmic solution is available in concentrations of 0.25 and 0.5 per cent. The recommended starting dose is one drop of 0.25 per cent solution in each eye twice daily, increasing to one drop of 0.5 per cent solution in each eye twice daily. The response of some patients to timolol may require a few weeks to stabilize. The manufacturer suggests that when intraocular pressure is controlled, a single dose per day can be tried, but there is no published evidence that such a regimen is effective. If a further reduction in intraocular pressure is considered necessary, concomitant therapy with miotics, epinephrine, or systemic carbonic anhydrase inhibitors may be instituted.[33] The wholesale price of timolol (per milliliter) is approximately $1.30 for the 0.25 per cent solution and $1.50 for the 0.5 per cent solution, as compared with $0.21 for 1 per cent pilocarpine and $0.60 for 1 per cent epinephrine. However, since a smaller volume of timolol is used clinically, the comparative wholesale costs for a month of treatment are approximately $10.40 for timolol (0.25 per cent), $3.30 for pilocarpine (1 per cent), and $9.40 for epinephrine (1 per cent).

Timolol ophthalmic solution is usually well tolerated. Mild eye irritation occurs occasionally, and a few patients have reported blurred vision after initial doses. Objective measurements of ophthalmic status during topical timolol treatment have shown few changes.[33] The oral dose of timolol maleate for treatment of systemic hypertension is 20 to 60 mg per day. In contrast, the amount of timolol in four drops of 0.5 per cent ophthalmic solution (the maximal daily dose) is only about 1 mg. Plasma levels of the drug after ocular administration are far below those of the cardiovascular therapeutic-dose range. However, aggravation or precipitation of certain cardiovascular and pulmonary disorders has been reported and is presumably related to the systemic effects of β-adrenoceptor blockade.[33] These include bradycardia, hypotension, syncope, confusion, and bronchospasm (predominantly in patients with bronchospastic disease). The manufacturer recommends caution in prescribing timolol eye drops when a systemic β-adrenergic blocking drug may be contraindicated, as in patients with preexisting asthmatic conditions, heart block, or heart failure. No data are available on the use of the drug for more than two years, use in children, or use during pregnancy. Patients who are taking an oral β-adrenergic drug and are given topical timolol should be observed for a potential additive effect on intraocular pressure and on the known systemic effects of β-blockade.

Prophylaxis of Migraine

The use of β-adrenergic blocking drugs to prevent migraine headache was first suggested by Rabkin et al. in 1966.[35] These investigators and others reported a beneficial effect of propranolol on migraine headaches in patients being treated for angina pectoris or arrhythmia. These early observations led to clinical trials that confirmed the safety and efficacy of propranolol (Inderal) for the prophylaxis of common migraine[36,37]; the FDA approved the drug for this indication in 1979. Propranolol is not approved for the treatment of migraine headache or for the prevention and treatment of cluster headaches.

The causes of vascular-headache syndromes, including common migraine, are not well defined.[38] Therefore, the exact mechanisms of propranolol activity in prevention of migraine are not known. Other β-blockers may also be effective in migraine, but they need more intensive study. The use of propranolol for migraine is based on the fact that the drug concentrates in brain and presumably inhibits β-adrenoceptor-mediated vasodilatation. Dilatation of branches of the external carotid artery is assumed to be one source of pain during an episode of migraine.[39] Propranolol may also prevent the uptake of serotonin by platelets and thereby increase the amount of extracellular serotonin, which is then available for vasotonic actions on cerebral blood flow.[39]

Propranolol decreases the frequency of common migraine and can completely suppress headaches in some patients. One third of patients with common migraine have an excellent response to propranolol, with more than a 50 per cent reduction in the number of attacks and a markedly reduced need for ergotamine and analgesic medication; another third have a smaller reduction in the number of attacks; and the remaining third either have no response or become worse.[40] In a recent comparative trial, propranolol was demonstrated to be as effective as methysergide in reducing the frequency and severity of migraine headaches.[41] However, fewer adverse reactions were seen during propranolol treatment.[41] Direct comparisons with other prophylactic regimens for migraine (cyproheptadine, tricyclic antidepressants, papaverine, and monoamine oxidase inhibitors) have not been made.

Daily administration of any prophylactic medication is warranted only when headaches of moderate to severe intensity occur several times a month. For prevention of migraine, the initial amount is 80 mg daily in divided doses. The usual range of effective doses is 160 to 240 mg per day; the dose may be increased gradually to 480 mg per day to achieve a better response. Several reports have appeared on the combined use of propranolol and ergot preparations; this combination apparently had no untoward effects.[41] Severe migraine attacks have been reported to follow abrupt withdrawal from propranolol. It is recommended that the drug be gradually withdrawn over a two-week period if the maximal dosage has not produced a satisfactory response within four to six weeks. Adverse reactions in patients receiving propranolol for migraine are similar to those in patients given this drug for hypertension or angina pectoris.

I am indebted to Drs. Edmund Sonnenblick, Seymour Solomon, and Daniel Weiss of the Albert Einstein College of Medicine for critical reviews of the manuscript, and to Ms. Nina Scotti for valuable assistance.

References

1. Ahlquist RP. A study of the adrenotropic receptors. Am J Physiol. 1948; 153:586-600.
2. Powell CE, Slater IH. Blocking of inhibitory adrenergic receptors by a dichloro analog of isoproterenol. J Pharmacol Exp Ther. 1958; 122:480-8.
3. Frishman W, Silverman R. Clinical pharmacology of the new beta-adrenergic blocking drugs. Part 3. Comparative clinical experience and new therapeutic applications. Am Heart J. 1979; 98:119-31.
4. Conolly ME, Kersting F, Dollery CT. The clinical pharmacology of beta-adrenoceptor-blocking drugs. Prog Cardiovasc Dis. 1976; 19:203-34.
5. Frishman W. Clinical pharmacology of the new beta-adrenergic block-

ing drugs. Part I. Pharmacodynamic and pharmacokinetic properties. Am Heart J. 1979; 97:663-70.

6. Waal-Manning HJ. Hypertension: which beta-blocker? Drugs. 1976; 12:412-41.

7. Opie LH. Drugs and the heart. I. Beta-blocking agents. Lancet. 1980; 1:693-8.

8. Koch-Weser J. Metoprolol. N Engl J Med. 1979; 301:698-703.

9. Thadani U, Davidson C, Singleton W, Taylor SH. Comparison of the immediate effects of five β-adrenoceptor-blocking drugs with different ancillary properties in angina pectoris. N Engl J Med. 1979; 300: 750-5.

10. Frishman W, Silverman R, Strom J, Elkayam U, Sonnenblick E. Clinical pharmacology of the new beta-adrenergic blocking drugs. Part 4. Adverse effects. Choosing a β-adrenoceptor blocker. Am Heart J. 1979; 98:256-62.

11. Frishman WH. Clinical pharmacology of the beta-adrenoceptor blocking drugs. New York: Appleton-Century-Crofts, 1980:209-10.

12. Cruickshank JM. The clinical importance of cardioselectivity and lipophilicity in beta blockers. Am Heart J. 1980; 100:160-78.

13. Barrett AM, Cullum VA. The biological properties of the optical isomers of propranolol and their effects on cardiac arrhythmias. Br J Pharmacol. 1968; 34:43-55.

14. Singh BN, Jewitt DE. B-Adrenergic receptor blocking drugs in cardiac arrhythmias. Drugs. 1974; 7:426-61.

15. Buiumsohn A, Eisenberg ES, Jacob H, Rosen N, Bock J, Frishman WH. Seizures and intraventricular conduction defect in propranolol poisoning: a report of two cases. Ann Intern Med. 1979; 91:860-2.

16. Lands AM, Arnold A, McAuliff JP, Luduena FP, Brown TG Jr. Differentiation of receptor systems activated by sympathomimetic amines. Nature. 1967; 214:597-8.

17. Dunlop D, Shanks RG. Selective blockade of adrenoceptive beta receptors in the heart. Br J Pharmacol. 1968; 32:201-18.

18. Sinclair DJM. Comparison of effects of propranolol and metoprolol on airways obstruction in chronic bronchitis. Br Med J. 1979; 1:168.

19. Sannerstedt R, Wasir H. Acute haemodynamic effects of metoprolol in hypertensive patients. Br J Clin Pharmacol. 1977; 4:23-6.

20. McSorley PD, Warren DJ. Effects of propranolol and metoprolol on the peripheral circulation. Br Med J. 1978; 2:1598-1600.

21. Cocco G, Burkart F, Chu D, Follath F. Intrinsic sympathomimetic activity of β-adrenoceptor blocking agents. Eur J Clin Pharmacol. 1978; 13:1-4.

22. Aronow WS, Uyeyama RR. Treatment of arrhythmias with pindolol. Clin Pharmacol Ther. 1972; 13:15-22.

23. Frishman W, Kostis J, Strom J, et al. Clinical pharmacology of the new beta-adrenergic blocking drugs. Part 6. A comparison of pindolol and propranolol in treatment of patients with angina pectoris. The role of intrinsic sympathomimetic activity. Am Heart J. 1979; 98:526-35.

24. Atterhög J-H, Dunér H, Pernow B. Experience with pindolol, a beta-receptor blocker, in the treatment of hypertension. Am J Med. 1976; 60:872-6.

25. Frishman W, Silverman R. Clinical pharmacology of the new beta-adrenergic blocking drugs. Part 2. Physiologic and metabolic effects. Am Heart J. 1979; 97:797-807.

26. Johnsson G, Regárdh CG. Clinical pharmacokinetics of β-adrenoceptor blocking drugs. Clin Pharmacokinet. 1976; 1:233-63.

27. Heel RC, Brogden RN, Pakes GE, Speight TM, Avery GS. Nadolol: a review of its pharmacological properties and therapeutic efficacy in hypertension and angina pectoris. Drugs. 1980; 20:1-23.

28. Heel RC, Brogden RN, Speight TM, Avery GS. Atenolol: a review of its pharmacological properties and therapeutic efficacy in angina pectoris and hypertension. Drugs. 1979; 17:425-60.

29. Koch-Weser J, Sellers EM. Binding of drugs to serum albumin. N Engl J Med. 1976; 294:311-6, 526-31.

30. Greenblatt DJ, Koch-Weser J. Adverse reactions to β-adrenergic receptor blocking drugs: a report from the Boston collaborative drug surveillance program. Drugs. 1974; 7:118-29.

31. Phillips CI, Howitt G, Rowlands DJ. Propranolol as ocular hypotensive agent. Br J Ophthalmol. 1967; 51:222-6.

32. Bucci MG, Missiroli A, Giraldi JP, Virno M. Local administration of propranolol in the treatment of glaucoma. Boll Oculist. 1968; 47:51-80.

33. Heel RC, Brogden RN, Speight TM, Avery GS. Timolol: a review of its therapeutic efficacy in the topical treatment of glaucoma. Drugs. 1979; 17:38-55.

34. Boger WP III, Steinert RF, Puliafito CA, Pavan-Langston D. Clinical trial comparing timolol ophthalmic solution to pilocarpine in open-angle glaucoma. Am J Ophthalmol. 1978; 86:8-18.

35. Rabkin R, Stables DP, Levin NW, Suzman MM. The prophylactic value of propranolol in angina pectoris. Am J Cardiol. 1966; 18:370-83.

36. Weber RB, Reinmuth OM. The treatment of migraine with propranolol. Neurology. 1972; 22:366-9.

37. Diamond S, Medina JL. Double blind study of propranolol for migraine prophylaxis. Headache. 1976; 16:24-7.

38. Caviness VS Jr, O'Brien P. Headache. N Engl J Med. 1980; 302:446-50.

39. Børgesen SE. Propranolol for migraine. Compr Ther. 1977; 3(4):53-8.

40. Forssman B, Henriksson K-G, Johannsson V, Lindvall L, Lundin H. Propranolol for migraine prophylaxis. Headache. 1976; 16:238-45.

41. Behan PO, Reid M. Propranolol in the treatment of migraine. Practitioner. 1980; 224:201-4.

Badia Fiesdanar, Tuscany   Ernest L. Levinger, M.D.

MEDICAL INTELLIGENCE

DRUG THERAPY

JAN KOCH-WESER, M.D., *Editor*

β-Adrenergic Blockade for Survivors of Acute Myocardial Infarction

WILLIAM H. FRISHMAN, M.D.,
CURT D. FURBERG, M.D.,
AND WILLIAM T. FRIEDEWALD, M.D.

THE β-adrenoceptor antagonists have been shown to be both safe and effective for the treatment of systemic hypertension, arrhythmia, angina pectoris, hypertrophic cardiomyopathy, thyrotoxicosis, and open-angle glaucoma, and for prophylaxis against migraine headache.[1] Recent clinical trials with one to four years of active treatment have demonstrated that some orally active β-blockers can reduce the risk of cardiovascular mortality in patients recovering from acute myocardial infarction.[2-15] On the basis of the results of the Norwegian Multicenter Study[10] and the Beta-Blocker Heart Attack Trial[11] in North America, the Food and Drug Administration has recently approved two nonselective β-blockers, timolol maleate (Blocadren) and propranolol (Inderal) for this indication. Metoprolol (Lopressor), a β_1-selective adrenergic blocker, is now under consideration for this same use. β-Blockers have also been suggested as a treatment for reducing the extent of myocardial injury and mortality during the acute phase of myocardial infarction,[16-18] but their role in this situation remains unclear.[19,20] This article assesses the current state of knowledge regarding the value of long-term β-blocker therapy in survivors of acute myocardial infarction and the implications for clinical practice.

THE CLINICAL PROBLEM

Despite a decline in the incidence of coronary heart disease, more than 600,000 patients a year are admitted to hospitals in the United States, with a diagnosis of acute myocardial infarction.[21] For patients having their first infarction, there is a 15 per cent mortality during hospitalization, and the figure is somewhat higher in patients with recurrent infarctions.[22]

From the Department of Medicine, Albert Einstein College of Medicine, Bronx, N.Y., and the Clinical Applications and Prevention Program of the National Heart, Lung, and Blood Institute, Bethesda, Md. Address reprint requests to Dr. Frishman at the Hospital of Albert Einstein College of Medicine, 1825 Eastchester Rd., Bronx, NY 10461.

Dr. Frishman is a recipient of a Preventive Cardiology Academic Award (Grant HL-00653-4) from the National Institutes of Health.

Upon discharge from the hospital, patients continue to have an increased risk of cardiovascular morbidity and mortality. Patients under 70 years of age who survive a myocardial infarction have a 10 per cent mortality rate in the first year, with the highest proportion of deaths occurring in the first three months.[22] Subsequently, there is a five per cent annual mortality rate, which is six times higher than the expected rate in an age-matched population without coronary disease.[22] Approximately 85 per cent of the deaths that occur after hospitalization for myocardial infarction are related to coronary heart disease, and almost half of these are sudden deaths. Ventricular fibrillation appears to be the primary mechanism for sudden death.

Prospective epidemiologic studies have identified subsets of patients who have survived a myocardial infarction with a high, intermediate, or low risk of mortality.[23,24] The high-risk subset represents 15 per cent of the postinfarction population. This patient group has a mortality ranging from 20 to 40 per cent in the first year after hospital discharge and is characterized by the presence of cardiac symptoms before the index coronary event, by frequent ventricular ectopy on in-hospital 24-hour ambulatory electrocardiographic recordings, and by left ventricular dysfunction on physical examination and radionuclide evaluation.[24] In contrast, the low-risk subgroup, which makes up 30 per cent of the postinfarction population, has a 2 per cent mortality in the first year after discharge. This subgroup is characterized by the absence of infarction or cardiac symptoms before the index cardiac event, the absence of high-grade ventricular ectopy and congestive heart failure during hospitalization, and a negative submaximal exercise test performed just before discharge.[23-26] Between these two subgroups is the remaining 55 per cent of the postinfarction population. This intermediate-risk subgroup has one or two characteristics of the high-risk subset and a first-year mortality rate of approximately 10 per cent.[24]

Prolonging life in this heterogeneous group of patients is a major goal of preventive therapy. To reach this goal, a variety of therapeutic approaches have been evaluated, including life-style measures (dietary modifications, weight reduction, cessation of smoking, and physical exercise) and coronary-artery reconstructive surgery.[22] Specific pharmacologic agents have included anticoagulants,[27] drugs that inhibit platelet aggregation,[28] lipid-lowering agents,[29] calcium-channel blockers,[30] and antiarrhythmic drugs.[22] Among the multiple interventions evaluated to date, only β-adrenergic blockade has been clearly demonstrated to be efficacious in reducing cardiovascular mortality in patients surviving the acute phase of myocardial infarction.[22]

β-ADRENERGIC BLOCKADE IN THE POSTINFARCTION PERIOD

The presumed major mechanisms for increased cardiovascular mortality during the postinfarction period include persistent myocardial ischemia, cardiac arrhythmias, and left ventricular dysfunction.[22-24,31-33] Raised levels of circulating catecholamines or enhanced sympathetic drive can increase both the severity of myocardial ischemia[34] and the frequency of ventricular arrhythmias.[35] After the clinical introduction of propranolol for angina pectoris and arrhythmias in 1963, it was conceived that β-blocker administration might favorably influence the natural history of patients with myocardial infarction by attenuating the undesirable consequences of increased sympathetic-nervous-system activity.[36] However, since these drugs could also depress left ventricular function — the other major factor contributing to mortality after infarction — β-blockers were initially avoided in patients with myocardial infarction or were used in small doses for fear of causing congestive heart failure.[36-40] Only recently have the results of large long-term clinical trials conclusively demonstrated the efficacy and safety of β-blocker therapy.

The Long-Term β-Blocker Trials

Since 1974, 13 major randomized controlled trials with β-blockers after acute myocardial infarction have been reported, with treatment and mean patient follow-up extending from nine months to four years.[2-15,41,42] Over 16,000 survivors of acute myocardial infarction were studied in attempts to document reductions in total mortality, cardiovascular mortality, coronary mortality, sudden death, and nonfatal reinfarction.

Seven different β-blockers have been evaluated in these studies: alprenolol, oxprenolol, pindolol, practolol, propranolol, sotalol, and timolol (Table 1).[2-15,41,42] A long-term trial evaluating metoprolol has been completed, but the findings are not yet available.[43]

The 13 trials met the following criteria for study design: a trial end point of total mortality or of a clearly defined cause-specific mortality, a total sample size of at least 200, and random assignment of patients to either the β-blocker group or a concurrently followed control group. The study populations of the 13 trials contained from 230 to 3837 patients.[2-15,41,42] Twelve of the 13 trials used a placebo-treated control group and had a double-blind design. The time between the infarction and the start of β-blocker or placebo treatment ranged from under 24 hours to 7½ years. In 11 trials, patients in the low-risk and intermediate-risk groups were predominantly studied,[2-11,13,14,41,42] and in two trials only high-risk patients were evaluated.[12,15]

The results from 11 of the 13 long-term trials showed a lower mortality rate in the β-blocker group than in the placebo group.[2-15] In the three largest studies, the reduction in mortality with β-blocker treatment was statistically significant.[8-11] In the remaining eight trials, the results were not conclusive with regard to overall mortality.

The most convincing long-term data emerged from the Norwegian timolol trial[10] and the Beta-Blocker

Table 1. Pharmacologic Properties of the β-Adrenergic Blocking Drugs Tested in Long-Term Trials.

Drug	Relative β₁ Selectivity	Intrinsic Sympathomimetic Activity	Membrane-Stabilizing Activity
Alprenolol *	0	+	+
Metoprolol †	+	0	0
Oxprenolol *	0	+	+
Pindolol	0	+ +	0
Practolol *	+	+	0
Propranolol	0	0	+ +
Sotalol *	0	0	0
Timolol	0	0	0

*Not available for clinical use in the United States.
†Results of study not available.

Heart Attack Trial, which employed propranolol hydrochloride.[11,44] The Norwegian trial, involving 1884 patients, demonstrated that timolol maleate, given orally at a dosage of 10 mg twice daily for an average of 17 months and for up to 33 months, reduced total mortality by 36 per cent and reduced the rate of nonfatal reinfarction by 34 per cent. The benefit of timolol was evident regardless of the patient's age or heart size or the site of the infarct. The Beta-Blocker Heart Attack Trial, involving 3837 patients, indicated that propranolol, given orally at a dosage of 60 to 80 mg three times daily for an average of 25 months and for up to 39 months, reduced total mortality by 26 per cent, cardiovascular mortality by 26 per cent, sudden cardiac death by 28 per cent, and nonfatal reinfarction by 16 per cent.[11,44,45] The protective effect was primarily seen in the first 12 to 18 months of intervention — an observation similar to the findings of the Norwegian timolol study. The first-year mortality rate of 11.3 per cent in the placebo group of the timolol study[10] was about twice the rate in placebo recipients in the propranolol study,[11] suggesting that a higher-risk population was studied in Norway. In spite of this difference in study populations, the treatment effect was similar: the reduction in the first-year mortality rate was approximately 33 per cent with timolol and 39 per cent with propranolol (in both trials, patients were followed for a minimum of one year).

The estimate of mortality benefit obtained after combining the results of all 13 β-blocker trials is 22 per cent. However, caution is advisable in interpreting such results, because in pooling data one disregards certain differences — for example, in the patient populations, the types of β-blocker and dosage, and the time of initiation and the duration of treatment.

Nine of the 10 trials[2,5,9,10,13-15,41,44,45] reporting on the incidence of nonfatal reinfarction showed lower rates in the actively treated group. In only one of the trials was this lower incidence statistically significant.[10,45] A comparison of the effect of treatment on the incidence of nonfatal reinfarction is complicated for many reasons. For example, the diagnostic criteria for infarction differed between the trials, resulting in large differences in incidence. However, a statistical test for homogeneity indicated that the result of each trial was consistent with those of the others. When all the findings from the nine placebo-controlled, double-blind trials are pooled, the reduction in nonfatal reinfarction is 22 per cent — a benefit almost identical to that for overall mortality.

Mechanisms of Benefit

An analysis of cause-specific mortality in the β-blocker trials indicates that the reductions in total mortality were due to a reduction in cardiovascular deaths.[2-15] Although different definitions of sudden death were employed in the trials, the benefit from β-blocker treatment appears to have stemmed particularly from the prevention of these deaths. In the seven trials that reported on sudden death,[2,5,8-13] pooled data revealed that treatment led to a 28 per cent reduction in mortality — a 33 per cent reduction in sudden cardiac death, and a 20 per cent reduction in nonsudden cardiac death. These figures suggest a primary antiarrhythmic effect to explain the beneficial actions of β-blockers. However, the reduction in nonsudden cardiac death, coupled with the observed reduction in nonfatal reinfarctions with β-blocker therapy, cannot be explained by an antiarrhythmic effect alone and raises questions about whether other protective mechanisms were also involved.

Antiarrhythmic Effects

The β-blockers as a group, although not powerful antiarrhythmic agents, can attenuate cardiac stimulation by the sympathetic nervous system and can perhaps attenuate the potential for reentrant ventricular arrhythmias and sudden death.[46,47] The β-blockers can also inhibit lipolysis and thereby reduce the stress-induced increase in free fatty acids — a metabolic factor capable of inducing ventricular arrhythmias in the ischemic myocardium.[48,49]

In experimental studies, β-blockers have been demonstrated to raise the ventricular-fibrillation threshold in the ischemic myocardium.[47] In placebo-controlled clinical trials, the drugs have reduced the number of episodes of ventricular fibrillation and cardiac arrest during the acute phase of myocardial infarction.[50,51] In studies of long-term β-blocker treatment after infarction, and in other studies, the occurrence of complex ventricular arrhythmias has been reduced by these drugs.[13,52-55]

In the Beta-Blocker Heart Attack Trial, 24-hour ambulatory electrocardiographic monitoring was performed at base line in all patients and after six weeks of therapy in a subgroup of patients. In the placebo group, the incidence of ventricular arrhythmias was higher at six weeks than at the base line. This increase was blunted by propranolol therapy.[53] It was recently reported that among the placebo recipients in that study, patients with complex ventricular arrhythmias had a mortality rate almost 2.5 times that of patients without ventricular arrhythmias (15.3 per cent vs. 6.4

per cent).[56] The placebo–propranolol difference in mortality rate was 4.5 per cent among patients with complex arrhythmias, but only 1.6 per cent among patients without arrhythmia.[56]

Antiischemic Effects

Since the incidences of nonsudden cardiovascular deaths and nonfatal reinfarction were reduced by β-blockers in the long-term trials, the antiischemic actions of the drugs may also have contributed to their beneficial effects in the postinfarction period.

Stimulation of cardiac β-adrenergic receptors by endogenous catecholamines increases myocardial oxygen consumption and can thereby aggravate the ischemic process. Drugs that block the β-adrenergic receptor reduce the effects of catecholamines and decrease myocardial oxygen requirements by reducing systemic arterial pressure, heart rate, and myocardial contractility at rest and during exercise.[17,57] The effects of these drugs on coronary blood flow are less well defined. β-Blockers may decrease coronary blood flow by allowing the unopposed influence of coronary vasoconstrictor impulses to prevail; however, the drugs may also augment or maintain overall coronary blood flow by slowing the heart rate and increasing diastolic perfusion time.[17,18,57,58] More controversial are studies reporting favorable effects of β-blockers on myocardial metabolism, the coronary microvasculature, collateral blood flow, the distribution of myocardial blood flow, oxygen–hemoglobin affinity, and platelet function.[17,57,59-61] One or several of these antiischemic mechanisms may underlie the beneficial effects of β-blocker therapy in survivors of myocardial infarction.

CLINICAL USE

It has been demonstrated conclusively that β-blockers can prolong life in many patients who have had infarction, yet a number of important questions regarding the clinical application of these drugs remain to be answered: Should all patients receive β-blockers after myocardial infarction? When should therapy be instituted and for how long? Which β-blocker should be used and at what dose? What are the risks of therapy?

Which Patients Should Receive β-Blockers?

Results from recruitment efforts in long-term postinfarction trials have demonstrated that one to two weeks after the acute event, up to 20 per cent of survivors have absolute or relative contraindications to β-blockade, such as severe congestive heart failure, bronchial asthma, disorders of atrioventricular and sinus-node function, hypotension, vasospastic angina, and Raynaud's phenomenon.[62,63] It appears from the findings of the Norwegian timolol trial and the Beta-Blocker Heart Attack Trial that a large proportion of the remaining patients stand to benefit from β-blocker therapy.[10,11,44,64-66] A relative reduction of approxi-

Vol. 310   No. 13   MEDICAL INTELLIGENCE — FRISHMAN ET AL.   833

mately 20 to 25 per cent in total mortality in this population can be expected during one to two years of such therapy. A trend toward an even greater benefit has been observed in patients 60 years of age or older and in patients with complicated infarctions (ventricular tachyarrhythmias or mild left ventricular dysfunction).[10,65-68]

In the subgroup of survivors of infarction in whom the risk of mortality is high (i.e., 30 per cent in the first year), β-blocker treatment of 100 such patients for at least one year would prolong the lives of 7, assuming a 25 per cent benefit from therapy. In the low-risk subgroup (2 per cent mortality in the first year), 1400 patients would have to be treated to prolong the lives of 7, assuming the same relative benefit. The clinician may therefore question the need to treat low-risk survivors of infarction, since the hazards and costs of β-blocker therapy may outweigh the potential reduction of cardiovascular mortality.[68,69] In making this decision, one must also consider that the risk of nonfatal reinfarction is favorably influenced by these drugs, and that the occurrence of this morbid event cannot be predicted as reliably as cardiovascular mortality.

The decision to start β-blocker treatment should probably not be based on any consideration of performing coronary arteriography for assessing the potential benefit of coronary-artery surgery. Information is not available to determine whether β-blockers are useful in patients who have undergone successful coronary-bypass surgery after their infarction. However, considering that the risk of mortality and morbidity in the postinfarction population has multiple causes that may not be altogether eliminated by coronary-artery surgery, it would seem reasonable to administer β-blockers to this population as well. The decision to treat patients who have had an infarction is certainly easiest when other proved indications for β-blockade exist (e.g., angina pectoris, hypertension, and supraventricular tachyarrhythmias).

When Should Treatment Be Started?

In most of the long-term trials, β-blocker treatment was initiated one to three weeks after the infarction. By that time patients had begun to recover and were in a relatively stable condition. It was clearly advantageous to begin treatment while patients were hospitalized. In two trials, the International Multicentre Study with practolol and the Beta-Blocker Heart Attack Trial with propranolol, the results of early and late initiation of treatment were compared in hospitalized patients. In both trials it appeared, though it was not proved, that therapy initiated early (six to nine days after acute infarction) was more advantageous than therapy initiated after two to three weeks.[70]

It has been suggested that β-blocker treatment should be started upon admission to the hospital to reduce the high rate of early mortality among inpatients.[17] It has also been argued that treatment started within 6 to 12 hours may limit infarct size and subsequent mortality.[17] An analysis of the reported trials of acute intervention with β-blockers can provide information on this matter.

There have been 18 controlled trials of the effects of acute intervention with a β-blocker on early (usually four-week) mortality.[6,7,37-40,51,52,71-80] In 10 trials, an oral treatment regimen was used, which was probably started too late to have a favorable effect on the size of the infarct or on the eventual development of acute infarction.[7,37-40,71-75] In 7 of these 10 trials, total mortality was higher in the β-blocker group than in the placebo group.[37-40,72,74,75]

In the remaining eight trials, intravenous β-blocker treatment was started immediately and followed by oral treatment, to assess whether early intervention could favorably affect mortality, presumably by limiting infarct size.[6,51,52,76-78] Three of these trials demonstrated a higher mortality in the β-blocker group than in the placebo group,[6,76,77] four showed a lower mortality in the β-blocker group,[51,52,78,80] and one showed no difference.[79] In one of the trials, using metoprolol, there was a statistically significant reduction in mortality,[52] predominantly in patients with anterior-wall infarcts. Metoprolol also appeared to reduce serum levels of lactate dehydrogenase isoenzyme, when treatment was started within 12 hours,[81] and to reduce the incidence of in-hospital ventricular fibrillation.[50] The effect on mortality was the same whether treatment was started before or after 12 hours, suggesting that a reduction of infarct size did not contribute to the benefit. Judging from the mortality curves, which did not start to diverge until after five to seven days of therapy, the benefit seen with metoprolol may have been related to the 90-day oral maintenance regimen rather than to early intravenous treatment. A second study of metoprolol at the same dosage, in which patients were enrolled within six hours after the onset of symptoms and were also treated for 90 days, did not show any clear benefit.[76] An acute-intervention trial using intravenous and oral atenolol showed a favorable effect on in-hospital mortality, a reduction in repetitive ventricular arrhythmias, and a reduction in serum levels of creatine kinase MB isoenzyme.[51] Despite these favorable findings, however, there was no significant difference in long-term mortality (up to two years of follow-up) between placebo-treated and atenolol-treated patients.[51] Two recent reports[79,80] have highlighted the importance of administering active treatment very early after the onset of infarction: the indexes of infarct size were favorably reduced when timolol was given within an average of four hours after the onset of symptoms,[80] whereas no such effect was observed when propranolol was given within an average of 8.9 hours after the onset of chest pain.[79]

The clinical value of treatment with a β-adrenergic blocker within 18 hours of a myocardial infarction is now being reexamined in three cooperative trials in Europe and in the United States.[43] One of these studies (the Metoprolol in Acute Myocardial Infarction trial) is assessing intravenous and oral metoprolol; the results should be available in late 1984. Another (the International Study of Infarct Survival) will be evaluating intravenous and oral atenolol in 18,000 patients.[43]

To date, β-blockers have not received FDA approval for early intravenous use in patients with myocardial infarction, except for the treatment of supraventricular tachyarrhythmias. Thus, on the basis of the evidence available, oral β-blocker therapy should be started six to nine days after acute myocardial infarction in patients who are hemodynamically stable and have no contraindications to this treatment.

No conclusive data are available regarding a benefit on long-term survival when β-blocker therapy is begun months to years after an acute infarction. Nonetheless, it seems reasonable to assume that a favorable effect on mortality and morbidity will occur if treatment is initiated within a few months after hospitalization. Support of this view arises from retrospective subgroup analyses of a trial of oxprenolol, which suggested a beneficial effect on survival if treatment was started within four months after myocardial infarction, but no benefit if treatment was started at four months or later.[14]

When to Stop Therapy?

Studies of timolol and propranolol treatment have demonstrated a continuously increasing effect on mortality over approximately 18 months.[10,11,44] Beyond that point, interpretation of the data is more difficult because there were fewer deaths. It should be noted that cumulative mortality curves can give misleading visual impressions and that a small number of late deaths in either treatment group can substantially change the slope of the curve. Nevertheless, the mortality curves for the control and intervention groups in the propranolol trial remained essentially parallel from 18 to 36 months. In addition, whether the accruing benefit over 18 months would disappear if treatment were stopped at that time is not known. It is possible that some members of the intervention group who were saved initially by β-blocker treatment would still receive benefit from continuous therapy. As Rose has asked, "Do β-blockers merely keep the wolf from the door, and when protection is withdrawn, does he return?"[82]

Considering the available evidence, any decision to continue β-blocker therapy beyond 18 months has to be based on clinical judgment rather than on hard scientific data. The limited information available from the trials shows more deaths in the placebo group than in the β-blocker group after as long as 48 months.[10,11,14] This suggests that there is sustained benefit from continued therapy. One may be concerned about the extended use of these drugs in the general postinfarction population. However, patients in the intermediate-risk and high-risk subsets, who could potentially benefit the most from β-blocker

treatment, may be the group to consider for longer courses of therapy.

An argument for stopping β-blocker treatment after a fixed period is the recent observation that β-blockers can lower plasma levels of high-density-lipoprotein cholesterol and raise levels of triglycerides, potentially increasing the risk of accelerated atherogenesis.[83-85] Whether this should be a matter of concern in patients who already have advanced coronary-artery disease is debatable. Finally, in the long-term trials there was no evidence of a β-blocker "withdrawal reaction" in patients who discontinued active treatment — an early concern that has not been confirmed in the postinfarction population.[70]

Which β-Blocker and at What Dosage?

Each of the long-term postinfarction trials compared a single β-blocking drug with a placebo. Since no direct comparisons of drugs are available, it is not known whether any specific β-blocking compound has advantages over another when used after infarction. Some investigators have argued that the pharmacodynamic differences that these drugs manifest (such as β_1-selectivity, membrane-stabilizing properties, and partial agonist activity) may be important, so that β-blockers are not interchangeable. Other investigators believe that the benefit of β-blockers is conferred by the β_1-adrenergic blockade that is common to the class, rather than by a specific compound.[86] The results of the individual trials suggest that differences in clinical efficacy do exist among the various β-blocking drugs, but whether these differences are real is not clear. The most favorable effects on mortality in all subgroups of patients have been observed with nonselective β-blockers without partial agonist activity (e.g., propranolol and timolol).[10,11] The two largest trials using β_1-selective adrenergic blockers showed a benefit that was predominant in patients with anterior-wall myocardial infarction.[8,9,52] The results of three recent trials with β-blockers having partial agonist activity revealed little or no benefit.[14,15,42]

Evidence is strongest at present for the use of oral timolol or propranolol, which are both nonselective β-blockers with similar pharmacokinetics. Both drugs have been shown to reduce total mortality, cardiovascular mortality, sudden death, and nonfatal reinfarction. Timolol maleate was the first orally active β-blocker to be approved for reducing the long-term risk of cardiovascular mortality in hemodynamically stable survivors of acute myocardial infarction who had no contraindications to β-blockade; a fixed daily dosage of 20 mg should be given in two divided doses.[87] Propranolol was recently approved for this use, primarily because of the favorable findings from the Beta-Blocker Heart Attack Trial. In that study, 180 to 240 mg of oral propranolol was employed in three divided doses, and plasma levels were used to monitor the dosage regimen.[88] The 180-mg dosage was assigned to 82 per cent of the patients[88]; this

Vol. 310   No. 13   MEDICAL INTELLIGENCE — FRISHMAN ET AL.   835

amount is approximately equivalent in pharmacological potency to 20 mg of timolol.[87]

A regimen of three daily doses was evaluated in the propranolol study; however, there are pharmacologic studies supporting a twice-daily regimen in survivors of myocardial infarction.[89] Both timolol and propranolol have plasma half-lives of four to five hours and pharmacodynamic half-lives that are substantially longer, allowing for twice-daily doses in patients with angina pectoris or systemic hypertension.[87,88,90-92] Pharmacodynamic studies with propranolol in normal volunteers indicate that clinical β-blockade, as assessed by blunting of exercise-induced tachycardia, is well maintained whether the drug is administered twice or three times daily at a dosage of 160 to 240 mg per day.[89]

On the basis of these observations and data from the Beta-Blocker Heart Attack Trial, propranolol was approved for use in survivors of acute myocardial infarction at a dosage range of 180 to 240 mg per day in two or three divided doses. The Beta-Blocker Trial showed no significant correlation between trough plasma propranolol levels and beneficial effect, indicating that the lower trough level that occurred with two daily doses should not compromise drug efficacy. Whether the new sustained-release propranolol preparation (Inderal LA)[93] will allow effective single daily doses in postinfarction patients is not known.

The trials have still not indicated what the optimal dosage of a β-blocker is, or whether it is preferable to use a fixed-dosage regimen for all postinfarction patients or to titrate the dosage until clinical β-adrenergic blockade is achieved.[88] Neither issue was carefully assessed in the reported trials. In some acute-intervention and long-term trials with propranolol, there was evidence that with lower doses than those used in the Beta-Blocker Heart Attack Trial, no clinical benefit occurred.[41] In addition, up to 480 mg per day may be needed to treat coexisting conditions, such as hypertension, arrhythmia, and angina pectoris.[88] In determining clinical efficacy, following plasma drug levels is not helpful, except for monitoring patient compliance with the prescribed drug regimen.

Side Effects

In deciding whether or not to treat patients with β-blockers after infarction, the risks of therapy must be weighed against the potential benefits. In studies of patients with no absolute or relative contraindications to β-blocker treatment, severe adverse reactions leading to discontinuation of therapy were fairly infrequent. The proportion of patients taken off active treatment for medical reasons ranged from 5.7 to 20.7 per cent.[2-15,63] The composition of the patient populations, the drug dosages and durations of treatment, and the methods of ascertaining and reporting adverse effects are factors that need to be considered in comparing these numbers. A remarkable finding was the observation that side effects were common with placebo treatment; in fact, the frequencies were similar to those with active treatment.[10,11,63]

Cardiovascular problems accounted for the greatest number of severe reactions in the β-blocker groups. These included symptomatic congestive heart failure, hypotension with and without dizziness, bradycardia, and atrioventricular block.[63] Heart failure was much less common than expected, perhaps because most of the studies excluded patients with even moderate heart failure at entry.[94,95] Nonetheless, patients with a history of heart failure are more likely to have problems.[68] The high-risk patients assigned to the propranolol group in a Norwegian study had a transient increase in heart failure within the first two weeks of therapy.[12]

Caution should therefore be exercised when using β-blockers in patients whose myocardial and bronchial function may depend on adequate stimulation from the sympathetic nervous system. Overall, the different β-blockers used in these trials were remarkably well tolerated and demonstrated similar safety profiles[2-7,10-15,41]; the exception was practolol, which caused a unique set of adverse reactions leading to its removal from the world market.[9]

The trials also showed a high frequency of minor side effects with β-blockers, which did not lead to discontinuation of the treatment. These included cases of cold extremities, nausea, constipation, asthma, fatigue, mental depression, impotence, and dry eyes.[2-15] The excess reporting of these effects in the patients treated with β-blockers was relatively small.

PUBLIC-HEALTH IMPACT

The reduction in cardiovascular mortality and recurrent infarction in survivors of myocardial infarction who are treated with β-blockers represents an important breakthrough in the treatment of coronary-artery disease.[96] For the first time, a pharmacologic therapy has had a clearly demonstrated favorable effect on survival in the period after infarction. This comes after years of testing different therapeutic regimens with benefits that remain unproved. β-Blockers act by delaying recurrent fatal and nonfatal coronary events. Patients who are "saved" by β-blockade have an uncertain prognosis, since their underlying atherosclerotic heart disease is generally progressive and most will ultimately die from it. β-Blockers appear to be of only partial and temporary benefit in preventing death from coronary-artery disease. The primary prevention of coronary-artery disease and the control of factors that precipitate coronary events remain our strongest hopes for the future.

REFERENCES

1. Frishman WH. β-Adrenoceptor antagonists: new drugs and new indications. N Engl J Med 1981; 305:500-6.
2. Wilhelmsson C, Vedin JA, Wilhelmsen L, Tibblin G, Werkö L. Reduction of sudden deaths after myocardial infarction by treatment with alprenolol: preliminary results. Lancet 1974; 2:1157-60.

836   THE NEW ENGLAND JOURNAL OF MEDICINE   March 29, 1984

3. Vedin A, Wilhelmsson C, Werkö L. Chronic alprenolol treatment of patients with acute myocardial infarction after discharge from hospital: effects on mortality and morbidity. Acta Med Scand [Suppl] 1975; 575:1-40.

4. Ahlmark G, Saetre H, Korsgren M. Reduction of sudden deaths after myocardial infarction. Lancet 1974; 2:1563.

5. Ahlmark G, Saetre H. Long-term treatment with β-blockers after myocardial infarction. Eur J Clin Pharmacol 1976; 10:77-83.

6. Andersen MP, Bechsgaard P, Frederiksen J, et al. Effect of alprenolol on mortality among patients with definite or suspected acute myocardial infarction: preliminary results. Lancet 1979; 2:865-8.

7. Barber JM, Boyle DMcC, Chaturvedi NC, Singh N, Walsh MJ. Practolol in acute myocardial infarction. Acta Med Scand [Suppl] 1975; 587:213-9.

8. Improvement in prognosis of myocardial infarction by long-term beta-adrenoreceptor blockade using practolol: a multicentre international study. Br Med J 1975; 3:735-40.

9. Reduction in mortality after myocardial infarction with long-term beta-adrenoceptor blockade: multicentre international study. Supplementary report. Br Med J 1977; 2:419-21.

10. Norwegian Multicenter Study Group. Timolol-induced reduction in mortality and reinfarction in patients surviving acute myocardial infarction. N Engl J Med 1981; 304:801-7.

11. β-Blocker Heart Attack Trial Research Group. A randomized trial of propranolol in patients with acute myocardial infarction. I. Mortality results. JAMA 1982; 247:1707-14.

12. Hansteen V, Møinichen E, Lorentsen E, et al. One year's treatment with propranolol after myocardial infarction: preliminary report of Norwegian multicentre trial. Br Med J 1982; 284:155-60.

13. Julian DG, Prescott RJ, Jackson FS, Szekely P. A controlled trial of sotalol for one year after myocardial infarction. Lancet 1982; 1:1142-7.

14. Taylor SH, Silke B, Ebbutt A, Sutton GC, Prout BJ, Burley DM. A long-term prevention study with oxprenolol in coronary heart disease. N Engl J Med 1982; 307:1293-301.

15. Australian and Swedish Pindolol Study Group. The effect of pindolol on the two-year mortality after complicated myocardial infarction. Eur Heart J 1983; 4:367-75.

16. Frishman WH. Clinical pharmacology of the new beta-adrenergic blocking drugs. Part 12. Beta-adrenoceptor blockade in myocardial infarction: the continuing controversy. Am Heart J 1980; 99:528-36.

17. Braunwald E, Muller JE, Kloner RA, Maroko PR. Role of beta-adrenergic blockade in the therapy of patients with myocardial infarction. Am J Med 1983; 74:113-23.

18. Turi ZG, Braunwald E. The use of β-blockers after myocardial infarction. JAMA 1983; 249:2512-6.

19. Hampton JR. Should every survivor of a heart attack be given a beta-blocker? I. Evidence from clinical trials. Br Med J 1982; 285:33-6.

20. Long-term and short-term beta-blockade after myocardial infarction. Lancet 1982; 1:1159-61.

21. May GS, Furberg CD, Eberlein KA, Geraci BJ. Secondary prevention after myocardial infarction: a review of short-term acute phase trials. Prog Cardiovasc Dis 1983; 25:335-59.

22. May GS, Eberlein KA, Furberg CD, Passamani ER, DeMets DL. Secondary prevention after myocardial infarction: a review of long-term trials. Prog Cardiovasc Dis 1982; 24:331-52.

23. Davis HT, DeCamilla J, Bayer LW, Moss AJ. Survivorship patterns in the posthospital phase of myocardial infarction. Circulation 1979; 60:1252-8.

24. Multicenter Postinfarction Research Group. Risk stratification after myocardial infarction. N Engl J Med 1983; 309:331-6.

25. Théroux P, Waters DD, Halphen C, Debaisieux J-C, Mizgala HF. Prognostic value of exercise testing soon after myocardial infarction. N Engl J Med 1979; 301:341-5.

26. Fein SA, Klein NA, Frishman WH. Exercise testing soon after uncomplicated myocardial infarction: prognostic value and safety. JAMA 1981; 245:1863-8.

27. Frishman WH, Ribner HS. Anticoagulation in myocardial infarction: a modern approach to an old problem. Am J Cardiol 1979; 43:1207-13.

28. Persantine-Aspirin Reinfarction Study Research Group. Persantine and aspirin in coronary heart disease. Circulation 1980; 62:449-61.

29. The Coronary Drug Project Research Group. Clofibrate and niacin in coronary heart disease. JAMA 1975; 231:360-81.

30. Myocardial Infarction Study Group. Secondary prevention of ischaemic heart disease: a long-term controlled lidoflazine study. Acta Cardiol [Suppl] (Brux) 1979; 24:1-116.

31. Weinblatt E, Shapiro S, Frank CW, Sager RV. Prognosis of men after first myocardial infarction: mortality and first recurrence in relation to selected parameters. Am J Public Health 1968; 58:1329-47.

32. Coronary Drug Project Research Group. Factors influencing long-term prognosis after recovery from myocardial infarction — three-year findings of the Coronary Drug Project. J Chronic Dis 1974; 27:267-85.

33. Vedin A, Wilhelmsson L, Wedel H, et al. Prediction of cardiovascular deaths and non-fatal reinfarction after myocardial infarction. Acta Med Scand 1977; 201:309-16.

34. Vatner SF, McRitchie RJ, Maroko PR, Patrick TA, Braunwald E. Effects of

35. Han J. Mechanisms of ventricular arrhythmias associated with myocardial infarction. Am J Cardiol 1969; 24:800-13.

36. Snow PJD. Effect of propranolol in myocardial infarction. Lancet 1965; 2:551-3.

37. Balcon R, Jewitt DE, Davies JPH, Oram S. A controlled trial of propranolol in acute myocardial infarction. Lancet 1966; 2:917-20.

38. Clausen J, Felsby M, Jørgensen FS, Nielsen BL, Roin J, Strange B. Absence of prophylactic effect of propranolol in myocardial infarction. Lancet 1966; 2:920-4.

39. Propranolol in acute myocardial infarction: a multicentre trial. Lancet 1966; 2:1435-7.

40. Norris RM, Caughey DE, Scott PJ. Trial of propranolol in acute myocardial infarction. Br Med J 1968; 2:398-400.

41. Baber NS, Wainwright-Evans D, Howitt G, et al. Multicentre post-infarction trial of propranolol in 49 hospitals in the United Kingdom, Italy, and Yugoslavia. Br Heart J 1980; 44:96-100.

42. European Infarction Study Group. European Infarction Study — a secondary beta-blocker prevention trial after myocardial infarction. Circulation 1983; 68:Suppl 3:III-294. abstract.

43. Cutler JA. A review of on-going trials of beta-blockers in the secondary prevention of coronary heart disease. Circulation 1983; 67 (6:Part 2):I-62-5.

44. Goldstein S. Propranolol therapy in patients with acute myocardial infarction: the Beta-Blocker Heart Attack Trial. Circulation 1983; 67 (6:Part 2):I-53-7.

45. Furberg CD, Bell RL. Effect of beta-blocker therapy on recurrent non-fatal myocardial infarction. Circulation 1983; 67 (6:Part 2):I-83-5.

46. Pratt C, Lichstein E. Ventricular antiarrhythmic effects of beta-adrenergic blocking drugs: a review of mechanism and clinical studies. J Clin Pharmacol 1982; 22:335-47.

47. Anderson JL, Rodier HE, Green LS. Comparative effects of beta-adrenergic blocking drugs on experimental ventricular fibrillation threshold. Am J Cardiol 1983; 51:1196-1202.

48. Opie LH. Myocardial infarct size. Part 1. Basic considerations. Am Heart J 1980; 100:355-72.

49. Hjalmarson Å. Myocardial metabolic changes related to ventricular fibrillation. Cardiology 1980; 65:226-47.

50. Rydén L, Ariniego R, Arnman K, et al. A double-blind trial of metoprolol in acute myocardial infarction: effects on ventricular tachyarrhythmias. N Engl J Med 1983; 308:614-8.

51. Yusuf S, Sleight P, Rossi P, et al. Reduction in infarct size, arrhythmias and chest pain by early intravenous beta-blockade in suspected acute myocardial infarction. Circulation 1983; 67 (6: Part 2):I-32-41.

52. Hjalmarson Å, Elmfeldt D, Herlitz J, et al. Effect on mortality of metoprolol in acute myocardial infarction: a double-blind randomised trial. Lancet 1981; 2:823-7.

53. Lichstein E, Morganroth J, Harrist R, Hubble E. Effect of propranolol on ventricular arrhythmia. The Beta-Blocker Heart Attack Trial experience: preliminary data from the Heart Attack Trial experience. Circulation 1983; 67 (6:Part 2):I-5-10.

54. Koppes GM, Beckmann CH, Jones FG. Propranolol therapy for ventricular arrhythmias 2 months after myocardial infarction. Am J Cardiol 1980; 46:322-8.

55. von der Lippe G, Lund-Johansen P, Kjekshus J. Effects of timolol on late ventricular arrhythmias after acute myocardial infarction. Acta Med Scand (Suppl) 1981; 651:253-63.

56. Capone R, Friedman L, Byington R. The effect of propranolol on mortality in patients following acute myocardial infarction with complex ventricular arrhythmias. Circulation 1983; 68:Suppl III:III-294. abstract.

57. Frishman WH. Multifactorial actions of β-adrenergic blocking drugs in ischemic heart disease: current concepts. Circulation 1983; 67 (6:Part 2):I-11-8.

58. Kirk ES, Sonnenblick EH. Newer concepts in the pathophysiology of ischemic heart disease. Am Heart J 1982; 103:756-67.

59. Opie LH. Myocardial infarct size. Part 2. Comparison of anti-infarct effects of beta-blockade, glucose-insulin-potassium, nitrates and hyaluronidase. Am Heart J 1980; 100:531-52.

60. Frishman WH, Weksler BB. Effects of β-adrenoceptor blocking drugs on platelet function in normal subjects and patients with angina pectoris. In: Roskamm H, Graefe KH, eds. Advances in β-blocker therapy: proceedings of an international symposium. Amsterdam: Excerpta Medica 1980: 164-90.

61. Schrumpf JD, Sheps DS, Wolfson S, Aronson AL, Cohen LS. Altered hemoglobin-oxygen affinity with long-term propranolol therapy in patients with coronary artery disease. Am J Cardiol 1977; 40:76-82.

62. Frishman W, Silverman R, Strom J, Elkayam U, Sonnenblick E. Clinical pharmacology of the new beta-adrenergic blocking drugs. Part 4. Adverse effects: choosing a β-adrenoreceptor blocker. Am Heart J 1979; 98:256-62.

63. Friedman LM. How do the various beta-blockers compare in type, frequency and severity of their adverse effects? Circulation 1983; 67 (6:Part 2):I-89-90.

catecholamines, exercise, and nitroglycerin on the normal and ischemic myocardium in conscious dogs. J Clin Invest 1974; 54:563-75.

64. Pedersen TR. The Norwegian multicenter study of timolol after myocardial infarction. Circulation 1983; 67 (6:Part 2):I-49-53.

65. Furberg CD, Byington RP. What do subgroup analyses reveal about differential response to beta-blocker therapy: the Beta-Blocker Heart Attack Trial experience. Circulation 1983; 67 (6:Part 2):I-98-101.

66. Rodda BE. The Timolol Myocardial Infarction Study: an evaluation of selected variables. Circulation 1983; 67 (6:Part 2):I-101-6.

67. Hawkins CM, Richardson DW, Vokonas PS. Effect on propranolol in reducing mortality in older myocardial infarction patients: the Beta-Blocker Heart Attack Trial experience. Circulation 1983; 67 (6:Suppl 2):I-94-7.

68. Furberg CD, Hawkins CM, Lichstein E. Effect of propranolol in post-infarction patients with mechanical or electrical complications. Circulation (in press).

69. Griggs TR, Wagner GS, Gettes LS. Beta-adrenergic blocking agents after myocardial infarction: an undocumented need in patients at lowest risk. J Am Coll Cardiol 1983; 1:1530-3.

70. Baber NS, Lewis JA. Beta-adrenoceptor blockade and myocardial infarction: when should treatment start and for how long should it continue? Circulation 1983; 67 (6:Part 2):I-71-7.

71. Barber JM, Murphy FM, Merrett JD. Clinical trial of propranolol in acute myocardial infarction. Ulster Med J 1967; 36:127-30.

72. Briant RB, Norris RM. Alprenolol in acute myocardial infarction: double-blind trial. NZ Med J 1970; 71:135-8.

73. Wilcox RG, Roland JM, Banks DC, Hampton JR, Mitchell JRA. Randomised trial comparing propranolol with atenolol in immediate treatment of suspected myocardial infarction. Br Med J 1980; 280:885-8.

74. Wilcox RG, Rowley JM, Hampton JR, Mitchell JRA, Roland JM, Banks DC. Randomised placebo-controlled trial comparing oxprenolol with disopyramide phosphate in immediate treatment of suspected myocardial infarction. Lancet 1980; 2:765-9.

75. Coronary Prevention Research Group. An early intervention secondary prevention study with oxprenolol following myocardial infarction. Eur Heart J 1981; 2:389-93.

76. Evemy KL, Pentecost BL. Intravenous and oral practolol in the acute stages of myocardial infarction. Eur J Cardiol 1978; 7:391-8.

77. Johansson BW. A comparative study of cardioselective β-blockade and diazepam in patients with acute myocardial infarction and tachycardia. Acta Med Scand 1980; 207:47-53.

78. McIlmoyle L, Evans A, Boyle DMcC, et al. Early intervention in myocardial ischaemia. Br Heart J 1982; 47:189. abstract.

79. Muller J, Roberts R, Stone P, et al. Failure of propranolol administration to limit infarct size in patients with acute myocardial infarction. Circulation 1983; 68: Suppl 3:III-294. abstract.

80. International Collaborative Study Group. Reduction of infarct size with the early use of timolol in acute myocardial infarction. N Engl J Med 1984; 310:9-15.

81. Hjalmarson Å, Herlitz J. Limitation of infarct size by beta-blockers and its potential role for prognosis. Circulation 1983; 67 (6:Part 2):I-68-71.

82. Rose G. Prophylaxis with β-blockers and the community. Br J Clin Pharmacol 1982; 14:45S-48S.

83. Leren P, Foss PO, Helgeland A, Hjermann I, Holme I, Lund-Larsen PG. Effect of propranolol and prazosin on blood lipids: the Oslo study. Lancet 1980; 2:4-6.

84. Shulman RS, Herbert PN, Capone RJ, et al. Effects of propranolol on blood lipids and lipoproteins in myocardial infarction. Circulation 1983; 67 (6:Part 2):I-19-21.

85. Johnson BF. The emerging problem of plasma lipid changes during antihypertensive therapy. J Cardiovasc Pharmacol 1982; 4: Suppl 2:213s-21s.

86. Harrison DC. Beneficial effects of beta-blockers: a class action or individual pharmacologic spectrum? Circulation 1983; 67 (6:Part 2):I-77-82.

87. Frishman WH. Atenolol and timolol: two new systemic β-adrenoceptor antagonists. N Engl J Med 1982; 306:1456-62.

88. Shand DG. How should the proper dose of a beta blocker be determined? Circulation 1983; 67 (6:Part 2):I-86-8.

89. Mullane JF, Kaufman J, Dvornik D, Coelho J. Propranolol dosage, plasma concentration, and beta blockade. Clin Pharmacol Ther 1982; 32:692-700.

90. Thadani U, Parker JO. Propranolol in angina pectoris: comparison of therapy given two and four times daily. Am J Cardiol 1980; 46:117-23.

91. Berglund G, Andersson O, Hansson R, Olander R. Propranolol given twice daily in hypertension. Acta Med Scand 1973; 194:513-5.

92. MacLeod SM, Hamet P, Kaplan H, et al. Antihypertensive efficacy of propranolol given twice daily. Can Med Assoc J 1979; 121:737-40.

93. Leahey WJ, Neill JD, Varma MPS, Shanks RG. Comparison of the efficacy and pharmacokinetics of conventional propranolol and a long acting preparation of propranolol. Br J Clin Pharmacol 1980; 9:33-40.

94. Julian DG. Can beta-blockers be safely used in patients with recent acute myocardial infarction who also have congestive heart failure? Circulation 1983; 67 (6:Part 2):I-91.

95. Gundersen T. Influence of heart size on mortality and reinfarction in patients treated with timolol after myocardial infarction. Br Heart J 1983; 50:135-9.

96. Friedewald WT. Beta-adrenergic blockade after myocardial infarction: clinical and public health implications of the reported beta-blocker clinical trials. Circulation 1983; 67 (6:Part 2):I-110-1.

DRUG THERAPY

Drug Therapy

ALASTAIR J.J. WOOD, M.D., *Editor*

CARVEDILOL

WILLIAM H. FRISHMAN, M.D.

CARVEDILOL is a β-adrenoreceptor–antagonist drug with α_1-adrenoreceptor–antagonist activity. It was approved in the United States in September 1995 for the treatment of patients with essential hypertension and in May 1997, on the basis of the results of several clinical trials,[1-8] became the first adrenoreceptor-blocking drug to receive approval for the treatment of symptomatic heart failure.

PHARMACODYNAMIC AND PHARMACOKINETIC PROPERTIES

Carvedilol is a racemic lipophilic aryloxypropanolamine (Fig. 1) that causes both precapillary vasodilatation by means of α_1-adrenoreceptor blockade and nonselective β-adrenoreceptor blockade and is devoid of intrinsic sympathomimetic activity.[9] Its membrane-stabilizing activity is less than that of propranolol. Milligram for milligram, carvedilol is about two to four times as potent as propranolol as a β-adrenoreceptor antagonist.[10] The ratio of α_1- to β-adrenoreceptor blockade for carvedilol is 1:10,[11] as compared with 1:4 for labetalol, another α- and β-adrenoreceptor–antagonist drug used in treating hypertension.[12] Thus, carvedilol may cause fewer side effects resulting from α_1-adrenoreceptor blockade than labetalol.[9]

Most of the vasodilator activity of carvedilol is due to its ability to block α_1-adrenoreceptors,[13] although at high concentrations it also blocks calcium entry.[14] The drug has no effect on angiotensin receptors.[15] Other β-adrenoreceptor antagonists with peripheral vasodilator action include those that have partial β_2-adrenoreceptor–agonist activity (e.g., pindolol) and those that have direct vasodilator action (e.g., bucindolol) (Table 1).[16,17] Carvedilol also has in vitro antioxidant activity, the importance of which is unknown.[18]

In normal subjects and patients with hypertension, carvedilol is rapidly and completely absorbed after oral administration.[9] The volume of distribution is about 1.5 to 2 liters per kilogram of body weight, indicating substantial distribution into extravascular tissues.[13] Peak plasma drug concentrations are reached in one to two hours. Absorption is delayed an additional 60 to 135 minutes when the drug is administered with food.[19] Carvedilol undergoes extensive stereoselective first-pass hepatic metabolism.[20] In plasma, 98 percent of the drug is bound to plasma proteins, predominantly to albumin.[9] The terminal elimination half-life of carvedilol ranges from 7 to 10 hours in most subjects.[9]

Carvedilol is cleared by aromatic-ring oxidation and glucuronidation in the liver.[20] The oxidative metabolites are then conjugated with glucuronide and sulfate,[13] and the resulting conjugates are excreted in the bile and eliminated in the feces; only 16 percent is excreted in the urine.[21] Some of the metabolites of carvedilol have β-adrenoreceptor–antagonist activity, and one 4-hydroxyphenyl metabolite is approximately 13 times as potent as carvedilol in this regard.[13] The metabolites also have weak vasodilator activity, but the clinical importance of this property is unknown. The metabolism of carvedilol is affected by genetic polymorphism of cytochrome P-450 2D6 activity, in that patients with low activity have higher plasma concentrations of *R*-carvedilol, a stereoisomer that has both α- and β-adrenoreceptor–antagonist activity.[22] Drugs that inhibit cytochrome P-450 2D6 activity, such as quinidine, paroxetine, fluoxetine, and propafenone, may also increase plasma carvedilol concentrations. Thus, patients taking these drugs may be at particularly high risk of hypotension due to excessive α-adrenoreceptor blockade. In contrast, plasma concentrations of *S*-carvedilol, which has only β-adrenoreceptor–antagonist activity, are increased only slightly in patients with low cytochrome P-450 2D6 activity.[23]

Clearance of carvedilol is delayed in patients over 65 years of age. On average, their plasma carvedilol concentrations are 50 percent higher than in younger patients. Patients with liver disease also have high plasma carvedilol concentrations,[24] but the half-life of the drug is unchanged. Patients with renal disease have slightly increased plasma carvedilol concentrations[25]; the pharmacokinetics of carvedilol are not altered in patients undergoing hemodialysis.[26] Drugs

From the Departments of Medicine and Pharmacology, New York Medical College, Valhalla. Address reprint requests to Dr. Frishman at the New York Medical College–Westchester Medical Center, Department of Medicine, Munger Pavilion, Valhalla, NY 10595.

The New England Journal of Medicine

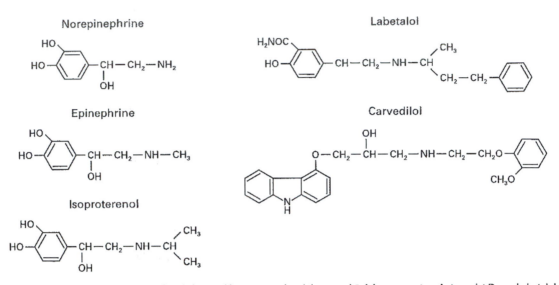

Figure 1. Structure of Norepinephrine, Epinephrine, and Isoproterenol and the α- and β-Adrenoreceptor–Antagonist Drugs Labetalol and Carvedilol.

that increase cytochrome P-450 activity, such as rifampin, can accelerate the clearance of carvedilol. Hydrochlorothiazide does not influence the pharmacokinetics of carvedilol,[9] and the pharmacokinetics of warfarin are not affected by carvedilol. Plasma digoxin concentrations rise slightly in patients given carvedilol.[27]

Patients with heart failure (particularly patients with New York Heart Association [NYHA] functional class IV heart failure) have higher plasma carvedilol concentrations than normal subjects of the same age, but the values overlap considerably between the two groups. The increase is higher for *S*-carvedilol than for *R*-carvedilol. Heart failure, by causing intestinal edema, may also reduce absorption of the drug.[28] Since heart failure causes reduced cardiac output, depressed hepatic perfusion, and hepatic congestion, it could interfere with hepatic drug metabolism; these factors could influence the pharmacokinetics of carvedilol.[29] However, in one study that assessed the pharmacokinetics of carvedilol in patients with heart failure, the stereoselective disposition of the drug was proportional to the dose over the therapeutic range (6.25 to 50 mg per day).[30]

CLINICAL EFFECTIVENESS

Carvedilol has been studied in patients with heart failure, hypertension, and ischemic heart disease.

Congestive Heart Failure

Because of their known negative inotropic effects, β-adrenoreceptor antagonists were thought for many years to be contraindicated in patients with heart failure.[31] However, we now know that the course of chronic heart failure can be adversely influenced by neurohormonal activation of the renin–angiotensin–aldosterone system and activation of the sympathetic nervous system.[32,23] Therapy with angiotensin-converting–enzyme inhibitors has improved survival and decreased morbidity among patients with heart failure,[34] and there is growing evidence that modulation of the sympathetic nervous system by β-adrenoreceptor blockade can also favorably affect patients with heart failure.[35]

Patients with heart failure have increased sympathetic activity that is associated with exercise intolerance,[36] hemodynamic abnormalities,[37] and increased mortality.[33] Increases in sympathetic tone can potentiate the activity of renin and angiotensin in such patients, leading to retention of salt and water, arterial and venous constriction, and increased ventricular preload and afterload.[35] Excess catecholamines can increase the heart rate and cause coronary vasoconstriction, thereby diminishing myocardial blood flow,[38] and they can decrease myocardial contractility on the cellular level.[39,40] Catecholamines can also stimulate growth and provoke oxidative stress in terminally differentiated cardiac-muscle cells; these two factors can trigger the process of programmed cell death (apoptosis).[41] Finally, catecholamines can increase the risk of sudden death in patients with heart failure by adversely influencing the electrophysiologic properties of the failing heart[42] and by inducing hypokalemia,[43] thereby lowering the threshold for ventricular fibrillation.

In 1975, β-adrenoreceptor blockade with prac-

DRUG THERAPY

TABLE 1. PHARMACOLOGIC PROPERTIES OF VARIOUS β-ADRENORECEPTOR–ANTAGONIST DRUGS WITH VASODILATOR ACTIVITY.

DRUG	β-ADRENORECEPTOR–ANTAGONIST POTENCY*	β_1-ADRENORECEPTOR SELECTIVITY	INTRINSIC SYMPATHOMIMETIC ACTIVITY AT β-ADRENORECEPTORS	α-ADRENORECEPTOR–ANTAGONIST ACTIVITY	DIRECT VASODILATOR ACTION
Bucindolol	1.0	No	No	No	Yes
Carvedilol	2.4	No	No	Yes	No
Labetalol	0.3	No	Yes	Yes	No
Pindolol	6.0	No	Yes	No	No

*Potency is expressed relative to that of propranolol, which is defined as 1.0.

tolol or alprenolol was reported to alleviate symptoms and to improve exercise tolerance and left ventricular function in patients with dilated cardiomyopathy.[44] This report was followed by a series of placebo-controlled studies involving the use of various β-adrenoreceptor antagonists in patients with idiopathic dilated cardiomyopathy and ischemic cardiomyopathy. The drugs studied included the selective β_1-adrenoreceptor–antagonist drugs metoprolol[45-47] and bisoprolol,[48] the partial β-adrenoreceptor agonists and antagonists practolol,[45] alprenolol,[45] and acebutolol,[49] and the nonselective β-adrenoreceptor antagonists and vasodilators bucindolol,[50] labetalol,[51] and carvedilol.[1-3,52] Most of these studies, which lasted one to six months, found either no benefit or some improvement in hemodynamic function, reduced symptoms, reduced hospitalizations, increased exercise tolerance, and an improved neurohormonal milieu.[1-3,44-55] Although there was no benefit in terms of survival, these studies provided evidence that β-adrenoreceptor–antagonist drugs could be administered to patients with heart failure with a reasonable degree of safety and some clinical benefit. In addition, several placebo-controlled studies suggested that β-adrenoreceptor–antagonist drugs reduced mortality, especially the risk of sudden death, in patients who had survived myocardial infarction with moderately severe left ventricular dysfunction.[56,57]

The evidence of the efficacy of carvedilol in patients with heart failure comes primarily from the U.S. Carvedilol Heart Failure Program, which consisted of four coordinated studies of a total of 1094 patients who had ventricular ejection fractions of less than 35 percent and NYHA class II, III, or IV symptoms,[4-7] and from a study of 415 patients in Australia and New Zealand who had a history of myocardial infarction, ejection fractions of less than 45 percent, and NYHA class I, II, or III symptoms.[8]

In the U.S. program, patients were entered into one of the four placebo-controlled studies, which lasted 6 to 12 months, on the basis of their ability to complete a six-minute-walk test.[58] At base line

they had to have a resting heart rate of at least 68 beats per minute and a systolic blood pressure of at least 85 mm Hg and had to be able to complete the walk test. Patients were entered into a study of mild heart failure if they could walk 450 to 550 m on the six-minute-walk test at base line,[6] into two studies of moderate heart failure if they could walk 150 to 425 m,[4,5] and into a study of severe heart failure if they could walk less than 150 m.[7] Most patients were receiving conventional therapy for heart failure, including an angiotensin-converting–enzyme inhibitor, a diuretic, and digoxin.[59] Irrespective of the severity of symptoms, their condition had to be clinically stable, as manifested by the absence of hospitalization or a change in heart-failure medication within the preceding month. They then had to be able to tolerate a two-week run-in period while taking 6.25 mg of carvedilol twice daily, after which they were randomly assigned to receive placebo or carvedilol in doses adjusted up to 25 or 50 mg twice daily, depending on the study.

The primary end point in the study of mild heart failure (slowing of the progression of heart failure, defined as death or hospitalization for heart failure, or a sustained increase in heart-failure medication) was reduced by 48 percent during treatment for an average of seven months ($P=0.008$).[6] Exercise tolerance, a primary end point in the two studies of patients with moderate heart failure, was not changed by carvedilol.[4,5] The primary end point in the study of patients with severe heart failure, quality of life as measured by a standard questionnaire, was unaffected by carvedilol.[7,60]

Many secondary end points were prospectively specified in these studies, including a change in the NYHA functional class, patients' and physicians' global assessments of clinical status, and hospitalization for cardiovascular problems.[4-7] In all the studies, there was at least a trend toward improvement in the NYHA class, which was associated with an increase in the left ventricular ejection fraction.[4-7] Global assessment by patients and physicians was significantly higher when patients received carvedilol, as compared with placebo, in most studies.[4-7]

Mortality was not a preplanned primary efficacy end point in any of the four studies.[4-7] However, the U.S. Carvedilol Heart Failure Program was terminated in February 1995 on the recommendation of the data and safety monitoring board, because of a reduction in mortality among the patients treated with carvedilol.[59] According to an intention-to-treat analysis, overall mortality risk was reduced significantly (by 65 percent) in the carvedilol group as compared with the placebo group (3.2 percent vs. 7.8 percent). Mortality was 68 percent lower among patients with NYHA class II symptoms (1.9 percent vs. 5.9 percent) and 65 percent lower among those with NYHA class III symptoms (4.2 percent vs. 11 percent).[59] The reduction in mortality with carvedilol was similar for patients with ischemic cardiomyopathy and those with nonischemic cardiomyopathy.[59] These analyses were based on a total of 53 deaths among the 1094 patients studied, occurring over a mean of 6.5 months. These results, when initially reported, were criticized because deaths that occurred during the prerandomization run-in period with carvedilol were not included[61]; however, when these events were included, the analysis still showed a benefit of carvedilol in terms of mortality.

Nevertheless, the interpretation of the findings of the U.S. Carvedilol Heart Failure Program remains problematic.[61,62] The reported reduction in total mortality includes data from some trials in which the primary results did not show a significant benefit of treatment. In such situations, assignment of significance values to the other results is complex, and such values need to be interpreted cautiously.

The study in Australia and New Zealand[8] was designed to evaluate the clinical and physiologic effects of carvedilol in patients with mild-to-moderate heart failure due to ischemic cardiomyopathy who were already being treated with a diuretic and with an angiotensin-converting–enzyme inhibitor and whose condition was stable for at least one month before enrollment. All patients were initially treated with open-label carvedilol (3.125 mg twice daily, followed by 6.25 mg twice daily, each given for 1 to 2 weeks), followed by 1:1 random assignment to carvedilol or placebo, with the highest tolerated dose (up to 25 mg twice daily) maintained for 18 to 24 months. The end point was death or hospitalization for any reason. After 18 months or more of treatment, the rate of death or hospitalization was 26 percent lower in the carvedilol group than the placebo group (P=0.02).[8]

On the basis of the results of the U.S. Carvedilol Heart Failure Program and the study in Australia and New Zealand,[8] which showed that the drug had a beneficial effect in patients with chronic mild or moderate heart failure, the Food and Drug Administration approved carvedilol for reducing the clinical progression of heart failure, as evidenced by the reduction in rates of hospitalization and mortality and the decreased need for adjustments in medications for heart failure.[62]

Therapy with β-adrenoreceptor antagonists, including carvedilol, has no known beneficial effects on diastolic dysfunction in patients with heart failure. No information is available that suggests a use for carvedilol or other β-adrenoreceptor–antagonist drugs in asymptomatic patients with compromised left ventricular function. However, the results of the postinfarction trials suggest a benefit in these patients.[55,56]

Carvedilol is a β-adrenoreceptor–antagonist vasodilatory drug. It is not known whether its effects in patients with heart failure are unique or are shared by a specific subclass of β-adrenoreceptor antagonists or by β-adrenoreceptor antagonists in general. Carvedilol is the β-adrenoreceptor antagonist that has been most extensively studied for the treatment of heart failure. However, the results of ongoing studies comparing it with other β-adrenoreceptor antagonists should answer these questions. In two small, placebo-controlled trials of the effects of carvedilol (25 to 50 mg daily) and metoprolol (125 to 150 mg daily), carvedilol was associated with a greater improvement among patients with NYHA class III heart failure.[63]

The mechanisms by which β-adrenoreceptor–antagonist drugs slow the progression of heart failure are not known. Possible mechanisms include upregulation of β-adrenergic receptors in the heart, modulation of postreceptor inhibitory G proteins,[64] an effect on left ventricular remodeling, and an improvement in baroreceptor function, which normally can inhibit excess sympathetic outflow.[40,55,64,65] In addition, the drugs may attenuate apoptosis, a process implicated in the progression of heart failure.[66]

Hypertension

On the basis of extensive clinical study,[13,67] carvedilol was also approved for use in patients with mild-to-moderate systemic hypertension, in whom it is used alone in doses of 6.25 to 25 mg twice daily or in combination with other antihypertensive drugs. In comparative clinical trials, the antihypertensive action of carvedilol was quantitatively similar to that of labetalol and other β-adrenoreceptor antagonists, diuretics, captopril, and nifedipine.[67-72] However, because of its higher cost, carvedilol should not be considered as a first-line treatment for patients with uncomplicated hypertension.

Ischemic Heart Disease

Carvedilol reduces the frequency of chest pain and exercise-induced myocardial ischemia in patients with chronic stable angina.[73] In small comparative studies, its efficacy was similar to that of other β-adrenoreceptor antagonists and nifedipine.[52,74,75] In a study of 151 patients with acute myocardial infarction, carvedilol reduced the frequency of cardiac events, including death, reinfarction, and the need for urgent coronary-artery revascularization, as compared with the rates with placebo.[76] However, carvedilol has not been approved for these indications in the United States.

CLINICAL USE IN HEART FAILURE

Carvedilol is indicated to slow the clinical progression of heart failure, as evidenced by reductions in hospitalization rates and mortality and the decreased need for adjustments in medications for heart failure among patients with mild-to-moderate (NYHA class II or III) heart failure of ischemic or cardiomyopathic origin whose condition is stable but who continue to have symptoms despite receiving standard therapy with angiotensin-converting–enzyme inhibitors and diuretics. Carvedilol may also be given to patients who cannot be treated with an angiotensin-converting–enzyme inhibitor. Such patients may or may not be taking digoxin, hydralazine, or a nitrate. The drug is available in 3.125-, 6.25-, 12.5-, and 25-mg tablets at a cost to patients of approximately $100 for a month's supply.

For the treatment of heart failure, the dosage must be individualized and monitored closely. Before therapy with carvedilol is begun, the dosage of angiotensin-converting–enzyme inhibitor and of diuretics (and digoxin) should be stabilized. The recommended starting dose of carvedilol is 3.125 mg twice daily for at least two weeks. If this amount is tolerated, the dose can be doubled at a minimum of every two weeks to the maximal recommended dose of 25 mg twice daily in patients weighing up to 85 kg and 50 mg twice daily in patients weighing more than 85 kg. The drug should be taken with food to slow the rate of absorption and reduce the incidence of side effects.

Before any increase in the carvedilol dose is prescribed, heart-failure status, vital signs, and body weight should be evaluated, since patients may have symptoms (usually transient) of worsening heart failure or dizziness while adjusting to the effects of α- or β-adrenoreceptor blockade. Fluid retention or worsening symptoms of heart failure (such as increasing dyspnea) may be treated with a higher dose of diuretics, although it may be necessary to reduce or discontinue carvedilol. Dizziness or hypotension often responds to a reduction in the dose of the diuretic or angiotensin-converting–enzyme inhibitor, but these symptoms, if persistent, may also require a reduction in the dose of carvedilol. The dose of carvedilol should not be increased until worsening heart failure, hypotension, or bradycardia is stabilized. Improvement in symptoms may become apparent only after carvedilol therapy has been main-tained for several weeks or months. In patients whose symptoms neither improve nor worsen, carvedilol should be continued because of a possible benefit in terms of survival.

For patients who are already receiving relatively high doses of β-adrenoreceptor antagonists, particularly those with ischemic heart disease or those who are likely to have dizziness after the institution of α-adrenoreceptor blockade, adjustment of the dose of carvedilol from a starting dose of 3.125 mg and simultaneous reduction of the dose of the other β-adrenoreceptor antagonist (rather than discontinuation) over one to two weeks are most likely to ensure tolerance. If carvedilol is tolerated, the dose can then be increased as recommended.

Carvedilol is contraindicated in patients with severe decompensated heart failure, including those requiring intravenous inotropic therapy. Such patients are likely to be dependent on sympathetic stimulation and therefore will not tolerate a β-adrenoreceptor–antagonist drug. In addition, the patient's volume status may not be sufficiently stabilized, so that symptoms of vasodilatation or worsening heart failure are likely to appear. Carvedilol may be given to patients who cannot tolerate angiotensin-converting–enzyme inhibitors. It is equally effective in black and white patients[77] and as effective in elderly patients as in younger ones.

Other contraindications to carvedilol therapy in patients with heart failure include marked bradycardia, the sick sinus syndrome, and partial or complete atrioventricular block, unless a permanent pacemaker is in place. Carvedilol had no adverse effects on pulmonary function in normal subjects; however, the drug is contraindicated in patients with asthma. Patients with diabetes mellitus should be treated cautiously, because the drug can mask the symptoms of hypoglycemia. The safety of carvedilol in pregnant and lactating women and its safety and effectiveness in children with heart failure have not been established.

SIDE EFFECTS

In the U.S. Carvedilol Heart Failure Program, carvedilol was discontinued in 5 percent of patients because of worsening heart failure, dizziness, or bradycardia.[59] The most common adverse reactions in this and other studies were edema, dizziness, bradycardia, hypotension, nausea, diarrhea, and blurred vision.[59] The incidence of adverse reactions does not differ between patients with heart failure who are 65 years of age or older and those who are younger.

Rarely, carvedilol has caused reversible deterioration of renal function, usually in patients with low blood pressure, underlying renal insufficiency, or diffuse vascular disease. Patients at risk for renal dysfunction should be monitored and the drug discontinued if renal function worsens.

Mild hepatocellular injury confirmed by carvedilol challenge after the discontinuation of treatment has occurred in a few patients, but no deaths due to liver failure have been reported. The incidence of abnormalities in liver function with carvedilol in the clinical trials was 1.1 percent, as compared with 0.9 percent with placebo. However, in patients receiving carvedilol in whom results of liver-function tests become abnormal, the drug should be discontinued. Moreover, it should not be given to patients with preexisting liver disease.

Overdoses of carvedilol, alone or in combination with other drugs, have been reported. The symptoms include hypotension and bradycardia. For excessive bradycardia, atropine can be given. Intravenous glucagon, dobutamine, or isoproterenol is recommended to support impaired ventricular function. For severe hypotension, norepinephrine or epinephrine can be given, and for drug-induced bronchospasm, isoproterenol or intravenous aminophylline is recommended.

CONCLUSIONS

Carvedilol is an α- and β-adrenoreceptor–antagonist drug that has proven therapeutic value when given as adjunctive therapy with diuretics and angiotensin-converting–enzyme inhibitors, with or without digoxin, in patients with mild or moderate heart failure. In such patients, it appears to reduce the progression of the disease, as reflected by the combined risk of cardiovascular morbidity (the need for hospitalization and for adjustment of other heart-failure medications) or death from cardiovascular causes.

REFERENCES

1. Metra M, Nardi M, Giubbini R, Dei Cas L. Effects of short- and long-term carvedilol administration on rest and exercise hemodynamic variables, exercise capacity and clinical conditions in patients with idiopathic dilated cardiomyopathy. J Am Coll Cardiol 1994;24:1678-87.
2. Krum H, Sackner-Bernstein JD, Goldsmith RL, et al. Double-blind, placebo-controlled study of the long-term efficacy of carvedilol in patients with severe chronic heart failure. Circulation 1995;92:1499-506.
3. Olsen SL, Gilbert EM, Renlund DG, Taylor DO, Yanowitz FD, Bristow MR. Carvedilol improves left ventricular function and symptoms in chronic heart failure: a double-blind randomized study. J Am Coll Cardiol 1995; 25:1225-31.
4. Bristow MR, Gilbert EM, Abraham WT, et al. Carvedilol produces dose-related improvements in left ventricular function and survival in subjects with chronic heart failure. Circulation 1996;94:2807-16.
5. Packer M, Colucci WS, Sackner-Bernstein JD, et al. Double-blind, placebo-controlled study of the effects of carvedilol in patients with moderate to severe heart failure: the PRECISE trial: Prospective Randomized Evaluation of Carvedilol on Symptoms and Exercise. Circulation 1996;94: 2793-9.
6. Colucci WS, Packer M, Bristow MR, et al. Carvedilol inhibits clinical progression in patients with mild symptoms of heart failure. Circulation 1996;94:2800-6.
7. Cohn JN, Fowler MB, Bristow MR, et al. Safety and efficacy of carvedilol in severe heart failure. J Card Fail 1997;3:173-9.
8. Australia/New Zealand Heart Failure Research Collaborative Group. Randomised, placebo-controlled trial of carvedilol in patients with congestive heart failure due to ischaemic heart disease. Lancet 1997;349:375-80.
9. Morgan T. Clinical pharmacokinetics and pharmacodynamics of carvedilol. Clin Pharmacokinet 1994;26:335-46.
10. Bartsch W, Sponer G, Strein K, Muller-Beckmann B, von Mollendorf

E, Abshagen U. Pharmakologie und klinische pharmakologie des neuen vasodila tierenden beta-rezeptoren blockers BM 14190. Therapiewoche 1982;32:5714.
11. Ruffolo RR Jr, Sauermelch CF, Willette RN. Hemodynamic differences between carvedilol and labetalol in the cutaneous circulation. Eur J Pharmacol 1990;38:Suppl 2:S112-S114.
12. Baum T, Sybertz EJ. Pharmacology of labetalol in experimental animals. Am J Med 1983;75:Suppl 4A:15-23.
13. Dunn CJ, Lea AP, Wagstaff AJ. Carvedilol: a reappraisal of its pharmacological properties and therapeutic use in cardiovascular disorders. Drugs 1997;54:161-85.
14. Nichols AJ, Gellai M, Ruffolo RR Jr. Studies on the mechanism of arterial vasodilation produced by the novel antihypertensive agent, carvedilol. Fundam Clin Pharmacol 1991;5:25-38.
15. Tomlinson B, Bompart F, Graham BR, Liu J-B, Prichard BNC. Vasodilating mechanism and response to physiological pressor stimuli of acute doses of carvedilol compared with labetalol, propranolol and hydralazine. Drugs 1988;36:Suppl 6:37-47.
16. Frishman WH. Pindolol: a new β-adrenoceptor antagonist with partial agonist activity. N Engl J Med 1983;308:940-4.
17. Deitchman D, Perhach JL, Snyder RW. Beta-adrenoceptor and cardiovascular effects of MJ 13105 (bucindolol) in anesthetized dogs and rats. Eur J Pharmacol 1980;61:263-77.
18. Yue T-L, Cheng H-Y, Lysko PG, et al. Carvedilol, a new vasodilator and beta adrenoceptor antagonist, is an antioxidant and free radical scavenger. J Pharmacol Exp Ther 1992;263:92-8.
19. Louis WJ, McNeil JJ, Workman BS, Drummer OH, Conway EL. A pharmacokinetic study of carvedilol (BM 14.190) in elderly subjects: preliminary report. J Cardiovasc Pharmacol 1987;10:Suppl 11:S89-S93.
20. Neugebauer G, Akpan W, von Mollendorff E, Neubert P, Reiff K. Pharmacokinetics and disposition of carvedilol in humans. J Cardiovasc Pharmacol 1987;10:Suppl 11:S85-S88.
21. Fujimaki M, Murakoshi Y, Hakusui H. Assay and disposition of carvedilol enantiomers in humans and monkeys: evidence of stereoselective presystemic metabolism. J Pharm Sci 1990;79:568-72.
22. Zhou HH, Wood AJ. Stereoselective disposition of carvedilol is determined by CYP2D6. Clin Pharmacol Ther 1995;57:518-24.
23. Fujimaki M. Oxidation of the R(+)- and S(-)-carvedilol by rat liver microsomes: evidence for stereoselective oxidation and characterization of the cytochrome P450 isozymes involved. Drug Metab Dispos 1994;22: 700-8.
24. Neugebauer G, Gabor M, Reiff K. Pharmacokinetics and bioavailability of carvedilol in patients with liver cirrhosis. Drugs 1988;36:Suppl 6: 148-54.
25. Kramer BK, Ress KM, Erley CM, Risler T. Pharmacokinetic and blood pressure effects of carvedilol in patients with chronic renal failure. Eur J Clin Pharmacol 1992;43:85-8.
26. Miki S, Masumura H, Kaifu Y, Yuasa S. Pharmacokinetics and efficacy of carvedilol in chronic hemodialysis patients with hypertension. J Cardiovasc Pharmacol 1991;18:Suppl 4:S62-S68.
27. De Mey C, Brendel E, Enterling D. Carvedilol increases the systemic bioavailability of oral digoxin. Br J Clin Pharmacol 1990;29:486-90.
28. Frishman WH, Sokol SI. Cardiovascular drug therapy in patients with intrinsic hepatic disease and impaired hepatic function secondary to congestive heart failure. In: Frishman WH, Sonnenblick EH, eds. Cardiovascular pharmacotherapeutics. New York: McGraw-Hill, 1997:1561-76.
29. Shammas FV, Dickstein K. Clinical pharmacokinetics in heart failure: an updated review. Clin Pharmacokinet 1988;15:94-113.
30. Tenero D, Ilson B, Boyle D, et al. Dose-proportional stereoselective kinetics of carvedilol in patients with CHF. Clin Pharmacol Ther 1996;59: 201. abstract.
31. Frishman WH. Alpha- and beta-adrenergic blocking drugs. In: Frishman WH, Sonnenblick EH, eds. Cardiovascular pharmacotherapeutics. New York: McGraw-Hill, 1997:59-94.
32. Packer M, Lee WH, Kessler PD, Gottlieb SS, Bernstein JL, Kukin ML. Role of neurohormonal mechanisms in determining survival in patients with severe chronic heart failure. Circulation 1987;75:Suppl IV:IV-80–IV-92.
33. Cohn JN, Levine TB, Olivari MT, et al. Plasma norepinephrine as a guide to prognosis in patients with chronic heart failure. N Engl J Med 1984;311:819-23.
34. The SOLVD Investigators. Effect of enalapril on survival in patients with reduced left ventricular ejection fractions and congestive heart failure. N Engl J Med 1991;325:293-302.
35. Sackner-Bernstein JD, Mancini DM. Rationale for treatment of patients with chronic heart failure with adrenergic blockade. JAMA 1995; 274:1462-7. [Erratum, JAMA 1996;275:686.]
36. Francis GS, Goldsmith SR, Cohn JN. Relationship of exercise capacity to resting left ventricular performance and basal plasma norepinephrine levels in patients with congestive heart failure. Am Heart J 1982;104:725-31.

DRUG THERAPY

37. Viquerat CE, Daly P, Swedberg K, et al. Endogenous catecholamine levels in chronic heart failure: relation to the severity of hemodynamic abnormalities. Am J Med 1985;78:455-60.

38. Frishman WH. Multifactorial actions of β-adrenergic blocking drugs in ischemic heart disease: current concepts. Circulation 1983;67:Suppl I:I-11–I-18.

39. Daly PA, Sole MJ. Myocardial catecholamines and the pathophysiology of heart failure. Circulation 1990;82:Suppl I:I-35–I-43.

40. Henderson EB, Kahn JK, Corbett JR, et al. Abnormal I-123 metaiodobenzylguanidine myocardial washout and distribution may reflect myocardial adrenergic derangement in patients with congestive cardiomyopathy. Circulation 1988;78:1192-9.

41. Zimmer HG, Kolbeck-Ruhmkoff C, Zierhut W. Cardiac hypertrophy induced by alpha- and beta-adrenergic receptor stimulation. Cardioscience 1995;6:47-57.

42. Podrid PJ, Fuchs T, Candinas R. Role of the sympathetic nervous system in the genesis of ventricular arrhythmia. Circulation 1990;82:Suppl I:I-103–I-113.

43. Packer M, Gottlieb SS, Kessler PD. Hormone-electrolyte interactions in the pathogenesis of lethal cardiac arrhythmias in patients with congestive heart failure: basis of a new physiologic approach to control of arrhythmia. Am J Med 1986;80:Suppl 4A:23-90.

44. Waagstein F, Hjalmarson Å, Varnauskas E, Wallentin I. Effect of chronic beta-adrenergic receptor blockade in congestive cardiomyopathy. Br Heart J 1975;37:1022-36.

45. Anderson JL, Lutz JR, Gilbert EM, et al. A randomized trial of low-dose beta-blockade therapy for idiopathic dilated cardiomyopathy. Am J Cardiol 1985;55:471-5.

46. Engelmeier RS, O'Connell JB, Walsh R, Rad N, Scanlon PJ, Gunnar RM. Improvement in symptoms and exercise tolerance by metoprolol in patients with dilated cardiomyopathy: a double-blind, randomized, placebo-controlled trial. Circulation 1985;72:536-46.

47. Fisher ML, Gottlieb SS, Plotnick GD, et al. Beneficial effects of metoprolol in heart failure associated with coronary artery disease: a randomized trial. J Am Coll Cardiol 1994;23:943-50.

48. The CIBIS Investigators and Committees. A randomized trial of beta-blockade in heart failure: the Cardiac Insufficiency Bisoprolol Study. Circulation 1994;90:1765-73.

49. Ikram H, Fitzpatrick D. Double-blind trial of chronic oral beta blockade in congestive cardiomyopathy. Lancet 1981;2:490-3.

50. Bristow MR, O'Connell JB, Gilbert EM, et al. Dose-response of chronic beta-blocker treatment in heart failure from either idiopathic dilated or ischemic cardiomyopathy. Circulation 1994;89:1632-42.

51. Leung WH, Lau CP, Wong CK, Cheng CH, Tai YT, Lim SP. Improvement in exercise performance and hemodynamics by labetalol in patients with idiopathic dilated cardiomyopathy. Am Heart J 1990;119:884-90.

52. The Australia/New Zealand Heart Failure Collaborative Group. Effects of carvedilol, a vasodilator-beta-blocker, in patients with congestive heart failure due to ischemic heart disease. Circulation 1995;92:212-8.

53. Eichhorn EJ. Restoring function in failing hearts: the effects of beta blockers. Am J Med 1998;104:163-9.

54. Zarembski DG, Nolan PE Jr, Slack MK, Lui CY. Meta-analysis of the use of low-dose beta-adrenergic blocking therapy in idiopathic or ischemic dilated cardiomyopathy. Am J Cardiol 1996;77:1247-50.

55. Hjalmarson Å, Kneider M, Waagstein F. The role of β-blockers in left ventricular dysfunction and heart failure. Drugs 1997;54:501-10.

56. The Beta-Blocker Pooling Project Research Group. The Beta-Blocker Pooling Project (BBPP): subgroup findings from randomized trials in post infarction patients. Eur Heart J 1988;9:8-16.

57. Frishman WH. Role of β-adrenergic blockers. In: Fuster V, Ross R,

Topol EJ, eds. Atherosclerosis and coronary artery disease. Vol. 2. Philadelphia: Lippincott-Raven, 1996:1205-14.

58. Guyatt GH, Sullivan MJ, Thompson PJ, et al. The 6-minute walk: a new measure of exercise capacity in patients with chronic heart failure. Can Med Assoc J 1985;132:919-23.

59. Packer M, Bristow MR, Cohn JN, et al. The effect of carvedilol on morbidity and mortality in patients with chronic heart failure. N Engl J Med 1996;334:1349-55.

60. Rector TS, Kubo SH, Cohn JN. Patients self-assessment of their congestive heart failure. 2. Content, reliability and validity of a new measure, the Minnesota Living with Heart Failure Questionnaire. Heart Fail 1987;3:198-209.

61. Pfeffer MA, Stevenson LW. β-Adrenergic blockers and survival in heart failure. N Engl J Med 1996;334:1396-7.

62. Roden DM. Cardiovascular and Renal Advisory Panel of the US Food and Drug Administration considers four drugs. Circulation 1997;95:2335.

63. Gilbert EM, Abraham WT, Olsen S, et al. Comparative hemodynamic, left ventricular functional, and antiadrenergic effects of chronic treatment with metoprolol versus carvedilol in the failing heart. Circulation 1996;94:2817-25.

64. Bohm M, Deutsch HJ, Hartmann D, Rosee KL, Stablein A. Improvement of postreceptor events by metoprolol treatment in patients with chronic heart failure. J Am Coll Cardiol 1997;30:992-6.

65. Doughty RN, Whalley GA, Gamble G, MacMahon S, Sharpe N. Left ventricular remodeling with carvedilol in patients with congestive heart failure due to ischemic heart disease. J Am Coll Cardiol 1997;29:1060-6.

66. Olivetti G, Abbi R, Quaini F, et al. Apoptosis in the failing human heart. N Engl J Med 1997;336:1131-41.

67. Moser M, Frishman WH. Results of therapy with carvedilol, a β-blocker vasodilator with antioxidant properties, in hypertensive patients. Am J Hypertens 1998;11:15S-22S.

68. Ollivier JP, Durier P, Bussiere JL, Gayet JL. Safety and efficacy of once-daily carvedilol vs twice-daily labetalol in mild to moderate hypertension. Eur J Clin Pharmacol 1990;38:Suppl 2:S164-S166.

69. Young PH. A comparison of carvedilol with atenolol in the treatment of mild-to-moderate essential hypertension. J Cardiovasc Pharmacol 1992;19:Suppl 1:S82-S85.

70. Hall S, Prescott RI, Hallman RJ, Dixon S, Harvey RE, Ball SG. A comparative study of carvedilol, slow-release nifedipine, and atenolol in the management of essential hypertension. J Cardiovasc Pharmacol 1991;18:Suppl 4:S35-S38.

71. Langdon CG, Baxter GA, Young PH. A multicenter comparison of carvedilol with hydrochlorothiazide in the treatment of mild-to-moderate essential hypertension. J Cardiovasc Pharmacol 1991;18:Suppl 4:S51-S56.

72. Hauf-Zachariou U, Widmann L, Zulsdorf B, Hennig M, Lang PD. A double-blind comparison of the effects of carvedilol and captopril on serum lipid concentrations in patients with mild to moderate essential hypertension and dyslipidaemia. Eur J Clin Pharmacol 1993;45:95-100.

73. Weiss R, Ferry D, Pickering E, et al. Effectiveness of three different doses of carvedilol for exertional angina. Am J Cardiol 1998;82:927-31.

74. van der Does R, Eberhardt R, Derr I, Ehmer B, Rudorf J, Uberbacher HJ. Treatment of chronic stable angina with carvedilol in comparison with nifedipine s.r. Eur Heart J 1991;12:60-4.

75. Freedman SB, Jamal SM, Harris PJ, Kelly DT. Comparison of carvedilol and atenolol for angina pectoris. Am J Cardiol 1987;60:499-502.

76. Basu S, Senior R, Raval U, van der Does R, Bruckner T, Lahiri A. Beneficial effects of intravenous and oral carvedilol treatment in acute myocardial infarction: a placebo-controlled, randomized trial. Circulation 1997;96:183-91.

77. Yancy C, Fowler MB, Colucci WS, Gilbert EM, Lukas MA, Young ST. Response of black heart failure patients to carvedilol. J Am Coll Cardiol 1997;29:Suppl A:284A. abstract.

An Odyssey of a Clinical Researcher

William H. Frishman, MD

You are about to embark on a great odyssey, as grand an adventure and as spectacular as that of Ulysses, the Greek warrior from Homer's classic epic, *The Odyssey*. Each of you is looking forward to a rich, fulfilling life with accomplishments in clinical medicine and biomedical research. You all want to be good husbands or wives, devoted parents, and grateful children. You also want to achieve basic material comforts in payment for your education and hard work and be respected as paragons of the community. In fact, many of you want to have it all (Table 1), and you will suffer for it. However, at the same time, you will experience an exhilaration that comes with a life devoted to helping humankind. I often draw parallels between the odyssey or voyage that Ulysses took with that which your physician predecessors have taken and which you will take. The voyage will be an adventure, but one lined with obstacles and challenges that will test your very mettle and soul. There are dangers that lie ahead that can blow you off course, and rocks that can even destroy your ship. You will be measured on how you stay the course and focus on your life's goals.

As a devotee of history and literature, Homer's *Odyssey* was one of my favorite books. The story is about a marvelous journey of an individual who had the best of all possible experiences as a soldier, adventurer, and lover. Ulysses is one of the heroes of the Trojan War, and on his return voyage to Greece and his home in Ithaca over a 10-year period, he had to undergo a series of adventures, challenges, and near disasters (Table 2). Ulysses faced continuous battles, ill winds that frustrated him within reach of his goal, storms that threatened to pull him under, whirlpools and wandering rocks that would smash his ship to bits, temptations that could compromise his integrity, jealousy and envy from ruthless rivals, giants who could swallow him whole, and personal despair. However, he had strengths that helped him face these obstacles head on and ultimately succeed in life (Table 3).

These are qualities that every medical student and prospective physician must have to embark successfully on their voyage. It is the equipment that you need to steer your ship as it traverses the waves and whirlpools that lie ahead? What are some of the obstacles that will test your

Heart Disease 2002;4:392–396
Copyright © 2002 Lippincott Williams & Wilkins, Inc.

From the Department of Medicine, New York Medical College and Westchester Medical Center, Valhalla, New York.

Address correspondence and reprint requests to William H. Frishman, MD, Department of Medicine, New York Medical College and Westchester Medical Center, Valhalla, NY 10595; e-mail: William_Frishman@nymc.edu

very inner core and essence and how does one get around them (Table 4)? As your teachers, we can share our own stories with you, just as Ulysses related his own adventures to his son Telamechus.

You will be confronted with dogmatism. When I was a medical student 30 years ago in the 1960s, there was no such entity as evidence-based medicine. Evidence was the word our professors, who often had no scientific basis to support their practices, used to describe their personal anecdotes and experiences. These professors were models to emulate at the bedside, but if one would inquire "why are we doing this" or "what is the evidence that this surgical approach or approach is beneficial," you would usually get a stern reply (such as "what is your name?"), but not an answer to your specific question. Clinical research was not much different in 1965 than it was in 1365—a treatment was used because it made sense, because patients seemed to improve. Throughout history, a clinical study often used historical controls. As an example, radical mastectomy was performed because it made sense to remove all cancerous tissue around a malignant breast. The controls were those patients too far gone to consider surgery and already near death, and this operation became the standard treatment for over 80 years. As a medical student in 1968, try asking your surgical professor about the need for or rationale behind radical mastectomy!

Throughout the history of medicine, we have been faced with established dogmas for treatment where there was no scientific proof. We are seeing this now with coronary angioplasty and stenting, a procedure being carried out across the country in increasing frequency for stable angina pectoris with no conclusive evidence that the intervention changes the natural history of coronary artery disease in most patients, and despite disturbing new evidence that it may even make some individuals worse. How can we then combat clinical dogmatism? We do that with our curiosity and the modern placebo-controlled trial, a research development of the last 30 years. Twelve years ago I participated in a study to evaluate a new drug treatment modality for angina pectoris. To approve such a treatment, the FDA requires 20% improvement in exercise tolerance until the time of pain. Indeed, in this study, a 20% improvement was seen in exercise tolerance over time.[1] What was this new treatment? Well, this was the benefit seen with placebo. Patients will often respond to kindness, reassurance, and comforting words, and this must be controlled for so we can be sure that a new treatment modality is of therapeutic benefit. As a cardiologist and clinical trialist, I have wit-

TABLE 1
What every physician wants

Love
Security
Acting on dreams
A happy family
Adventure and intrigue

TABLE 3
Ulysses' strengths

Intelligence and curiosity
Strength of character
A loving family and devotion to family
Devoted teacher (mentor)
A life plan
Ambition
Enriched by his interactions with others
Compassion
Courage
Divine intervention (Athena), faith

---

nessed a placebo effect in angina pectoris, hypertension, arrhythmia, and heart failure.[2] Any new treatment deemed to be an advance must withstand the rigors of a placebo- or sham-controlled clinical trial, and old treatments and clinical recommendations must be reexamined with similar scrutiny.

We have already witnessed numerous drugs and operative procedures that were considered the rages of their time fall along the wayside in the era of the modern controlled clinical trial. Female reproductive hormones are no longer considered fountains of youth.[3–5] Major procedures, such as radical mastectomy, the most feared operation by women, and the thoracic repair of hiatus hernia, are only painful memories now. Recently arthroplastic knee surgery for osteoarthritis was shown to have no benefit compared to "sham" surgery.[6] Dogmatism is the greatest threat to the care of patients when irresponsible, unproven treatment approaches are used. The following story serves to illustrate this point. When coronary bypass operations were done in the 1970s, there was a dogma that β-adrenergic blockers should be stopped 2 days to a week before surgery, based on the notion that as a myocardial depressant, the blocker might prevent postoperative recovery of the heart. What was the evidence to support this practice? Well, there was none. In 1975 the incidence of postoperative infarction after coronary bypass was up to 30%. That year I had a patient, a 48-year-old father of three young daughters, who needed a bypass because we couldn't control his symptoms with medication. Three days before surgery, we followed the practice of the time and stopped his β-blocker therapy. He had continued pain and worsening pain on the morning of surgery, and although he underwent a successful operation, he had a massive myocardial infarction during surgery and died on the operating table. When his distraught children, wife, and mother asked me what had happened, I really had no answer, but suspected that β-blocker withdrawal was the problem. Subsequently, several colleagues and I carried out a controlled study which showed that β-blockers could and should be given until the time of

surgery, not as a myocardial depressant, but as a myocardial protectant, which ultimately was shown to reduce the risk of myocardial infarction from 30% to about 1%. When I first presented my findings at the American Heart Association's Annual Scientific Session in 1979, I was attacked unmercifully. Subsequently, our work was corroborated and it is now standard clinical practice all over the world[7,8] to maintain β-blockade in the perioperative period, an intervention that has done more to assure the safety of bypass surgery than any other pharmacologic approach.

You too, in your career as a physician, will face dogma. Attack it head on. Ask the question "why are we doing this?" Not only ask questions, but answer them yourselves in the laboratory or in the clinic if you don't get the right response. One of the exhilarating experiences that Ulysses had on his journey was the joy of discovery. If you are not going to answer the question yourself, be part of the answer by encouraging your patients to participate in clinical trials.

As you do battle against dogmatism on behalf of your patients, you will experience one of the greatest joys of medical science: the satisfaction of discovery. Indeed, some of you may even have the privilege of being one of the first people to uncover a truth that is only known to God.

As you do battle against dogmatism, you will be faced with denial. Despite the advances of medicine that have been proven beyond a doubt in controlled studies, there are physicians and patients who will ignore the results. We have studies to prove beyond a doubt that aggressive reduction of cholesterol will prevent heart attack, that reduction of blood pressure will reduce the risk of stroke and heart attack, that aspirin will reduce the risk of heart attack, and that ACE inhibitors can prevent and successfully treat congestive heart failure. Despite this evidence from well-done, placebo-controlled trials, a minority of patients with hyperlipidemia in the US are prescribed cholesterol-lowering drugs, most patients are not having their blood pressure controlled,[9] yet thousands of patients undergo expensive

TABLE 2
Obstacles facing Ulysses

War
Ill winds
Storms
Giants (Cyclopes)
Whirlpools (Charybdis)
Temptation (The Sirens)
Jealousy and envy (Poseidon)
Wandering rocks
Despair

TABLE 4
Obstacles facing physicians

Jealousy and envy
Conflicting oaths
Apathy
Dogmatism
Denial
Big technology
Healthcare reimbursement and government controls

operative procedures where there is no clear evidence of benefit. There is no greater omission that a physician can make than ignoring the truth. Ulysses lost all members of his crew because they ignored the precepts of the gods. Ulysses persevered because he followed these precepts. We are truly in the prevention era, where we can impact favorably on the risk of cancer, heart disease, and stroke, and not to avail our patients of these proven therapies is doing them the greatest disservice.

Beware of apathy. Our responsibilities as healthcare providers and biomedical scientists extend well beyond the study and treatment of disease. As healthcare providers, we must speak out on behalf of those issues that can benefit universal health. Years ago, it was said that clinicians and scientists should avoid involvement in politics. I could not disagree more. Who is better qualified to speak to the healthcare needs of the country? It was political pressures from the scientific community that changed the attitudes of Congress to increase financing for biomedical research. It is the courage of physician-leaders like David Kessler and Everett Koop, two pediatricians who helped to contain the Seven Merchants of Death: the American Tobacco companies whose lethal mass media campaigns have been aimed at hooking 6,000 new teenage smokers daily to replace those Americans ready to kick the habit or die of tobacco-related illnesses. However, we need to go beyond our own borders in this battle. America has now become the leading exporter of death through our tobacco exports, while at the same time calling itself the leading spokesman for international health. This can no longer be tolerated, and physicians must become the true guardians of national and international health, and through our activities in this pursuit, we will gain even greater respect in the eyes of our patients.

Regarding apathy, we also cannot remain blind to the problems of the uninsured. In a country that is enjoying such economic success, no individual should be without food and shelter, and no individual should be denied healthcare. Good health is a right and not a privilege. As future leaders in the healthcare system, you must demand a universal healthcare policy. It is the right thing to do. In a market economy there has to be losers; those who cannot compete, who must be cared for with mercy and without prejudice.

Beware of jealousy and envy. In *The Odyssey*, Ulysses is constantly being victimized by his enemy, Poseidon, the god of the sea who wants to destroy him. It is for this reason that his ship is exposed to violent storms, whirlpools, and ill winds. Throughout everything that Poseidon throws at him, Ulysses persists. Ulysses knows where he wants to go, and he has a clear vision of the future. If you always maintain a high level of integrity and intellectual and professional honesty, the lightning bolts and waves that will be thrown at you will only bounce off. If you always remain responsive to the needs of your patients and treat them with compassion and respect, you will remain intact despite the violent storms that rage around you.

Medicine is now becoming very competitive, and the research and clinical dollar can only be split so many ways. However, there will always be room in the system for good physicians and researchers. Never lose your idealism or compromise your integrity and you will always be successful. You must be able to withstand the ill winds of greed and cynicism that will pull at you from all sides. At the end of every day, you should feel the contentment that comes from a job well done. Every day you should make someone feel better. Every day you should learn something new. Every day you should teach. This will help make the voyage smooth, and you will drift into a restful slumber each night and wake up energized to take on the challenges of the next day.

In the competitive healthcare system, we are now dealing with a monster as cruel and compromising as the Cyclops, Managed Care, which has the ability to compromise a successful healthcare system in the name of corporate profit taking. Most of us are now dealing with managed care, but not necessarily liking it. Part of the problem was brought on by ourselves, by not being able to manage the costs of care we provide. Managed care, however, has led to a perverse transformation of the health system in which cash-rich, profit-driven, often poorly managed corporate giants with monopolistic tendencies are circumscribing the medical profession. They view medical care as a cost rather than as the purpose of the business, the so-called medical loss ratio. It is an extreme irony, given all the progress we have made, that necessary medical care should be counted as a loss.

Obsession with cost or price has had the desired effect of raising national consciousness and restraining the upward spiral. But this too has had its price. For example, pressures to reduce hospital costs have become so great that it is difficult for these institutions to support research, education, charity service, or community care. This poses enormous ethical conflicts for physicians and other professionals. Our ethical responsibility to patients is contested by the economic pressures imposed by the business entity. Hospitals and physicians are squeezed between the patient who needs rational, high-quality care and the for-profit company demanding tight control, and therefore limiting patient access to care. Simply stated, the survival of physicians as professionals is at stake. The relationship between the physician and patient is threatened as employers switch healthcare plans for their employees. This perverse effect is just one of the many in the new medical environment that runs counter to the original health philosophy of the health management organization, which was to foster prevention of illness through long-term patient-physician relationships and continuity of care.

I agree that the system needs to be overhauled and I would recommend the single-payor system, similar to Medicare, with financial constraints to contain costs. Despite the criticisms of the systems, Medicaid and Medicare were significant pieces of social legislation that allowed two segments of the population, the poor and the elderly, to become entitled by law to all the healthcare they need while maintaining physician-patient continuity. I am optimistic we will solve this problem, just as Ulysses was able to escape from the Cyclops. We are a group of powerful, resilient, and wonderfully bright people, and there is no group more resourceful for solving the problems at hand. Always remember that healthcare is a ministry, not an industry.

Another giant that will confront you on your journey is big technology. As a clinical investigator over the past 30 years, I have certainly been impressed with many of the technological advances in diagnostics and therapeutics. The translational research that will now come out of the current biomedical research efforts in genetics and molecular biology offers great promise in future diagnostic and therapeutic approaches to disease and its prevention. However, beware of big technology. We have the ability with impressive imaging techniques to diagnose tumors we still cannot cure. This technology is called "half-way technology," one that has no clinical payoff. We also don't know if the molecular genetic approaches will lead to effective treatments. Also, none of these technological advances will ever replace what patients throughout history have demanded: a physician who has compassion and a love of humanity. Despite the promises of big technology, there will always be a necessity for caring people in medicine, which will satisfy that moral and human need—the hope of relief, for sympathy, for appropriate action in the time of suffering. We also need to be realistic with our patients, that we can't return them to eternal youth, and nature must often take its course. I have often felt as if I was a boatman on a turbulent river with responsibility for a patient on his way to recovery or death. My primary job was to be there and assure that the journey for the patient was as smooth as possible, no matter what the outcome. So again, be cautious when embracing big technology; it can never replace the good physician who listens to and cares for patients.

Finally, there is the river of conflicting oaths where you will have the greatest challenge. With its many rapids, whirlpools, logjams, and hidden, hovering rocks, there is no way you won't be hurt along the way. It is a river you have already begun to travel, and you will have to navigate its obstacles with great care throughout your professional life.

An oath is a sacred vow, usually given in the name of a deity and pronounced in a public forum. You are never the same person after making yours vows, and its obligates you to a lifetime of commitment to the precepts you swore to uphold. An oath is different from a promise, which does not obligate one to a lifetime commitment. Promises are constantly broken, as when a child promises never to lie again. However, an oath goes much further and has greater moral obligation. The Scout oath, which is pronounced in front of friends and parents, commits one to a life of dedicated teamwork and reverence for family. With our religious oaths made at Bar Mitzvahs and Confirmations, we are suddenly changed from children to young adults with all the responsibilities that come with adult life. The oath you make as a physician is one of dedication to the care of patients throughout your professional life. At graduation from medical school, some students recite modifications of the Hippocratic oath, some the oath of Maimonides, some the Helsinki Accord pledge—but once our oath is taken as

physicians, we are never the same. I was told by my professors that medicine is a priesthood with one's life dedicated in its entirety to the care of patients, and my graduation oath committed me to this obligation.

However, most of us take another public oath, our marriage vows, which commits us to the care of our families "until death do us part," and it is here that the river takes a violent turn. I think this conflict contributes more to ruined marriages and the breakup of families. Every one of you will face the conflict between medical school vows and marriage vows, with the long work hours and commitment that a medical career demands. You will not always make it home to dinner on time, you will not be able to see every one of the baseball games or concerts your children will perform in, and anger and conflict will occur, often aimed at you. Although it won't make the voyage perfectly smooth, remember to thank your spouse every day. Remember to hug your children daily and make every spare moment with them count. Be there for your parents as they were for you. The conflict between the vows of marriage and medicine will test your very mettle throughout your life, but remember this adage, "happy home, happy doctor, unhappy home, nothing in medicine will be good, your patients will suffer, and your very core values will be compromised." Medicine is not a priesthood, and although it requires a dedication and commitment that no other profession requires, your most sacred oath is to your family and yourself.

There will be other oaths that may put you in conflict with your medical vows. Some of us have had to take a military oath when we entered the service during war time, and you might be asked to pursue a path that goes against both religious and medical vows, such as physician-assisted suicide. The clinical investigator faces another obstacle. We often need to try new but unproven treatments in our quest to improve medical care. Is a blinded study where placebo is used a confirmation of our medical vows or are we conflicted? The ethics of clinical investigation will often put one in a precarious position, but the obligation to do what is best for patients includes the requirement to seek the truth, and as I showed before, placebo often is associated with its own benefits and patients are not put at risk in studies as long as appropriate safeguards are maintained. I have maintained that the medical care patients receive in trials is more focused and responsible than traditional care approaches. We have the responsibility that is built into our medical vows to support the research mission, and the applications of molecular biology and molecular genetics provide opportunities for patient treatment that could never be imagined only 5 years ago. We must remain committed to the medical research mission more than ever, allowing our patients to participate in studies. This is not a conflict of our medical vows, but a reaffirmation.

As you can see, one can survive the river of conflicted oaths if your vision is clear and you prioritize what is important. First, you must take care of yourself and be responsible to your physical, psychological, and spiritual wellbeing. Second, you must take care of your spouse, children, parents, and grandparents. Third, you should try to be the best physician you can be, hopefully both as caregiver and researcher. Don't lost sight of the fact that your medical vows are sacred but they are not priestly vows that should take preference over anything else you do in your life. It is alright to take multiple oaths, even those that may be in conflict at one time, but your own basic values and beliefs should always come first. If one is able to keep the ship balanced, the ride can be exhilarating and you will reach your final destination, albeit somewhat scarred, somewhat tattered, somewhat compromised, but in gentle waters with the satisfaction of having lived a life as a good husband or wife, a good parent, a good son or daughter, a good friend, a good physician, a good scientist, and a spiritually enriched human being. Although there will be some low points, even moments of despair, along the voyage, like Ulysses, you will have grown, matured, and found the inner peace that comes from a job well done.

REFERENCES

1. Steering Committee. Transdermal Nitroglycerin Cooperative Study Group: acute and chronic antianginal efficacy of continuous twenty-four hour application of transdermal nitroglycerin. *Am J Cardiol* 1991;68:1263–1273.

2. Frishman W, Lee W-N, Glasser SP, et al. The placebo effect in cardiovascular disease. In: Frishman WH, Sonnenblick EH, Sica D (eds): *Cardiovascular Pharmacotherapeutics*, 2nd ed. New York: McGraw Hill, in press; 2003.

3. Grady D, Herrington D, Bittner V, et al, for the HERS Research Group. Cardiovascular disease outcomes during 6.8 years of hormone therapy. Heart and Estrogen/Progestin Replacement Study Follow-up (HERS II). *JAMA* 2002; 288:49–57.

4. Hulley S, Furberg C, Barrett-Connor E, et al, for the HERS Research Group. Noncardiovascular disease outcomes during 6.8 years of hormone therapy. Heart and Estrogen/Progestin Replacement Study Follow-up (HERS II). *JAMA* 2002;288:58–66.

5. Writing. Group for the Women's Health Initiative Investigators: risks and benefits of estrogen plus progestin in healthy postmenopausal women. Principal results from the Women's Health Initiative Randomized Controlled Trial. *JAMA* 2002;288:321–333.

6. Moseley JB, O'Malley K, Petersen NJ, et al. A controlled trial of arthroscopic surgery for osteo-arthritis of the knee. *N Engl J Med* 2002;347:81–88.

7. Fogel DH, Amar D. Cardiovascular pharmacotherapeutic considerations in anesthesia. In: Frishman WH, Sonnenblick EH (eds). *Cardiovascular Pharmacotherapeutics*. New York: McGraw Hill, 1997:1423–1437.

8. Oka Y, Frishman W, Becker RM, et al. Clinical pharmacology of the new beta blocking agents. Part 10: beta-adrenoceptor blockade and coronary artery surgery. *Am Heart J* 1980;99:255–269.

9. The Sixth Report of the Joint National Committee on Prevention, Detection, Evaluation and Treatment of High Blood Pressure. *Arch Intern Med* 1997;157: 2413–2446.

A Day of Remembrance*

A year has passed since the terrorist attacks in New York, Pennsylvania and at the Pentagon. We have assembled today as a healthcare and research community to remember those souls who were lost in those disasters, and to also recognize the firemen, policemen and paramedics who gave up their lives in the rescue attempts at the World Trade Center.

The entire world witnessed two aspects of human nature on September 11, 2001: the capability to do great harm and the capability to do great good. New York Medical College (NYMC) and its affiliated teaching hospitals in Manhattan were on the front line that day. St. Vincent's Medical Center-Manhattan was the closest trauma center to the World Trade Center. If you stood outside St. Vincent's emergency room on that bright clear morning, just before the attack, and lifted your hands, you could almost touch the towers as they rose majestically out of lower Manhattan.

On that day, 80 third- and fourth-year NYMC medical students were at St. Vincent's participating in required clinical clerkships and various elective rotations. For many of the students, it was their first clinical experience in a hospital, and for others, their first assignment in Manhattan. Another 200 of our students were working in what were to be the back-up hospitals in mid-Manhattan (Metropolitan Hospital) and other facilities located in the Bronx, Staten Island, and in Westchester County. Many of the students at St. Vincent's were direct witnesses to the airplane attacks and watched the collapse of the Twin Towers. The students became part of the triage and emergency treatment teams joining residents, fellows, attending physicians, nurses, and other healthcare personnel in treating hundreds of individuals, including the most severely injured during those first hours after the attack. They saw the entire hospital mobilize itself in response to the disaster with a calm efficiency, treating those injured with great competence and poise. Mayor Rudy Giuliani would say that day, "Thank God for St. Vincent's Hospital."

The whole world will also remember the news videotapes taken that night outside St. Vincent's emergency room with emergency staff waiting for additional injured from the collapsed buildings who would never come. Indeed, it was those television images that made the world aware of the extent of the tragedy, that those thousands of individuals caught in the collapse of the towers were not injured, but dead.

We were greatly affected by September 11, 2001. Clearly, our feeling of security in this country was breached. However, we have also suffered as a medical community. Many of our hospital nurses lost their husbands who were firemen and policemen. Members of other hospital staffs lost loved ones. The husband of a medic from our helicopter ambulance service at Westchester Medical Center was killed. One of our medicine attending physicians lost his sister. The only physician to die at the World Trade Center was one of our medical residents who lived in the area of the World Trade Center

and by chance happened to be off that day. She had been on call Monday night and the Bell Commission 405 requirements in New York mandate a day off for a house officer after an overnight call.[1,2] She was last seen by witnesses running from her apartment toward a makeshift first aid station that had been set up at the base of the North Tower. She was never seen again.

Needless to say, the events on September 11 also affected our medical research projects and our clinical practices. I am a coprincipal investigator of the Women's Health Initiative Trial in New York. Five of our study subjects lost children, and our head research nurse lost her husband. For weeks, because of fear, many of the study subjects refused to come for follow-up visits to our research clinic at Union Square in lower Manhattan. Our cardiology practices were crowded with an increased number of individuals with palpitations and atypical chest pain, which was part of the posttraumatic stress syndrome seen in so many New Yorkers. We saw disabled firemen in our offices with chronic cough that would soon be described in the *New England Journal of Medicine* as "World Trade Center Cough."[3,4] One of my female patients lost a son who had his birthday on September 11. He had gone to work earlier than usual that day so he could leave his office early in the afternoon to celebrate with his wife and children. Subsequently, his only sibling, an Army officer, was deployed for Afghanistan days later.

In the aftermath of this national tragedy, we must rededicate ourselves to doing good in our clinics and hospitals where we care for the sick and infirm, in our laboratories where we search for the cures for human ailments, and in our pursuit of world peace. Our institutions and staff were examples for the world in demonstrating the capacity of the human spirit and their actions will forever be enshrined with the memories of those who were lost. Just after September 11, 2001, the St. Vincent's students and house officers who were clearly shaken by the event asked me if everything will be all right. "As in the past," I replied, "if we dedicate ourselves to improving the human condition, we will not only be all right, but we will be stronger and more resilient in the future." That being said, we can no longer walk outside St. Vincent's emergency room and lift our hands to touch the World Trade Center towers. However, if you do lift your hands in the direction where the towers stood, you will feel a gentle breeze caressing both your fingers and your face.

William H. Frishman, MD
Editor in Chief

REFERENCES

1. Weinstein DF. Duty hours for resident physicians: tough choices for teaching hospitals. N Engl J Med 2002;347:1275–1277.
2. Steinbrook R. The debate over residents' work hours. *N Engl J Med* 2002;347:1296–1302.
3. Scanlon PD. World Trade Center Cough: a lingering legacy and a cautionary tale. *N Engl J Med* 2002;347:840–842.
4. Prezant DJ, Weiden M, Banauch GI, et al. Cough and bronchial responsiveness in firefighters at the World Trade Center site. *N Engl J Med* 2002;347:806–815. publications and frequently changing "guidelines."

*Given at the September 11, 2002 Memorial Prayer Service at New York Medical College

COMMENTARY

THE AMERICAN
JOURNAL *of*
MEDICINE®

Fifty Years of Beta-adrenergic Blockade: A Golden Era in Clinical Medicine and Molecular Pharmacology

The development and subsequent clinical application of various beta-adrenergic receptor blocking drugs during the past 50 years has represented one of the major advances in human pharmacotherapy. Beginning in 1958 with the introduction of dichloroisoproterenol, no other class of synthetic drugs has demonstrated such widespread clinical utility in the treatment of both cardiovascular and noncardiovascular diseases. In addition, these agents have served as molecular probes that contributed greatly to our understanding of both the structure and workings of the ubiquitous 7 transmembrane G protein-coupled receptors, which mediate the actions of many hormones, neurotransmitters, and drugs.

Beta-adrenergic blockers are competitive pharmacologic inhibitors of catecholamine actions that influence a wide number of physiologic and metabolic activities in human beings. It has been shown that the effects of catecholamines ultimately depend on their chemical interactions with specific adrenergic receptors, membrane-bound macromolecular glycoprotein structures located on cell membranes, conceptual entities that were not well defined until the 1980s. More than 100 years ago, early investigators conceived that catecholamines were binding selectively to receptor-like structures in mediating their pharmacologic actions. In 1948, Ahlquist conducted a series of classic pharmacologic studies and concluded from his findings that there were 2 distinct organ responses to catecholamine drugs that he called alpha- and beta-receptor mediated.[1]

In 1958, the compound dichloroisoproterenol, synthesized by Eli Lilly Laboratories, was found to inhibit the activities of epinephrine and was thus considered the first beta-adrenergic blocker.[2] However, its potential clinical application was not initially appreciated. In the early 1960s, Black et al at Imperial Chemical Industries in Great Britain were working on a series of beta-adrenergic blocking compounds, pronethanol and propranolol, that they hypothesized would lower myocardial oxygen consumption by interfering with the effects of catecholamines, and, therefore, would be useful for the treatment of angina pectoris, hypertension, and arrhythmia.[3] Although pronethanol was effective in patients with angina pectoris, it was propranolol that became the prototype beta-blocker with proven efficacy in both intravenous and oral forms for the treatment of cardiovascular disease. In 1964, propranolol became the first major advance in the treatment of angina pectoris since the introduction of nitroglycerin almost 100 years earlier.

In addition, it quickly became an accepted treatment for arrhythmia, hypertension, and hypertrophic cardiomyopathy.

The potential adverse reactions related to the anti-catecholamine effects of propranolol on heart rate, myocardial contractility, and bronchial tone led to ongoing refinements in the pharmacologic structure of beta-blockers and subsequent advances in drug delivery.[4] The evolution in drug development led to the introduction of drugs having relative selectivity for cardiac beta$_1$-receptors (metoprolol, atenolol), partial adrenergic agonist activity (pindolol), concomitant alpha-adrenergic blocking activity (labetalol, carvedilol), and direct vasodilator activity (nebivolol). In addition, long-acting and ultra-short formulations of beta-blockers were developed.

Years after propranolol was introduced, studies showed the class of drugs also was useful for treating patients with mitral valve prolapse, pheochromocytoma (labetalol), the hereditary QT prolongation syndrome, hypertensive emergencies and urgencies (labetalol), and for the treatment and prevention of acute aortic dissection. Moreover, both intravenous and oral forms were able to reduce mortality in survivors of myocardial infarction, the first class of drugs shown to do so.[5,6]

Remarkably, in the 1990s, some beta-blockers also were shown to reduce morbidity and mortality in symptomatic patients with congestive heart failure, a clinical diagnosis for which beta-blockers had been contraindicated previously.[7] This revelation has led to a complete rethinking of the pathophysiology of heart failure, thought now to be aggravated by the adverse effects of increased neurohormonal stimulation of the heart.

Beta-blockers now have application that extends beyond cardiovascular use, to the prevention of migraine headache, the treatment of benign essential tremor, for patients with pheochromocytoma and thyrotoxicosis, and in topical ophthalmic formulations for reducing intraocular pressure in patients with open-angle glaucoma. The drugs also have been used to reduce portal hypertension in patients with liver cirrhosis and to aid in the management of delirium tremens and stage fright.

After decades of clinical use, the beta-blocking drugs have demonstrated a remarkable record of clinical safety in patients of all ages, and the ability to be combined successfully with other drug classes for the treatment of cardiovascular disease. Their continued use in patients undergoing

934   The American Journal of Medicine, Vol 121, No 11, November 2008

cardiovascular and noncardiovascular surgery also has been shown to reduce both intra-operative and peri-operative mortality and morbidity.

Almost in parallel with the clinical introduction of beta-adrenergic blockers came an explosion of research studies that contributed to the scientific understanding of receptor structure, function, and regulation on the molecular level. Beta-adrenergic receptor agonists and blockers have served as the biologic probes to help answer fundamental molecular pharmacology questions.

The concept of adrenergic receptor stimulation for mediating catecholamine actions had been recognized throughout the 20th century, and during the past 35 years, scientists began to study the molecular steps that lay between the putative receptors and agonists and the response elements within the cell.[8] It was found that adrenergic receptors, when stimulated, can trigger the production of second messengers (eg, adenyl cyclase) via an interaction with the coupling proteins attached to the beta receptor. The beta- and alpha-receptors are part of a major class of G protein-coupled receptors or 7 transmembrane receptors—the most important targets of clinically used drugs—that also zero in on serotonin receptors, histamine receptors, and angiotensin-II receptors.[8]

Using radioligand labeling techniques and purification methods, Lefkowitz and his colleagues[8] helped to identify the structures of the adrenergic receptors as membrane-bound polypeptide chains with a molecular weight of about 67,000 Da. The beta-receptors consist of 7 transmembrane alpha-helices of 20-28 amino acids joined by alternating extracellular and cytoplasmic loops.[8] Lefkowitz was successful in reconstituting the beta-receptors and demonstrated that the receptors could convey catecholamine responsiveness when transplanted to previously unresponsive organic systems.[8] Subsequently, the receptor genes and cDNAs for beta-receptors were cloned in 1986, and the 3-dimensional crystalline structure of the beta$_2$ receptor was recently described in 2007.

A major contribution to our understanding of beta-receptor functioning came with the fundamental description of receptor desensitization.[8] In contrast to the older concepts of adrenergic receptors as static entities on cell membranes that simply serve to initiate a chain of events, newer concepts suggest that adrenergic receptors are subject to a wide variety of controlling influences, resulting in the dynamic regulation of receptor sites and their sensitivity to catecholamine agonists. Changes in tissue concentration or sensitivity of receptors are important in drug activity and in the pathophysiology of disease. This desensitization phenomenon has been shown to be caused not by a change in receptor function or degradation, but rather by catecholamine-induced changes in the conformation of the receptor sites, which renders them ineffective. Rapid desensitization of beta receptors was proved to be mediated by agonist stimulation of beta-adrenergic receptor kinases (βARK) or GRK2, which phosphorylate receptors and decrease the coupling of G proteins to adenyl cyclase.[8]

However, it also was found that phosphorylation of the receptor itself was not sufficient to fully desensitize receptor function. A second reaction must occur that involves an arresting protein known as beta-arrestin.[8] Through this desensitization process, internalization of receptors on the cell membrane also occurs. In contrast to adrenergic agonists, beta-adrenergic blocking drugs by themselves do not induce desensitization or changes in the conformation of receptors. They also can block the ability of catecholamines to desensitize receptors. More work is being carried out with beta-arrestin agonists to form "super" beta-blockers that can turn off G protein-mediated signaling of the beta receptor but still maintain the benefits of continued beta-arrestin-mediated signaling on cell survival systems.[8]

Based on the concept of a functional adrenergic receptor that mediated the effects of catecholamines, the introduction of the first beta-blocker caused a revolution in human pharmacotherapy that has impacted favorably on the health of millions of patients with a wide variety of cardiovascular and noncardiovascular diseases. Their introduction further opened the door to fundamental discoveries of basic receptor structure and function, which have influenced the development of other drug classes for other medical conditions. In addition, the 50 years of beta-blocker experience, with the ability to modulate successfully excessive catecholamine activity, has reaffirmed the early observations and descriptions of the "ancients" who believed that imbalances in naturally occurring humors could cause disease, while the reestablishment of humoral balance would contribute to health. Indeed, how golden is the legacy the beta-blockers have given us.

William H. Frishman, MD
Departments of Medicine and Pharmacology
New York Medical College
Department of Medicine
Westchester Medical Center
Valhalla, NY

References

1. Ahlquist RP. A study of the adrenotropic receptors. *Am J Physiol.* 1948;153:586-600.
2. Powell CE, Slater IH. Blocking of inhibitory adrenergic receptors by a dichloro analogue of isoproterenol. *J Pharmacol Exp Ther.* 1958;122:480-488.
3. Black JW, Crowther AF, Shanks RG, et al. A new adrenergic beta receptor antagonist. *Lancet.* 1964;1:1080-1081.
4. Frishman WH. beta-Adrenoceptor antagonists. New drugs and new indications. *N Engl J Med.* 1981;305:505-506.
5. Frishman WH, Furberg CD, Friedewald WT. beta-Adrenergic blockade in survivors of acute myocardial infarction. *N Engl J Med.* 1984;310:830-837.
6. Frishman WH. Alpha and beta-adrenergic blocking drugs. In: Frishman WH, Sonnenblick EH, Sica DA, eds. *Cardiovascular Pharmacotherapeutics,* 2nd edn. New York: McGraw-Hill; 2003:67-97.
7. Frishman WH. Carvedilol. *N Engl J Med.* 1998;339:1759-1765.
8. Lefkowitz RJ. Seven transmembrane receptors: something old, something new. *Acta Physiol.* 2007;190:9-19.

EDITORIAL

THE AMERICAN
JOURNAL *of*
MEDICINE ®

The Patient–Physician–Industry–Government Partnership: A Societal Good

I recently celebrated the 40th anniversary of my graduation from medical school at a class reunion in Boston. While reminiscing with my former classmates about the joys and tribulations of living as a student during the 1960s, a discussion arose regarding what was available to us then in the area of pharmacotherapeutics compared with what is now available for practicing physicians. In regard to treatments for cardiovascular disease, my area of internal medicine subspecialty, we had nitrates for angina pectoris; digitalis preparations and furosemide for heart failure; hydrochlorothiazide, reserpine, guanethidine, hydralazine, and alpha-methyldopa for hypertension; quinidine, lidocaine, and procainamide for arrhythmias; and bile acid resins for hypercholesterolemia. Since 1969, with the advances in basic research supported by the National Institutes of Health (NIH) and the development of new drugs by the pharmaceutical industry, we now have available for clinical use the beta-adrenergic blockers and calcium-entry blockers for the treatment of angina pectoris; angiotensin-converting enzyme inhibitors and angiotensin receptor blockers for heart failure; new drugs for systemic and pulmonary hypertension; thrombolytics for myocardial infarction; statins for hypercholesterolemia; and new antiplatelet drugs. These newer therapies have favorably affected both the prevention and treatment of cardiovascular disease.

As examples, over the past 40 years, major reductions have occurred in the numbers of acute myocardial infarctions, in part related to innovative drug therapies for cholesterol elevations, hypertension, and smoking addiction. If an acute myocardial infarction does occur, there is now a highly significant chance a patient will survive the event with the use of thrombolytics, antiplatelet drugs, beta-blockers, and drug-eluting stents. In individuals with class IV heart failure, a condition with an extremely high 1-year mortality rate if left untreated, angiotensin-converting en-

zyme inhibitors, angiotensin receptor blockers, and beta-blockers have been shown to reduce the mortality rate while improving the functional capacity of patients.

As a Chief of Medicine at a Bronx teaching hospital in 1982, I was an early eyewitness to the horrors of the human acquired immunodeficiency disease syndrome (AIDS). It was the intense drug development efforts by the pharmaceutical industry, in tandem with the discoveries by investigators at the NIH and elsewhere, that has made AIDS an outpatient condition with a significantly reduced mortality risk. Similar advances have occurred in the therapy of cancer, rheumatologic diseases, infectious diseases, and almost every other area of medicine. Indeed, for more than 100 years there has been an unwritten understanding in the United States that the pharmaceutical industry, in a market economy, would develop the treatments that patients and their physicians require, and that the government would supervise the approval process and regulate the marketing and manufacturing of drugs.

At the same time, industry also has helped to support an unfunded educational mandate from our professional accrediting organizations by providing the missing financial support for graduate and continuing medical education, while helping to support our scientific societies, scientific meetings, and our erudite and not-so-erudite medical publications. Clearly, in the past there were marketing excesses by industry and major physician and physician–researcher conflicts of interest that needed to be reined in.[1-3] Overall, however, the patient–physician–industry–government partnership has been a great success, a union that has benefited many.

In this issue of *The American Journal of Medicine,* Ross et al.,[4] using a survey research methodology, demonstrated at one major academic medical center that academic faculty appreciate the collaborations that exist between physicians and the pharmaceutical industry; they do not perceive this interaction as an innate evil, as long as conflicts of interest are addressed and the relationships between physicians and industry are transparent.

If the pharmaceutical industry stopped developing drugs because they had no incentive to do so, what would replace it? The government, struggling with a world economic crisis, cannot fill in the gap. I am certain that our politicians do not want to nationalize the pharmaceutical industry as they did General Motors and Chrysler. Similarly, the NIH, which

Funding: None.

Conflict of Interest: Dr Frishman is Chairman of Medicine at the New York Medical College in Valhalla, New York. He is also a member of the Speakers Bureau for Bristol Myers Squibb and Forest Laboratories, and has served as a paid consultant for Glaxo Laboratories and Boehringer Ingelheim.

has been in the forefront of basic science research, could not step in without a major overhaul of its mission.

In my view, and that of many of my colleagues, society clearly benefited from the drug discovery process sponsored by industry over the past century. With the appropriate regulatory safeguards by the government on industry and physicians, society should continue to benefit from the ongoing partnership of patients, physicians, industry, and government. However, that beneficial relationship is now being threatened by attacks from some uninformed pundits who have demonized all physicians and the pharmaceutical industry as co-conspirators in some unholy cabal aimed at exploiting and injuring patients. These persistent, and at times irresponsible attacks, can potentially bring down a US pharmaceutical industry that has for years been looked on by the entire world as a source of strength in medical research and in the advancement of clinical therapeutics. With the threatened breakdown of the partnership, what new drugs will be available for our patients when my classmates and I reassemble in Boston for our 50th reunion in 2019?

William H. Frishman, MD
Department of Medicine
New York Medical College
Valhalla, New York

References

1. Relman AS, Angell M. America's other drug problem. *The New Republic*. December 16, 2002:27-41.
2. Alpert JS. Doctors and the drug industry: how can we handle potential conflicts of interest? (editorial). *Am J Med*. 2005;118:99-100.
3. Blumenthal D. Doctors and drug companies. *N Engl J Med*. 2004;351: 1885-1890.
4. Ross JS, Keyhani S, Korenstein D. Appropriateness of collaborations between industry and the medical profession: physicians' perceptions. *Am J Med*. 2009;122:955-960.

EDITORIAL

THE AMERICAN
JOURNAL *of*
MEDICINE®

A Bridge too Far: A Critique of the New ACGME Duty Hour Requirements

SEE RELATED ARTICLE p. 104

The issue of resident work hours has been discussed extensively for more than 25 years.[1-11] Errors and signs of sleep deprivation in residents have been catalogued in a few single institution studies with a limited number of residents and a modest number of observations.[5,8,9,11] The results have been contradictory with some studies showing fewer errors with more mandated sleep time and one recent study showing increased length of stay and lower quality of care for patients with shorter duty shifts.[8,9,11] Over recent years, resident on-call duty hours spent in the hospital have been progressively reduced in response to requirements imposed by the Accreditation Council for Graduate Medical Education (ACGME), a non-governmental regulatory agency. These mandated changes in residency hours are being strictly enforced even though there is a remarkable paucity of outcomes data supporting these new rules. This year, the rules have become so stringent that they have forced training programs into what we and many others think may be a detrimental and dangerous situation for our patients. The number of consecutive hours and the number of patients that can be seen in a 24-hour period have been so restricted that many, if not most, patients admitted by residents are subjected to multiple physician changes during their first 24 hours in the hospital. This process of multiple patient hand-offs reminds me (JA) of what an old friend who was a high school football coach once told me: "The more hand-offs that are called for in a single play, the more likely there will be fumbles."

We are convinced that this is now the situation on the in-patient services of all US post-graduate hospital training programs. We have yet to speak with anyone involved in resident training in any specialty that supports the new highly restrictive on-call hour requirements. Surgical faculty are particularly disturbed by shift work in the operating room. These colleagues and professional acquaintances are convinced that the new system will inevitably lead to many "fumbles" with increased likelihood of patient harm.

Funding: None.
Conflict of Interest: None.
Authorship: Both authors had access to the data and played a role in writing this manuscript.

Like many of the current readers of *The American Journal of Medicine*, we trained in a very different era when residents spent 36 out of every 48 hours in the hospital taking care of in-patients. Please do not misunderstand us: we are not calling for the return of this form of cruel and unusual punishment in our training programs. What we are calling for are studies to examine the impact of the currently mandated system in comparison to what was required just 1 year ago. At that time residents were allowed to work only 80 hours per week, spending every 5th night in the hospital. In addition, residents were allowed to remain in the hospital, taking continuous on-call, for a maximum of 30 hours. In my opinion, this system allowed ample time off from call to recover from the 30-hour stint in the hospital.

Why have we seen this continuing pressure from the ACGME to restrict resident on-call time in the hospital? What data or studies support this curtailment of duty hours? Primarily, the information supporting duty hour restrictions comes from a limited number of studies of residents on call taken together with an extensive literature resulting from studies of airline pilots and long-haul truck drivers who work long and continuous hours at night. Sleep deprivation in these individuals was shown to impair their judgment and their performance. It is alleged that residents performing long on-call shifts in the hospital are subject to the same sleep deprivation with resultant error-prone performances. The small number of studies in residents mentioned earlier were all unblinded, performed in single institutions, and involved a limited number of observations of patient outcomes. In this issue of the *Journal*, Mueller et al report multi-center survey data provided by 169 hospitals that have internal medicine residency training programs. They found that "variations in resident workload are not associated with differences in quality of care, readmission, or mortality rates for common inpatient diagnoses."[12] In the current era of evidence-based medicine, in order to make major policy decisions, more studies are needed.[8,9,11]

In addition, we reject the analogy of observations made on airline pilots and truck drivers as models for medical residency duty hour modeling. There is a huge difference between sitting in a small, darkened enclosure surrounding

2   The American Journal of Medicine, Vol 125, No 1, January 2012

by continuously droning noise and long stretches of monotony. The situation for the resident on-call is the opposite of the situation for the pilot or truck driver: the hospital is fully lighted, there is constant stimulation and interaction with patients, nurses, pharmacists, and technicians, and there is continuous demand for intellectual decision-making. All of these factors contribute to a state of wakefulness that makes sleepiness and incorrect judgment much less likely compared with the aviation and highway situation. Unfortunately, as already noted, there is a paucity of scientifically rigorous, controlled study of sleep deprivation in residents who are on-call in the hospital.

What is clearly required are a number of carefully controlled, randomized, long-term studies of different resident on-call schedules with errors committed as the primary outcome being evaluated. We would like to suggest the following multicenter trial to produce the information we need in order to set requirements for the number of hours that residents spend in the hospital on-call. Large numbers of US training hospitals would participate in this study and would be randomly assigned to 1 of 2 duty hour protocols. This experiment would last for 2 years and would monitor the number and the seriousness of any medical errors committed when residents were assigned to one of these 2 duty hour regimens: A. The currently mandated duty hour schedule and, B. The formerly employed, every 5th night on-call schedule. In this protocol, half the hospitals would use program A the first year followed by program B in the second year while the other half of the hospitals would start with program B during the first year and then switch to program A during the second year. An independent events committee would monitor patient charts for error events and would be blinded as to which program was being employed at the time of a patient's admission to the hospital. At the end of 2 years, it would be possible to compare the total number of medical errors that had occurred with the 2 systems as well as the severity of the errors with any potential harm to patients. At that point, it would be possible to select the duty hour training schedule that led to the least number of errors. Such studies also could be repeated in the future using other novel and innovative resident duty call schedules in an attempt to arrive at the best solution to this vexing issue in resident training.

In current medical training and practice, we always attempt to make medical care as evidenced-based as possible.

Why are we not doing the same thing with respect to resident duty hours?

We look forward to responses to this editorial on our blog at http://amjmed.blogspot.com.

Joseph S. Alpert, MD
Professor of Medicine
University of Arizona College of Medicine
Tucson, Arizona
Editor-in-Chief
The American Journal of Medicine

William H. Frishman, MD
Rosenthal Professor and Chairman of Medicine
Professor of Pharmacology
New York Medical College
Director of Medicine, Westchester Medical Center
Valhalla, New York
Supplements Editor
The American Journal of Medicine

Bibliography

1. Asken MJ, Raham DC. Resident performance and sleep deprivation: A review. *J Med Ed.* 1983;58:382-388.
2. Friedman RC, Bigger JT, Kornfeld DS. The intern and sleep loss. *N Engl J Med.* 1971;285:201-203.
3. American College of Physicians: Working conditions and supervision for residents in internal medicine programs: Recommendations. *Ann Int Med.* 1989;110:657-663.
4. Asch DA, Parker RM. The Libby Zion Case—One step forward and two steps backward? *N Engl J Med.* 1988;318:771-775.
5. McCall T. The impact of long working hours on resident physicians. *N Engl J Med.* 1988;318:775-778.
6. Levinsky NG. Compounding the error. *N Engl J Med.* 1988;318:778-780.
7. Glickman RM. House staff training—The need for careful reform. *N Engl J Med.* 1988;318:780-782.
8. Lockley SW, Cronin JW, Evans EE, Cade BE, Lee CJ, Landrigan CP, et al. Effect of reducing interns' weekly work hours on sleep and attentional failures. *N Engl J Med.* 2004;351:1829-1837.
9. Landrigan CP, Rothschild JM, Cronin JW, Kaushal R, Burdick E, Katz JT, et al. Effect of reducing intern's work hours on serious medical errors in intensive care units. *N Engl J Med.* 2004;351:1838-1848.
10. Mukherjee S. A precarious exchange. *N Engl J Med.* 2004;351:1822-1824.
11. Schuberth JL, Elasy TA, Butler J, Greevy R, Speroff T, Dittus RS, et al. Effect of short call admissions on length of stay and quality of care for acute decompensated heart failure. *Circulation.* 2008;117:2637-2644.
12. Mueller SK, Call SA, McDonald FS, Halvorsen AJ, Schnipper JL, Hicks LS. Impact of resident workload and handoff training on patient outcomes. *Am J Med.* 2012;125:104-110.

COMMENTARY

THE AMERICAN
JOURNAL *of*
MEDICINE ®

The Closing of St Vincent's Hospital in New York City: What Happened to the House Staff Orphans?

During a time when a significant percentage of the population is uninsured and the cost of medical care has become unmanageable, it is no surprise that hospitals have recently fallen prey to mounting debt and financial woes.

As one of New York City's longest-standing hospitals, St Vincent's Hospital in Manhattan was no different. After losing a several-year-long battle with financial hardship, the institution closed on April 30, 2010. Founded in 1849, St Vincent's had been the major site for the triage of survivors from the 9/11 World Trade Center attacks in 2001[1] and the receiving hospital for the survivors of the Titanic in 1912. Located in Greenwich Village, the hospital was at the clinical forefront of the early acquired immunodeficiency syndrome epidemic.

Although the public often wonders what will happen to the people the hospital once served, it is just as important to consider the people who once served the hospital. When a hospital shuts down, what happens to one of its largest work forces, its house staff? For these young doctors who have not yet completed their medical education but are in the last chapter of their training, what lies ahead?

These are the questions that revolved around the house officers at St Vincent's when they abruptly learned that with the hospital's closing, they would no longer have a job and, perhaps more important, could not complete their medical training.

Although the closing was met with great surprise, the hospital had been under much financial distress for years, with its final debt mounting to more than $1 billion. Having already declared bankruptcy in July of 2005, executives at St Vincent's worked aggressively to keep the hospital afloat. However, after many failed business deals and possible mergers, the institution was sinking by early 2010 and eventually folded on April 30, 2011.[2]

While St Vincent's fate was still being debated, one thing eventually became certain—the Accreditation Council for Graduate Medical Education confirmed that all residency programs would be voluntarily withdrawn,

putting 253 residents and 104 fellows out of a job. It would be the largest closure of a house staff program in the history of Graduate Medical Education in the United States. This announcement came approximately 1 month before the hospital's closing.

Given the short notice, residents had few options for acquiring a new program in a hurry. The primary methods used were as follows: residents contacted programs themselves; St Vincent's program directors contacted directors at other hospitals; the designated institutional official from St Vincent's communicated with the designated institutional officials from other institutions; residents found open positions from a national database created by the Accreditation Council for Graduate Medical Education.

Although the odds seemed to be stacked against them, the residents had one significant advantage: Because Medicare provides reimbursement funding for each resident, the house staff provides financial incentive to any hospital that is in need of labor. So when a program closes, each enrolled resident is placed under "orphan" status and the money that was originally allotted for the resident can be transferred to the new hospital. The money is available to the receiving program for each year that is needed to complete the residency.

Although this served the majority of residents well, it placed others in a tougher situation, particularly those who had matched at St Vincent's for neurology, anesthesiology, and radiology starting in July 2010, but were at a different program for their preliminary or transitional year at the time the hospital closed. Because they had not yet started training at the St Vincent's program in which they matched, they were not considered orphans. Therefore, no funding was available for these residents.

However, when St Vincent's Hospital finally closed its doors, all but 2 residents and all the fellows were offered positions at other training program.

After accepting offers, the residents started their new training programs just as quickly as their former one had ended. Their last day at St Vincent's was Friday, April 30, and for most, the first day on the new job was Monday, May 3.

Today, the empty St Vincent's Hospital building still stands in Greenwich Village, a mere shadow of what it once

Funding: None.
Conflict of Interest: None.
Authorship: All authors had access to the data and played a role in writing this manuscript.

e6   The American Journal of Medicine, Vol 125, No 5, May 2012

was, a fate that other teaching hospitals may be facing in a cloudy economic environment. However, despite the death of St Vincent's, the orphaned house staff found new homes.

Elizabeth Zheng, MD[a]
William H. Frishman, MD[b]
[a]*Department of Medicine*
Albert Einstein College of Medicine/Montefiore Medical Center
Bronx, NY

[b]*Department of Medicine*
New York Medical College/Westchester Medical Center
Valhalla

References

1. Frishman WH. A day of remembrance (editorial). *Heart Dis.* 2003;5:1.
2. Levine M. St. Vincent's is the Lehman Brothers of hospitals. *New York Magazine*, October 17, 2010.

COMMENTARY

THE AMERICAN
JOURNAL *of*
MEDICINE ®

Faculty Supervision of the House Staff Handoff Process: The Time Has Come

The Accreditation Council for Graduate Medical Education is taking bold new initiatives to make residency education more accountable to the public. If this is not done by the Accreditation Council for Graduate Medical Education, it will surely be legislated by governmental agencies that are paying the bill for Graduate Medical Education training, which would include requirements for more direct observation of a trainee's performance, documentation of the trainee's individual clinical outcomes, and educational outcomes of the residency training program. The creation of "the milestones" makes it easier to document specific behaviors and performance on specific tasks.

Previously, some of our faculty ratings were a result of supervisory "gestalt" rather than direct observation of the task by the trainee/learner. Direct observation is the only way to discern the difference between what the learner "can do" versus what the learner "actually does." This has been well described in faculty development sessions at our institution with Dr Eric Holmboe of the American Board of Internal Medicine, as well as by Dr Louis Pangaro at the Clerkship Directors of Internal Medicine meeting in October, 2005. The fact that a learner has the knowledge, skills, and attitude of a particular task does not mean this automatically translates into desired behaviors at the bedside, thus the need for more direct supervision and direct observation in all of our training programs. This is the essence of competency-based education. This direct observation will be applied to the Entrustable Patient Activities. No Entrustable Patient Activity is more important than the process of "handoffs." No Entrustable Patient Activity requires more direct observation and supervision than the handoff process if we are to increase the patient safety culture and environments in our teaching hospitals.

The process of handoffs has been studied for some time.[1-8] As a consequence of the mandated changes in house staff duty hours,[9] we have an average of 5.2 handoffs per day per patient in the United States. This number is chilling in the mathematic calculation of risk for each patient in the

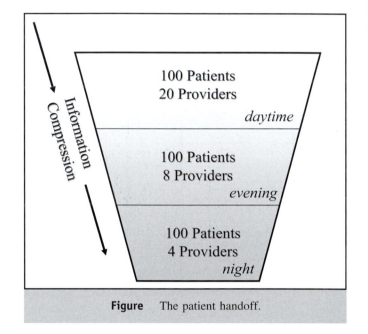

Figure   The patient handoff.

process. Programs have tried selecting the faculty members who best model the knowledge, skills, and attitudes of the handoff process to teach and define this process for residents with various success rates. The handoff process gets more complicated with fewer people to sign out to as we approach night float or night medicine (**Figure**). Of note, sign-outs at 4:30 PM take approximately the same amount of time as sign-outs at 9:30 PM and sign-ins at 7:30 AM. This quickly becomes a game of "telephone" with great potential to forget or drop important information that should have been passed along to the next provider. There also is great variability of faculty involvement in the handoff process in most programs. This has to be addressed in the new era of milestones, landmarks, and Entrustable Patient Activities, and is particularly important in light of the rapid expansion of hospitalist programs across the country. Hospitalists on the teaching service are generally assigned to resident-specific teams. Each team averages 16 or 17 patients. The maximum for any team as per the Residency Review Committee guidelines is 20. The physician who knows each patient the best is the supervisory hospitalist faculty member. Why have they not been drawn more into the sign-out process? We believe that this is the paradigm shift that must

Funding: Supported in part by the Educational Innovations Project of the Accreditation Council for Graduate Medical Education.

Conflict of Interest: None.

Authorship: All authors had access to the data and played a role in writing this manuscript.

take place and be evaluated in the Next Accreditation System. We have tried this in our own residency training program.[10,11] All patients were signed out by the resident team in our electronic sign-out system (Patient Documentation Transfer System).[10] As in most programs, sign-outs are supervised by our fourth-year Chief Residents. Unlike most programs, face-to-face sign-outs cannot and will not proceed until the sign-outs are reviewed, corrected, and approved by the faculty. This is followed by constructive feedback on accuracy given to the trainee. The faculty are not present at the actual sign-outs, but they are entirely responsible for the information entered into the electronic handoff system. Our faculty initially were not happy about this new requirement until they saw the rate of unacceptable errors, which was reduced once they participated. Direct observation of this process was an eye-opening experience for the faculty in our program. We have created this as a required milestone evaluation for the trainee to develop individual "process improvement." This will eventually be a certified Entrustable Patient Activity in our program.

The next step in information flow was to require feedback to the hospitalist the following morning on the results or follow-up of each sign-out from the day before. This was supplemented by any additional information on change of status (eg, a code, a rapid response, an adverse event, or a critical laboratory test) that occurred since the handoff. The program requires that this information be entered into the electronic system, again supervised by nocturnists from our Night Medicine Program. Each hospitalist on the service, teaching and nonteaching, receives a summary before entering the hospital the following morning. They, in turn, can review the events and the required documentation in each patient's chart, with feedback to the trainee on how to improve both the flow and the accuracy of information in this important legal record.

To be sure, a considerable amount of work is required for supervision and documentation.[12] But this is the "process improvement" in housestaff supervision we are all being challenged with. With the duty hours requirements, fatigue prevention systems (all in the name of safety), and exponential increase in the number of handoffs in our academic medical centers, the only way to achieve "process improve-

ment" is direct observation and supervision of the handoff information by our own faculty. We suggest that the continuous quality improvement required of each program accepts handoffs as the most important and challenging topic for us to show the public that we are absolutely serious about patient safety at our academic medical centers.

William H. Frishman, MD
Christopher Nabors, MD
Stephen J. Peterson, MD
Department of Medicine
New York Medical College/Westchester Medical Center
Valhalla, NY

References

1. Arora V, Johnson J, Lovinger D, Humphrey HJ, Meltzer DO. Communication failures in patient sign-out and suggestions for improvement: a critical incident analysis. *Qual Saf Health Care*. 2005;14:401-407.
2. Salerno SM, Arnett MV, Domanski JP. Standardized sign-out reduces intern perception of medical errors on the general internal medicine ward. *Teach Learn Med*. 2009;21:121-126.
3. Petersen LA, Orav EJ, Teich JM, O'Neil AC, Brennan TA. Using a computerized sign-out program to improve continuity of inpatient care and prevent adverse events. *Jt Comm J Qual Improv*. 1998;24:77-87.
4. Foster PN, Sidhu R, Gadhia DA, DeMusis M. Leveraging computerized sign-out to increase error reporting and addressing patient safety in graduate medical education. *J Gen Intern Med*. 2008;23:481-484.
5. Farnan JM, Paro JA, Rodriguez RM, et al. Hand-off education and evaluation: Piloting the observed simulated hand-off experience (OSHE). *J Gen Intern Med*. 2010;25:129-134.
6. Arora V, Johnson J. A model for building a standardized hand-off protocol. *Jt Comm J Qual Patient Saf*. 2006;32:646-655.
7. Gakhar B, Spencer AL. Using direct observation, formal evaluation, and an interactive curriculum to improve the sign-out practices of internal medicine interns. *Acad Med*. 2010;85:1182-1188.
8. Vidyarthi AR, Arora V, Schnipper JL, Wall SD, Wachter RM. Managing discontinuity in academic medical centers: strategies for a safe and effective resident sign-out. *J Hosp Med*. 2006;1:257-266.
9. Alpert JA, Frishman WH. A bridge too far: a critique of the new ACGME duty hour requirements. *Am J Med*. 2012;125:1-2.
10. Nabors C, Peterson SJ, Lee WN, et al. Experience with faculty supervision of an electronic resident sign-out system. *Am J Med*. 2010;123:376-381.
11. Nabors C, Peterson SJ, Aronow WS, et al. Physician reporting of clinically significant events through a computerized patient sign-out system. *J Patient Saf*. 2011;7:155-161.
12. Nabors C, Peterson SJ, Forman L, et al. Operationalizing the internal medicine milestones —an early status report. *J Grad Med Ed*. In press.

COMMENTARY

THE AMERICAN
JOURNAL *of*
MEDICINE ®

Medical Residency Training and Hospital Care During and After a Natural Disaster: Hurricane Sandy and Its Effects

During natural disasters, resident physicians in teaching hospitals play an integral role in ensuring continuous patient care. The challenges that a residency program experiences as a referral hospital after such calamities have not been documented in the past. However, there is literature addressing the demands faced by hospital programs that were forced to close down temporarily, such as what happened during Hurricane Katrina in New Orleans in 2005.[1-3] In this article, we highlight some of what occurred during and after Hurricane Sandy in New York City.

On October 29, 2012, the wind started to blow in New York City. Hurricane Sandy was expected. The implications of this disturbing storm were uncertain. It had been 1 year since Hurricane Irene passed by New York City. Metropolitan Hospital Center (MHC), a public hospital located in East Harlem, in Manhattan, suffered minimal disruptions at that time.

A state of emergency was declared days before Hurricane Sandy, which included the suspension of all public transportation, mandatory evacuation of Zone A (where the MHC staff housing building was located), and closing of all major bridges and tunnels. Likewise, the Department of Medicine at MHC started planning for this natural disaster. A plan for a medical resident backup system was developed. Medical interns and residents who lived near the hospital were identified and informed ahead of time that they would serve as first-line responders as the need arose during this time of anticipated calamity. All residents living outside Manhattan and those evacuated from the hospital's housing building were encouraged to stay within the city with peers or friends. The program leadership advocated for the solidarity of the house-staff and faculty.

During the day of the storm, volunteer residents were asked to stay in the hospital. At 5:00 PM, we put in place a ward team composed of 1 senior resident, 3 junior residents, and 3 interns, and a medical intensive care unit team of 2 senior residents and 2 interns. Also in-house were 1 of the chief medical residents, 4 medical attending physicians, and the chief of medicine. Everyone volunteered to stay and to work overnight without hesitation despite the fact that

they also had families left behind. At 7:00 PM when the winds were very strong, we advised the on-call teams to remain inside the hospital. The night float team was notified not to report for their regular 9:00 PM shift out of concern for their safety. At 9:00 PM, we learned that New York University Hospital was being evacuated and that possibly our institution would accept patient transfers from them.[4] At 9:30 PM, First Avenue was flooded and the winds were fierce. Lights on the street gradually faded within the buildings, and the cars were under water. Our institution's command center provided information by the minute. At 9:45 PM, the lights of MHC went off for the first time. After half a minute, the main emergency generator started to work and the lights came back. The flooding continued and 45 minutes later, the main generator failed, leaving the hospital in darkness. Critical supportive equipment was working with the backup system. The backup generator started to work 15 minutes later; however, large portions of the hospital, including the medical floors and medical intensive care unit, had no electrical power. The transfer of critical patients was coordinated from the medical intensive care unit on the 9th floor to the recovery room (the only unit with full power at that time) on the 10th floor. One by one the patients were transferred by one of our interns and a senior resident accompanied by the nursing staff and an intensivist, by the use of the one and only functioning elevator. On the medical floors, everything was dark. Calls to assess patients became a challenge. At midnight, we received news that we would continue admitting patients. That night, with no electrical power, attention to the patients continued nonstop. The clinical skills of the medical staff were challenged continuously by the absence of full laboratory support and by the lack of electronic medical records until early morning when we got our main generator back.

On the morning of October 30, the flooding subsided, but we saw the damage the storm left behind. We learned that Bellevue Hospital (BH), a 700+ bed facility in the Kips Bay neighborhood of Manhattan, was being evacuated and many of the patients would be transferred to MHC,[4] which at the time had the physical capacity to accept new patients.

On the night of October 31st, we had an influx of patients from BH and needed to construct an additional night float team for the care of these patients. Two medicine senior residents and 1 attending physician volunteered for the job. This team

---

Funding: None.

Conflict of Interest: None.

Authorship: All authors had access to the data and played a role in writing this manuscript.

admitted a total of 22 patients, in addition to the regular over-night admissions. The patients were triaged by the chief of medicine and supportive staff sometimes in the hallways near the admitting office and then brought safely to the appropriate services, including the medical intensive care unit.

On November 1st, a new "emergency" team of medical residents from MHC was created to take care of these patients in units newly opened to accommodate the increased patient volume. Later, a medical team from BH was deployed to MHC so as not to lose the continuity of their residency training. A MHC senior resident was assigned to coach the BH team in their transition. During this time, close lines of communication with our MHC and the new BH staff were vital. We ensured that all of our residents were supported and that their work and living conditions would not be disrupted in the aftermath of the storm.

The BH teams that came in different groups at different times generated added stress to the program leadership because orientation, credentialing, and access to our hospital needed to be addressed. During the following weeks, our admission rate increased up to 40%. An increased number of overnight admissions with limited bed availabilities were problems that our house-staff and faculty members faced daily, especially when the BH emergency department reopened without an inpatient facility 8 weeks after the disaster. The closing of nursing homes flooded by the storm also became a hurdle, because we were unable to discharge patients in a timely manner.

The outpatient clinics were closed during the days after the storm, which provided additional physicians to attend to hospitalized patients. One week later, the outpatient clinic was fully operational. During the time that the hospital did not have full power, the academic activities that depended on electronic devices were suspended, but bedside teaching continued daily.

THE CHALLENGES FOR THE PROGRAM

1. Although daily scheduled conferences were resumed 1 week after the storm, because of prioritization of essential patient care activities, residents had to be excused, at times, from attending noon conferences. However, there was a noticeable change of learning patterns from classroom to bedside.
2. The inaccessibility of the hospital housing building for a prolonged period of time contributed to additional stress for our house-staff.
3. There needed to be increased numbers of emergency meetings to coordinate and to address Accreditation Council for Graduate Medical Education cap limits, patient redistribution, and team assignments, among other matters.
4. The Department of Medicine strategy to integrate the BH teams into our activities to have a homogenous group of physicians sometimes created problems because the

interpretation of the Accreditation Council for Graduate Medical Education rules between the program's leadership differed.
5. The BH emergency department reopened on December 27, and the accepting MHC residents were unable to assess the patients before they were transferred to the MHC medical floors.

OPPORTUNITIES FOR THE PROGRAM

1. Working closely with trainees and faculty members from another residency program provided a unique opportunity for our residents to be exposed to another style of medical education. BH house-staff interacted with MHC house-staff during conferences and with the consulting services. The BH residents returned to the main BH campus in early February after 3 months at MHC.
2. Having BH faculty members as teachers for some of our academic activities was beneficial.
3. Working for a short time in *crisis mode* was viewed as a learning opportunity and a chance for personal and professional growth.

LESSONS LEARNED

The burdens of this crisis proved to be a unique opportunity for learning. We noticed tremendous collegiality, professionalism, and a willingness to help our guest colleagues and to continue to excel in patient care. In the era of modern technology, the residents demonstrated their basic clinical skills, efficiency, and ability to take care of patients without laboratory support and electronic medical records. All the physicians in the Department of Medicine demonstrated a great commitment in continuing the academic activities despite the increase of workload, keeping our program alive and fresh.

Christian Espana-Schmidt, MD
Erwyn C. Ong, MD
William Frishman, MD
Nora V. Bergasa, MD, FACP
Shobhana Chaudhari, MD, FACP, AGSF
Department of Medicine
New York Medical College/Metropolitan Hospital Center
New York

References

1. Pero CD, Pou AM, Arriaga MA, Nuss DW. Post-Katrina: study in crisis-related program adaptability. *Otolaryngol Head Neck Surg*. 2008;138:394-397.
2. Cefalu CA, Schwartz RS. Salvaging a geriatric medicine academic program in disaster mode-the LSU training program post-Katrina. *J Natl Med Assoc*. 2007;99:590-596.
3. Ayyala R. Lessons from Katrina: a program director's perspective. *Ophthalmology*. 2007;114:1425-1426.
4. Ofri D. The storm and the aftermath. *N Engl J Med*. 2012;367:2265-2267.

COMMENTARY

THE AMERICAN
JOURNAL *of*
MEDICINE ®

Milestones: Direct Observation May Be the Key to Accelerated Training

The United States faces a worsening shortage of physicians, particularly in primary care.[1,2] The number of medical school positions has increased, but without a corresponding expansion of residency slots. As such, the number of American medical graduates is rising while the total number of postgraduate positions remains stable. Short of turning over primary care to nurse practitioners and physician assistants, we must be open to the idea of accelerating the pace of medical training. Emanuel and Fuchs[3] recently made this argument, pointing out that reductions in medical school and residency duration are already underway. They suggested that certain aspects of third-year medicine residency, such as supervising interns and taking electives, are "hardly essential to becoming a knowledgeable practitioner." And they concluded that "the third year of internal medicine or pediatric residencies or the research year in surgical specialties could be eliminated without compromising the clinical quality of trainees." While their contentions may be largely correct, few would disagree that some medical residents require more than 2 years of supervised clinical experience before being deemed ready for fellowship or entry into independent practice. The challenge to the medical system, then, is to tailor training duration to *actual* clinical ability. In turn, educators must be able to assess trainee competence confidently and accurately.

The Outcomes Project, which was introduced over 10 years ago, appeared to be the logical framework for such determinations. Yet full implementation has been slowed by a number of factors[4-6] and the premise of the Outcomes Project challenged.[7-9] Lurie et al[9] argued that with the exception of medical knowledge, assessments of residents could not reliably distinguish between levels of competence within the 6 general domains. On the other hand, Green and Holmboe[4] have contended that "the inconsistent use and interpretation of [available instruments] by unskilled faculty" is more contributory to Lurie's findings than a lack of suitable evaluation tools.

To address concerns with the Outcomes Project, the American Board of Internal Medicine and Accreditation Council for Graduate Medical Education (ACGME) jointly developed educational milestones.[10] By subdividing the general competencies into more specific components, the milestones were intended to permit more convincing measures of clinical competence. Shortly after their introduction, our program, in collaboration with other members of the Educational Innovations Project (EIP),[11] began to use them for clinical assessments. The EIP initiative used 8 milestones to guide direct observations of clinic performance that informed the entrustment decision for "ready for distance supervision."[12] At the same time, our program broadly incorporated milestones within all clinical rotations, except certain subspecialty electives. Our initiative engaged faculty in all phases of curricular redesign, development, implementation, tool construction and use, and data management and consideration at higher-order summative evaluations (eg, clinical competency committee deliberations).

For almost 3 years, we have considered curricular-milestones-based data at a series of landmark assessments (Entrustable Professional Activities[13]) to evaluate resident progress. Both faculty and residents have indicated through surveys and end-of-rotation feedback that milestones promoted a common understanding of what knowledge, skills, and attitudes should be displayed at particular stages of training, permitted greater specificity in performance feedback, and enhanced uniformity and fairness in promotion decisions. We successfully utilized *curricular*-milestones-based data to complete synthetic evaluations of trainee progress at the clinical competency level, where the use of curricular milestones allowed us to discern statistically significant differences in milestones-defined domains of clinical competence.[14] Surveyed committee members indicated that milestones improved the quality of information, promoted more uniform evaluation standards, and enhanced the ability of the committee to discriminate between specific strengths and weaknesses of individual residents. More recently, we conducted a pilot test of the Alliance for Academic Internal Medicine redesign group's recently released *reporting* milestones.[15] Using *curricular*-milestones-data organized by *reporting* milestone narrative, core competency and ACGME competency, we were able to effectively identify training attainment levels for a sample of our current residents.

Two years ago, when Green and Holmboe[4] asked whether the toolbox for competency-based assessment was

Funding: CN has received funding as a principal investigator on 2 research grants from the Foundation for Innovation in Medical Education.

Conflict of Interest: In 2012, CN served as a paid consultant to the Greater New York Hospital Association. SJP and WHF have no disclosures.

Authorship: All authors had access to the data and a role in writing the Commentary.

half full or half empty, the answer was uncertain. Since then, the *curricular* milestones have identified the medical community's belief as to what knowledge, skills, and attitudes a trainee should display at particular times in medical training. These represent the "explicitly stated set of expectations that... link the ideals of the general competencies to the realities of measurement" called for by Lurie et al.[9] Programs are now rapidly developing milestones-based evaluation tools within a unifying framework that allows for innovative approaches while also promoting standardization. Given the scope of the project, best practices and favored evaluation strategies should be identified quickly. The *reporting* milestones carry competency assessments one step further by providing the descriptive language by which *curricular* milestones-based data can be synthesized at higher-order summative evaluations to accurately mark the course of resident skill acquisition.[16]

In order for this new outcomes-based model of evaluation to reach its full potential, we believe that programs will require additional support for development of expert faculty evaluators who will be able to spend more time directly observing, guiding, and rating resident clinical activities. Program directors and clinical competency committees must then be able to fully consider the new stream of evaluation data. While calls for more resources in a time of belt tightening might seem whimsical, this training model has worked well within the EIP, where all program directors were guaranteed a minimum 0.75 Full-Time Equivalent. Our institution's EIP-related support made possible robust faculty participation that was critical to the development of a shared mental framework that guided evaluation tool construction and promoted focused and more numerous direct observations of clinical performance. This allowed us to integrate curricular milestones into our training 2 years ahead of the Next Accreditation System mandate while carrying out other quality improvement and patient safety initiatives at the same time.[17-19] We are convinced that the tools needed for accurate identification of trainees suitable for rapid advancement are at hand. As such, resources devoted to making sound promotion decisions would be well utilized. If each training program fast-tracks one fourth of its residents to graduate in 2 rather than 3 years, the nation's physician shortage will be mitigated and funds allocated to more effective outcomes assessments will be repaid.

In short, the suite of evaluation tools now available to medicine residency program directors tips the half-full/half-empty balance far towards full. As residency programs integrate curricular and narrative milestones-based assessments into their training, they also should give thought to the next phase of outcomes-based assessment that will involve short-track pathways for suitably competent residents.

ACKNOWLEDGMENT

Dr Nabors thanks Dr Howard Kerpen, Director of the Lorber Center for the Advancement of Medical Education, Long Island Jewish Medical Center, Lorber Professor of Medicine, Albert Einstein College of Medicine, Clinical Professor of Medicine, Hofstra North Shore-Long Island Jewish Health System, and the Foundation for Innovation in Medical Education for generously supporting our efforts to advance competency-based medical education.

Stephen J. Peterson, MD
Christopher Nabors, MD, PhD
William H. Frishman, MD
Department of Medicine
New York Medical College/Westchester Medical Center
Valhalla

References

1. Petterson SM, Liaw WR, Phillips RL Jr, Rabin DL, Meyers DS, Bazemore AW. Projecting US primary care physician workforce needs: 2010-2025. *Ann Fam Med.* 2012;10(6):503-509.
2. Carek PJ, Peterson L, Shokar NK, Johnson SP, Knoll ME, Mainous AG 3rd. Graduate medical education and primary care workforce: a CERA study. *Fam Med.* 2012;44(10):712-715.
3. Emanuel EJ, Fuchs VR. Shortening medical training by 30%. *JAMA.* 2012;307(11):1143-1144.
4. Green ML, Holmboe E. The ACGME toolbox: half empty or half full? *Acad Med.* 2010;85(5):787.
5. Heard JK, Allen RM, Clardy J. Assessing the needs of residency program directors to meet the ACGME general competencies. *Acad Med.* 2002;77(7):750.
6. Malik MU, Diaz VV, Stewart CM, et al. Barriers to implementing the ACGME outcome project: a systematic review of program director surveys. *Journal of Graduate Medical Education.* 2012;4(4): 425-433.
7. Huddle TS, Heudebert GR. Taking apart the art: the risk of anatomizing clinical competence. *Acad Med.* 2007;82(6):536-541.
8. Whitcomb ME. Redirecting the assessment of clinical competence. *Acad Med.* 2007;82(6):527-528.
9. Lurie SJ, Mooney CJ, Lyness JM. Measurement of the general competencies of the accreditation council for graduate medical education: a systematic review. *Acad Med.* 2009;84(3):301-309.
10. Green ML, Aagaard EM, Caverzagie KJ, et al. Charting the road to competence: Developmental milestones for internal medicine residency training. *J Grad Med Educ.* 2009;1(1):5-20.
11. Accreditation Council for Graduate Medical Education. Educational Innovation Project. Available at: http://www.acgme.org/acWebsite/ RRC_140/140_EIPindex.asp. Accessed April 2, 2013.
12. Heist K, Post J, Meade L, Brandenburg S. Milestones: do learners and teachers agree? *Am J Med.* 2013;126(3):270-274.
13. ten Cate O. Entrustability of professional activities and competency-based training. *Med Educ.* 2005;39(12):1176-1177.
14. Nabors C, Peterson SJ, Forman L, et al. Operationalizing the internal medicine milestones-an early status report. *J Grad Med Educ.* 2013;5(1):130-137.
15. Caverzagie KJ, Iobst WF, Aagaard EM, et al. The internal medicine reporting milestones and the next accreditation system. *Ann Intern Med.* 2013;158(7):557-559.
16. Nasca TJ, Philibert I, Brigham T, Flynn TC. The next GME accreditation system—rationale and benefits. *N Engl J Med.* 2012;366(11): 1051-1056.
17. Nabors C, Peterson SJ, Weems R, et al. A multidisciplinary approach for teaching systems-based practice to internal medicine residents. *J Grad Med Educ.* 2011;3(1):75-80.
18. Nabors C, Peterson SJ, Lee WN, et al. Experience with faculty supervision of an electronic resident sign-out system. *Am J Med.* 2010;123(4):376-381.
19. Nabors C, Peterson SJ, Aronow WS, et al. Physician reporting of clinically significant events through a computerized patient sign-out system. *J Patient Saf.* 2011;7(3):155-161.

REVIEW ARTICLE

Vascular and Heart Diseases in the Incumbent Presidents and Vice Presidents of the United States of America

A Medical-Historical Perspective

William H. Frishman, MD,* Franklin H. Zimmerman, MD,*§ and Robert G. Lerner, MD*

Abstract: Vascular diseases have been the major cause of death and disability in presidents and vice presidents of the United States. Untreated hypertension and cigarette smoking have contributed greatly to this increased morbidity and mortality risk, which has impacted on historical events, especially in the 20th century. In this article, the medical histories of those incumbent Presidents and Vice Presidents who suffered from coronary artery and cerebrovascular diseases will be reviewed. A discussion of how atrial fibrillation has affected the Presidents is also included.

Key Words: Presidents, Vice Presidents, cardiovascular disease, presidential health

(*Cardiology in Review* 2013;21:1–8)

Atherosclerotic vascular disease has been the most common serious illness affecting presidents and vice presidents of the United States in the 20th century. There have been suggestions that this also was a problem in the 19th century, however, diagnostic modalities have become more sophisticated over the last 100 years since Herrick in 1912 described coronary thrombosis as the cause of myocardial infarction (MI) and sudden death[1] and with the introduction of the electrocardiogram (ECG).

During the 20th century 1 president died in office from a probable MI and 2 incumbent presidents suffered strokes (both of the World War presidents), 1 of which was seriously disabling and 1 fatal. One president and 1 vice president had known coronary artery disease (CAD) before being elected to national office, and 1 president sustained a transmural MI while in office and was re-elected. CAD also affected multiple president after they left office (1 former president was diagnosed with triple vessel CAD at our hospital).

Coronary and cerebrovascular disease of the presidents has also had a major impact on 20th century history and highlights the importance of cardiovascular and cerebrovascular risk factor modification, especially in the management of systemic hypertension, cigarette smoking, and hyperlipidemia.

In this article, the known medical histories of those incumbent presidents and vice presidents who suffered from CAD, cerebral artery disease, and atrial fibrillation and how these medical conditions may have impacted on world events will be discussed. At the same time, a discussion of the care provided to the presidents

From the *Department of Medicine, New York Medical College/Westchester Medical Center, Valhalla, NY and §Department of Medicine, Phelps Memorial Hospital Center, Sleepy Hollow, NY.
Disclosure: The authors declare no conflicts of interest.
Correspondence: William H. Frishman, MD, Department of Medicine, New York Medical College, Munger 263, Valhalla, NY 10595. E-mail: William_Frishman@nymc.edu
ISSN: 1061-5377/13/2101-01
DOI: 10.1097/CRD.0b013e31827303b5

and vice presidents will serve to illustrate the remarkable advances in diagnostics and therapeutics of atherosclerotic vascular disease, which have taken place over the last 100 years.

THE PRESIDENTS

Woodrow Wilson

Thomas Woodrow Wilson, the 28th President (Fig. 1), was the most disabled Chief Executive to serve, having suffered a major stroke in 1919 while well into his second term of office.[2] Wilson's neurovascular history probably began many years earlier.

In May 1906, at the age of 49, while serving as President of Princeton, Wilson awoke from sleep and found that he was blind in his left eye, the result of a retinal hemorrhage.[3] He consulted with 2 prominent Philadelphia physicians who diagnosed arteriosclerosis and recommended that Wilson follow a more relaxed lifestyle.[3,4] He clearly did not follow this recommendation, and ultimately was elected Governor of New Jersey in 1910 and President of the United States in 1912.

Wilson was found to have hypertension and suffered from recurrent headaches.[4] He had no known history of cigarette smoking. From 1906 to 1915 he experienced multiple episodes of transitory weakness and numbness of his right hand, but these were most likely not related to a vascular etiology.[5]

Wilson's labors reached a pinnacle during America's entry into World War I in 1917 and its aftermath. He worked 18 hours a day, developing the covenant for the League of Nations, while at the same time trying to overcome isolationist opposition in the US Senate.[2] He began a national speaking campaign in September 1919 to try to win popular support for his foreign policy program.[2] On September 25, in Pueblo, Colorado, Wilson suffered a headache, slurred speech, and temporary left-sided weakness, a probable transient cerebral ischemic attack.[6] He improved the next day, cancelled the rest of his speaking tour, and returned to Washington, DC. On October 2, 1919 he was found by his wife in a White House bathroom, lying on the floor. Wilson had a massive stroke that left him with complete paralysis of his left arm and leg; he had left hemianopsia, difficulty in swallowing, impairment of speech, and a change in both his cognition and emotional state.[6]

Prominent civilian consultants were called in, however, the condition of the President was kept a secret from his Vice President, his cabinet, and the public.[6-8] During Wilson's disability, his physician, Admiral Cary Grayson, the President's wife Edith Galt Bolling Wilson, and a few trusted aides ran the activities of the White House.[6] The press was told Wilson was suffering from nervous exhaustion and the gravity of his illness was not disclosed.[6] The First Lady saw that no one was admitted to Wilson's sick room. She screened the papers that were brought to his attention and reported the President's decisions to other government officials when necessary.[7] For 3 months after his stroke, Wilson had contact only with his family and physicians. He did not meet with his cabinet until April 1920, 6 months after his stroke.[7,8] After several months Wilson's condition improved, and he was able to walk with assistance.

FIGURE 1. President Woodrow Wilson with First Lady Edith Galt Bolling Wilson. Courtesy of Library of Congress.

The United States never joined the League of Nations. One wonders what would have happened in world history had antihypertensive drug therapy been available for Wilson. Perhaps the second World War would have been averted.

Wilson remained physically frail and mentally and emotionally impaired for the rest of his presidential term, which ended in March 1921.[9] Considering the extent of his illness, Wilson should have resigned or temporarily relinquished his presidential power, turning the office over to Vice President Thomas Marshall.

It was Wilson's disability as President that, in part, ultimately would lead to the 25th Amendment to the constitution over 45 years later, which includes the criteria for removing an impaired president.[10] Wilson's illness also raises the issue of what should be publicly disclosed about an incumbent president's health problems.

Warren G. Harding

Warren Gamaliel Harding was the 29th President of the United States, elected by a large plurality in 1920 with the campaign theme "Return to Normalcy."[11] He was the first president to die in office from a probable MI. He was also the only president to have parents who were both doctors; both his mother and father were homeopathic physicians. His presidential physician was Dr. Charles Sawyer, a homeopathic physician who ran a clinic in Harding's hometown of Marion, Ohio.[12]

To induce Dr. Sawyer to come to Washington, DC to become the presidential physician, he was appointed by Harding from civilian status to Brigadier General in the Army Reserves[12] (an author of this article [W.H.F.] served as a Lieutenant-Colonel and cardiologist on active duty and in the Army Reserves, and also as a civilian consultant in cardiology for the Army).

Before beginning his presidency in 1921, Harding was reported to be in excellent health, although he had been treated 20 years prior for fatigue and nervous illness at the Battle Creek, Michigan Sanitarium run by Dr. J.H. Kellogg of "cornflakes" fame.[13] There is no history of premature heart disease in his family, and Harding was an avid golfer throughout his presidency. However, Harding had multiple risk factors for CAD. He had high blood pressure with systolic blood pressure readings of 195 mm Hg.[13] He was overweight and consumed tobacco in all forms, including cigarettes, cigars, pipes, and chewing tobacco.[13]

During his presidency, Harding had an episode of influenza, which weakened him, but he seemed to recover.[14] He was said to work 15 hours a day in his presidential role. He periodically complained of chest and abdominal pain, exhaustion, and he had episodes of mental depression.[13,14]

In June 1923 Harding took a political vacation trip to the West Coast, which included a visit to the Alaska territory. After visiting Alaska, the President's health seemed to deteriorate. Upon his return to the United States, he developed upper abdominal pain and nausea. His physician, Dr. Sawyer, suspected indigestion and food poisoning. The assistant presidential physician, Dr. Joel Boone, noted he had a pulse of 120 and a respiratory rate of 40. Harding's Secretary of the Interior, Hubert Work, was also a physician, and he and Dr. Boone, without Dr. Sawyer's knowledge, wired Dr. Ray Lyman Wilbur, a President of Stanford, past Dean of its medical school, and President of the American Medical Association, to meet the presidential train in San Francisco. Wilbur brought with him Dr. Charles Cooper, a well-known San Francisco cardiologist.[14-16]

Harding was brought to the Palace Hotel in San Francisco. Bronchopneumonia was suspected and he was treated with digitalis and caffeine. On August 1, it was noted that his heart action had improved, his lungs were clearing, and his pulse and blood pressure were improving. He never had an ECG and there are no reports of blood tests. However, the next day he died suddenly in his bed at the age of 57 years.[14-16] The cause of death was said to be "apoplexy stroke."[17] An autopsy was never carried out.

Of note, Harding was never hospitalized and his symptoms and physical findings suggested a severe cardiorespiratory illness, most likely an MI with preinfarction angina and congestive heart failure.[18] The cause of his sudden death was probably an arrhythmia.

His presidential successor, Calvin Coolidge, had a fear of cardiac disease. As President, he would have his pulse monitored twice daily by a White House physician.[19] A smoker, he ultimately would die in his sleep at age 60 years, 4 years after his term of office was completed.

Franklin Delano Roosevelt

Franklin Roosevelt, who was the 32nd President, led the country through the Great Depression and most of World War II.[20,21] He suffered from poliomyelitis at the age of 39 years, which left him with atrophic dysfunctional lower extremities. He also had a significant cardiovascular history, which was not well known publicly until 1970, at which time his presidential cardiologist, Howard Bruenn reported on Roosevelt's medical conditions in the *Annals of Internal Medicine*, 25 years after the President's death in 1945 from a probable cerebral hemorrhage with brain herniation.[22-24]

Roosevelt was elected President in 1932 and chose as his presidential physician, Dr. Ross McIntire, an otolaryngologist who was in the Navy Medical Corp.[23] Roosevelt was a long-time cigarette smoker and had chronic sinusitis.[23] He was first noted to have an elevated systolic and diastolic blood pressure in 1937 at the age of 55 years.[22] At that time there was no known effective therapy available for chronic hypertension. Roosevelt had no history of diabetes mellitus, but his father died at the age of 72 years from a probable MI.[25]

In 1941 Roosevelt developed severe iron deficiency anemia (hemoglobin 4.5 g/100 dL) caused by bleeding hemorrhoids that were

228   *Appendix Q*

Cardiology in Review • Volume 21, Number 1, January/February 2013   *Vascular/Heart Disease in Presidents/Vice Presidents*

treated with ferrous sulfate. He had no cardiac symptoms at the time. In 1943 he had a severe episode of probable influenza with recurrent respiratory infections and fatigue. In 1944 Dr. Howard Bruenn, a Navy cardiologist and Chief of the ECG Lab at Bethesda Naval Hospital, was asked by Dr. McIntire to examine Roosevelt as an outpatient at the hospital. During the examination, Bruenn found Roosevelt to be in moderate respiratory distress with a blood pressure of 188/108 and pulse of 72. He noted rales on the pulmonary examination and an enlarged heart by palpation. A blowing systolic murmur was also heard at the apex. Roosevelt's ECG revealed diffuse T wave inversions (Fig. 2).[22]

On the basis of his examination of the President, Bruenn made the diagnoses of hypertension, hypertensive heart disease, and left ventricular cardiac failure.[22] Bruenn reported his findings to McIntire, who at the time was also the Surgeon General for the Navy. Bruenn's recommendations for Roosevelt were digitalization, sedation with barbiturates, a weight-reducing diet, and curtailment of cigarette smoking.[22] Bruenn also reviewed his findings with the civilian medical consultants and a board of Naval physicians, who, despite early skepticism, ultimately agreed with the diagnosis and treatment plan.[22,23] Bruenn was assigned to care for the President, and did so right until Roosevelt's death a year later.[22] McIntire, acting as the public spokesperson, as did past presidential physicians, was secretive regarding Roosevelt's health, and the public did not realize the gravity of Roosevelt's illness at the time.[23]

Over the next number of months, under Bruenn's constant supervision (he would examine the President almost every morning), the President's health declined steadily. He lost over 20 lb and had a decreased appetite. He received digitalis leaf 0.1 mg daily with an additional dose twice a week. His blood pressure readings were reported to be as high as 240/150 mm Hg, however, his ECG remained stable.[22] He was never hospitalized (the first President to be hospitalized was Harry Truman years later).[26,27] Bruenn accompanied Roosevelt on his subsequent trips to Hawaii, Alaska, and Quebec in 1944 and to Yalta in 1945.

Roosevelt did not attend his final Democratic nomination convention in 1944, but made an acceptance speech on the radio. At his final inaugural in early 1945, he made a brief speech at the White House. Most of his political speeches were now made in the sitting position; no longer standing with his leg braces.[22] At the Yalta conference in February 1945, a weakened Roosevelt seemed to have let Stalin have the upper hand in their negotiations, which ultimately could have led to the Cold War (Fig. 3).[20]

Roosevelt seemed exhausted in late March 1945 (Fig. 4) and went to Warm Springs in Georgia, a major rehabilitation institution for polio victims, which he had sponsored and visited frequently.[22,24] That month it was also noted by Bruenn that

Roosevelt's systolic blood pressure rose 50 mmHg after talking on the telephone to his wife Eleanor.[24] At Warm Springs he seemed to improve, although his blood pressure ranged from 110/88 mm Hg to 240/130 mm Hg. Bruenn made his usual daily morning visits to Roosevelt. On the morning of April 12, the President complained of a slight headache. In the early afternoon while sitting for a portrait in the cabin where he stayed, he complained of a severe occipital headache and lapsed into a coma within a few minutes. Bruenn examined the President within 15 minutes and his blood pressure was noted to be more than 300/190 mm Hg. Roosevelt died of a cardiac arrest within 2 hours, despite closed chest massage and the use of intracardiac epinephrine.[22,24] He was 63 years old.[21]

In summary, Franklin Roosevelt suffered from severe hypertension and developed multiple complications from untreated hypertensive disease, including hypertensive cardiomyopathy, and ultimately a fatal cerebral hemorrhage. There was no long-term treatment available for hypertension until the introduction of oral reserpine after World War II. It is of interest that both World War Presidents, Wilson and Roosevelt, developed cerebrovascular complications of hypertension at pivotal points in history. Subsequent world events could well have been very different had there been effective treatment of hypertension for these 2 wartime presidents.

Should Roosevelt have been allowed to run for his fourth term? His diagnoses and the medical care provided were kept secret from the public, which was also was the situation with Woodrow Wilson. Eisenhower's illnesses were revealed somewhat to the public. How much information should be disclosed regarding the health of the president and presidential candidates is still an issue being debated today.

Dwight Eisenhower

Dwight Eisenhower was a World War II hero who served as the 34th President of the United States.[28] During his first term as President in 1955, he sustained an anterior wall MI, and 7 months later underwent intestinal surgery for obstruction related to probable Crohn disease, which he tolerated well.[29] In his second term he sustained a transient cerebral ischemic event or a mild stroke, which he seemed to have recovered from.[30] He ultimately would die in retirement in 1969, after suffering multiple MIs from ischemic

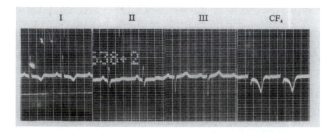

FIGURE 2. Roosevelt's electrocardiogram (ECG) taken March 28, 1944 before digitalization. The ECG shows sinus rhythm with deep inversion of the T waves in leads I and CF$_4$ (only 1 precordial lead was used with ST segment depression in the other lead). Bruenn HG: Clinical notes on the illness and death of President Franklin D. Roosevelt. *Ann Intern Med* 1970; 72: 579–91 with permission.

FIGURE 3. Winston Churchill, Franklin D. Roosevelt (with cigarette in hand) and Joseph Stalin at Yalta, February 1945. Courtesy of Roosevelt Library, Hyde Park, New York.

FIGURE 4. Franklin D. Roosevelt on the day before his death. Courtesy of Roosevelt Library, Hyde Park, New York.

cardiomyopathy, and intestinal obstructions, and undergoing successful electrocardioversions and treatment with bretylium.[31,32] The year he died he was considered to be an early candidate for the newly introduced intra-aortic balloon.[32]

Eisenhower had been a heavy smoker, consuming 3 packs daily.[33] During the final planning for the D-Day Invasion of mainland Europe in 1944, he was noted to be lighting up 1 cigarette after another.[34] In 1949 he stopped smoking completely.[32] He had no history of diabetes, hypertension, nor a family history of premature CAD. He was noted to have sporadic blood pressure elevations and an elevated plasma cholesterol level.

While vacationing in Colorado in September 1955, Eisenhower developed "indigestion" while playing golf. The following evening he complained of chest pain and his physician, General Dr. Howard Snyder, an Army colleague since World War II, treated him at Eisenhower's in-law's house in Denver. He was treated with oxygen, amyl nitrate, morphine, heparin, and papaverine (a vascular dilator). The President's blood pressure fell. Inexplicably, his physician did not recommend immediate hospitalization, and Eisenhower spent the night in bed with his wife. The following day a cardiologist came to the house and administered an ECG, which showed changes suggestive of an anterior wall MI. Eisenhower was brought to Fitzsimmons Army Hospital in Denver in a car after walking with aid to the automobile. At the hospital he was placed in an oxygen tent and then told he was having "a heart attack." Eisenhower was treated in the manner of the times (Fig. 5), and spent 7 weeks in the hospital[29,31,35] (the author W.H.F. remembers reciting a national prayer for the President's recovery in his third-grade public school

classroom). Eisenhower did not meet with the public for 5 weeks. His Army cardiologist, Dr. Thomas Mattingly, suggested that Eisenhower not seek re-election in 1956.[29] However, the civilian cardiology consult, Paul Dudley White, was much more optimistic about the President's prognosis, and Eisenhower would ultimately be re-elected a year later.[29] Over time, subsequent cardiac exams would reveal that Eisenhower had a left ventricular aneurysm.[31] During Eisenhower's illness, his personal physician, Dr. Snyder, was always reassuring, telling the public that the President would make a full recovery.[29]

Eisenhower spent some time convalescing at his farm in Gettysburg, Pennsylvania. He returned to work in November 1955. He remained on oral anticoagulation. At no time did he relinquish power to Vice President Richard Nixon.

In June 1956, at Walter Reed Army Hospital, Eisenhower underwent an intestinal resection by Army surgeon Leonard Heaton without cardiac complications.[36]

While speaking to his secretary in 1957 during his second term, Eisenhower sustained a transient cerebral ischemic attack on coumadin.[30] He had lost the ability to hold a pen and sustained an acute memory loss and difficulty in speaking.[30] He recovered most if not all of his function within 3 days, but had considered resigning if he could not function cognitively. Ultimately he would complete his second term as President with no further disability from his illnesses. He did have an episode of atrial fibrillation in 1960 while campaigning for Richard Nixon, and was treated with quinidine.[31]

In conclusion, once admitted to the hospital, Eisenhower received the usual recommended treatment for MI, prolonged bed rest followed by a long convalescence. However, he was able to function as President and was re-elected. In retrospect, his personal physician tried to minimize the severity of Eisenhower's illness, as did the physicians of Woodrow Wilson and Franklin Roosevelt. There was also a controversy between his military and civilian cardiologists regarding Eisenhower's ability to serve as president. Clearly, most survivors of uncomplicated MI today can return to work after a much shorter convalescence than Eisenhower had undergone.

Lyndon Baines Johnson

Lyndon Johnson, the 36th President, suffered from CAD before his elections as Vice President in 1960 and as President in

FIGURE 5. Past President Dwight D. Eisenhower (in wheelchair) convalescing from his myocardial infarction at Fitzsimmons Army Hospital, Denver, Colorado.

1964.[37] Johnson became the Majority Leader of the Senate in 1954. In 1955 he was noted to be overweight (he consumed a high-fat diet), and had a smoking history of at least 60 unfiltered cigarettes a day. He had nicotine-stained fingernails.[38] Johnson also had a strong family history of premature death including his father who died at the age of 60 years from complications of CAD, 1 uncle who died suddenly at the age of 57 years from an MI, and another uncle who died from complications related to an MI at the age of 65 years.[39,40] It was said in his family that all Johnson men had bad hearts and died young.[40] Johnson was always worried that he himself would die before the age of 60 years from cardiac disease, and it affected his driving ambition to succeed in national politics at a young age.[39]

Johnson sustained an MI in July 1955, 1 month before his 47th birthday.[41] He was being considered a strong candidate for either the vice presidency or presidency in 1956. He had a prior history of having episodes of chest pain and palpitations at rest and during intercourse. Just before his MI, Johnson was noted to have had multiple "temper tantrums" in the Senate. While being driven to a friend's house in Virginia, he developed severe chest pains, which were thought by him to be indigestion. A physician was called to the house, and Johnson was told he was having "a heart attack." He was told to go to Washington, DC to be hospitalized, and was driven by ambulance, which took over 90 minutes while Johnson had crushing chest pain. He was hospitalized at Bethesda Naval Hospital. Dr. J. Willis Hurst, who was in the Navy at the time, became Johnson's cardiologist and Hurst would continue to serve as his civilian cardiologist for the next 18 years until Johnson's death from CAD in 1973.[38]

Similar to Eisenhower, Johnson received the usual care being provided for post-MI patients. He had to stop smoking (he initially said he would rather have his "pecker cut off than stop smoking") and he was hospitalized for 5 weeks. He was given a diet of 1500 calories a day, which ultimately brought his weight down 50 lb, and he was told to watch the amount of fat intake (diet studies were already demonstrating the relationship between cholesterol intake and heart disease).[38]

Johnson also suffered from a severe postmyocardial depression.[38] He went home to his ranch in Texas to recover, where he would spend 4 months before returning to his job as Senate Majority Leader in January 1956. Johnson did talk about his experience in an article "My Heart Taught Me How to Live" which was published in the *American* magazine. In the article he described how he was driven in his political life before his MI, and that now he paid more attention to family and the world around him.[42] After his MI, he began to develop an interest in reading. Although he would work with great intensity and drive for the rest of his political life, he learned to outwardly control his temper and to modify his emotions.

In December 1955, Johnson's doctors told him he had fully recovered, although for the rest of his life he feared having another heart attack.[38] His fellow senators were impressed with how well he looked when he returned to the Senate. He was elected Vice President in 1960 and there were no further episodes of cardiac symptoms noted during that time. In 1963, when he assumed the presidency after Kennedy's assassination, he was found fit to serve by Dr. Hurst.[43] He underwent gallbladder surgery with no problems, and seemed to function well during his own elected term as President in 1964. With the stresses of the war in Vietnam and the political challenges that constrained him, Johnson retired from political life in 1969. There were questions whether his cardiac history or cardiac symptoms contributed to his not seeking a second elected term as President.[44]

Johnson's presidential physicians were physiatrist Janet Travell, who had cared for John Kennedy, and Vice Admiral George Burkley (who was in the Dallas motorcade with Kennedy and Johnson when Kennedy was shot).[45]

During retirement in Texas, Johnson would have multiple episodes of chest pain, and he sustained another MI in 1972 and was treated at the University of Virginia Hospital in Charlottesville. He had resumed cigarette smoking, and in January 1973 he was found dead by a telephone in his bedroom, probably from a recurrent MI and a fatal arrhythmia.[46] Johnson was 64 years old. Because of his anginal symptoms, a coronary angiography had been recommended before his death, but he had refused.[47] An autopsy of Johnson revealed that 2 of the 3 major arteries were completely occluded, and the third was 60% restricted.[47]

Johnson's cardiac history was classic for premature CAD, but it did not seem to affect his roles as Vice President and President. However, his disease process probably did affect decisions he made about his own future political life.

As an aside, the author (W.H.F.) got to know Dr. Willis Hurst, Johnson's cardiologist, very well, having contributed to multiple editions of his textbook *The Heart,* and after having made many trips to Emory as a visiting professor where Hurst served as Chairman of Medicine. Hurst was also a past president of the American Heart Association. Hurst, like Johnson, was a "bear of a man," tall and imposing. Similar to Johnson, Hurst would persuade you to do something by grabbing your arm, and pulling your body close to his (Fig. 6). I remember him telling me (W.H.F.), "Frishman, I'm counting on you to have your chapters done on time and with updated references." Dr. Willis Hurst died recently at the age of 90 years,[48] and he will be missed.

George H.W. Bush

George H.W. Bush, the 41st President, collapsed in 1991 while jogging at Camp David, Maryland, the presidential retreat. He was brought to Bethesda Naval Hospital by helicopter and was found to be in atrial fibrillation.[49,50] It was difficult to control his heart rate with medication, which included digitalis, procainamide, and warfarin, and electrocardioversion was considered.[45,46] Before cardioversion, Bush was found to be hyperthyroid, and he was successfully treated with radioactive thyroid (leaving him with hypothyroidism requiring replacement therapy) and converted to normal sinus rhythm.[51,52] His presidential physician, Dr. Burton Lee, an oncologist, was criticized for not obtaining earlier thyroid function tests as part of Bush's annual exam.[51]

Of interest, Barbara Bush, the First Lady, was also found to be hyperthyroid, as well as their pet dog Millie (who also had lupus erythematosis).[49]

Other Presidents, including William Taft and Eisenhower, had atrial fibrillation after their terms of office were complete. At the end of his life, Richard Nixon, the 37th President, had a probable embolic stroke as a consequence of new onset atrial fibrillation. During his hospitalization at New York Hospital (where W.H.F. trained), Nixon developed a cerebral hemorrhage and coma as a complication of anticoagulation, and life-support therapy was ultimately terminated in response to his living will.[53,54]

George W. Bush

In 2002 Bush had a syncopal episode in the White House living quarters while sitting on the couch, watching a football game.[55,56] He fell, hitting his head on the floor, and resumed consciousness within a few minutes. It was felt to be a vasovagal syncope (a common faint) and there were no recurrences. Bush had not been feeling well for a few days before the event, and it was thought that a pretzel he was eating may have caused esophageal irritation and a vagal discharge.[55,56]

Barack Obama

As an aside, President Obama has undergone a nuclear cardiac stress test as part of an annual physical exam, which was normal.[57,58] He has a history of cigarette smoking and has used nicorette gum for cigarette cessation.

FIGURE 6. Senator Majority Leader, Lyndon Baines Johnson, corners Senator Theadore Francis Green of Rhode Island, 1957. Courtesy of *New York Times.*

THE VICE PRESIDENTS

Seven American vice presidents have died in office between 1812 and 1912, and there has not been an incumbent vice presidential death for 100 years. Unlike the presidency, where no known vascular disease was documented in a candidate before election, 2 vice president were elected with known histories of CAD: Lyndon Johnson in 1960 and Richard Cheney in 2000. Joseph Biden, elected Vice President in 2008, had a previous history of cerebral hemorrhage from a ruptured berry aneurysm, and a history of a documented pulmonary embolism. He underwent 2 surgical procedures for repair of aneurysms in 1988. Since 1899, no incumbent vice president has died from complications of vascular disease. During the 19th century, 4 incumbent vice presidents probably died in office from vascular disease, and their courses are described below.

Elbridge Gerry

Elbridge Gerry was elected Vice President in 1812 during the second presidential term of James Madison. Madison's first term Vice President, George Clinton, died in 1812 of probable pneumonia. Clinton had also served as Vice President under President Thomas Jefferson, one of 2 vice presidents to serve with 2 different presidents. Clinton was the first national leader to die in office.[59,60]

Gerry was 68 years old when he was elected Vice President. He had previously served as a Congressman, Ambassador and as Governor of Massachusetts. The term "gerrymander" is named after him. In 1813 he was reported to have had a "stroke" and was sent home to Massachusetts to recover. In 1814, while serving in Washington where he presided over the Senate, he developed chest pains and over a short period of time died in the bed of his boarding home residence, minutes after arriving.[61,62] With the information available to us today, Gerry probably had unstable angina with an MI and sudden death. It is of interest that President Madison lost both his vice presidents, and during his two terms in office, the country had no vice president from 1812–1813 and 1814–1817.

Henry Wilson

Henry Wilson from Massachusetts was the second Vice President to serve with President Ulysses S. Grant. Elected in 1873 at the age of 61 years, he had a stroke 3 months into office with paralysis of the right side of his face and slurred speech.[63,64] He convalesced at home in Massachusetts and never spent much time in Washington. In 1875 he had a second stroke characterized by vertigo, slurring of his speech, and difficulty swallowing.[63,64] During that same year he had a third stroke while sitting in the Capitol barbershop, and died 12 days later.[63,64] He was presumed to have died from atherosclerosis of the base of the brain, although from an autopsy study, he may have had a cerebral hemorrhage.[65] With Wilson's death, Grant would have no vice president during his second term from 1875 to 1877.

Thomas Hendricks

Thomas Hendricks from Indiana died within 9 months of serving as President Grover Cleveland's first Vice President in 1885 (Adlai Stevenson of Illinois would serve as Cleveland's Vice President during his second term as President). Early in his term, Hendricks suffered a stroke from which he recovered.[66,67] In November 1885 he suddenly complained of pain in his chest and stomach.[66] A physician treated him with emetics, bromides, and cupping of the chest, and he died suddenly the same day. His final diagnosis was said to be paralysis of the brain with heart complications. After Hendricks' death, Cleveland would have no vice president for over 3 years of his first presidential term.

Garret Hobart

Garret Hobart of New Jersey was President William McKinley's first Vice President, elected in 1896 (Theodore Roosevelt was McKinley's second Vice President, elected in 1900). Early in 1899 Hobart developed severe episodes of chest pain, presumably angina pectoris and symptoms of congestive heart failure, characterized by fatigue and orthopnea.[68,69] He expired in November 1899, presumably of an MI, although the cause of death was said to be angina pectoris.[70]

Walter Mondale

Walter Mondale, Vice President to President Jimmy Carter, was elected in 1976 and was defeated for re-election in 1980. He subsequently ran for the presidency in 1984 on his own, and lost to Ronald Reagan in the general election

Mondale was a known hypertensive who was treated with 3 antihypertensive drugs that included a diuretic, combination hydralazine and the beta-blocker atenolol. His father, a Protestant minister, had died of a stroke. Mondale served as Vice President with no medical issues. The author (W.H.F.) was one of multiple physicians interviewed for a *New York Times* article during the presidential campaign of 1984, and was asked whether Mondale's relaxed demeanor was related to his beta-adrenergic blocker treatment. I disagreed with this premise because it was reported by his family internist, Dr. Milton Hurwitz, that Mondale's demeanor was the same well before he was started on beta blockers.[71]

FIGURE 7. Richard Cheney.

Richard Cheney

Richard Cheney was another Vice President elected with a very significant history of CAD (Fig. 7). With his health at a vulnerable level, he required close medical surveillance by both military physicians and civilian physicians at George Washington University Hospital in Washington. Cheney, who had been a heavy smoker, had his first MI at 37 years of age and had 3 subsequent episodes, including 1 just after the election of 2000.[72–74]

Cheney was treated with diet and exercise, and had undergone a 4-vessel coronary bypass operation in 1988 by Dr. Benjamin Aaron, who had previously operated on Ronald Reagan in 1981 after he was shot in an assassination attempt. As Vice President, Cheney also underwent 2 coronary stent procedures,[72,75,76] the placement of an implantable defibrillator,[77] surgery for popliteal artery aneurysms,[75] and treatment for deep vein thrombosis.[75] With his various cardiac problems, he would go on to serve as Vice President under George W. Bush for 8 years. Cheney's coronary disease did not stop him from being one of the most proactive vice presidents in history, however, his disease probably prohibited him from making a run for the presidency in 2008. After his retirement from the vice presidency, Cheney wrote his memoirs, which also included a description of his multiple cardiovascular illnesses.[78] Because of deteriorating left ventricular function from a possible ischemic cardiomyopathy, he subsequently had a left ventricular assist device placed and ultimately underwent heart transplantation.[72] His medical history reflects the advances in the treatment of CAD and heart failure, which have been made over the past 40 years.

Joseph Biden

Joseph Biden from Delaware is the current Vice President, and seems to be in vigorous health at age 70 years. Before his election as Vice President, while serving as a US Senator in Delaware, Biden had a ruptured berry aneurysm and a cerebral hemorrhage, which required surgery at Walter Reed Army Hospital in 1988. His course was complicated by a pulmonary embolism. He underwent a second elective operation for another berry aneurysm in 1988,[79] and did not return to the Senate for 7 months from the time the original diagnosis was made.

Comment

Unlike the election of a new president, where the voters expect an individual to be in excellent health, the same standard has not been true for newly elected vice presidents. Lyndon Johnson and Richard Cheney were elected Vice Presidents with known histories of MI. Joseph Biden was elected with a known history of a ruptured berry aneurysm. Walter Mondale had known hypertension. Unlike the vice presidents of the 19th century, where 4 were impaired and

probably died in office from stroke and MI, no vice president since 1912, except for Richard Cheney, has either died or has had serious vascular complications while in office.

Final Commentary

During the 20th century, CAD and cerebrovascular disease were major causes of morbidity and mortality for the American presidents, before, during, and after their terms in office. Risk factors such as hypertension, obesity, and cigarette smoking were highly prevalent in many of the presidents. The care the presidents received was somewhat comparable to the standard of care given to the general population. Of interest, Presidents Wilson, Harding, and Roosevelt were never hospitalized with their life-threatening illnesses, in part to prevent the public from knowing about the gravity of their conditions. William McKinley, who was assassinated in 1901 in Buffalo, was operated on in a hospital tent, not at a hospital.

Vice President Richard Cheney certainly benefited from advances in cardiac care during his lifetime, and is a success story, in part, because of what can be accomplished today in cardiac care and prevention. After multiple MIs, Cheney underwent coronary artery bypass surgery. As Vice President he underwent coronary stenting, surgery for popliteal aneurysms, treatment for deep vein thrombosis, and the placement of an implantable cardiac defibrillator. After his term in office he underwent placement of a left ventricular assist device and heart transplantation. He also stopped smoking, takes a statin drug, and other cardiac medications.

CONCLUSIONS

The presidents and vice presidents, with the help of their physicians, have a responsibility to the public to be sure that their cardiovascular and cerebrovascular health is attended to, especially in an era where effective preventive therapies are available. It is of interest that most of the presidents of the early 20th century suffered from complications of premature cerbrovascular and cardiovascular disease (Fig. 8). In the latter part of the 20th century, the presidents as a whole have done much better. Reagan and Ford each lived to 93 years. Carter and George H.W. Bush are both 88. None of these 4 Presidents were smokers, or had a history of hypertension, hyperlipidemia, or diabetes mellitus.

Firm medical criteria need to be established to determine when presidents and vice presidents should relinquish their duties of office, especially when a major disability occurs in these individuals related to vascular disease and/or myocardial disease.

Presidents 1-8 (1789-1841):
5 lived over 80 years (1 of whom lived over 90 years)

Presidents 9-30 (1841-1929):
1 lived over 75 years (although 3 were assassinated)
None lived over 80 years

Presidents 31-41 (1929-1992):
8 of 11 lived over 75 years (1 was assassinated)
3 lived 85-88 years (1 lived 88 years, 2 are alive at 88 years)
3 lived over 90 years

Presidents 42-44 are still alive, under 70 years

FIGURE 8. Age at death of the American Presidents related to different eras in American history.

REFERENCES

1. Herrick JB. Clinical features of suden obstruction of the coronary arteries. *JAMA* 1912;59:2015.

2. Moore K. *The American President*. New York: Fall River Press; 2007: 478.

3. Marmor MF. The eyes of Woodrow Wilson. Retinal vascular disease and George de Schweinitz. *Ophthalmology*. 1985;92:454–465.

4. The health and medical history of President Woodrow Wilson. Available at: http://www.doctorzebra.com/prez/t28.htm. ©2000–2009 by DoctorZebra. com. Accessed July 3, 2012.

5. Marmor MF. Wilson, strokes, and zebras. *N Engl J Med*. 1982;307:528–535.

6. Deppisch LM. *The White House Physician*. North Carolina: McFarland & Co. Inc.; 2007: 93–94.

7. Ferrell RH. *Ill-Advised Presidential Health and Public Trust*. Columbia: Univ of Missouri Press; 1992:16–17.

8. Weinstein EA: *Woodrow Wilson. A Medical and Psychological Biography*. Princeton, NJ: Princeton University Press; 1981:279.

9. Friedlander WJ. About 3 old men: an inquiry into how cerebral arteriosclerosis has altered world politics. A neurologist's view. (Woodrow Wilson, Paul von Hindenberg, and Nikolai Lenin). *Stroke*. 1972;3:467–473.

10. Deppisch, p 159–166.

11. Moore, p 342.

12. Deppisch, p 82

13. The health and medical history of President Warren Harding. Available at: http://www.doctorzebra.com/prez/t29.htm. ©200–2009 by DoctorZebra. com. Accessed July 3, 2012.

14. Dean JW. *Warren G. Harding*. New York: Times Books; 2004:138–152.

15. Murray RK. *The Harding Era. Warren G. Harding and His Administration*. Minneapolis: University of Minnesota Press; 1969:447–451.

16. Ferrell RH. *The Strange Death of President Harding*. Columbia: University of Missouri Press; 1996:31–49.

17. President Harding dies suddenly; stroke of apoplexy at 7:30 pm; Calvin Coolidge is President. *The New York Times*. August 2, 1923.

18. Wilbur RL, Cooper CM. President Harding's last illness. *JAMA*. 1923; 81:603.

19. Heller MF. *The President's Doctor: An Insider View of Three First Families*. New York: Vantage Press; 2000:38.

20. Moore, p 392

21. Krack A. "President Roosevelt is Dead; Truman to Continue Policies". 9th Crosses Elbe Near Berlin. *The New York Times*. April 12, 1945.

22. Bruenn HG. Clinical notes on the illness and death of President Franklin D. Roosevelt. *Ann Intern Med*. 1970;72:579–591.

23. Deppisch, p 88

24. Black C. *Franklin Delano Roosevelt*. New York: Public Affairs; 2003:1110–1101.

25. Black, p 28

26. McCullough D. *Truman*. New York: Simon & Schuster; 1992:902.

27. Leviero A. "Truman in hospital for health check". *The New York Times*. July 17, 1952.

28. Dwight DE. A leader in world peace (obituary). *The New York Times*. March 29, 1969.

29. Deppisch, p 100–101

30. Phelps RH. "Eisenhower says he considered resigning after stroke in 1957". *The New York Times*. September 13, 1965.

31. The health and medical history of President Dwight Eisenhower. Available at: http://www.doctorzebra.com/prez/t34.htm. © 2000–2009 by DoctorZebra. com. Accessed March 7, 2012.

32. Messerli FH, Messerli AW, Lüscher TF. Eisenhower's billion-dollar heart attack–50 years later. *N Engl J Med*. 2005;353:1205–1207.

33. Eisenhower DD. *At Ease*. New York: Doubleday & Co.; 1967;354–355.

34. Korda M. *Ike*. New York: Harper Collins; 2007:473.

35. In: Ferrell RH, ed. *The Eisenhower Diaries*. New York: WW Norton & Co.; 1981:302–304.

36. McLean RB. Leonard D. Heaton–military surgeon. *Mil Med*. 1982;147:717–727.

37. Moore, p 478

38. Caro R. *Master of the Senate*. New York: Alfred A. Knopf; 2002:619–636.

39. Caro R. *The Years of Lyndon Johnson. The Passage of Power*. New York: Alfred A. Knoph; 2012:370–371.

40. Ibid. p 112

41. Lyndon J. 3rd Out for this session; johnson suffers heart attack; will miss rest of senate session. *Associated Press*. July 3, 1955.

42. Johnson LB. My heart attack taught me how to live. *American Magazine*, July 1956.

43. Hurst J, Cain JC. *LBJ: To Know Him Better*. Austin, Texas: LBJ Library; 1994:7.

44. Califano JA. *The Triumph and Tragedy of Lyndon Johnson: The White House Years*. New York: Simon & Schuster; 1991.

45. Deppisch, p 128–129

46. Kearns GD. *Lyndon Johnson and the American Dream*. New York: Harper & Row; 1976:366.

47. Lyndon Johnson, 36th President is dead; was architect of "Great Society" Program. *The New York Times*. January 23, 1973.

48. Sperling LS. Lessons about the heart, of the heart, and from the heart: remembering J. Willis Hurst. *Clin Cardiol*. 2012;35:199.

49. The health and medial history of President George Bush. Available at: http://www.DoctorZebra.com/prez/t41.htm. © 2000–2009 by DoctorZebra.com. Accessed July 3, 2012.

50. The health and medical history of President George H.W. Bush: atrial fibrillation. Available at: http://www.DoctorZebra.com/prez/t41.htm. © 2000–2009 by DoctorZebra.com. Accessed July 3, 2012.

51. Altman LK. Bush begins tests to treat thyroid that disrupted heart rhythm. *The New York Times*. May 9, 1991.

52. Naftali T. *George H.W. Bush*. New York: Times Books, Div. of Henry Holt & Co.; 2007:130–131.

53. Herbers "The 37th President; In Three Decades". *The New York Times*. April 24, 1994.

54. Apple RW, Jr "The 37th President; Richard Nixon, 81, Dies; A Master of Politics Undone by Watergate". *The New York Times*. April 22, 1992.

55. "Report on President Bush's Physical Examination". *The New York Times*. August 2, 2006.

56. The health and medical history of President George W. Bush. Available at: http://www.DoctorZebra.com/prez/t43.htm. ©2000–2009 by DoctorZebra. com. Accessed July 3, 2012.

57. Redberg RF. First physical. *Arch Intern Med*. 2010;170:583.

58. Einstein AJ. President Obama's coronary calcium scan. *Arch Intern Med*. 2010;170:1175; author reply 1175–1175; author reply 1176.

59. Deppisch, p 180

60. In: Hatfield MO, Ritchie DA, Quatannens JAM, et al., eds. *Vice Presidents of the United States*. Washington DC: US Govt Printing Office; 1997:58.

61. ibid, p 67–68

62. Deppisch, p 181

63. Deppisch, p 182–183

64. Hatfield, p 238–239

65. Hammon WA: On the cause of Vice President Wilson's death. *The Boston Med Surg J*. 1875;93:693–704.

66. Deppisch, p 183–184

67. Hatfield, p 265

68. Deppisch, p 184–185

69. Hatfield, p 292–293

70. "Vice President Hobart Dead". *The New York Times*. November 22, 1899.

71. Altman LK. "Mondale's Health Termed Excellent by Physician". *The New York Times*. September 30, 1984.

72. Altman LK. "Cheney File Traces Heart Care Milestones". *The New York Times*. April 23, 2012.

73. Fournier R. "Doctor: Cheney Okay After Heart Attack". *Associated Press*, November 22, 2000.

74. Deppisch, p 187–189.

75. The health and medical history of Richard "Dick" Cheney. Availavle at: http://www.doctorzebra.com/prez/a_cheney.htm. ©2000–2009 by DoctorZebra. com. Accessed July 23, 2012.

76. Schmitt E. "Cheney Complains of Pains in Chest. Artery is Cleared". *The New York Times*. March 6, 2001.

77. Sanger DE, Altman LK. "Doctors Implant Heart Regulator in Cheney's Chest". *The New York Times*. July 1, 2001.

78. Cheney D, Cheney L. *In My Times: A Personal and Political Memoir*. New York: Threshold Editions, a Div. of Simon & Schuster Inc.; 2011:524–525.

79. "Biden Resting After Surgery for Second Aneurysm". *Associated Press*, May 4, 1988.

80. Rasky SF. "Biden Return Brings Purrs to Senate". *The New York Times*. September 8, 1988.

EDITORIAL

THE AMERICAN JOURNAL *of* MEDICINE ®

Is the Stethoscope Becoming an Outdated Diagnostic Tool?

During the past hundred years, the 3 major symbols representing the bedside physician have been the "black bag," the white coat, and the stethoscope. It was a badge of honor during my second year of medical school to obtain all 3 items in anticipation of seeing patients on the hospital wards after the preclinical lecture hall experience. The stethoscope dangling from the pocket of the white coat or wrapped around the back of the neck meant to the outside world that you were now a member of the healing profession.

The "black bag" is no longer a physician symbol because house calls are no longer part of routine clinical care. Will the stethoscope also meet the same fate, given that handheld ultrasound devices have now become available to better define cardiac anatomy, hemodynamics, and pathophysiology?[1]

Since the time of its introduction in 1816, the stethoscope has been an invaluable bedside tool for auscultating heart sounds.[2] During the golden age of early 19th century French medicine, with the use of the stethoscope, the physical examination became an integral part of clinical assessment.[3] Dr. René Laennec would become the leading proponent of this diagnostic approach. Laennec was a student of Dr. Jean-Nicolas Corvisart at the Charité in Paris, one of the leading teaching hospitals in Europe.[3] Subsequently, as an attending physician at the Necker-Enfants Malades Hospital in Paris, Laennec introduced a cylindrical device, open at each end, to auscultate the thorax. He called this device a stethoscope, whose name derived from the Greek word for chest, stethos, and the word for observer, skopos.[3] With his discovery, Laennec, an accomplished musician, was able to differentiate various diseases of the chest by physical examination and correlate his findings with autopsy studies.[3] He reported

on his work with the early stethoscope in the classic text *De l'Auscultation Médiate*,[4] which was published in 2 editions. Ultimately, the cylindrical stethoscope was improved upon by Dr. George Cammann 40 years later, after the introduction of rubber, by introducing a device having hearing pieces that fit into the examiner's ears.[5] Other refinements included the bell to discern low-pitched sounds, and the diaphragm, to better hear high-pitched sounds. Most recently electronic stethoscopes with microphone amplifiers have become available. For almost 200 years the stethoscope, the first bedside diagnostic tool, has remained a central part of the thoracic examination. Many of the great clinicians made their reputations as masters of auscultation. Whether these physicians actually heard everything they claimed to hear was always a question.

During my career in academic cardiology, the introduction of ultrasound devices has provided the ability to visualize both anatomic structures of the heart and to assess myocardial function, technologies going well beyond the capabilities of the stethoscope. Most recently handheld ultrasound devices, which can fit into the pocket of a physician's white coat, have demonstrated the ability to make more accurate diagnoses at the bedside when compared with standard examination using the stethoscope.[6] In some medical schools students are being trained to use these handheld devices as part of their curriculum.[7] Physicians working in the emergency room and critical care units are being trained on this technology.[8] Primary care physicians are also potential operators of these handheld devices.[9,10]

The stethoscope may indeed be replaced by handheld ultrasound devices, at least for cardiac examination. It will still be necessary to use the stethoscope for pulmonary examination and for auscultation of the abdomen to hear bowel sounds and bruits.

At present the handheld devices are expensive when compared with the cost of a stethoscope. However, their use could save money for the healthcare system if the need for conventional ultrasound studies or other diagnostic tests can be lowered.[6,10]

We may also see a return of the "black bag," to store the handheld ultrasound devices when they are not being used.

Funding: None.

Conflict of Interest: None.

Authorship: The author is solely responsible for the content of this manuscript.

Requests for reprints should be addressed to William H. Frishman, MD, New York Medical College, Department of Medicine, Valhalla, NY 10595.

E-mail address: William_Frishman@nymc.edu

William H. Frishman, MD
Chairman, Department of Medicine
New York Medical College
Valhalla
Supplements Editor, American Journal of Medicine

References

1. Liebo MJ, Isreal RL, Lillie EO, et al. Is pocket mobile echocardiography the next-generation stethoscope? A cross-sectional comparison of rapidly acquired images with standard transthoracic echocardiography. *Ann Intern Med.* 2011;155:33-38.

2. Weinbergo F. The history of the stethoscope. *Can Fam Physician.* 1993;34:2223-2224.

3. Nuland SB. Rene Laennec, inventor of the stethoscope. In: *Doctors.* New York: Vintage Books; 1988:200-235.

4. Laennec RTH. *De l'Auscultation Médiate.* London: T.G. Underwood; 1821 (French); Birmingham, AL: Classics of Medicine Library; 1979 (English).

5. Peck P. Dr. Cammann and the binaural stethoscope. *J Kansas Med Soc.* 1963;64:121-129.

6. Mehta M, Jacobson T, Peters D, et al. Handheld ultrasound versus physical examination in patients referred for transthoracic echocardiography for a suspected cardiac condition. *JACC Cardiovasc Imaging.* 2014;7:983-990.

7. Panoulas VF, Daigeler AL, Malaweer AS, et al. Pocket-size hand-held cardiac ultrasound as an adjunct to clinical examination in the hands of medical students and junior doctors. *Eur Heart J Cardiovasc Imaging.* 2013;14:323-330.

8. Testuz A, Muller H, Keller PF, et al. Diagnostic accuracy of pocket-size handheld echocardiographs used by cardiologists in the acute care setting. *Eur Heart J Cardiovasc Imaging.* 2013;14:38-42.

9. Alpert JS, Mladenovic J, Hellmann DB. Should a hand-carried ultrasound machine become standard equipment for every internist? *Am J Med.* 2009;122:1-3.

10. Rosenthal E. The odd math of medical tests: one scan, two prices, both high. *The New York Times.* December 16, 2014:1, A22.

EDITORIAL

Forty Years in Academic Cardiology

Last July I participated in the orientation of our newest cardiology fellows at Westchester Medical Center, while at the same time reflecting on the 40th anniversary of the start of my own cardiology fellowship in 1972 at New York Hospital-Cornell Medical Center. The day before my fellowship had begun, I had just completed an internal medicine residency at a large New York City public hospital, and had recently finished sitting for the board exam (the first without orals).

Our Chief of Cardiology at New York Hospital was Dr Thomas Killip III, "the father of acute coronary care,"[1] and we were part of the National Institutes of Health (NIH)-funded Myocardial Infarction Research Unit program. The Swan-Ganz catheter was a byproduct of the program,[2] and all the eight participating Myocardial Infarction Research Unit research sites using this new technology with advanced computer applications were active in the hemodynamic descriptions of patients with myocardial infarction. Diagnostic coronary angiography and coronary artery bypass surgery were still in the early stages of development. There were many patients with rheumatic heart disease, who required valvular surgery.

Echocardiography was in its most primitive stage of development, and Feigenbaum's textbook was only a thin volume then.[3] We taught ourselves how to use the echo probe on patients while photographing the M-mode images we obtained off an oscilloscope with a Polaroid camera. We were still performing and interpreting phonocardiograms, apex cardiograms, and vectorcardiograms, and measuring systolic time intervals from a simultaneous electrocardiogram, carotid pulse tracing, and phonocardiogram.[4–6] We had advanced from the Masters Step Test to treadmill and bicycle ergometer exercise protocols for cardiac stress testing. Nuclear imaging of the heart was at its earliest stage. Electrophysiologic testing consisted of bundle of His recordings, and all permanent cardiac pacemakers were being inserted by cardiothoracic surgeons.

At New York Hospital in 1972 there were other "Giants who walked the Halls." The pioneers of heart surgery, Drs C. Walton Lillehei and Paul Ebert, were our lead cardiac surgeons. Dr Mary Allen Engel, an early disciple of Dr Helen Taussig, ran the pediatric cardiology service where we rotated. Next door at Rockefeller University, Drs Edward Ahrens and Scott Grundy were involved in seminal studies in cholesterol metabolism.[6A]

The cardiology fellowship at Cornell was 2 years in duration, of which 1 year was spent in research. It was felt that 1 year was enough time to learn all of clinical cardiology, including cardiac catheterization. Additional years of cardiology fellowship training were dedicated predominantly for research. There were no sub-sub-specialty cardiology societies. The oral exam for the American Board of Internal Medicine (ABIM) cardiology boards had just been terminated in 1975, and the passing of a written exam was all that was required for certification.

With regard to the pharmacotherapy of cardiovascular disease, my life-long area of research, we had available to us only nitrates for angina pectoris; various digitalis preparations, and loop diuretics for treatment of congestive heart failure; hydrochlorothiazide, reserpine, guanethidine, hydralazine, and alpha-methyldopa for hypertension; catecholamine pressors for shock, atropine, and isoproterenol for bradycardia; quinidine, lidocaine, and procainamide for arrhythmias; and bile acid resins and the fibric-acid derivative clofibrate for the treatment of hypercholesterolemia and hypertriglyceridemia.

Over the last 40 years, with advances in basic research supported by the NIH and the introduction of new drugs by the pharmaceutical industry, we became part of a "golden era" in cardiovascular drug development. In 1972, with Dr Killip, I helped carry out the first pivotal US clinical trial evaluating the beta-adrenergic blocker propranolol for the treatment of angina pectoris, which led to subsequent studies by our group of new beta blockers and new clinical indications for their use.[7–13] After serving as Chief of Cardiology of a large army hospital, I worked at Einstein-Montefiore Hospital, where we participated in the clinical development of the calcium channel blockers, the alpha-adrenergic blockers, the inhibitors of the renin-angiotensin-aldosterone system, new inotropic agents such as dobutamine,[14] the statins, thrombolytics, new antiplatelet, and antithrombotic drugs, new drugs for pulmonary hypertension, and new drugs for peripheral vascular disease.[15] In our basic science studies work, we helped identify a hyperthrombotic state in patients with atherosclerosis.[16]

The author has no conflicts of interest to report.
Copyright © 2012 by Lippincott Williams & Wilkins
ISSN: 1061-5377/12/265-267
DOI: 10.1097/CRD.0b013e31826b3454

Editorial   *Cardiology in Review* • Volume 20, Number 6, November/December 2012

We would also participate in some of the major NIH-funded clinical trials such as Systolic Hypertension in the Elderly Program,[17] Studies of Left Ventricular Dysfunction,[18,19] Antihypertensive Lipid Lowering Heart Attack Trial,[20] and the Womens Health Initiative,[21] where thousands of subjects were recruited from our Bronx, Manhattan, and Westchester clinical research centers. In all, over the past 40 years (at New York Hospital/Cornell, Einstein/Montefiore, and New York Medical College/Westchester Medical Center), I have participated in more than 200 clinical trials and played a role in the evaluation of almost every cardiovascular drug approved for clinical use since 1972. I also coedited and coauthored a standard textbook on cardiovascular pharmacology, now in its third edition.[15]

In academic cardiology, teaching has an important role, and I received early career development support in medical education as a recipient of both the Teaching Scholar Award from the American Heart Association and the Preventive Cardiology Academic Award of the National Heart Blood and Lung Institute. Ultimately, I would be the recipient of both the Distinguished Teacher and Humanism in Medicine awards from the Association of American Medical Colleges in recognition of my research in medical education.

As a novice cardiovascular epidemiologist, I also served as the coprincipal investigator of the federally funded Bronx Longitudinal Aging Study, a Framingham-like study, where we helped identify risk factors for cardiovascular disease, cerebrovascular disease, and cognitive decline in elderly subjects over the age of 75 years.[22,23]

I am gratified to see that over the past 40 years in academic cardiology, we have also added to our practices an emphasis on the prevention of disease, in addition to our clinical roles as diagnosticians and therapists of critically ill patients. I am also pleased that we have not lost our core foundations in general internal medicine. As bedside cardiologists, we still take care of the whole patient, not just a body system.

For the first time during these past decades, the incidence rate of coronary artery disease is going down, and cardiology fellows undergoing clinical training in 2012 will be as well versed in prevention of disease as they will be in diagnostics and treatment. In 2012 we are also at a better place in our overall health care system in the United States compared with 1972 when I began my cardiology training. In the future, more individuals will have their own health insurance to help cover the costs of prevention and treatment services,[24] so that in the decades to come patients can benefit from those therapies developed over the past 40 years, as well as those advances in treatment from current and future breakthroughs in molecular medicine, pharmacogenetics, and stem cell biology.[25,26]

William H. Frishman MD
New York Medical College/Westchester Medical Center
Valhalla, NY

REFERENCES

1. Killip T, Kimball JT. A survey of the coronary care unit: concept and results. *Prog Cardiovasc Dis*. 1968;11:45–52.

2. Swan HJ, Ganz W, Forrester J, et al. Catheterization of the heart in man with use of a flow-directed balloon-tipped catheter. *N Engl J Med*. 1970;283:447–451.

3. Feigenbaum H. *Echocardiography 1st ed*. Philadelphia: Lea & Febiger, 1972.

4. Tavel M: *Clinical Phonocardiography and External Pulse Recording 2nd ed*. Chicago: Year Book Medical Publishers, Inc., 1972.

5. Frishman W, Smithen C, Befler B, et al. Noninvasive assessment of clinical response to oral propranolol therapy. *Am J Cardiol*. 1975;35:635–644.

6. Weissler AM, Garrard CL Jr. Systolic time intervals in cardiac disease. I. *Mod Concepts Cardiovasc Dis*. 1971;40:1–4.

6A. Grundy SM, Ahrens EH Jr., Salen G, et al: Mechanisms of action of clofibrate on cholesterol metabolism in patients with hyperlipidemia. *J Lipid Res* 1972; 13: 531–551.

7. Koch-Weser J, Frishman WH. beta-Adrenoceptor antagonists: new drugs and new indications. *N Engl J Med*. 1981;305:500–506.

8. Frishman WH. Drug therapy: atenolol and timolol, two new systemic beta-adrenoceptor antagonists. *N Engl J Med*. 1982;306:1456–1462.

9. Frishman WH. Nadolol: a new beta-adrenoceptor antagonist. *N Engl J Med*. 1981;305:678–682.

10. Frishman WH. Drug therapy. Pindolol: a new beta-adrenoceptor antagonist with partial agonist activity. *N Engl J Med*. 1983;308:940–944.

11. Frishman WH, Furberg CD, Friedewald WT. Beta-adrenergic blockade for survivors of acute myocardial infarction. *N Engl J Med*. 1984;310:830–837.

12. Frishman WH. Carvedilol. *N Engl J Med*. 1998;339:1759–1765.

13. Frishman W, Halprin S. Clinical pharmacology of the new beta-adrenergic blocking drugs. Part 7. New horizons in beta-adrenoceptor blockade therapy: labetalol. *Am Heart J*. 1979;98:660–665.

14. Sonnenblick EH, Frishman WH, LeJemtel TH. Dobutamine: a new synthetic cardioactive sympathetic amine. *N Engl J Med*. 1979;300:17–22.

15. Frishman WH, Sica DA (eds). *Cardiovascular Pharmacotherapeutics 3rd ed*. Minneapolis: Cardiotext, 2011.

16. Frishman WH, Weksler B, Christodoulou JP, et al. Reversal of abnormal platelet aggregability and change in exercise tolerance in patients with angina pectoris following oral propranolol. *Circulation.* 1974;50:887–896.

17. The SHEP Cooperative Research Group. Prevention of stroke by antihypertensive drug treatment in older persons with isolated systolic hypertension: Final results of Systolic Hyper-tension in the Elderly Program (SHEP). *JAMA.* 1991;265:3255–3264.

18. SOLVD Investigators: Effects of angiotensin converting enzyme inhibition with enalapril on survival in patients with reduced left ventricular ejection fraction and congestive heart failure. *N Engl J Med.* 1991;325:293–302.

19. SOLVD Investigators: Effect of enalapril on mortality and the development of heart failure in asymptomatic patients with reduced left ventricular ejection fractions. *N Engl J Med.* 1992;327:685–691.

20. Davis BR, Cutler JA, Gordon DJ, et al. Rationale and design for the Antihypertensive and Lipid Lowering Treatment to Prevent Heart Attack Trial (ALLHAT). ALLHAT Research Group. *Am J Hypertens.* 1996;9(4 Pt 1):342–360.

21. The Womens' Health Initiative Study Group: Design of the Womens' Health Initiative clinical trial and observational study. *Controlled Clin Trials.* 1998;18:61–109.

22. Frishman WH, Sokol S, Aronson MK, et al. Risk factors for cardiovascular and cerebrovascular diseases and dementia in the elderly. *Curr Probl Cardiol.* 1998;23:1–62.

23. Zimetbaum P, Frishman WH, Ooi WL, et al. Plasma lipids and lipoproteins and the incidence of cardiovascular disease in the very elderly. The Bronx Aging Study. *Arterioscler Thromb.* 1992;12:416–423.

24. Jaffe S. US Supreme Court makes historic health ruling. *Lancet.* 2012;380:14.

25. Leri A, Anversa P, Frishman WH (eds): *Cardiovascular Regeneration and Stem Cell Therapy.* UK/New York: Blackwell/Futura, 2007.

26. Leri A, Kajstura J, Anversa P, et al. Myocardial regeneration and stem cell repair. *Curr Probl Cardiol.* 2008;33:91–153.

A thirty-five-year odyssey of an Alpha Omega Alpha chapter councilor

William H. Frishman, MD, MACP

The author (AΩA, Albert Einstein College of Medicine, 1978) is the Barbara and William Rosenthal Professor and Chair of the Department of Medicine at New York Medical College, and Director of Medicine at the Westchester Medical Center, Valhalla, New York. He was the councilor of the Kappa New York chapter at the Albert Einstein College of Medicine from 1978 to 1997 and has served as the Iota New York chapter councilor at New York Medical College since 1998.

In June 2013 I will be completing my thirty-fifth year as an Alpha Omega Alpha (AΩA) chapter councilor. According to the AΩA constitution, the councilor is a member of the faculty and of the society appointed by the Dean on the recommendation of the chapter to serve a term of three years. The councilor may be reappointed to successive three-year terms, and is responsible to the school's faculty and the national officers of the society for the operations and well being of the chapter. The councilor guides the chapter's election process of new members and works with student members to plan and conduct chapter activities.

I have served as chapter councilor at two medical schools: Albert Einstein College of Medicine (Kappa New York) from 1978 through 1997, and New York Medical College (Iota New York) from 1998 until now. Over my years as councilor, I have helped to officiate in the induction into AΩA of more than 1,100 students at these two schools. Most of them have gone on to brilliant careers in academic medicine or clinical practice.

I became an AΩA councilor in the late 1970s, a time that saw rising opposition among students on many medical school campuses to the concept of comparative ranking of students, including the very idea of an honor society. In 1978, the viability of the AΩA chapter at Einstein was threatened, with students clamoring to dissolve the chapter. In a panic, Dean Ephraim Friedman, who had been my ophthalmology professor in medical school, asked me to address the newly elected AΩA students to try to save the chapter. I was a thirty-one-year-old internist-cardiologist and assistant professor of Medicine, two years out of the Army Medical Corps, and a popular teacher. In my meeting with the students, I told them there was nothing wrong with exceptionalism and being recognized for a job well done. I gave examples from the military, where medals and citations are often awarded for extreme heroism and for going the extra mile. I pointed out that the granting of an award made all soldiers try to perform better, and that this was also true for medical students.

The students agreed to keep the chapter active, and laid out two conditions for the dean: they stipulated that I should be the AΩA faculty initiate, and wanted me to be their AΩA councilor. They also insisted that the induction ceremony be modest in scope, and for many years the AΩA lecture and induction ceremony was held in the school's auditorium, followed by a dinner at the school's cafeteria (albeit with white linens and flowers on the tables). The AΩA induction speaker during my first year as councilor was Dr. Edmund Pellegrino, a noted bioethicist from Georgetown.

In 1997, when I moved to New York Medical College (NYMC) to become chairman of Medicine, world-famous trauma surgeon Louis Del Guercio was the AΩA councilor. Within a few months he stepped down, and given my experience as councilor at Einstein, the dean approved me as his replacement, just in time to plan the induction ceremony.

My experiences as AΩA councilor at two different medical schools give me a unique vantage point from which to comment on the roles of the councilor in guiding the chapter, and to offer some perspective on the successes and failures the society has had with its various activities, such as student and faculty elections and community service projects.

Student elections

Election to AΩA recognizes students in the third and fourth years of medical school who have excelled academically, demonstrated professionalism, and have shown the promise of becoming leaders in the profession.

When I started at Einstein, a faculty group of all course leaders, both in basic science and clinical rotations, served as electors. I oversaw the election but was not a voting member. The process was fair, in that every student had at least one advocate, but at the end class rank was the largest contributing factor. There was always great difficulty in deciding on the last two or three students to be elected, as they often had academic records quite similar to those just below them. It was here that we looked at other qualifications, such as community service, to set some candidates apart. (Even though we were an active research school, research accomplishments were not part of our AΩA election process.)

Initially, election to junior AΩA membership at Einstein was based on basic science grades only, but we quickly learned that some of these students performed less well on ward rotations. Election of seniors to AΩA included information from the third-year clerkship combined with basic science scores. Every AΩA nominee had to have passed USMLE Part 1. Ultimately, we decided to hold one election in the early part of the senior year and to not elect juniors. We eventually developed a point system formula in which the first two years of basic science counted for a maximum of one-third of the points, and the clinical clerkship year counted for two-thirds of the points. A student thus could be elected on a strong clinical performance alone, but could not be elected on a strong basic science performance alone. At NYMC, the election process also uses a point system, giving a greater weight to the clinical clerkship year than basic science course work, even for the third-year elections.

The main problem with the Einstein election process of only seniors was that it occurred late; with the pressures of finding house staff jobs, this resulted in the chapter becoming less active. Electing only seniors also meant that Einstein had no AΩA student officers and no chapter continuity other than faculty and house staff.

Thus, when I became councilor at NYMC, I had already recognized the value to a chapter of electing junior AΩA members, both in chapter activity and continuity. In 1999, the NYMC chapter was awarded the AΩA Chapter of the Year Award because of our service efforts.

Election of other categories

At the same time the chapter inducts students, it also nominates two faculty and two alumni. Faculty who do small group teaching can miss being nominated because they are not known to the entire student class. To balance the nomination process, students choose one faculty nominee and the faculty and administration recommend another with the students' consent.

Alumni nominees are identified through the Alumni Association and by faculty and students who might be familiar with the nominee's accomplishments.

The chapter has nominated distinguished individuals for honorary membership. One who was elected by the board of directors of the society to honorary membership was Dr. Attilio Maseri, a noted cardiologist from Italy, and the physician to Pope John Paul II.

Chapter finances

Local AΩA chapters do not receive funds for their campus activities from the national organization, except for specific awards programs. At Einstein, the AΩA chapter was supported by the dean, especially to fund the induction banquet and the induction speaker if we had no AΩA Visiting Professorship grant. At NYMC we do not receive direct support from the school because we are not an organization that includes all students. We raise money by assessing all AΩA faculty members on campus and the different academic departments. These funds support some community service programs on campus sponsored by AΩA and pay for the induction banquet, which is a grand affair.

Awards from the national office

AΩA national headquarters supports a number of programs on campus, including the Carolyn Kuckein Student Research Fellowship and the Administrative Recognition Award. The NYMC chapter coordinator and my administrative secretary, Carol Ruggiero, has received *two* Administrative Recognition awards for her outstanding work at both the Kappa Chapter of Einstein and the Iota Chapter at NYMC, the only coordinator in the country to receive this award for work at two chapters. In previous years we received the Medical Student Service Project awards to support a highly successful AΩA tutoring program on campus, and a smoking cessation program at local community schools.

At NYMC, the most popular AΩA program has been the Visiting Professorship Program, which has allowed us to host a distinguished medical educator, scientist, or health policy leader each year. The visiting professors have included national and international figures; the chapter and councilor expend much effort in selecting each year's visiting professor. The visiting professor gives the valedictory address at the induction ceremony and banquet where NYMC's third- and fourth-year AΩA nominees are inducted.

NYMC also elects an individual for a volunteer clinical faculty award, usually a small group teacher. These individuals are presented at the AΩA induction ceremony. We do not elect residents to AΩA, because NYMC has half a dozen hospital sites for student training, making it difficult to objectively select a resident for induction. The same situation existed at Einstein.

AΩA national headquarters

presents the Robert J. Glaser Distinguished Teacher Award at the annual meeting of the Association of American Medical Colleges. I was a recipient of the award in 1997 as I left Einstein to join NYMC.

Other service projects

NYMC's AΩA chapter also prepares the school's student handbook and a directory of off-campus student electives. The chapter also sponsors a successful advisory program for students applying for various house staff programs. The councilor helps to oversee these activities, which are undertaken independently of the AΩA national office.

Relationships with other societies on campus and nationwide

The Gold Humanism Society recently instituted a chapter at NYMC. As AΩA councilor, I work closely with the Gold Society's faculty advisor to plan common programs and to avoid redundancy.

The AΩA councilor represents his school's chapter, but also maintains frequent communication with other chapters and the national headquarters. Chapter councilors serve as sources of information for other councilors, and can mentor new councilors. I served as a Councilor Director on the Board of Directors of AΩA from 2004 to 2007, and also was the regional councilor for the Northeast region (which included the American University in Beirut) when that program was in place. While serving on the Board of Directors, I reviewed applications for the Carolyn Kuckein Student Research Fellowships, and, as a past recipient of the Glaser Award, have been a member of the selection committee for the Distinguished Teacher Award.

Final thoughts

What a grand adventure and privilege it has been to serve as an AΩA chapter councilor at two medical schools over a thirty-five-year period!

I have worked with more than 1,100 student inductees, many of whom have gone on to the distinguished careers predicted by their election to AΩA. The president of our university was a student inductee of mine at Einstein in 1979. In addition, I have worked with another 5,500 students who were not elected to AΩA as undergraduates, but who have distinguished themselves and hopefully will be recognized for their accomplishments by election as faculty and alumni members. Later recognition by AΩA may even be more significant since it reflects a lifetime of achievement.

Among my accomplishments as an AΩA councilor: I saved a chapter from being dismantled and helped to see that chapter flourish, and I served at another chapter that flourished as well. After all these years I think we have developed a good election process for students and faculty. I watched the great changes in medical education and health care that have occurred since 1978, and I can reiterate what I told the students at Einstein: there is nothing wrong with receiving a medal for working hard, aspiring to do your best, and going the extra distance. Election to AΩA is a great honor and makes all of medicine better at the end. The AΩA chapters at Einstein and NYMC have truly raised the academic standards of each school for all students and faculty.

I served for six full terms as councilor at Einstein and was well into my seventh term when I left for NYMC. I am now completing my fifth term in the NYMC chapter and wouldn't mind serving another thirty-five years if the dean and students will have me. Being an AΩA chapter councilor has been one of the best jobs I have had in my academic medicine career.

The author's address is:
New York Medical College
Department of Medicine
Munger Pavilion, Room 263
Valhalla, New York 10595
E-mail: william_frishman@nymc.edu

"A Perfect Match"
Specialty Choice and Residency Selection

William H. Frishman, M.D.
Eliot J.Lazar, M.D.
Stanley Luftschein, M.D.

Medical school faculty have a unique opportunity to discuss the approach to "Match Day" with students. Although there have been a number of publications on this subject(Wagoner & Gray 1979, Calhoun et al 1990), few are recent and most deal with the factors that affect students' choices,(Sacks et al, 1983), rather than advise students about the match process. We thought it might be helpful to share our thoughts on this process with the entire student community. We caution the reader that these are our opinions, not scientifically derived recommendations. The student must evaluate his/her particular circumstances. What follows is a brief summary of our views on choosing a specialty and then matching successfully.

THE SPECIALTY DECISION

During March or April of each year, a time that coincides with the 4th year course lottery, many students become acutely distressed by the prospect of having to decide on a specialty. It is easier to be sure, if one is certain that he/she is a future pediatrician or cardiac surgeon, but our experience suggests that although many students have narrowed down their choices, they are by no means finalized. There are however, several points to keep in mind which may alleviate the anxiety. First, although it is helpful to make a firm decision on specialty by the time the interview season begins, it is by no means mandatory. There are several options. A few students opt to take a year off but this is a decision that should be carefully weighed. Alternatively, some decide to apply for one year Medicine programs or a flexible year. If, however you are an individual who wants, needs, etc. to make a firm decision, we recommend that you generate a list with three categories. One category should include the definite ruleouts, i.e. those fields that you cannot see yourself pursuing as a career. These need not be fields that you don't enjoy or find interesting, merely those that you could not see yourself in long term, perhaps because of lifestyle, routine, etc. The next category should include those fields that are possibilities albeit unlikely ones. The final category should include those specialties in which you are definitely interested. Most students ultimately choose a specialty from the latter list. Usually this last list contains no more than two or three options and for some this simple process of classification serves to focus ones' true interest. If after formulating the list several choices remain viable, than one should design an elective schedule which will not only aid you in obtaining the desired residency spot, but will help you make a final decision on specialty. The exact schedule for each student depends on a variety of factors. These include third year grades, competitiveness of specialty fields and the likelihood of obtaining desired electives at specific times. We believe that it is extremely important for students to speak with faculty members in the specialties one is interested in. Issues such as the importance of particular electives, research, letters etc., may vary from specialty to specialty. It may also be extremely helpful to spend some time with a practitioner in the area one is considering. Electives often do not provide the full flavor of the field.

The final career decision is rarely as painful or traumatic as expected. It is important not to become too frazzled by the thought of having to go through the process.

THE APPROACH TO THE MATCH

We believe that there are four essential components of a successful residency application. These include 1)Grades 2)Letters of recommendation 3) Research/publications 4)Interview. Some also feel a professional appearing Curriculum Vitae is helpful while the importance of National Board scores remains variable.

Grades

By the spring of the third year most students have a fairly defined pattern of grades. An oft asked question is whether the basic science grades matter? Although the exact answer may vary from field to field and program to program, the basic science grades do reflect a level of academic achievement. On balance we suspect that the clinical grades may carry more weight, but a transcript that shows tremendous disparity between the basic science and clinical years might raise an eyebrow. Additionally, both basic science and clinical grades are evaluated in determining election to Alpha Omega Alpha which remains important for the most competitive programs. We are not suggesting that learning should be for the sake of a grade or that the transcript is more important than ones education. Unfortunately in a Pass-Fail system a few students take a "just enough to pass" attitude in which both knowledge and transcript suffer, particularly in regard to the basic sciences.

Board Scores

The importance of National Board scores in the application process remains controversial. In our experience the actual scores have not had a tremendous impact on a students' candidacy, although this is not a universal observation. Calhoun et al (1990) reported on a study examining thirty one variables in which National Board part I scores greater than 650 (as one measure of academic excellence) were significantly correlated with a successful match in otolaryngology. McCollister conducted a survey of program directors in ophthalmology and otolaryngology to determine the importance of National Board scores. Two hundred eighteen surveys representing 90% of U.S programs in these fields were analyzed. Part I scores were employed by over 75% of respondents, in the selection process and were considered by more than 50% in deciding on whom to interview. His conclusion was that the "use of NBME scores in the residency application process is widespread...". It is less clear how important NBME scores are in other specialties such as Internal Medicine. Generally, we feel that Board scores are often evaluated in the context of a student's overall academic performance. In some specialties they may be especially important and are sometimes utilized as a factor in the decision to interview.

Letters of Recommendation

This is the area that students neglect more than any other. It is not uncommon to meet with a student in the Fall and inquire as to who will be writing letters of recommendation, only to find that the student is not sure. It is equally common is to review a student's list and find that some of the choices do not appear optimal, based on the chosen specialty. There are no absolute rules, but the following suggestions regarding selection of letter writers may be helpful. In general, the more senior the academic rank the better. Someone who is involved in running a program, i.e., a special unit or a division or department may be particularly good choice. It is usually advisable to stay within one's chosen area to the extent possible. An interviewer who sees a Medicine applicant with letters only from other specialties will wonder why the student did not know anyone in Medicine to request a letter from. The length of time that a letter writer knows the applicant is also important as is the situation under which the student has been observed, i.e. classroom or lab versus direct patient care experience. The critical question however, is whether the potential letter writer has a good sense of your strengths and abilities. A vague non-descript letter from a senior faculty member is probably less helpful than an in-depth, insightful letter from a junior faculty member.

What of the uncertainty regarding a particular faculty member's opinion of you i.e. will he/she write a very strong letter. We have been suggesting for some time that a student phrase their request in terms such as the following-"Do you know me well enough to write a strong letter?" This allows the faculty member who doesn't think highly of you to plead lack of familiarity and thus allow both of you to save face. Certainly not all faculty will follow this script, but perhaps after this article more will.

Research/Publications

This is an area that is rarely considered in the context of residency application, even by students who are interested in research. We have discussed this topic with many faculty, and they differ in their views on the importance of research to the application process. If one accepts the premise that research experience or publication is helpful, students who have done significant investigations and/or published before medical school have a head start. The majority of students are not in this position and unless you have participated in research during the first two years of medical school, you face the end of third year with the last page of your Curriculum Vitae blank.

Many would agree that it is extremely important for students to have research experience, even if this is not a future career path. Designing a project, writing a protocol, carrying out the study and analyzing the results is an extremely valuable experience, which at the very least will facilitate the clinician's ability to critically analyze scientific data throughout his/her career. Nonetheless, if a student has no interest in such an endeavor, engaging in one only for the sake of one's Curriculum Vitae would hardly be appropriate. A more reasonable approach is to make use of the opportunities and talent available at a renown academic center to investigate an area of one's interest.

Once the decision is made to undertake a scholarly project, what are the available options? We think it is unrealistic to expect a student to be the principal investigator in a major bench or clinical research project in addition to the responsibilities of a normal course load. A more viable alternative is to develop a long lasting association with a faculty preceptor investigating an area of mutual interest, and to pursue this investigation over some years in a part time fashion. Alternatively one may pursue: 1) A relatively brief, uncomplicated clinical study with a short term goal of submitting results in abstract form, 2) A case report and review of the literature 3) A scholarly review on a topic of interest. Case reports are of course limited by the likelihood of coming across an unusual case. Clinical studies, require submission of the proposal to the Committee on Clinical Investigation, which adds considerable time to the process, not to mention the difficulty in finding a faculty member who is able and willing to guide the project under your time constraints. A scholarly review lends itself most easily to completion by the student, but here the choice of topic is extremely important. There is already an abundance of medical literature and the 200th review on the same topic probably adds little. However, a discrete area which has not been previously examined, particularly when one can pool data or perform a meta analysis, may be of significant value. The key here again, is to find a faculty member with the expertise to guide you appropriately.

Interview

The interview is an extremely important aspect of the application process. For some programs it may be more important than the academic record (Garden & Smith 1989). In other specialties, the interview may significantly alter a program's ranking of a candidate. Gong et al (1984) reported on a series of 236 applicants who were ranked before and after the interview. They found that after the interview approximately a third were ranked more favorably, a third less favorably and a third remained unchanged(Gong et al 1984). Our experience and at least one published report (Featherstone & Ramsey 1983) suggests that negative personal characteristics (of the applicant) perceived by the interviewer, have a significantly adverse effect on a candidates ranking.

Preparation for the interview starts well in advance. It is important to learn as much about the program-demographics, sites, strengths and weaknesses-before one arrives at the interview. It may also be useful to review a couple of interesting case histories for the proverbial "Tell me about the most interesting case you saw" question. Try to determine the interviewer's specialty and interest e.g. clinical or research, primary care or specialist, basic science or clinical. If this cannot be determined before the interview, glance at any certificates on the wall (if it can be done unobtrusively). While touring, pay particular attention to the atmosphere. Is the tour leader (usually a house officer) happy or morose? He/she may be tired but most residents are. Does he/she have a good rapport with attendings, nurses, and other house officers met during the tour? Does the staff seem happy? This reveals a lot about the program. At one program an author observed that the two Chief Residents could not agree on a particular issue during the presentation. This raised a red flag about the relationship between residents. Once the interview starts, relax and be yourself. Be ready with answers to commonly asked questions such as "Where do you expect to be in 10 years?" Even if the answer is I don't know, decide this in advance. Keep your answers short. The next time the television is on and a public figure is asked a question, time the answer. You'll see that most are expressed in "sound bites" of thirty seconds or less. If the interviewer wants you to expand he/she'll prompt you. Do not ask questions about your chances for acceptance, etc. Use the interview to obtain answers to questions that concern you, but keep in mind that queries about on call schedules or how many days off one gets, tend to be viewed unfavorably. Don't ask questions just for the sake of asking them. One does not visit a tertiary center and ask if they do research, or how the conferences are. It would not be inappropriate however, to ask how many residents actually find time to do research or publish or what are the unique elements of the program. As the interview season winds down, or if you are convinced about your interest in a particular program early on, it may be helpful to write a thank you letter to the program director. In your letter you may wish to point out features of the residency which make it particularly attractive to you. This also demonstrates a thorough knowledge of the program.

The Decision

The interview season may last several months and it is a challenge to accurately recall every program visited. One very helpful suggestion is to record your opinions of each on a small tape recorder immediately after the interview. One author chose to rank all the programs after each interview as if the "Match" list had to be submitted that day. An added benefit of this latter technique is that one's rank list evolves rather painlessly. A week before the list is due one should sit down with the tape in a quiet place and review your thoughts. Subtleties in your language and intonation are very valuable to listen to, particularly months after the interview. An alternative approach is to take careful notes but most people seem to confine these to objective data, number of patients, on-call etc. Your own subjective thoughts, which become the essence of your decision, may be lost if one is not careful.

As suggested above, a week or two before the deadline for submission of your "Match" list is the time to take out your notes or tape and trace the process from the beginning, ruling out programs and including others as you proceed. For students whose top one or two choices have been evident for some time, this process is already nearly completed. For others the review process serves to crystallize one's thoughts. A small number may have some difficult decisions to make but we feel that by following the approach outlined, the process will be considerably easier. Finally, we suggest that you not rank a program that you really don't wish to be at.

Conclusion

In this brief article we've tried to present an outline of the process of deciding on a specialty and how to go approach the match. We emphasize that this represents only one approach and acknowledge that this treatise may meet with some serious disagreement and stimulate considerable comment. If so, then our mission is successful. Good luck and relax.

References

Calhoun KH, Martinez SA, Stevens MH, Hokanson JA, Bailey BJ: The resident selection process in otolaryngology-head and neck surgery. Arch Otolaryngology Head and Neck Surgery 116:1041-1043, 1990

Featherstone HJ, Ramsey PG: Analysis of selection criteria for medical residents. Differences between primary care and traditional pathway committees. American Journal of Medicine 75(4):687-690, 1983

Garden FH, Smith BS: Criteria for selection of physical medicine and rehabilitation residents. A survey of current practices and suggested changes. American Journal of Physical Medicine & Rehabilitation 68(3):123-127, 1989

Gong H, Parker NH, Apgar FA, Shank C: Influence of the interview on ranking in the residency selection process. Medical Education. 18(5):366-369, 1984

McCollister RJ: The use of part I National Board scores in the selection of residents in ophthalmology and otolaryngology. JAMA 259:240-242, 1988

Wagoner NE, Gray GT: Report on a survey of program directors regarding selection factors in graduate medical education. Journal of Medical Education 54:445-452, 1979

In Memoriam

Edmund H. Sonnenblick, MD, 1932–2007

Dr. Edmund H. Sonnenblick died in 2007 after a long and courageous battle with cancer. He was just shy of his 75th birthday. He had been coeditor of the first and second editions of *Cardiovascular Pharmacotherapeutics* and the supplementary handbooks and has been an inspiration for this third edition.

Ed was a towering figure in academic cardiology who made seminal contributions in the areas of cardiovascular physiology and energetics, pathophysiology, and therapeutics. The clinical approaches we use now to treat patients with ventricular dysfunction, heart failure, valvular heart disease, and coronary artery disease stem, in great part, from Ed's pioneering research work.

Ed graduated *cum laude* from Harvard Medical School. He completed his postgraduate training in medicine at Columbia Presbyterian Hospital in New York City where he worked directly with Drs. John Laragh and Paul Cannon. At Columbia, Ed was credited as being the first individual to use the electron microscope to image heart muscle structure and the force of its contractions. Subsequently he joined the Cardiovascular Research Laboratories at the National Institutes of Health in Washington DC, working with Drs. Stanley Sarnoff and Eugene Braunwald. At the NIH, Ed carried out fundamental studies on the structure and function of heart muscle that has formed the basis of our current understanding of cardiac ventricular function under normal physiologic and pathophysiologic conditions. In addition to Drs. Sarnoff and Braunwald, his collaborators at the NIH included Drs. John Ross Jr., Dean Mason, William Parmley, Henry Spotnitz, and James Spann.

In 1968 Ed joined Dr. Richard Gorlin at the Peter Bent Brigham Hospital in Boston, where he served as Codirector of Cardiovascular Research and as Associate Professor of Medicine at Harvard Medical School. At Harvard he continued much of the work started at the NIH, while helping to train many of the future leaders of academic cardiology.

In 1975 Ed moved to the Albert Einstein College of Medicine in the Bronx, New York as the Olson Professor of Medicine and Chief of the Division of Cardiology. He was also Director of the Cardiovascular Center. In 1996 he stepped down as Division Chief after 21 years of distinguished leadership, but remained active as a clinical cardiologist and investigator. At Einstein he held the position of the Edmond Safra Distinguished Professor of Medicine until the time of his death.

During his 30 years at Einstein, Ed branched out into translational medicine. Working with collaborators at Einstein, he helped to demonstrate the efficacy and safety of both beta-adrenergic blockers and inhibitors of the renin-angiotensin system in the treatment of congestive heart failure. In reaction to the results of trials with catecholamines and phosphodiesterase inhibitors, Ed was instrumental in overturning the inotropic therapy approach as a first-line therapy for chronic heart failure. In collaboration with Dr. Piero Anversa at New York Medical College in Valhalla, New York, he proposed new theories regarding cardiomyocyte growth and death and the etiology of heart failure. Ed was also involved with Dr. Anversa in the fundamental studies of myocardial regeneration and cardiac stem cell therapy, and he lived to see the early application of these experimental findings applied in clinical medicine.

Ed was a major contributor to the basic science and clinical literature, authoring and coauthoring more than 650 original scientific articles, reviews, and chapters. He was the coeditor of *Progress in Cardiovascular Diseases* with Dr. Michael Lesch and an editor of *Hurst's The Heart* for 4 editions. He was the coauthor with John Ross Jr. and

Eugene Braunwald of the text *Mechanisms of Contraction of the Normal and Failing Heart*, which appeared in 2 editions.

Ed received numerous honors, including the Distinguished Scientific Award of the American College of Cardiology and the Research Achievement Award from the American Heart Association, given posthumously at its 2007 Annual Scientific Sessions.

I had the good fortune to work closely with Ed Sonnenblick for more than 30 years. I joined him as a faculty member at Einstein in 1976. Previously I had followed his remarkable career at the NIH and at Harvard while I was both a medical student and house officer. Ed was an exceptional mentor, whose knowledge of cardiac pathophysiology dramatically influenced my own academic career and that of hundreds of colleagues and trainees. He helped train many of the first heart failure clinical specialists, including Drs. Thierry LeJemtel, Donna Mancini, Uri Elkayam, Joel Strom, Stuart Katz, Hillel Ribner, and Marc Klapholz. He helped form the first academic program in molecular cardiology with Drs. James Scheuer, Leslie Leinwand, Richard Kitsis, and Glenn Fishman. Ed had the ability to bring basic physiologic principles, new concepts in molecular medicine, with a logical clinical approach, to the bedside. He was a revered teacher who was just as excited to be with patients, students and clinical trainees as he was with his colleagues in the basic science laboratory.

After 20 years as colleagues at Einstein, I continued my interactions with him at New York Medical College where I had moved to be Chairman of Medicine in 1997. Fortunately for me, Ed maintained his status as an Adjunct Professor at New York Medical College where he worked with Piero Anversa. It was a privilege to watch him participate at Piero's weekly research meetings, until the time of his death.

Ed was a remarkable intellect. He had the ability to integrate basic physiologic principles with quantitative parameters of the diseased heart. He brought us such terms as "preload" and "afterload." His tremendous curiosity and interest in new ideas was contagious and an inspiration to young trainees and colleagues. He had the ability to make the most difficult concepts understandable, both at the lectern and in one-on-one interactions.

Ed was also a true "Renaissance Man," a "Man for All Seasons." He had an interest in everything and everybody. He was an avid reader, especially of history, and was a connoisseur of the arts. He did not suffer fools lightly and set the highest standards for himself and those around him. His favorite phrase at our research meetings was "I wonder," and he left a great legacy and personal example for all of us in cardiovascular medicine.

—*William H. Frishman*

New York Medical College
150 YEARS OF EXCELLENCE (1860-2010)
William H. Frishman, M.D., M.A.C.P.
Rosenthal Professor and Chairman of Medicine

The 150th anniversary of any institution is naturally a time of great celebration. Since this year is New York Medical College's sesquicentennial, we strove not to be exceptions to this maxim. We recall that ours is a special school, with an impressive history that, in itself, chronicles the evolution of American medicine, bioscience and public health.

The school was founded in 1860 by New York City civic leaders, among them the reformer and New York Tribune editor William Cullen Bryant, because of a glaring need to address major deficiencies in medical education, and to alleviate the city's overcrowding, poor nutrition, pollution, and resulting epidemics. The founders envisioned a new kind of medical school based on the latest scientific knowledge, combined with principles of healthy living and patient-centered care that would address these issues.

When the College opened its doors, during the year of Abraham Lincoln's election to the Presidency at the dawning of the Civil War, 59 students and 8 faculty members assembled at the school's first facility located at the corner of 20th Street and Third Avenue, near Gramercy Square in a building on the top three floors above a grocery store. The annual tuition was approximately $100.00, and a college degree was not a prerequisite for admission.

After attending two courses of lectures, studying medicine for three years and having "apprenticed oneself to a respectable practitioner of medicine," a student became a candidate for graduation-contingent upon demonstrating good moral character and attaining the age of 21.

New York Medical College would become the first United States medical school to require an entrance exam, and its innovative three-year curriculum was ultimately adopted by other medical schools including Harvard and the newly formed Johns Hopkins University whose first President, Ira Remsen, was a graduate of the College's Class of 1865.

Innovative in education from its beginnings, New York Medical College created the first Department of Pediatrics in the United States led by Dr. Abraham Jacobi, who was also the founder of the specialty. In 1875, NYMC became the first private medical school in the nation to train its students at an urban hospital when it affiliated with Metropolitan Hospital Center, located first on Ward's Island in the middle of the East River, then Welfare Island (Roosevelt Island) and ultimately, in 1957 on Manhattan Island. For over 75 years, NYMC students were ferried by boat to their clinical rotations at Met on Welfare Island. Legend had it that some NYMC students skipped taking the boat and swam to Welfare Island on top of the water, some did it underwater, and a few were said to have walked on water. The College's 135-year-old continuous affiliation with Metropolitan remains the oldest partnership between a freestanding private medical school and a public hospital in the United States.

NYMC also recognized the need to own its own teaching hospital. It became the first American medical school to do so, opening the Flower Free Surgical Hospital in 1989, next to the newly relocated medical school on 63rd Street and York Avenue. The student magazine, "The Chironian" had the following quote describing Flower Hospital: "to embrace under its New York Medical College jurisdiction, a free hospital to care for the poor and the clinical instruction of its students." Flower Hospital would serve as the model a few years later for the newly created Johns Hopkins Hospital and other medical school-owned university hospitals.

Front Yard of New York Medical College with Flower Hospital in background

Ambulance Call in the Nineteen Twenties

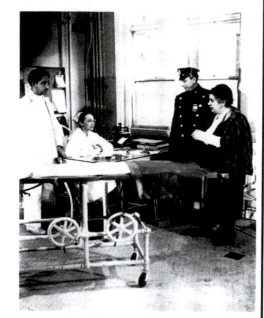

The site of the new building was Sixty-fourth Street and York Avenue in the shadow of the Queensboro Bridge. A surgical hospital was erected next to the College and was named in honor of Governor Flower.

The hospital had two hundred beds and provided care for both private and charity patients. It maintained very active ambulance and emergency services.

Emergency Room

Early Operating Room

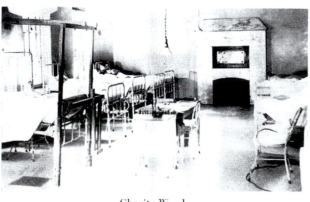

Charity Ward

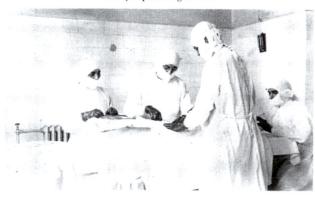

25

At its new location, the medical school and hospital flourished. In 1896, it was noted that NYMC had the highest grade performance among all schools on the New York State licensure exam, a tradition that continues today by our student performances on the National Board Exams. The College was the nation's first medical school to implement a three-year (in 1870), and later a four-year curriculum, and was among the first to accept women and minority students as far back as the 1870's. The school would ultimately merge in 1918 with a sister school, the New York Medical College for Women which started in 1863. A NYMC graduate, Franklin Gardiner, was the family physician for President Benjamin Harrison from 1889-1993 and diagnosed the first lady, Mrs. Harrison, with the tuberculosis that ultimately, caused her premature death.

One hundred years ago, in 1910, all American medical schools were inspected by a national commission led by Abraham Flexner. At the time, the school's dean was Dr. Royal Copeland, an ophthalmologist and the first physician to perform a corneal transplant. He would ultimately go on to serve as the Commissioner of Health in New York City during the 1918-1919 Spanish influenza pandemic, and later served as a United States Senator for three terms. Under Copeland's leadership, the school passed the Flexner inspection with commendation, especially regarding the superior performance of NYMC students on the state licensure exams. The mission of the school, as stated in 1910 and only somewhat modified in subsequent years, was and is "to train superior clinical physicians with strong scientific underpinnings." In 1910, the school's research enterprise began to flourish both on campus and at the affiliated hospitals. In 2010, a century after the Flexner Report, the school continues to enjoy the highest level of medical school and health university accreditation by all the national certifying organizations.

It's OK in the halls but it's murder on the stairs

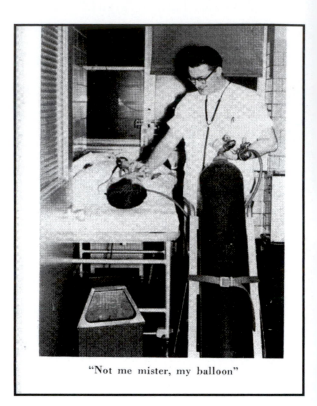

"Not me mister, my balloon"

Beyond influenza, NYMC also has risen to the challenges of other 20th century crises. The College dispatched a special medical unit of physicians and nurses during World War I, and it introduced an accelerated three-year M.D. program that supplied 650 urgently-needed physicians during World War II. The latter program lasted through 1946, and the school was commended by the United States Army and Navy for its role in expanding the medical corps during wartime.

In 1936, the decision was made to move the medical school and its hospital from 63rd Street and to merge with Fifth Avenue Hospital at 105th Street across from Central Park. The facility, which became known as New York Medical College/Flower and Fifth Avenue Hospitals, had a new instructional building, modern research facilities and a state-of-the-art 600-bed university teaching hospital. Educational innovations continued at the new facility and at nearby affiliated Metropolitan Hospital, including a fourth-year year medicine subinternship where students would work as interns—a totally new concept at that time.

Hmm...must be lupus.

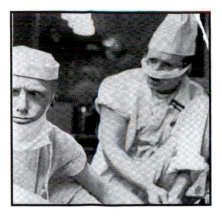

This is not what was meant by intern matching

When they tell us to scrub, we scrub!

In the 1970s, after serving as a landmark New York City institution for more than 100 years, the College, then under the sponsorship of the Archdiocese of New York, was invited by Westchester County leaders to move to its current location in Valhalla. At its new campus site, the school began its new affiliations with Westchester Medical Center, St. Vincent's Medical Center (with its own history dating back to 1849), Terence Cardinal Cooke Health Care Center (formerly the Flower and Fifth Avenue Hospital building complex) and Lenox Hill Hospital. In the Bronx were affiliated Lincoln Hospital and Our Lady of Mercy Hospital (now Montefiore North). The College became the only school to ever affiliate with the New York Eye & Ear Hospital, the first specialty hospital in the United States, dating back to the 1830's, and with other institutions in Queens, Staten Island, Southern and Western Connecticut, and throughout the entire Hudson Valley Region, including Keller Army Hospital and the Montrose VA. Since 1980, the school has also had an affiliation with the Westchester Institute for Human Development.

Today New York Medical College is the nation's third largest private medical school. Yet there is no other medical school in the country that can match the diversity of our patient population and the variety of our public, private, suburban, inner-city, county, tertiary care teaching hospitals and clinics.

The College has also been at the forefront of biomedical research and public health. During the past 50 years, the university opened its Graduate School of Basic Sciences, offering Masters and Ph.D. degrees, and the School of Health Sciences and Practice, an offshoot of the Graduate School of Medical Administration as it was first named. In recent years, a new instructional building (the Medical Education Center), the Learning Center (SHSP building), the Health Sciences Library and the Maria Fareri Children's Hospital were added to the Westchester/Valhalla Campus.

Among the recent accomplishments of faculty, Charles Kelman was awarded the Lasker Prize (sometimes called the American Nobel) for developing the modern cataract surgical extraction procedure. The seed vaccine for influenza and a cardiovascular niche in the field of regenerative medicine were developed through the efforts of its faculty and the help of student co-workers.

Today, New York Medical College provides 3,000 students and residents with an unparalleled variety of learning environments each year. With more than 3,000 faculty mentors and 12,700 living alumni, the school is well positioned for the challenges that lie ahead, as we all begin to write the next 150 years of the school's glorious history.

As a teacher at NYMC, it is a great privilege for me to work with such an outstanding group of students, who are clearly positioned to be the top physicians, healthcare leaders and bioscientists of the coming years. Congratulations to the Class of 2010, and to New York Medical College on its 150th anniversary. I am proud of you, and I rejoice in all of your accomplishments, past and present, and wholeheartedly predict a brilliant future ahead.

N.P. Flower, founder of th Flower hospital and the former governor of New York

William Cullen Bryant, first president of the college.